CANADIAN SOCCER'S 2024 MEN'S FOOTBALL ANNUAL AND WHO'S WHO GUIDE TO FOOTBALLERS

FOOTBALLMEDIA / BY RICHARD SCOTT
APRIL 2024

CANADIAN SOCCER'S 2024 MEN'S FOOTBALL ANNUAL
& WHO'S WHO GUIDE TO FOOTBALLERS

ISSUE 2 (APRIL 2024)

FOOTBALLMEDIA / BY RICHARD SCOTT
COPYRIGHT © 2024 UP NORTH PRODUCTIONS.
NO REPRODUCTION WITHOUT PERMISSION.
ALL RIGHTS RESERVED.

PUBLISHED IN CANADA BY:
UP NORTH PRODUCTIONS
1995 INDIAN CREEK ROAD
LIMOGES, ON   K0A 2M0
BOOKS@FOOTBALLMEDIA.CA

Cover design by Griffin Scott. Cover photos by Richard Scott.

CANADIAN SOCCER FOOTBALL ANNUAL

TABLE OF CONTENTS

CANADIAN SOCCER CLUBS, STATS & 2024 ROSTERS	4
2023 CANADIAN SOCCER STANDINGS & RESULTS	
CANADIAN CHAMPIONSHIP	28
CONCACAF CHAMPIONS LEAGUE	28
CANADIAN PREMIER LEAGUE	28
MAJOR LEAGUE SOCCER	31
LEAGUES CUP	33
MLS NEXT PRO	33
LEAGUE1 BRITISH COLUMBIA	34
LEAGUE1 ALBERTA	36
LEAGUE1 ONTARIO	36
LEAGUE1 QUÉBEC	41
WHO'S WHO GUIDE TO MEN'S FOOTBALLERS	
FOOTBALLERS A-Z	46
2024 CANADIAN SOCCER MATCH SCHEDULE	152

VANCOUVER WHITECAPS FC

FIVE MOST RECENT SEASONS (2019 - 2023)

YEAR	CONCACAF	MAJOR LEAGUE	PLAYOFFS	L.CUP	CANCHAMP
2023	QF (1-0-3)	W-6th (12-12-10)	L16 (0-0-2)	L32 (1-2-0)	1st (3-0-0)
2022	-	W-9th (12-7-15)	-	-	1st (2-2-0)
2021	-	W-6th (12-13-9)	(0-0-1)	-	(0-0-1)
2020	-	W-9th (9-0-14)	-	-	-
2019	-	W-12th (8-10-16)	-	-	(0-1-1)

* W-D-L from Concacaf Champions League, Major League Soccer, MLS Playoffs, Leagues Cup, Canadian Championship

2023 VANCOUVER WHITECAPS FC

Head Coach Vanni Sartini overall record in 2023 from 45 competitive matches : 16W - 14D - 15L
Assistant Coach Michael D'Agostino in charge for one match on 15 July 2023 : 1W - 0D - 0L

GOALKEEPERS	CONCACAF	MAJOR LEAGUE	MLS PLAYOFFS	LEAGUES CUP	CAN. CHAMP
18 Takaoka, Yohei	2/2 180	33/33 2970 CS 8	2/2 180	2/2 180	3/3 270 CS 1
1 Hasal, Thomas	2/2 180	1/1 90	- -	0/0 0	0/0 0
32 Boehmer, Isaac	0/0 0	0/0 0	0/0 0	1/1 90	- -

WHITECAPS FC	CONCACAF	MAJOR LEAGUE	MLS PLAYOFFS	LEAGUES CUP	CAN. CHAMP
4 Veselinovic, Ranko	3/3 214	32/31 2824 2g,2a	2/2 180	3/3 215	2/2 180
25 Gauld, Ryan	3/3 184	32/30 2640 11g,12a	2/2 180 1a	3/3 260 1a	2/2 158 1g
24 White, Brian	4/2 237 2g	32/30 2552 15g,5a	2/2 180 1g	3/2 225 1g	2/2 165 1g
6 Blackmon, Tristan	4/3 312 1g	30/28 2518 2g	2/2 180	3/2 225	3/3 262
45 Vite, Pedro	4/2 233 1g	34/24 2157 4g,3a	2/2 171	2/1 125 1g	3/0 79 2a
20 Cubas, Andrés	2/2 169	28/27 2144 3a	2/2 152 1a	3/3 270	2/2 180
8 Schöpf, Alessandro	- -	28/21 1783 1g,1a	2/1 80	3/3 226	1/1 64 1a
23 Brown, Javain	3/2 225 1a	25/21 1772 1g,2a	1/1 58	1/1 55	2/1 155
14 Luis Martins	1/0 22	20/18 1621 2a	1/0 32	1/1 90	2/0 57
2 Laborda, Mathias	3/2 211	23/17 1536 1g	1/1 21	3/2 215	2/2 180
27 Raposo, Ryan	4/4 293 1g	26/16 1335 2a	1/0 34	2/2 180	3/3 213
16 Berhalter, Sebastian	4/2 210 1a	28/11 1293 2g,2a	1/0 9	2/2 112 1a	2/1 107
22 Ahmed, Ali	3/2 177	22/12 1121 2g,2a	2/1 100	1/0 10	2/2 91 1g
7 Laryea, Richie	- -	12/12 953 1g,3a	2/2 146	- -	- -
29 Becher, Simon	2/0 42 1g	19/5 604 4g,1a	1/0 9	1/0 6	2/1 104 2g
3 Adekugbe, Samuel	- -	10/4 408 1a	2/2 171 1g	- -	- -
11 Hoilett, Junior	- -	7/2 231	2/0 88	- -	- -
28 Johnson, Levonte	0/0 0	7/2 199	1/0 9	2/1 59	2/1 90 1g
31 Teibert, Russell	3/2 171	7/0 147	0/0 0	2/0 30	3/3 217
26 Ngando, Jean-Claude	3/1 146	8/0 73	- -	2/2 139	1/0 8
66 Aguillar, Giovanni	- -	1/0 9	- -	- -	- -
12 Yao, Karifa	2/1 101	1/0 1	- -	1/0 55	1/0 8
52 Fry, Vasco	1/0 14	0/0 0	- -	- -	- -
30 Habibullah, Kamron	0/0 0	0/0 0	- -	- -	- -
61 Campagna, Matteo	1/0 3	0/0 0	- -	0/0 0	- -

X-WHITECAPS FC	CONCACAF	MAJOR LEAGUE	MLS PLAYOFFS	LEAGUES CUP	CAN. CHAMP
x-19 Gressel, Julian	3/2 195	18/16 1362 3g,5a	- -	- -	3/2 201 2g
x-9 Córdova, Sergio	2/2 138	19/9 837 2g,1a	- -	3/2 183 2g	- -
x-11 Dájome, Cristián	4/4 258	7/4 297	- -	- -	- -
x-7 Caicedo, Déiber	1/1 45	15/0 182 1a	- -	2/0 20	2/1 91

Matches played / started, Minutes played, Goals, Assists (or Clean Sheets for Goalkeepers)

CANADIAN SOCCER FOOTBALL ANNUAL

2024 VANCOUVER WHITECAPS FC
Vancouver Whitecaps FC roster as of 1 April 2024

GOALKEEPERS

#	Pos	Name	HT	S	YR	NAT
1	GK	Takoaka, Yohei	183	R	1996	JPN
17	GK	Bendik, Joe	191	L	1989	USA
32	GK	Boehmer, Isaac	188		2001	CAN
50	GK	Anchor, Max	183		2004	CAN

CENTRE BACKS & FULLBACKS

#	Pos	Name	HT	S	YR	NAT
2	CB	Laborda, Mathías	184	R	1999	URU
3	LB	Adekugbe, Sam	178	L	1995	CAN
4	CB	Veselinović, Ranko	186	R	1999	SRB
6	CB	Blackmon, Tristan	188	R	1996	USA
12	CB	Halbouni, Belal	188	R	1999	SYR
14	FB	Luis Martins	178	L	1992	POR
15	CB	Utvik, Bjørn Inge	183	R	1996	NOR
23	RB	Brown, Javain	180	R	1999	JAM

MIDFIELDERS & FORWARDS

#	Pos	Name	HT	S	YR	NAT
7	M / FB	Raposo, Ryan	170	R	1999	CAN
8	M	Schöpf, Alessandro	178	R	1994	AUT
11	W	Picault, Fafà	173	R	1991	HAI
13	M	Priso, Ralph	176		2002	CAN
16	M	Berhalter, Sebastian	175	R	2001	USA
19	F	Kreilach, Damir	186	R	1989	CRO
20	M	Cubas, Andrés	169	R	1996	PAR
22	M / FB	Ahmed, Ali	180	R	2000	CAN
24	F	White, Brian	180	R	1996	USA
25	AM	Gauld, Ryan	170	L	1995	SCO
28	W	Johnson, Levonte	178	R	1999	CAN
45	M	Vite, Pedro	168	L	2002	ECU

HEAD COACH : VANNI SARTINI
Fourth season as manager (appointed 27 August 2021)
Overall record across 98 matches : 37W - 28D - 33L

2024 TECHNICAL STAFF & COACHES

Sartini, Vanni	Head Coach & Director of Methodology
D'Agostino, Michael	Assistant Coach
Dahha, Youssef	Goalkeeper Coach
Foster, Andrew	Video Analyst

MAJOR LEAGUE SOCCER

WHITECAPS FC

FIXTURES (PACIFIC TIME)

Day	Date	Time	H/A	Result	Opponent
SA	02 MAR	16.30	HOME	D 1-1	vs. CHAR
SA	09 MAR	19.30	AWAY	W 2-0	@ SANJ
SA	16 MAR	17.30	AWAY	W 3-1	@ DALL
SA	23 MAR	16.30	HOME	L 1-2	vs. RSL
SA	30 MAR	19.30	HOME	W 3-2	vs. PORT
SA	06 APR	16.30	HOME	_____	vs. TORO
SA	13 APR	19.30	HOME	_____	vs. LAG
SA	20 APR	19.30	AWAY	_____	@ SEAT
SA	27 APR	16.30	AWAY	_____	@ NYRB
SA	04 MAY	19.30	HOME	_____	vs. AUST
SA	11 MAY	19.30	AWAY	_____	@ LAFC
WE	15 MAY	18.30	AWAY	_____	@ COLO
SA	18 MAY	19.30	AWAY	_____	@ SEAT
SA	25 MAY	19.30	HOME	_____	vs. MIAM
WE	29 MAY	17.30	AWAY	_____	@ KANS
SA	01 JUN	19.30	HOME	_____	vs. COLO
SA	15 JUN	16.30	AWAY	_____	@ NENG
SA	22 JUN	19.30	AWAY	_____	@ PORT
SA	29 JUN	19.30	HOME	_____	vs. SLOU
WE	03 JUL	17.30	AWAY	_____	@ MINN
SA	06 JUL	16.30	AWAY	_____	@ MONT
SA	13 JUL	20.30	AWAY	_____	@ SLOU
WE	17 JUL	19.30	HOME	_____	vs. KANS
SA	20 JUL	19.30	HOME	_____	vs. HOUS
SA	24 AUG	16.30	HOME	_____	vs. LAFC
SA	31 AUG	17.30	AWAY	_____	@ AUST
SA	07 SEP	19.30	HOME	_____	vs. DALL
SA	14 SEP	19.30	HOME	_____	vs. SANJ
WE	18 SEP	17.30	AWAY	_____	@ HOUS
SA	21 SEP	19.30	AWAY	_____	@ LAG
SA	28 SEP	19.30	HOME	_____	vs. PORT
WE	02 OCT	19.30	HOME	_____	vs. SEAT
SA	05 OCT	16.30	HOME	_____	vs. MINN
SA	19 OCT	18.00	AWAY	_____	@ RSL

CANADIAN CHAMPIONSHIP

Round	Year	Opponent
QF	2024	_____
QF	2024	_____
SF	2024	_____
SF	2024	_____
FINAL	2024	_____

PACIFIC FC

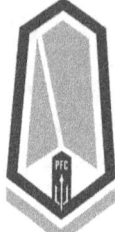

FIVE MOST RECENT SEASONS (2019 - 2023)

YEAR	C.LEAGUE	CAN. PREMIER	PLAYOFFS	CAN CHAMP
2023	-	4th (11-7-10)	3rd (2-0-1)	SF (1-1-1)
2022	L16 (2-1-1)	4th (13-7-8)	SF (0-1-1)	QF (0-1-0)
2021	-	3rd (13-6-9)	1st (2-0-0)	SF (2-0-1)
2020	-	1st (3-2-2)	3rd (1-0-2)	-
2019	-	5th (8-7-13)	-	(0-0-2)

* W-D-L from Concacaf League, Canadian Premier League, CPL Playoffs, Canadian Championship

2023 PACIFIC FC

Head Coach James Merriman overall record in 2023 from 33 competitive matches : 13W - 8D - 12L
Assistant Coach Armando Sá in charge for one match on 2 September 2023 : 1W - 0D - 0L

GOALKEEPERS	CONCACAF	CAN. PREMIER		CPL PLAYOFFS			CAN. CHAMP		
1 Gazdov, Emil		18/18	1620 CS 3	3/3	270	CS 2	2/2	180	
12 Baskett, Kieran		10/10	900 CS 3	0/0	0		1/1	90	CS 1

PACIFIC FC	CONCACAF	CAN. PREMIER		CPL PLAYOFFS			CAN. CHAMP		
26 Meilleur-Giguère, Thomas		26/26	2339 4g	3/3	270		2/2	180	
55 Didic, Amer		24/24	2159 4g,1a	3/3	238		3/3	270	
13 Dada-Luke, Olakunle		27/24	2149 1a	2/2	180		3/3	270	
34 Aparicio, Manuel		24/23	2046 4g,5a	3/3	270		3/3	202	
20 Young, Sean		26/22	1905 4g,3a	3/3	270		3/3	257	1a
11 Heard, Josh		25/20	1717 4g,1a	2/2	140		3/3	248	1g
28 Toussaint, Cédric		23/20	1672 1a	3/0	72		2/2	145	
7 Yeates, Steffen		28/19	1625 1g,1a	1/1	68		3/2	184	
21 Sellouf, Ayman		27/14	1616 7g,8a	3/1	107		3/2	137	
2 Mukumbilwa, Georges		21/17	1506	3/3	270		3/2	206	
10 Reid, Adonijah		23/16	1188 3g,3a	3/1	129	1g,1a	3/0	63	1g
9 Ongaro, Easton		26/9	1028 5g,2a	3/3	229		3/2	173	1g
23 Daniels, Djenairo		22/11	896 3g,3a	2/1	84		2/2	122	
5 Vliet, Bradley		14/9	842 2a	-	-		1/1	64	
31 Manneh, Kekuta		19/10	757 1g,1a	3/2	163	1g,1a	2/0	80	
4 Amedume, Paul		12/6	565	2/1	91		1/0	1	
3 Lajeunesse, Eric		6/5	455	-	-		1/0	67	
14 Brazão, David		12/2	335 2g,1a	0/0	0		2/0	18	1a
18 Bahous, Zakaria		4/1	136	2/1	119		-	-	
19 Binate, Abdul		3/0	35	-	-		-	-	
16 Watson, Jalen		0/0	0	-	-		-	-	
33 Marvasti, Sami		0/0	0	-	-		-	-	

X-PACIFIC FC	CONCACAF	CAN. PREMIER	CPL PLAYOFFS	CAN. CHAMP	
x-8 Lamothe, Pierre		6/2 196	- -	1/0	13

Matches played / started, Minutes played, Goals, Assists (or Clean Sheets for Goalkeepers)

CANADIAN SOCCER FOOTBALL ANNUAL

2024 PACIFIC FC
Pacific FC roster as of 1 April 2024

GOALKEEPERS

#	Pos	Name	HT	S	YR	NAT
1	GK	Gazdov, Emil	193		2003	CAN
-	GK	Melvin, Sean	193	R	1994	CAN

CENTRE BACKS & FULLBACKS

#	Pos	Name	HT	S	YR	NAT
2	FB / W	Mukumbilwa, Georges	180	R	1999	CAN
4	CB / M	Amedume, Paul	182		2003	CAN
26	CB	Meilleur-Giguère, Thomas	185	R	1997	CAN
-	FB/M	Greco-Taylor, Christian	175	L	2005	CAN
-	FB/M	Ndom, Aly	189	L	1996	FRA

MIDFIELDERS & FORWARDS

#	Pos	Name	HT	S	YR	NAT
7	M	Yeates, Steffen	175		2000	CAN
10	F	Reid, Adonijah	168	R	1999	CAN
11	LW	Heard, Josh	175		1994	CAN
13	M	Dada-Luke, Olakunle	183	R	2000	CAN
18	M	Bahous, Zakaria	180	R	2001	CAN
20	M	Young, Sean	186		2001	CAN
21	F	Sellouf, Ayman	177	L	2001	NED
28	DM	Toussaint, Cédric	173	R	2001	CAN
-	M	Lamothe, Pierre	173	R	1997	CAN
-	F	Moore, Reon	175	R	1996	TRI
-	M	Tircovean, Andrei	170	L	1997	ROU
-	F	Zanatta, Dario	175	R	1997	CAN

HEAD COACH : JAMES MERRIMAN
Third season as manager (appointed 21 January 2022)
Overall record across 70 matches since 2019 : 30W - 18D - 22L

2024 TECHNICAL STAFF & COACHES

Merriman, James	Head Coach
Sá, Armando	Assistant Coach
Stiles, Trevor	Goalkeeper Coach

PACIFIC FC

FIXTURES (PACIFIC TIME) — OPPONENT

Day	Date	Time	H/A		Opponent
SA	13 APR	16.00	HOME	___	vs. HALI
FR	19 APR	19.00	HOME	___	vs. WINN
SU	28 APR	14.00	AWAY	___	@ CALG
SA	04 MAY	16.00	HOME	___	vs. YORK
SA	11 MAY	14.00	HOME	___	vs. HAMI
FR	17 MAY	19.00	HOME	___	vs. OTTA
SA	25 MAY	13.00	AWAY	___	@ VFC
SA	01 JUN	16.00	HOME	___	vs. CALG
SA	08 JUN	11.00	AWAY	___	@ HALI
FR	14 JUN	17.00	AWAY	___	@ WINN
WE	19 JUN	16.00	AWAY	___	@ YORK
TH	27 JUN	19.30	HOME	___	vs. VFC
SU	07 JUL	11.00	AWAY	___	@ OTTA
TH	11 JUL	11.00	AWAY	___	@ HALI
SU	14 JUL	16.00	AWAY	___	@ HAMI
SU	28 JUL	14.00	HOME	___	vs. WINN
FR	02 AUG	19.00	HOME	___	vs. YORK
SU	11 AUG	14.00	AWAY	___	@ VFC
SA	17 AUG	13.00	HOME	___	vs. OTTA
SA	24 AUG	14.00	AWAY	___	@ CALG
FR	30 AUG	16.00	AWAY	___	@ HAMI
SA	07 SEP	19.00	HOME	___	vs. HALI
SA	14 SEP	14.00	HOME	___	vs. VFC
SU	22 SEP	11.00	AWAY	___	@ OTTA
MO	30 SEP	17.00	AWAY	___	@ WINN
SA	05 OCT	14.00	HOME	___	vs. CALG
TH	10 OCT	16.00	AWAY	___	@ YORK
SA	19 OCT	TBD	HOME	___	vs. HAMI

CANADIAN CHAMPIONSHIP — OPPONENT

Round	Year	H/A		Opponent
1R	2024	HOME	___	Victoria
QF	2024		___	
QF	2024		___	
SF	2024		___	
SF	2024		___	
FINAL	2024		___	

VANCOUVER FC

INAUGURAL YEAR (2023)

YEAR	CONCACAF	CAN. PREMIER	PLAYOFFS	CAN CHAMP
2023	-	7th (8-5-15)	-	(0-0-1)

* W-D-L from Concacaf Champions League, Canadian Premier League, CPL Playoffs, Canadian Championship

2023 VANCOUVER FC

Head Coach Afshin Ghotbi overall record in 2023 from 28 competitive matches : 8W - 5D - 15L
Assistant Coach Mark Village in charge for one match on 16 September 2023 : 0W - 0D - 1L

GOALKEEPERS	CONCACAF	CAN. PREMIER		CPL PLAYOFFS	CAN. CHAMP	
1 Irving, Callum		27/27	2430 CS 5		1/1	90
21 Zielinski, Jeremy		1/1	90		0/0	0
31 Schneider, Trevor		0/0	0		-	-

VANCOUVER FC	CONCACAF	CAN. PREMIER		CPL PLAYOFFS	CAN. CHAMP	
3 Romeo, Antonio Rocco		25/25	2189		1/1	90
11 Bitar, Gabriel		25/23	1968 6g,4a		1/0	45
9/10 Hundal, Shaan		28/20	1854 6g,1a		1/1	45
16 Simmons, Elliot		25/24	1832 1a		1/1	90
4 Bakaré, Ibrahim		25/18	1715		1/1	90
25 Cameron, James		19/17	1504 1g		-	-
20 White, Anthony		20/17	1500 1a		0/0	0
12 Crawford, Tyler		23/14	1318		0/0	0
17 Kwak, Minjae		26/13	1312 1g,2a		-	-
6 Garcia, Renan		14/14	1257 1g,1a		-	-
9 Diaz, Alejandro		14/14	1211 2g		-	-
19 Cantave, Mikaël		16/13	1100 4g,2a		-	-
2 Chung, Kadin		13/12	1002 1a		1/1	90
13 Fry, Vasco		10/10	868 1g,1a		-	-
8 Moazeni Zadeh, Nima		13/9	836		1/1	60
26 Tahid, Taryck		20/6	554 3g		-	-
18 Kinani, Ameer		20/2	466 1g,1a		1/1	60
14 Gyimah, Nicky		11/2	251		1/0	30
15 Kane, Mamadou		8/2	157		-	-
7 St. Louis, Nathaniel		4/1	71		1/0	9
24 Thompson, Lennon		3/0	48		-	-
33 Mejia, Ivan		1/0	11		-	-

X-VANCOUVER FC	CONCACAF	CAN. PREMIER		CPL PLAYOFFS	CAN. CHAMP	
x-5 Martínez, Eugene		11/11	906		1/1	90
x-10 Sandoval, Gael		12/9	777 1g,3a		1/1	81
x-22 Simmons, Marcus		5/2	127		-	-
x-19 Henry, Maël		3/1	121		-	-
x-13 Robe, Emmanuel		4/1	77		1/0	30

Matches played / started, Minutes played, Goals, Assists (or Clean Sheets for Goalkeepers)

CANADIAN SOCCER FOOTBALL ANNUAL

2024 VANCOUVER FC
Vancouver FC roster as of 1 April 2024

GOALKEEPERS

#	Pos	Name	HT	S	YR	NAT
1	GK	Irving, Callum	183	R	1993	CAN

CENTRE BACKS & FULLBACKS

#	Pos	Name	HT	S	YR	NAT
2	FB	Chung, Kadin	168		1998	CAN
3	CB	Romeo, Antonio Rocco	195	R	2000	CAN
12	LB	Crawford, Tyler	175	L	2004	CAN
20	CB	White, Anthony	188	L	2003	CAN
25	RB	Cameron, James	183	R	2005	CAN
-	RB	Bah, Elage	170	R	2004	CAN
-	FB / M	Gee, Paris	180	R	1994	CAN
-	CB / M	Norman, David	185	L	1998	CAN

MIDFIELDERS & FORWARDS

#	Pos	Name	HT	S	YR	NAT
6	M	Garcia, Renan	186	L	1986	BRA
9	F	Díaz, Alejandro	177	R	1996	MEX
11	M	Bitar, Gabriel	178	R	1998	LIB
13	M	Fry, Vasco	178	L	2000	PER
16	M	Simmons, Elliot	185	R	1998	CAN
19	M	Cantave, Mikaël	174	R	1996	HAI
26	M	Tahid, Taryck	178	R	2007	CAN
-	F	Dyer, Moses	178	R	1997	NZL
-	F	Fisk, Ben	178	L	1993	CAN
-	M	Kibato, Kembo	176	L	2000	CAN
-	AM	McDonnell, Grady	183	R	2008	IRL
-	F	Navarro, José	185		2003	MEX
-	M / FB	Verhoven, Zachary	175	R	1998	CAN

HEAD COACH : AFSHIN GHOTBI
Second season as manager (appointed 2 November 2022)
Overall record across 28 matches : 8W - 5D - 15L

2024 TECHNICAL STAFF & COACHES

Ghotbi, Afshin	Head Coach
Ferreira, Marco	Assistant Coach
Palani, Azad	Assistant Coach
Village, Mark	Goalkeeper Coach

CANADIAN PREMIER LEAGUE

VANCOUVER FC

FIXTURES (PACIFIC TIME)				OPPONENT
SU	14 APR	14.00	HOME ____	vs. WINN
TH	18 APR	19.00	HOME ____	vs. HALI
FR	26 APR	16.00	AWAY ____	@ YORK
FR	03 MAY	18.00	AWAY ____	@ CALG
SU	12 MAY	14.00	HOME ____	vs. OTTA
SA	18 MAY	13.00	AWAY ____	@ HAMI
SA	25 MAY	13.00	HOME ____	vs. PFC
SU	02 JUN	14.00	AWAY ____	@ WINN
SU	09 JUN	15.00	AWAY ____	@ YORK
SU	16 JUN	14.00	HOME ____	vs. CALG
SU	23 JUN	14.00	HOME ____	vs. HALI
TH	27 JUN	19.30	AWAY ____	@ PFC
FR	05 JUL	16.00	AWAY ____	@ HAMI
FR	12 JUL	19.00	HOME ____	vs. OTTA
SA	20 JUL	13.00	HOME ____	vs. YORK
FR	26 JUL	19.00	HOME ____	vs. CALG
MO	05 AUG	12.00	AWAY ____	@ HALI
SU	11 AUG	14.00	HOME ____	vs. PFC
SU	18 AUG	14.00	HOME ____	vs. HAMI
SU	25 AUG	12.00	AWAY ____	@ WINN
SA	31 AUG	16.00	AWAY ____	@ OTTA
FR	06 SEP	19.00	HOME ____	vs. YORK
SA	14 SEP	14.00	AWAY ____	@ PFC
SA	21 SEP	13.00	HOME ____	vs. HAMI
SA	28 SEP	16.00	AWAY ____	@ CALG
SA	05 OCT	11.00	AWAY ____	@ HALI
SU	13 OCT	14.00	HOME ____	vs. WINN
SA	19 OCT	TBD	AWAY ____	@ OTTA

CANADIAN CHAMPIONSHIP			OPPONENT
1R	2024	AWAY ____	@ CALG
QF	2024	____	
QF	2024	____	
SF	2024	____	
SF	2024	____	
FINAL 2024		____	

CALGARY CAVALRY FC

FIVE MOST RECENT SEASONS (2019 - 2023)

YEAR	C.LEAGUE	CAN. PREMIER	PLAYOFFS	CAN CHAMP
2023	-	1st (16-7-5)	2nd (1-0-2)	(0-1-0)
2022	-	3rd (14-5-9)	SF (0-1-1)	QF (1-1-0)
2021	-	2nd (14-8-6)	SF (0-0-1)	QF (1-0-1)
2020	-	1st (4-1-2)	4th (1-0-2)	-
2019	-	1st (19-5-4)	2nd (0-0-2)	SF (4-2-2)

* W-D-L from Concacaf League, Canadian Premier League, CPL Playoffs, Canadian Championship

2023 CAVALRY FC
Head Coach Tommy Wheeldon Jr. overall record in 2023 from 32 competitive matches : 17W - 8D - 7L

GOALKEEPERS	CONCACAF	CAN. PREMIER		CPL PLAYOFFS		CAN. CHAMP	
1 Carducci, Marco		28/28	2520 CS 8	3/3	300	1/1	90
21 Kerr, Sterling		0/0	0	0/0	0	0/0	0
31 Holliday, Joseph		0/0	0	0/0	0	-	-

CAVALRY FC	CONCACAF	CAN. PREMIER		CPL PLAYOFFS		CAN. CHAMP	
4 Klomp, Daan		28/28	2520 4g,1a	3/3	300 1g	1/1	90 1a
24 Kobza, Eryk		26/23	2068 2g	3/3	300	-	-
7 Musse, Ali		25/24	2030 5g,5a	3/3	245 2g,2a	1/1	78
9 Bevan, Myer		26/25	2017 11g,4a	3/3	299 1a	1/1	68 1g
5 Kamdem, Bradley		22/22	1947 2a	3/3	276	-	-
8 Daley, Jesse		24/20	1753 4a	3/3	266	1/0	22
6 Trafford, Charlie		25/21	1731 1a	3/3	300	1/1	68
33 Aird, Fraser		26/12	1435 2g,2a	3/2	222	1/0	12
10 Camargo, Sergio		25/20	1417 6g,1a	3/3	234 1a	-	-
26 Shome, Shamit		17/13	1245 1a	3/1	150	1/1	90
15 Chima, Udoka		13/9	838	-	-	0/0	0
3 Montgomery, Callum		11/6	656	2/0	34	1/1	90
19 Henry, Maël		12/6	559 2g	3/0	49	-	-
2 Alarcón, Roberto		11/7	547	INJ	-	1/1	90
23 Smith-Doyle, Gareth		16/7	532 1g,1a	0/0	0	-	-
20 Mason, Joe		17/4	518 2a	3/0	18 1g	1/1	33
17 Fisk, Ben		15/4	474 1g,2a	2/0	12	-	-
19 Akio, William		10/4	434 5g	3/3	295	-	-
14 Beckford, Ethan		14/0	254	-	-	1/0	22
12 Field, Tom		4/2	212	-	-	-	-
29 Harms, Michael		3/1	114	-	-	-	-
28 Myroniuk, Niko		1/0	3	-	-	1/0	57

X-CAVALRY FC	CONCACAF	CAN. PREMIER		CPL PLAYOFFS		CAN. CHAMP	
x-30 Ntignee, Goteh		17/8	883 2g,2a	-	-	1/0	12
x-11 Escalante, José		11/8	716	-	-	1/1	78
x-22 Cantave, Mikaël		10/6	543 2g	-	-	1/1	90
x-27 Omoreniye, William		0/0	0	-	-	-	-

Matches played / started, Minutes played, Goals, Assists (or Clean Sheets for Goalkeepers)

CANADIAN SOCCER FOOTBALL ANNUAL

2024 CAVALRY FC
Cavalry FC roster as of 1 April 2024

	GOALKEEPERS		HT	S	YR	NAT.
1	GK	Carducci, Marco	185	R	1996	CAN
21	GK	Barrett, Mitchell			2006	CAN
31	GK	Morrison, Blake			2008	CAN
-	GK	Barrett, Jack			2002	ENG

	CENTRE BACKS & FULLBACKS		HT	S	YR	NAT.
3	CB	Montgomery, Callum	190		1998	CAN
4	CB	Klomp, Daan	185	R	1998	NED
5	LB / M	Kamdem, Bradley	184	L	1994	CAN
12	LB	Field, Tom	183	L	1997	ENG
29	FB / CB	Harms, Michael	175	R	2005	CAN

	MIDFIELDERS & FORWARDS		HT	S	YR	NAT.
6	M	Trafford, Charlie	193	R	1992	CAN
7	W	Musse, Ali	183	L	1996	SOM
8	M	Daley, Jesse	175	R	1997	AUS
9	F	Bevan, Myer	188	R	1997	NZL
10	CM	Camargo, Sergio	170	R	1994	CAN
16	F	Warschewski, Tobias	188	R	1998	GER
18	M	Henry, Maël	178	R	2004	CAN
19	F	Akio, William	180	R	1998	SSD
24	F / M	Kobza, Eryk	188	R	2001	CAN
26	CM	Shome, Shamit	178	R	1997	CAN
27	M / FB	Gutiérrez, Diego	178	R	1997	CAN
33	M / FB	Aird, Fraser	173	R	1995	CAN
-	W	Brooks, Lleyton	179	R	2001	AUS
-	AM	Dias, Lucas	180	R	2003	CAN

HEAD COACH : TOMMY WHEELDON, JR.
Sixth season as manager (appointed 18 May 2018)
Overall record across 141 matches : 74W - 30D - 37L

2024 TECHNICAL STAFF & COACHES
Wheeldon, Tommy Jr.	Head Coach & General Manager
Ledgerwood, Nik	Assistant Coach & Community Relations
Wheeldon, Jay	Assistant Coach
Davis, Jake	Goalkeeper Coach

CAVALRY FC

FIXTURES (MOUNTAIN TIME)					OPPONENT
SA	13 APR	14.00	AWAY	_____	@ HAMI
SA	20 APR	12.00	AWAY	_____	@ OTTA
SU	28 APR	15.00	HOME	_____	vs. PFC
FR	03 MAY	19.00	HOME	_____	vs. VFC
SA	11 MAY	12.00	AWAY	_____	@ HALI
SA	18 MAY	17.00	HOME	_____	vs. YORK
SU	26 MAY	15.00	HOME	_____	vs. WINN
SA	01 JUN	17.00	AWAY	_____	@ PFC
SA	08 JUN	15.00	HOME	_____	vs. HAMI
SU	16 JUN	15.00	AWAY	_____	@ VFC
FR	21 JUN	19.00	HOME	_____	vs. OTTA
MO	01 JUL	13.00	AWAY	_____	@ HALI
SU	07 JUL	15.00	AWAY	_____	@ WINN
SA	13 JUL	14.00	HOME	_____	vs. YORK
SU	21 JUL	15.00	HOME	_____	vs. HAMI
FR	26 JUL	20.00	AWAY	_____	@ VFC
SA	03 AUG	17.00	AWAY	_____	@ OTTA
SA	10 AUG	14.00	HOME	_____	vs. HALI
FR	16 AUG	17.00	AWAY	_____	@ YORK
SA	24 AUG	15.00	HOME	_____	vs. PFC
FR	30 AUG	19.00	HOME	_____	vs. WINN
SA	07 SEP	17.00	AWAY	_____	@ HAMI
SU	15 SEP	15.00	HOME	_____	vs. OTTA
FR	20 SEP	17.00	AWAY	_____	@ YORK
SA	28 SEP	17.00	HOME	_____	vs. VFC
SA	05 OCT	15.00	AWAY	_____	@ PFC
SA	12 OCT	17.00	HOME	_____	vs. HALI
SA	19 OCT	TBD	AWAY	_____	@ WINN

CANADIAN CHAMPIONSHIP				OPPONENT
1R	2024	HOME	_____	vs. VFC
QF	2024		_____	
QF	2024		_____	
SF	2024		_____	
SF	2024		_____	
FINAL	2024			

WINNIPEG VALOUR FC

FIVE MOST RECENT SEASONS (2019 - 2023)

YEAR	CONCACAF	CAN. PREMIER	PLAYOFFS	CAN CHAMP
2023	-	8th (6-8-14)	-	(0-0-1)
2022	-	5th (10-7-11)	-	(0-0-1)
2021	-	5th (10-5-13)	-	QF (1-0-1)
2020	-	6th (2-2-3)	-	-
2019	-	6th (8-4-16)	-	(0-0-2)

* W-D-L from Concacaf Champions League, Canadian Premier League, CPL Playoffs, Canadian Championship

2023 WINNIPEG VALOUR FC
Head Coach Philip Dos Santos overall record in 2023 from 28 competitive matches : 6W - 7D - 15L
Assistant Coach Jeyhan Bhindi in charge for one match on 20 May 2023 : 0W - 1D - 0L

GOALKEEPERS	CONCACAF	CAN. PREMIER		CPL PLAYOFFS	CAN. CHAMP	
99 Yesli, Rayane		26/26	2340 CS 7		1/1	90
1 Murasiranwa, Darlington		2/2	180		-	-

VALOUR FC	CONCACAF	CAN. PREMIER		CPL PLAYOFFS	CAN. CHAMP	
6 Campbell, Dante		25/25	2165 1g,1a		1/1	45
8 Gutiérrez, Diego		25/25	2113 4g,1a		1/0	45
7 Williams, Kian		23/22	1937 4g,5a		1/1	45
21 Polisi, Marcello		22/22	1912 1g		-	-
2 Baquero, Andy		26/18	1839		1/1	90
24 Niyongabire, Pacifique		25/21	1823 1g,3a		1/0	45
18 Cela, Klaidi		23/18	1712 2g,1a		-	-
19/22 deBrienne, Matteo		20/18	1571 3g,3a		1/1	90
5 Samaké, Abdoulaye		17/17	1457 1g		1/1	90
4 Pianelli, Guillaume		17/15	1292 1g		1/0	11
20 Sanchez, Juan		21/15	1256		1/0	45 1g
9 Ponce, Gallardo, Walter		22/14	1085 4g,1a		1/0	28
11 Ulloa, Jared		26/9	1047 1g,1a		1/1	45
23 Novak, Anthony		23/9	943 1g		1/1	90
3 Haynes, Jordan		14/11	902		-	-
32 Siaj, Jaime		12/5	517		0/0	0
19 Mzoughi, Eskander		14/5	516		-	-
35 Jean-Baptiste, Andrew		9/6	487		-	-
12 Selemani, Ahinga		10/3	376		-	-
10 Rendón, Kevin		8/1	136		1/1	90
27 Ohin, Raphael		1/1	79		1/1	90
15 Chandler, Matthew		1/0	7		1/1	90

X-VALOUR FC	CONCACAF	CAN. PREMIER	CPL PLAYOFFS	CAN. CHAMP	
x- 1 Tisseur, Jordan		0/0 0		0/0	0

Matches played / started, Minutes played, Goals, Assists (or Clean Sheets for Goalkeepers)

CANADIAN SOCCER FOOTBALL ANNUAL

2024 WINNIPEG VALOUR FC
Valour FC roster as of 1 April 2024

GOALKEEPERS

#	Pos	Name	HT	S	YR	NAT
1	GK	Murasiranwa, Darlington	178		2001	CAN
-	GK	Visconi, Jonathan	188	R	1991	CAN

CENTRE BACKS & FULLBACKS

#	Pos	Name	HT	S	YR	NAT
3	LB / M	Haynes, Jordan	178	L	1996	CAN
5	CB	Samaké, Abdoulaye	186	R	1996	CAN
-	RB	Alarcón, Roberto	173	R	1998	ESP
-	FB	Antonoglou, Themi	178	L	2001	CAN
-	CB	Chantzopoulos, Haris	194	R	1994	GER
-	CB	Mourdoukoutas, Tass	189	R	1999	AUS
-	FB	Sukunda, Zachary	174	R	1995	CAN

MIDFIELDERS & FORWARDS

#	Pos	Name	HT	S	YR	NAT
6	M	Campbell, Dante	178	R	1999	CAN
7	M	Williams, Kian	182	R	2000	ENG
20	M	Sánchez, Juan Pablo	170	R	2003	CAN
21	M	Polisi, Marcello	173	R	1997	CAN
27	M	Ohin, Raphael	170	R	1995	GHA
-	F	Binate, Abdul	180	R	2003	CAN
-	W	Faria, Jordan	168	R	2000	CAN
-	F	Hundal, Shaan	183	R	1999	CAN
-	F	Swibel, Jordan	181	R	1999	AUS
-	M	Verhoeven, Noah	173	L	1999	CAN

HEAD COACH : PHILLIP DOS SANTOS
Fourth season as manager (appointed 23 September 2021)
Overall record across 67 matches : 19W - 17D - 31L

2024 TECHNICAL STAFF & COACHES

Dos Santos, Phillip	Head Coach & General Manager
Di Stefani, Patrick	Goalkeeper Coach
Bhindi, Jay	Assistant Coach
Fordyce, Daryl	Assistant Coach

VALOUR FC

FIXTURES (CENTRAL TIME)

Day	Date	Time	H/A		Opponent
SU	14 APR	16.00	AWAY	____	@ VFC
FR	19 APR	21.00	AWAY	____	@ PFC
SA	27 APR	15.00	AWAY	____	@ HAMI
SU	05 MAY	13.00	AWAY	____	@ OTTA
FR	10 MAY	18.00	AWAY	____	@ YORK
MO	20 MAY	14.00	AWAY	____	@ HALI
SU	26 MAY	16.00	AWAY	____	@ CALG
SU	02 JUN	16.00	HOME	____	vs. VFC
SU	09 JUN	14.00	HOME	____	vs. OTTA
FR	14 JUN	19.00	HOME	____	vs. PFC
SU	23 JUN	15.00	AWAY	____	@ HAMI
TH	27 JUN	18.30	HOME	____	vs. YORK
SU	07 JUL	16.00	HOME	____	vs. CALG
TH	18 JUL	17.00	AWAY	____	@ HALI
SU	21 JUL	13.00	AWAY	____	@ OTTA
SU	28 JUL	16.00	AWAY	____	@ PFC
SU	04 AUG	14.00	HOME	____	vs. HAMI
SU	11 AUG	19.00	HOME	____	vs. YORK
SA	17 AUG	14.00	HOME	____	vs. HALI
SU	25 AUG	14.00	HOME	____	vs. VFC
FR	30 AUG	20.00	AWAY	____	@ CALG
MO	09 SEP	19.00	HOME	____	vs. OTTA
FR	13 SEP	18.00	AWAY	____	@ YORK
SA	21 SEP	14.00	HOME	____	vs. HALI
MO	30 SEP	19.00	HOME	____	vs. PFC
SU	06 OCT	13.00	HOME	____	vs. HAMI
SU	13 OCT	16.00	AWAY	____	@ VFC
SA	19 OCT	TBD	HOME	____	vs. CALG

CANADIAN CHAMPIONSHIP

Round	Year		H/A		Opponent
1R	2024		AWAY	____	@ OTTA
QF	2024			____	
QF	2024			____	
SF	2024			____	
SF	2024			____	
FINAL	2024			____	

FORGE FC HAMILTON

FIVE MOST RECENT SEASONS (2019 - 2023)

YEAR	CONCACAF	C.LEAGUE	CAN. PREMIER	PLAYOFFS	CANCHAMP
2023	-	-	2nd (11-9-8)	1st (2-0-0)	SF (1-1-1)
2022	L16 (0-0-2)	-	2nd (14-5-9)	1st (2-1-0)	QF (1-0-1)
* [2020 in 2022]					*2nd (0-1-0)
2021	-	SF (3-4-1)	1st (16-2-10)	2nd (1-0-1)	SF (1-1-0)
2020	-	QF (2-1-1)	3rd (3-3-1)	1st (3-0-1)	-
2019	-	L16 (2-1-1)	2nd (17-5-6)	1st (2-0-0)	(0-1-1)

* W-D-L from Concacaf League & Champions League, Canadian Premier League, CPL Playoffs, Canadian Championship

2023 FORGE FC HAMILTON

Head Coach Bobby Smyrniotis overall record in 2023 from 32 competitive matches : 14W - 10D - 8L
Assistant Coach Kyt Selaidopoulos in charge for one match on 7 October 2023 : 0W - 0D - 1L

GOALKEEPERS	CONCACAF	CAN. PREMIER			CPL PLAYOFFS		CAN. CHAMP		
1 Henry, Triston		27/27	2400	CS 9	2/2	210	3/3	270	CS 1
29 Kalongo, Christopher		2/1	120	CS 1	0/0	0	0/0	0	
42 Marmolejo, Emmanuel		0/0	0		-	-	0/0	0	

FORGE FC	CONCACAF	CAN. PREMIER			CPL PLAYOFFS			CAN. CHAMP		
5 James, Manjrekar		26/26	2340	2a	2/2	174		3/3	270	
13 Achinioti-Jönsson, Alexander		27/24	2189		2/2	210		3/3	270	1a
24 Rama, Rezart		26/25	2189	1g,2a	2/2	208		2/2	180	
10 Bekker, Kyle		26/24	2121	3g,7a	2/2	210	1g,1a	2/2	162	1g
14 Campbell, Terran		28/24	1918	10g,1a	2/2	190		3/3	171	
21 Hojabrpour, Alessandro		22/16	1417		2/2	193		3/2	172	
17 Pacius, Woobens		28/15	1403	10g,3a	INJ	-		3/3	248	1g,1a
33 Sissoko, Aboubacar		25/16	1345	2g,1a	2/0	4		3/2	205	
20 Poku, Kwasi		21/16	1337	2g,2a	2/2	114		1/0	25	
19 Borges, Tristan		26/11	1294	1g,4a	1/0	52	1g	3/3	223	
23 Metusala, Garven-Michée		17/14	1223		2/2	210		2/1	122	
4 Samuel, Dominic		19/12	1083		2/0	111		3/2	180	
7 Choinière, David		15/11	970	2g,3a	2/0	20		2/2	155	
22 Jensen, Noah		21/10	945	1g	2/2	137	1a	3/1	94	2g
39 Badibanga, Béni		10/9	828	2g	2/2	208	1g	-	-	
81 Owolabi-Belewu, Malik		16/9	809		2/0	23		1/0	14	
9 Hamilton, Jordan		17/7	602	4g,1a	2/0	36		3/0	73	
64 Kane, Khadim		16/6	518		-	-		0/0	0	
2 Duncan, Malcolm		10/2	249		-	-		-	-	
37 Tavernier, Kevaughn		2/1	72		-	-		-	-	
12 Castello, Sebastian		2/0	2		-	-		-	-	

X-FORGE FC	CONCACAF	CAN. PREMIER			CPL PLAYOFFS		CAN. CHAMP		
x-3 Morgan, Ashtone		11/2	339	1a	-	-	3/2	166	
x-36 Firek, Daniel		0/0	0		-	-	-	-	
x-30 Olatunji, Rimi		0/0	0		-	-	-	-	

Matches played / started, Minutes played, Goals, Assists (or Clean Sheets for Goalkeepers)

CANADIAN SOCCER FOOTBALL ANNUAL

2023 FORGE FC HAMILTON
Forge FC Hamilton roster as of 1 April 2024

GOALKEEPERS

#	Pos	Name	HT	S	YR	NAT
1	GK	Henry, Triston	183	R	1993	CAN
29	GK	Kalongo, Christopher	184	R	2002	CAN
36	GK	Bontis, Dino	179	R	2004	CAN

CENTRE BACKS & FULLBACKS

#	Pos	Name	HT	S	YR	NAT
2	FB	Duncan, Malcolm	178	R	1999	CAN
4	CB / FB	Samuel, Dominic	178	R	1994	CAN
13	CB / M	Achinioti Jönsson, Alex.	180	R	1996	SWE
20	FB / M	Poku, Kwasi	188	L	2003	CAN
23	CB	Metusala, Garven-Michée	185	R	1999	HAI
81	CB	Owolabi-Belewu, Malik	190	L	2002	CAN
-	FB	Parra, Daniel	182	L	1999	MEX

MIDFIELDERS & FORWARDS

#	Pos	Name	HT	S	YR	NAT
7	AM	Choinière, David	163	R	1997	CAN
8	M	Cissé, Elimane	175	R	1995	SEN
9	F	Hamilton, Jordan	185	L	1996	CAN
10	CM	Bekker, Kyle	178	R	1990	CAN
12	M	Castello, Sebastian	175	R	2003	CAN
14	F	Campbell, Terran	173	L	1998	CAN
19	F	Borges, Tristan	170	L	1998	CAN
21	CM	Hojabrpour, Alessandro	181	R	2000	CAN
22	M	Jensen, Noah	178	R	1999	CAN
32	M	Bruno, Zayne			2007	CAN
37	F	Tavernier, Kevaughn	175	R	2006	CAN
39	W	Badibanga, Béni	176	R	1996	BEL
41	W	Koné, Amadou	190	R	2005	CAN
64	M	Kane, Khadim	190	R	2005	CAN
-	W	Ampomah, Nana	175	R	1996	GHA
-	M	Schiavoni, Matteo	183	R	2005	CAN

HEAD COACH : BOBBY SMYRNIOTIS
Sixth season as manager (appointed 1 October 2018)
Overall record across 154 matches : 77W - 35D - 42L

2024 TECHNICAL STAFF & COACHES

Smyrniotis, Bobby	Head Coach & Sporting Director
Albert, Johan	Assistant Coach & Goalkeeper Coach
Selaidopoulos, Kyt	Assistant Coach
Edgar, David	Assistant Coach
Smith, Jelani	Director of Soccer Operations

FORGE FC HAMILTON

FIXTURES (EASTERN TIME)

Day	Date	Time	H/A	OPPONENT
SA	13 APR	16.00	HOME	vs. CALG
SU	21 APR	16.00	AWAY	@ YORK
SA	27 APR	16.00	HOME	vs. WINN
TU	07 MAY	11.00	HOME	vs. HALI
SA	11 MAY	17.00	AWAY	@ PFC
SA	18 MAY	16.00	HOME	vs. VFC
SA	25 MAY	15.00	AWAY	@ OTTA
SA	01 JUN	16.00	HOME	vs. YORK
SA	08 JUN	17.00	AWAY	@ CALG
SA	15 JUN	16.00	AWAY	@ HALI
SU	23 JUN	16.00	HOME	vs. WINN
FR	28 JUN	19.00	AWAY	@ OTTA
FR	05 JUL	19.00	HOME	vs. VFC
SU	14 JUL	19.00	HOME	vs. PFC
SU	21 JUL	17.00	AWAY	@ CALG
SA	27 JUL	19.00	HOME	vs. HALI
SU	04 AUG	15.00	AWAY	@ WINN
SA	10 AUG	19.00	HOME	vs. OTTA
SU	18 AUG	17.00	AWAY	@ VFC
FR	23 AUG	19.00	AWAY	@ YORK
FR	30 AUG	19.00	HOME	vs. PFC
SA	07 SEP	19.00	HOME	vs. CALG
SA	14 SEP	14.00	AWAY	@ HALI
SA	21 SEP	16.00	AWAY	@ VFC
SA	28 SEP	16.00	HOME	vs. YORK
SU	06 OCT	14.00	AWAY	@ WINN
SA	12 OCT	16.00	HOME	vs. OTTA
SA	19 OCT	TBD	AWAY	@ PFC

CANADIAN CHAMPIONSHIP

Round	Year	H/A	OPPONENT
1R	2024	HOME	vs. YORK
QF	2024		
QF	2024		
SF	2024		
SF	2024		
FINAL	2024		

TORONTO FC

FIVE MOST RECENT SEASONS (2019 - 2023)

YEAR	CONCACAF	MAJOR LEAGUE	PLAYOFFS	L.CUP	CANCHAMP
2023	-	E-15th (4-10-20)	-	GS (0-0-2)	QF (0-0-1)
2022	-	E-13th (9-7-18)	-	-	2nd (2-1-0)
* [2020 in 2022]					*1st (0-1-0)
2021	QF (1-0-3)	E-13th (6-10-18)	-	-	2nd (2-0-1)
2020	-	E-2nd (13-5-5)	(0-0-1)	-	-
2019	L16 (0-1-1)	E-4th (13-11-10)	2nd (3-0-1)	-	2nd (3-0-1)

* W-D-L from Concacaf Champions League, Major League Soccer, MLS Playoffs, Leagues Cup, Canadian Championship
Head Coach Bob Bradley overall record until 27 June 2023 from 21 competitive matches : 3W - 10D - 8L
Interim Head Coach Terry Dunfield overall record from 15 competitive matches : 0W - 1D - 14L
Head Coach John Herdman record from last match of the 2023 season: 0W - 0D - 1L

GOALKEEPERS	CONCACAF	MAJOR LEAGUE	MLS PLAYOFFS	LEAGUES CUP	CAN. CHAMP
1 Johnson, Sean		20/20 1800 CS 6		2/2 180	1/1 90
18 Ranjitsingh, Greg		4/4 360		- -	- -
30 Romero, Tomás		6/6 540		0/0 0	0/0 0
90 Gavran, Luka		4/4 360		- -	- -

TORONTO FC	CONCACAF	MAJOR LEAGUE	MLS PLAYOFFS	LEAGUES CUP	CAN. CHAMP
10 Bernardeschi, Federico		31/31 2608 5g,4a		1/1 45	1/1 90
19 Franklin, Kobe		27/23 2172 1a		1/1 45	1/1 59
21 Osorio, Jonathan		21/21 1877 4g,6a		2/2 90	- -
28 Petretta, Raoul		24/22 1747 2a		2/2 172	0/0 0
23 Servania, Brandon		28/21 1703 1g,1a		2/2 180	1/1 90
17 Rosted, Sigurd		21/18 1645		2/2 180	1/1 80
24 Insigne, Lorenzo		20/18 1523 4g,5a		- -	1/1 90 1g
6 Mabika, Aimé		21/17 1515		1/0 45	1/1 90
4 Bradley, Michael		17/17 1444 1g,1a		- -	- -
52 Coello, Alonso		21/13 1287 1a		2/1 110	1/1 22
9 Sapong, C.J.		20/15 1268 1g		1/0 24	1/1 80
29 Kerr, Deandre		23/16 1225 5g,1a		2/1 135	1/0 31
7 Marshall-Rutty, Jahkeele		22/11 1146 1a		2/1 109	1/0 68
27 O'Neill, Shane		14/10 939		1/1 84	- -
47 Thompson, Kosi		14/6 580 1g		1/0 32	1/0 10
81 Antonoglou, Themi		11/3 478		2/0 20	0/0 0
5 Ibarra, Franco		7/5 440		1/1 58	- -
25 Osei-Owusu, Prince		6/3 257		- -	- -
83 Mbongue, Hugo		11/1 255		2/0 53	- -
3 Gutiérrez, Cristián		6/4 244 1a		- -	- -
8 Vazquez, Victor		12/3 235		- -	- -
99 Diomande, Adama		5/2 166		- -	- -
11 Blessing, Latif		5/1 152		2/2 129	- -
77 Perruzza, Jordan		5/1 122		1/1 45	- -
76 Stefanovic, Lazar		2/0 78		1/1 90	- -
12 Mailula, Cassius		3/0 68		- -	- -
73 Batiz, Jesús		2/0 63		1/1 58	- -
72 Faria, Jordan		1/0 24		- -	- -
51 Pearlman, Adam		1/0 6		- -	- -
65 Ćurić, Antony		1/0 1		- -	- -
71 Cimermancic, Markus		0/0 0		- -	- -
82 Altobelli, Julian		0/0 0		- -	- -

X-TORONTO FC	CONCACAF	MAJOR LEAGUE	MLS PLAYOFFS	LEAGUES CUP	CAN. CHAMP
14 Kaye, Mark Anthony		21/21 1843 2g,3a		- -	1/1 90
22 Laryea, Richie		18/18 1611 2g,3a		- -	1/1 90 1a
2 Hedges, Matt		14/13 1068		- -	- -
20 Akinola, Ayo		14/4 555		- -	1/0 10
5 MacNaughton, Lukas		3/2 180		- -	- -

CANADIAN SOCCER FOOTBALL ANNUAL

2024 TORONTO FC
Toronto FC roster as of 1 April 2024

GOALKEEPERS

#	Pos	Name	HT	S	YR	NAT
1	GK	Johnson, Sean	190	R	1989	USA
18	GK	Ranjitsingh, Greg	188		1993	TRI
90	GK	Gavran, Luka	198	R	2000	CAN

CENTRE BACKS & FULLBACKS

#	Pos	Name	HT	S	YR	NAT
5	CB	Long, Kevin	188	R	1988	IRL
6	CB	Mabika, Aimé	193	R	1998	ZAM
15	FB	Gomis, Nicksoen	185	L	2002	FRA
17	CB	Rosted, Sigurd	188	R	1994	NOR
19	RB	Franklin, Kobe	170	R	2003	CAN
22	FB	Laryea, Richie	175	R	1995	CAN
27	CB	O'Neill, Shane	188	R	1993	USA
28	FB	Petretta, Raoul	175	L	1997	ITA
51	CB	Pearlman, Adam	185	R	2005	CAN

MIDFIELDERS & FORWARDS

#	Pos	Name	HT	S	YR	NAT
7	W	Marshall-Rutty, Jahkeele	170	R	2004	CAN
8	M	Longstaff, Matty	170	R	2000	ENG
9	F	Akinola, Ayo	178	R	2000	CAN
10	W	Bernardeschi, Federico	185	L	1994	ITA
12	F	Mailula, Cassius	173		2001	RSA
14	M	Coello, Alonso	185	R	1999	ESP
16	FB	Spicer, Tyrese	185	L	2000	TRI
20	M	Flores, Deybi	180	R	1996	HON
21	M	Osorio, Jonathan	175	R	1992	CAN
23	M	Servania, Brandon	179	R	1999	USA
24	F	Insigne, Lorenzo	163	R	1991	ITA
29	M	Kerr, Deandre	180	R	2002	CAN
47	M	Thompson, Kosi	180	R	2003	CAN
77	F	Perruzza, Jordan	183	L	2001	CAN
83	F	Mbongue, Hugo	180	R	2004	CAN
99	F	Osei Owusu, Prince	190	L	1997	GER

HEAD COACH : JOHN HERDMAN
First full season as manager (appointed 28 August 2023)
Record from the last match of the 2023 season: 0W - 0D - 1L

2024 TECHNICAL STAFF & COACHES

Herdman, John	Head Coach
Tenllado, Eric	Assistant Coach & Performance Lead
Eaddy, Simon	Tech Co-ordinator & Goalkeeper Coach
deVos, Jason	Assistant Coach
Dunfield, Terry	Assistant Coach

MAJOR LEAGUE SOCCER

TORONTO FC

FIXTURES (EASTERN TIME)

Day	Date	Time	H/A	Result	Opponent
SU	25 FEB	14.30	AWAY	D 0-0	@ CINC
SU	03 MAR	14.00	AWAY	W 1-0	@ NENG
SA	09 MAR	14.00	HOME	W 1-0	vs. CHAR
SA	16 MAR	19.30	AWAY	W 2-1	@ NYCFC
SA	23 MAR	19.30	HOME	W 2-0	vs. ATLA
SA	30 MAR	19.30	HOME	L 1-3	vs. KANS
SA	06 APR	16.30	AWAY	_____	@ VWFC
SA	13 APR	19.30	AWAY	_____	@ CHAR
SA	20 APR	19.30	HOME	_____	vs. NENG
SA	27 APR	19.30	AWAY	_____	@ ORLA
SA	04 MAY	19.30	HOME	_____	vs. DALL
SA	11 MAY	19.30	HOME	_____	vs. NYCFC
WE	15 MAY	20.30	AWAY	_____	@ NASH
SA	18 MAY	19.30	HOME	_____	vs. MONT
SA	25 MAY	19.30	HOME	_____	vs. CINC
WE	29 MAY	19.30	AWAY	_____	@ PHIL
SA	01 JUN	19.30	AWAY	_____	@ D.C.
SA	15 JUN	19.30	HOME	_____	vs. CHIC
WE	19 JUN	19.30	HOME	_____	vs. NASH
SA	22 JUN	19.30	AWAY	_____	@ NYRB
SA	29 JUN	19.30	AWAY	_____	@ ATLA
WE	03 JUL	19.30	HOME	_____	vs. ORLA
SA	06 JUL	19.30	AWAY	_____	@ COLU
SA	13 JUL	19.30	HOME	_____	vs. PHIL
WE	17 JUL	19.30	AWAY	_____	@ MIAM
SA	20 JUL	19.30	AWAY	_____	@ MONT
SA	24 AUG	20.30	AWAY	_____	@ HOUS
SA	31 AUG	19.30	HOME	_____	vs. D.C.
SA	14 SEP	19.30	HOME	_____	vs. AUST
WE	18 SEP	19.30	HOME	_____	vs. COLU
SA	21 SEP	21.30	AWAY	_____	@ COLO
SA	28 SEP	20.30	AWAY	_____	@ CHIC
WE	02 OCT	19.30	HOME	_____	vs. NYRB
SA	05 OCT	19.30	HOME	_____	vs. MIAM

CANADIAN CHAMPIONSHIP

Round	Year	H/A	Result	Opponent
1R	2024	HOME	_____	Simcoe
QF	2024		_____	
QF	2024		_____	
SF	2024		_____	
SF	2024		_____	
FINAL	2024			

YORK UNITED FC

FIVE MOST RECENT SEASONS (2019 - 2023)

YEAR	CONCACAF	CAN. PREMIER	PLAYOFFS	CAN CHAMP
2023	-	5th (11-5-12)	5th (0-0-1)	QF (1-0-1)
2022	-	6th (9-7-12)	-	SF (0-2-1)
2021	-	4th (8-12-8)	SF (0-0-1)	QF (1-0-1)
2020	-	5th (2-4-1)	-	-
2019	-	3rd (9-7-12)	-	(2-2-2)

*W-D-L from Concacaf Champions League, Canadian Premier League, CPL Playoffs, Canadian Championship

2023 YORK UNITED FC
Head Coach Martin Nash overall record in 2023 from 31 competitive matches : 12W - 5D - 14L

GOALKEEPERS	CONCACAF	CAN. PREMIER		CPL PLAYOFFS		CAN. CHAMP		
1 Giantsopoulos, Niko		22/22	1980 CS 5	1/1	90	2/2	180	CS 1
77 De Rosario, Adisa		4/4	360	-	-	-	-	
67 Himaras, Eleias		2/2	180	0/0	0	0/0	0	
76 Williams, Michael		0/0	0	-	-	-	-	
77 Pavela, Ivan		0/0	0	-	-	0/0	0	

YORK UNITED FC	CONCACAF	CAN. PREMIER		CPL PLAYOFFS		CAN. CHAMP		
2 Gee, Paris		25/25	2240 1a	1/1	90	2/2	180	
32 Soumaoro, Brem		24/24	1920 2g,1a	1/1	90	2/2	180	
16 Ferrari, Max		26/20	1864	1/1	89	2/2	158	
3 Mourdoukoutas, Tass		21/20	1759 1a	1/1	90	1/1	90	
18 Babouli, Molham		19/18	1574 6g,2a	1/1	90	1/1	90	1g
11 Santos, Kévin		26/18	1544 6g	1/1	90	2/1	135	
12 Bayiha, Clément		27/18	1533 2g,2a	1/1	76	2/1	83	
22 Ricci, Austin		26/18	1467 3g,2a	-	-	2/0	51	1g
28 Gagnon-Laparé, Jérémy		21/15	1410 5a	1/0	1	1/1	57	
9 Wright, Brian		26/15	1370 2g,2a	1/0	1	2/0	55	
24 De Rosario, Osaze		24/13	1278 6g,2a	1/1	89	2/2	158	
6 Thompson, Roger		15/13	1166 1g	-	-	1/1	25	
7 Grant, Johnny		15/12	1038 1a	1/0	14	1/1	90	
33 Baldisimo, Matthew		15/8	799 1g	1/1	90	2/1	111	
23 Abatneh, Noah		12/8	637	0/0	0	0/0	0	
8 Adekugbe, Elijah		15/5	562	-	-	1/1	90	
37 Esprit, Trivine		11/3	373	0/0	0	-	-	
30 Martin-Pereux, Kadin		5/2	228 2a	1/1	89	-	-	
70 Voytsekhovskyy, Marki		7/2	167 1g	-	-	1/0	13	
27 Buschman-Dormond, Carson		5/0	61	1/0	1	-	-	
14 Afework, Theo		0/0	0	-	-	-	-	
55 Richardson, Toby		0/0	0	-	-	-	-	
60 Morano, Anthony		0/0	0	-	-	-	-	

X-YORK UNITED FC	CONCACAF	CAN. PREMIER		CPL PLAYOFFS		CAN. CHAMP		
x-43 Faye, Lassana		12/11	943	-	-	2/1	103	1a
x-10 Alou, Oussama		16/11	908 2g,2a	-	-	2/2	145	
x-21 Petrasso, Michael		14/1	305	-	-	-	-	

Matches played / started, Minutes played, Goals, Assists (or Clean Sheets for Goalkeepers)

CANADIAN SOCCER FOOTBALL ANNUAL

2024 YORK UNITED FC
York United FC roster as of 1 April 2024

GOALKEEPERS

#	Pos	Name	HT	S	YR	NAT
67	GK	Himaras, Eleias	184	R	2002	CAN
-	GK	Vincensini, Thomas	185	R	1993	FRA

CENTRE BACKS & FULLBACKS

#	Pos	Name	HT	S	YR	NAT
23	RB	Abatneh, Noah	188	R	2004	CAN
30	FB	Martin-Pereux, Kadin	183	L	2002	CAN
-	FB	Córdova, Juan	166	R	1995	CAN
-	CB	León, Oswaldo	190	L	1999	MEX
-	CB	Sturing, Frank	186	R	1997	CAN

MIDFIELDERS & FORWARDS

#	Pos	Name	HT	S	YR	NAT
6	M	Botello, Orlando	181		2001	MEX
8	M/F	Adekugbe, Elijah	174	R	1996	CAN
9	F	Wright, Brian	183	R	1995	CAN
12	M/FB	Bayiha, Clément	174	R	1999	CAN
15	M	Martínez, Josué	175	R	2002	MEX
16	CM	Ferrari, Max	172	R	2000	CAN
17	LW	Afework, Theo	181	R	2004	CAN
18	M/F	Babouli, Molham	173	R	1993	SYR
22	F	Ricci, Austin	178	R	1996	CAN
32	DM	Soumaoro, Brem	187	R	1996	NED
33	M	Baldisimo, Matthew	177		1998	PHI
70	M	Voytsekhovskyy, Marki	183		2003	CAN
-	W	Salanović, Dennis	179	R	1996	LIE

HEAD COACH : MARTIN NASH
Third season as manager (appointed 21 December 2021)
Overall record across 61 matches : 21W - 14D - 25L

2024 TECHNICAL STAFF, COACHES & FOOTBALL

Nash, Martin	Head Coach
Eustáquio, Mauro	Assistant Coach
Benzi, Camilo	A.Coach / GK Coach
Villalpando, Jorge	Technical & Sporting Director
O'Rourke, Derek	Director, Football Operations

CANADIAN PREMIER LEAGUE

YORK UNITED FC

FIXTURES (EASTERN TIME) — OPPONENT

Day	Date	Time	H/A		Opponent
SA	13 APR	13.00	AWAY		@ OTTA
SU	21 APR	16.00	HOME		vs. HAMI
FR	26 APR	19.00	HOME		vs. VFC
SA	04 MAY	19.00	AWAY		@ PFC
FR	10 MAY	19.00	HOME		vs. WINN
SA	18 MAY	19.00	AWAY		@ CALG
FR	24 MAY	19.00	HOME		vs. HALI
SA	01 JUN	16.00	AWAY		@ HAMI
SU	09 JUN	18.00	HOME		vs. VFC
SA	15 JUN	13.00	AWAY		@ OTTA
WE	19 JUN	19.00	HOME		vs. PFC
TH	27 JUN	19.30	AWAY		@ WINN
SA	06 JUL	16.00	HOME		vs. HALI
SA	13 JUL	16.00	AWAY		@ CALG
SA	20 JUL	16.00	AWAY		@ VFC
FR	26 JUL	19.00	HOME		vs. OTTA
FR	02 AUG	22.00	AWAY		@ PFC
SU	11 AUG	20.00	AWAY		@ WINN
FR	16 AUG	19.00	HOME		vs. CALG
FR	23 AUG	19.00	HOME		vs. HAMI
MO	02 SEP	15.00	AWAY		@ HALI
FR	06 SEP	22.00	AWAY		@ VFC
FR	13 SEP	19.00	HOME		vs. WINN
FR	20 SEP	19.00	HOME		vs. CALG
SA	28 SEP	16.00	AWAY		@ HAMI
SU	06 OCT	17.00	HOME		vs. OTTA
TH	10 OCT	19.00	HOME		vs. PFC
SA	19 OCT	TBD	AWAY		@ HALI

CANADIAN CHAMPIONSHIP — OPPONENT

Round	Year		Opponent
1R	2024	AWAY	@HAMI
QF	2024		
QF	2024		
SF	2024		
SF	2024		
FINAL	2024		

ATLÉTICO OTTAWA

FOUR SEASONS SINCE INAUGURAL YEAR (2020 - 2023)

YEAR	CONCACAF	CAN. PREMIER	PLAYOFFS	CAN CHAMP
2023	-	6th (10-6-12)	-	QF (1-0-1)
2022	-	1st (13-10-5)	2nd (1-1-1)	(0-1-0)
2021	-	8th (6-8-14)	-	(0-0-1)
2020	-	7th (2-2-3)	-	-

W-D-L from Concacaf Champions League, Canadian Premier League, CPL Playoffs, Canadian Championship

2023 ATLÉTICO OTTAWA

Head Coach Patrice Gheisar overall record in 2023 from 30 competitive matches : 11W - 9D - 10L

GOALKEEPERS	CONCACAF	CAN. PREMIER		CPL PLAYOFFS	CAN. CHAMP	
29 Ingham, Nathan		22/22	1980 CS 7		1/1	90
1 Melvin, Sean		6/6	540 CS 2		1/1	90
25 Engbers, Brogan		0/0	0		0/0	0

ATLÉTICO OTTAWA	CONCACAF	CAN. PREMIER		CPL PLAYOFFS	CAN. CHAMP		
10 Bassett, Oliver		27/27	2329 11g,3a		2/2	105	1g
5 Singh, Luke		25/25	2223 1g		2/1	120	
20 Ouimette, Karl		26/24	2192		2/2	180	
17 Acosta, Miguel		25/24	2168 1g,2a		2/2	165	
14 Assi, Jean-Aniel		26/20	1743 1g,3a		2/2	172	1a
4 Espejo, Diego		19/18	1590 1g		2/2	180	1g
18 Salter, Samuel		27/18	1475 7g,1a		2/0	38	
21 Zapater, Alberto		16/15	1395		-	-	
11 Verhoeven, Noah		25/15	1323 1g,2a		2/1	105	
19 Shaw, Malcolm		22/12	1274 1g,1a		2/2	180	1g
15 Tissot, Maxim		15/12	1066 2g		1/1	90	1g
96 Iliadis, Ilias		12/9	886 1g		-	-	
7 dos Santos, Gianni		19/10	858 2g,2a		2/1	89	1a
16 Verhoven, Zachary		22/8	768 3g,2a		1/0	8	
30 Antinoro, Gabriel		23/8	720 2g		1/0	75	
9 Haworth, Carl		17/7	647 3g,4a		-	-	
3 Niba, MacDonald		12/9	645 1a		1/1	90	
99 del Campo, Ruben		16/6	610 2a		-	-	
91 Sacko, Abou		9/5	438		1/1	61	
23 Duhaney-Walker, Tyr		5/3	243		0/0	0	
46 Roy, Zachary		3/1	71		-	-	
26 Darwish, Omar		0/0	0		-	-	

X-ATLÉTICO OTTAWA	CONCACAF	CAN. PREMIER		CPL PLAYOFFS	CAN. CHAMP	
x-22 Bahous, Zakaria		12/4	528 1g		2/2	142
x-12 Agyekum, Junior		0/0	0		-	-

Matches played / started, Minutes played, Goals, Assists (or Clean Sheets for Goalkeepers)

CANADIAN SOCCER FOOTBALL ANNUAL

2024 ATLÉTICO OTTAWA
Atlético Ottawa roster as of 1 April 2024

GOALKEEPERS			HT	S	DoB	NAT.
29	GK	Ingham, Nathan	188	R	1993	CAN
-	GK	Yesli, Rayane	200	R	1999	CAN

CENTRE BACKS & FULLBACKS			HT	S	YR	NAT.
20	CB / FB	Ouimette, Karl W.	183	R	1992	CAN
23	CB / FB	Duhaney-Walker, Tyr	188	R	2003	CAN
46	RB	Roy, Zachary	183	R	2003	CAN
91	LB	Sacko, Abou	175	L	2003	FRA
-	CB	Singh, Luke	173	R	2000	TRI
-	CB	Torres, Liberman	186		2002	ECU

MIDFIELDERS & FORWARDS			HT	S	YR	NAT.
10	F	Bassett, Oliver	168	R	1998	NIR
13	AM / F	Tabla, Ballou	175	R	1999	CAN
15	M / FB	Tissot, Maxim	180	L	1992	CAN
18	F	Salter, Samuel	186	L	1999	CAN
21	M	Zapater, Alberto	180	R	1985	ESP
30	LM	Antinoro, Gabriel	175	R	2004	CAN
99	F	del Campo, Rubén	185	L	2000	SUI
-	M	Aparicio, Manuel	168	R	1995	CAN
-	W	de Brienne, Matteo	163	L	2002	CAN
-	LW	dos Santos, Kévin	170	L	1999	POR
-	M	Sissoko, Aboubacar	183	R	1995	MLI
-	W	Twardek, Kris	185	R	1997	CAN

HEAD COACH : CARLOS GONZÁLEZ
Third season as manager (appointed 24 February 2022)
Overall record across 61 matches : 25W - 17D - 19L

2024 TECHNICAL STAFF & COACHES
González, Carlos	Head Coach
Galan, David	Assistant Coach
Montero, Borja	Goalkeeper Coach

ATLÉTICO OTTAWA

FIXTURES (EASTERN TIME)				OPPONENT
SA	13 APR	13.00	HOME	vs. YORK
SA	20 APR	14.00	HOME	vs. CALG
SA	27 APR	13.00	AWAY	@ HALI
SU	05 MAY	14.00	HOME	vs. WINN
SU	12 MAY	17.00	AWAY	@ VFC
FR	17 MAY	22.00	AWAY	@ PFC
SA	25 MAY	15.00	HOME	vs. HAMI
SU	02 JUN	14.00	HOME	vs. HALI
SU	09 JUN	15.00	AWAY	@ WINN
SA	15 JUN	13.00	HOME	vs. YORK
FR	21 JUN	21.00	AWAY	@ CALG
FR	28 JUN	19.00	HOME	vs. HAMI
SU	07 JUL	14.00	HOME	vs. PFC
FR	12 JUL	22.00	AWAY	@ VFC
SU	21 JUL	14.00	HOME	vs. WINN
FR	26 JUL	19.00	AWAY	@ YORK
SA	03 AUG	19.00	HOME	vs. CALG
SA	10 AUG	19.00	AWAY	@ HAMI
SA	17 AUG	16.00	AWAY	@ PFC
SA	24 AUG	14.00	AWAY	@ HALI
SA	31 AUG	19.00	HOME	vs. VFC
MO	09 SEP	20.00	AWAY	@ WINN
SU	15 SEP	17.00	AWAY	@ CALG
SU	22 SEP	14.00	HOME	vs. PFC
SU	29 SEP	14.00	HOME	vs. HALI
SU	06 OCT	17.00	AWAY	@ YORK
SA	12 OCT	16.00	AWAY	@ HAMI
SA	19 OCT	TBD	HOME	vs. VFC

CANADIAN CHAMPIONSHIP			OPPONENT
1R	2024	HOME	vs. WINN
QF	2024		
QF	2024		
SF	2024		
SF	2024		
FINAL	2024		

CF MONTRÉAL

FIVE MOST RECENT SEASONS (2019 - 2023)

YEAR	CONCACAF	MAJOR LEAGUE	PLAYOFFS	L.CUP	CANCHAMP
2023	-	E-10th (12-5-17)	-	GS (0-1-1)	2nd (3-0-1)
2022	QF (1-1-2)	E-2nd (20-5-9)	QF (1-0-1)	-	SF (1-0-1)
2021	-	E-10th (12-10-12)	-	-	1st (2-1-0)
2020	QF (1-2-1)	E-9th (8-2-13)	(0-0-1)	-	-
2019	-	E-9th (12-5-17)	-	-	1st (4-1-1)

* W-D-L from Concacaf Champions League, Major League Soccer, MLS Playoffs, Leagues Cup, Canadian Championship

2023 CF MONTRÉAL

Head Coach Hernán Losada overall record in 2023 from 40 competitive matches : 15W - 6D - 19L

GOALKEEPERS	CONCACAF	MAJOR LEAGUE	MLS PLAYOFFS	LEAGUES CUP	CAN. CHAMP
40 Sirois, Jonathan		33/32 2887 CS 11		2/2 180	3/3 270 CS 1
41 Pantemis, James		2/2 173		0/0 0	0/0 0
1 Ketterer, Logan		0/0 0		0/0 0	1/1 90 CS 1

CF MONTRÉAL	CONCACAF	MAJOR LEAGUE	MLS PLAYOFFS	LEAGUES CUP	CAN. CHAMP
29 Choinière, Mathieu		28/27 2436 5g, 5a		2/2 180 1g,1a	4/4 315 2a
16 Waterman, Joel		28/27 2375 1g, 3a		2/2 180	3/3 270
25 Corbo, Gabriele		28/25 2285 2a		2/2 180	4/4 353 1a
24 Campbell, George		26/21 1852 1g, 1a		0/0 0	3/1 113
2 Wanyama, Victor		25/20 1788 1a		1/0 14	2/2 157
19 Saliba, Nathan-Dylan		28/20 1768 1a		2/1 120	3/0 65
11 Lassiter, Ariel		25/17 1600 1g, 2a		2/2 105 1a	4/3 251 1g,1a
9 Offor, Chinonso		30/14 1503 4g		2/2 127	4/2 238 1g
10 Duke, Bryce		26/20 1473 2g, 2a		2/2 158 1g	3/2 144
22 Herrera, Aaron		19/16 1410 2a		2/1 82	2/1 91
15 Brault-Guillard, Zachary		24/14 1307 1g, 1a		2/1 98	4/2 224 1a
14 Ibrahim, Sunusi		25/11 1174 3g, 3a		1/0 8	3/3 264 3g
6 Piette, Samuel		16/14 1098		1/1 77	- -
21 Lappalainen, Lassi		21/13 1034 2g, 3a		2/0 58	2/1 89
90 Opoku, Kwadwo		12/12 937 4g, 1a		2/2 167	- -
30 Quioto, Romell		13/10 796 3g, 1a		- -	1/1 75
27 Rea, Sean		15/7 744 2a		- -	3/2 174 1g
13 Toye, Mason		14/8 679 3g, 1a		1/0 22	1/0 12
7 Hamdi, Ahmed		13/4 470 1g		1/0 13	2/1 92
28 Vilsaint, Jules-Anthony		11/4 408 1g, 1a		1/0 31	1/0 6
4 Álvarez, Fernando		4/2 255		- -	- -
26 Thorkelsson, Róbert		9/2 222		0/0 0	1/1 90
17 Kwizera, Jojea		4/1 133		- -	- -
23 Jabang, Ousman		3/1 75		- -	0/0 0

X-CF MONTRÉAL	CONCACAF	MAJOR LEAGUE	MLS PLAYOFFS	LEAGUES CUP	CAN. CHAMP
4 Camacho, Rudy		20/19 1613 1g		2/2 180	4/4 337
3 Miller, Kamal		6/6 477		- -	- -
5 Iliadis, Ilias		6/4 251		- -	1/1 90
18 Zouhir, Rida		5/1 218		- -	1/1 90
8 Miljevic, Matko		8/0 124 1a		0/0 0	2/1 60

Matches played / started, Minutes played, Goals, Assists (or Clean Sheets for Goalkeepers)

MAJOR LEAGUE SOCCER

CANADIAN SOCCER FOOTBALL ANNUAL

2024 CF MONTRÉAL
CF Montréal roster as of 1 April 2024

GOALKEEPERS

#	Pos	Name	HT	S	YR	NAT
1	GK	Breza, Sebastian	196	R	1998	CAN
33	GK	Ketterer, Logan	190		1993	USA
40	GK	Sirois, Jonathan	180	R	2001	CAN

CENTRE BACKS & FULLBACKS

#	Pos	Name	HT	S	YR	NAT
3	CB	Sosa, Joaquín	189	L	2002	URU
4	CB	Álvarez, Fernando	188	L	2003	COL
16	CB	Waterman, Joel	185	R	1996	CAN
22	RB	Teixeira, Ruan	174	R	1995	BRA
24	CB	Campbell, George	188		2001	USA
25	CB	Corbo, Gabriele	185	R	2000	ITA
26	CB	Thorkelsson, Róbert	186	L	2002	ISL
27	RB	Doody, Grayson	178	R	2002	USA
44	FB / M	Edwards, Raheem	172	L	1995	CAN

MIDFIELDERS & FORWARDS

#	Pos	Name	HT	S	YR	NAT
2	M	Wanyama, Victor	188	R	1991	KEN
5	M	Iliadis, Ilias	175	L	2001	GRE
6	M	Piette, Samuel	171	R	1994	CAN
7	F	Opoku, Kwadwo	170	L	2001	GHA
8	M	Iankov, Dominik	180	R	2000	BUL
9	F	Cóccaro, Matías	178	R	178	URU
10	M	Duke, Bryce	170	R	2001	USA
11	LW	Lassiter, Ariel	178	L	1994	CRC
13	F	Toye, Mason	190	L	1998	USA
14	F	Ibrahim, Sunusi	165	R	2002	NGA
17	F	Martínez, Josef	173	R	1993	VEN
18	M	Zouhir, Rida	180	R	2003	CAN
19	M	Saliba, Nathan-Dylan	171		2004	CAN
21	F	Lappalainen, Lassi	183	R	1998	FIN
23	M / CB	Jabang, Ousman	188	R	2001	USA
28	F / W	Vilsaint, Jules-Anthony	190		2003	CAN
29	M	Choinière, Mathieu	173	R	1999	CAN
-	M	Biello, Alessandro	184	R	2006	CAN

HEAD COACH : LAURENT COURTOIS
First season as manager (appointed 9 January 2024)

2024 TECHNICAL STAFF & COACHES

Courtois, Laurent	Head Coach
Ciman, Laurent	Assistant Coach
Sauvry, David	Assistant Coach
Sebrango, Eduardo	Assistant Coach
Peiser, Romuald	Goalkeeper Coach
Renard, Olivier	Vice-President & Chief Sporting Director
Cremanzidis, Vassili	Assistant Sporting Director

CF MONTRÉAL

FIXTURES (EASTERN TIME)					OPPONENT
SA	24 FEB	19.30	AWAY	D 0-0	@ ORLA
SA	02 MAR	20.30	AWAY	W 2-1	@ DALL
SU	10 MAR	17.00	AWAY	W 3-2	@ MIAM
SA	16 MAR	14.00	AWAY	L 3-4	@ CHIC
SA	30 MAR	19.30	AWAY	L 0-1	@ D.C.
SA	06 APR	22.30	AWAY	_____	@ SEAT
SA	13 APR	19.30	HOME	_____	vs. CINC
SA	20 APR	19.30	HOME	_____	vs. ORLA
SA	27 APR	19.30	AWAY	_____	@ COLU
SA	04 MAY	20.30	AWAY	_____	@ NASH
SA	11 MAY	19.30	HOME	_____	vs. MIAM
WE	15 MAY	19.30	HOME	_____	vs. COLU
SA	18 MAY	19.30	AWAY	_____	@ TORO
SA	25 MAY	19.30	HOME	_____	vs. NASH
WE	29 MAY	19.30	HOME	_____	vs. D.C.
SA	01 JUN	19.30	AWAY	_____	@ PHIL
SA	15 JUN	19.30	HOME	_____	vs. RSL
WE	19 JUN	19.30	HOME	_____	vs. NYRB
SA	22 JUN	21.30	AWAY	_____	@ COLO
SA	29 JUN	19.30	HOME	_____	vs. PHIL
WE	03 JUL	19.30	AWAY	_____	@ NYCFC
SA	06 JUL	19.30	HOME	_____	vs. VWFC
SA	13 JUL	19.30	HOME	_____	vs. ATLA
WE	17 JUL	19.30	AWAY	_____	@ NYRB
SA	20 JUL	19.30	HOME	_____	vs. TORO
SA	24 AUG	19.30	HOME	_____	vs. NENG
SA	31 AUG	19.30	AWAY	_____	@ CINC
SA	14 SEP	19.30	HOME	_____	vs. CHAR
WE	18 SEP	19.30	AWAY	_____	@ NENG
SA	21 SEP	19.30	HOME	_____	vs. CHIC
SA	28 SEP	19.30	HOME	_____	vs. SANJ
WE	02 OCT	19.30	AWAY	_____	@ ATLA
SA	05 OCT	19.30	AWAY	_____	@ CHAR
SA	19 OCT	18.00	HOME	_____	vs. NYCFC

CANADIAN CHAMPIONSHIP		OPPONENT
QF	2024	_____
QF	2024	_____
SF	2024	_____
SF	2024	_____
FINAL	2024	_____

HALIFAX WANDERERS FC

FIVE MOST RECENT SEASONS (2019 - 2023)

YEAR	CONCACAF	CAN. PREMIER	PLAYOFFS	CAN CHAMP
2023	-	3rd (11-9-8)	4th (0-0-1)	(0-0-1)
2022	-	7th (8-5-15)	-	QF (1-0-1)
2021	-	6th (8-11-9)	-	QF (1-0-1)
2020	-	2nd (3-3-1)	2nd (1-1-2)	-
2019	-	7th (6-10-12)	-	(3-1-2)

* W-D-L from Concacaf Champions League, Canadian Premier League, CPL Playoffs, Canadian Championship

2023 HALIFAX WANDERERS FC
Head Coach Patrice Gheisar overall record in 2023 from 30 competitive matches : 11W - 9D - 10L

GOALKEEPERS	CONCACAF	CAN. PREMIER		CPL PLAYOFFS		CAN. CHAMP	
1 Fillion, Yann		28/28	2520 CS 7	1/1	90	1/1	90
66 Rushenas, Aiden		0/0	0	0/0	0	0/0	0

WANDERERS FC	CONCACAF	CAN. PREMIER		CPL PLAYOFFS		CAN. CHAMP	
2 Nimick, Dan		27/27	2430 6g,3a	1/1	90	1/1	90
6 Callegari, Lorenzo		26/26	2325 6a	1/1	90	1/1	90
8 Ferrin, Massimo		25/25	2186 8g,3a	1/1	90	1/1	67 1g
5 Loughrey, Cale		24/24	2145	1/1	80	0/0	0
3 Fernandez, Zachary		23/21	1857 3g,2a	1/1	90	1/0	15
10 Daniels, Aidan		28/21	1795 3g,5a	1/1	90	1/1	75
17 Timóteo, Wesley		24/17	1584 4a	1/0	32	1/1	75
22 Omar, Mohamed		25/17	1468	1/1	90	1/1	90
23 Ferrazzo, Riley		22/14	1198 1a	1/0	10	1/1	90
18 Rampersad, Andre		19/12	1149 2a	-	-	1/1	90
14 Watson, Callum		24/12	1089 3g,1a	1/1	58	1/0	15
19 Coimbra, Tiago		19/9	837 3g,1a	1/1	80	1/1	67
24 Giraldo, Tomas		19/10	814 2g	INJ	-	-	-
9 Collomb, Théo		13/7	586 4g	-	-	1/0	23
21 Perruzza, Jordan		10/7	563 2g	1/0	32	-	-
20 Ruby, Jake		8/7	557 1a	1/1	58	-	-
4 Campagna, Cristian		10/5	539	-	-	1/1	90
11 Morelli, João		9/4	435 4g,1a	INJ	-	-	-
15 Henry, Doneil		13/3	410	1/0	10	-	-
7 James, Ryan		6/4	394	-	-	0/0	0
13 Wilson, Armaan		11/3	336 1g	0/0	0	-	-
37 Mwandwe, Lifumpa		7/3	257 1a	-	-	-	-
41 Vasconcelos, Camilo		1/0	45	0/0	0	-	-

X-WANDERERS FC	CONCACAF	CAN. PREMIER		CPL PLAYOFFS		CAN. CHAMP	
x-11 Nwafornso, Kosi		7/2	233	-	-	1/0	23

Matches played / started, Minutes played, Goals, Assists (or Clean Sheets for Goalkeepers)

CANADIAN SOCCER FOOTBALL ANNUAL

2024 HALIFAX WANDERERS FC
Halifax Wanderers FC roster as of 1 April 2024

		GOALKEEPERS	HT	S	YR	NAT.
1	GK	Fillion, Yann	193	R	1996	CAN
66	GK	Rushenas, Aiden	188		2003	CAN

		CENTRE BACKS & FULLBACKS	HT	S	YR	NAT.
2	CB	Nimick, Dan	188	R	2000	CAN
3	FB / M	Fernandez, Zachary	158	R	2001	CAN
5	CB	Loughrey, Cale	190	L	2001	CAN
23	RB / M	Ferrazzo, Riley	178		1999	CAN
-	CB	Dunn, Julian	188		2000	CAN
-	FB	Sow, Kareem	185	L	2000	CAN

		MIDFIELDERS & FORWARDS	HT	S	YR	NAT.
6	M	Callegari, Lorenzo	175	R	1998	FRA
8	W	Ferrin, Massimo	178	R	1998	CAN
10	M	Daniels, Aidan	175	R	1998	CAN
17	M	Timóteo, Wesley	175	L	2000	CAN
18	M	Rampersad, Andre	185	R	1995	TRI
19	F	Coimbra, Tiago	188	R	2004	CAN
24	M	Giraldo, Tomas	184	R	2003	CAN
-	M	Dias, Vitor	178	L	1998	BRA
-	CM	Gagnon-Laparé, Jérémy	180	L	1995	CAN
-	M	Probo, Giorgio	170		1999	ITA
-	F / FB	Telfer, Ryan	180	L	1994	TRI
-	M	Vasconcelos, Camilo	170	R	2005	CAN

HEAD COACH : PATRICE GHEISAR
Second season as manager (appointed 30 November 2022)
Overall record across 30 matches : 11W - 9D - 10L

2024 TECHNICAL STAFF & COACHES
Gheiser, Patrice	Head Coach
Feliciano, Jorden	Assistant Coach
Davies, Jed	Assistant Coach
Williams, Jan Michael	Goalkeeper Coach

CANADIAN PREMIER LEAGUE

HALIFAX WANDERERS FC

FIXTURES (ATLANTIC TIME)				OPPONENT
SA	13 APR	20.00	AWAY _____	@ PFC
TH	18 APR	23.00	AWAY _____	@ VFC
SA	27 APR	14.00	HOME _____	vs. OTTA
TU	07 MAY	12.00	AWAY _____	@ HAMI
SA	11 MAY	15.00	HOME _____	vs. CALG
MO	20 MAY	16.00	HOME _____	vs. WINN
FR	24 MAY	20.00	AWAY _____	@ YORK
SU	02 JUN	15.00	AWAY _____	@ OTTA
SA	08 JUN	15.00	HOME _____	vs. PFC
SA	15 JUN	17.00	HOME _____	vs. HAMI
SU	23 JUN	18.00	AWAY _____	@ VFC
MO	01 JUL	16.00	HOME _____	vs. CALG
SA	06 JUL	17.00	AWAY _____	@ YORK
TH	11 JUL	19.00	HOME _____	vs. PFC
TH	18 JUL	19.00	HOME _____	vs. WINN
SA	27 JUL	20.00	AWAY _____	@ HAMI
MO	05 AUG	16.00	HOME _____	vs. VFC
SA	10 AUG	17.00	AWAY _____	@ CALG
SA	17 AUG	16.00	AWAY _____	@ WINN
SA	24 AUG	15.00	HOME _____	vs. OTTA
MO	02 SEP	16.00	HOME _____	vs. YORK
SA	07 SEP	23.00	AWAY _____	@ PFC
SA	14 SEP	15.00	HOME _____	vs. HAMI
SA	21 SEP	16.00	AWAY _____	@ WINN
SU	29 SEP	15.00	AWAY _____	@ OTTA
SA	05 OCT	15.00	HOME _____	vs. VFC
SA	12 OCT	20.00	AWAY _____	@ CALG
SA	19 OCT	TBD	HOME _____	vs. YORK

CANADIAN CHAMPIONSHIP			OPPONENT
1R	2024	HOME _____	St-Laurent
QF	2024	_____	
QF	2024	_____	
SF	2024	_____	
SF	2024	_____	
FINAL	2024	_____	

CANADIANS IN MAJOR LEAGUE SOCCER

Team / Player		MLS	MLS PLAYOFFS	LEAGUES CUP	US OPEN CUP
ST. LOUIS CITY SC		(WEST 1st)			
22 Hiebert, Kyle		27/24 2128 2g, 1a	2/1 121	1/1 90	1/1 90
LOS ANGELES FC	CONCACAF	(WEST 3rd)			
16 Crépeau, Maxime	INJ	7/7 630 2 CS	5/5 450 3 CS	0/0 0	0/0 0
FC DALLAS		(WEST 7th)			
18 Fraser, Liam		7/4 368	3/2 231		-
SPORTING KANSAS CITY		(WEST 8th)			
30 Afrifa, Stephen		3/1 50		0/0 0	1/1 45
SAN JOSE EARTHQUAKES		(WEST 9th)			
* 9 Akinola, Ayo		7/0 51	0/0 0	1/0 19	-
PORTLAND TIMBERS FC		(WEST 10th)			
18 McGraw, Zac		28/27 2423 1g, 1a		3/3 270	0/0 0
MINNESOTA UNITED FC		(WEST 11th)			
97 St. Clair, Dayne		30/30 2700 8 CS		5/5 450 1 CS	0/0 0
14 Oluwaseyi, Tani		2/0 11			1/0 13
LOS ANGELES GALAXY		(WEST 13th)			
44 Edwards, Raheem		30/21 1873 2g, 4a		2/1 89	3/1 114
COLORADO RAPIDS		(WEST 14th)			
97 Priso, Ralph		26/11 1028 2a		2/1 94	2/2 169 1a
64 Bombito, Moïse		11/8 751 1a		2/1 121	1/1 73
ORLANDO CITY SC	CONCACAF	(EAST 2nd)			
20 Petrasso, Luca	2/2 149	12/4 430		0/0 0	INJ
COLUMBUS CREW SC		(EAST 3rd)			
23 Farsi, Mohamed		31/23 2158 5a	5/4 371	3/2 173	3/1 81 1g
19 Russell-Rowe, Jacen		21/4 527 4g, 3a	2/0 2	2/0 25	3/2 225
NEW ENGLAND REVOLUTION		(EAST 5th)			
* 28 Kaye, Mark-Anthony		10/10 783 3a	2/2 90	4/4 289	-
NASHVILLE SC		(EAST 7th)			
14 Shaffelburg, Jacob		2815 1318 3g, 1a	2/1 103	6/4 199 1g, 5a	3/2 174
* 3 MacNaughton, Lukas		14/13 1077 1g	2/0 96	7/6 538	1/1 45
NEW YORK RED BULLS		(EAST 8th)			
88 Mullings, O'Vonte		2/0 43			1/0 40
CHARLOTTE FC		(EAST 9th)			
37 Arfield, Scott		13/2 403 2g	1/0 24	5/5 334 1g	-
36 Cambridge, Brandon		9/0 128 2g		2/0 12	2/1 117 1a
INTER MIAMI CF		(EAST 14th)			
* 31 Miller, Kamal		22/21 1845		7/7 614	6/6 538

Matches played / started, Minutes played, Goals, Assists (or Clean Sheets for Goalkeepers)

* Before joining American teams, Ayo Akinola, Mark-Anthony Kaye and Lukas MacNaughton all started the season with Toronto FC (see page 16 for early-season stats) while Kamal Miller started the season with CF Montréal (see page 22).

CANADIAN SOCCER FOOTBALL ANNUAL

		GOALKEEPERS	HT	S	YR	NAT.	TEAM
50	GK	Anchor, Max	183		2004	CAN	Vanc. Whitecaps FC
32	GK	Boehmer, Isaac	188		2001	CAN	Vanc. Whitecaps FC
1	GK	Breza, Sebastian	196	R	1998	CAN	CF Montréal
16	GK	Crépeau, Maxime	185	R	1994	CAN	Portland Timbers FC
90	GK	Gavran, Luka	198	R	2000	CAN	Toronto FC
41	GK	Pantemis, James	185		1997	CAN	Portland Timbers FC
40	GK	Sirois, Jonathan	180	R	2001	CAN	CF Montréal
97	GK	St. Clair, Dayne	191	L	1997	CAN	Minnesota United FC

		CENTRE BACKS & FULLBACKS	HT	S	YR	NAT.	TEAM
3	LB	Adekugbe, Sam	178	L	1995	CAN	Vanc. Whitecaps FC
19	FB	Bassong, Zorhan	178	L	1999	CAN	Sporting Kansas City
44	FB / M	Edwards, Raheem	172	L	1995	CAN	CF Montréal
23	FB	Farsi, Mohamed	180	R	1999	CAN	Columbus Crew SC
19	RB	Franklin, Kobe	170	R	2003	CAN	Toronto FC
22	CB	Hiebert, Kyle	178		1997	CAN	St. Louis CITY SC
22	FB	Laryea, Richie	175	R	1995	CAN	Toronto FC
3	CB	MacNaughton, Lukas	188		1995	CAN	Nashville SC
18	CB	McGraw, Zac	193	R	1997	CAN	Portland Timbers FC
4	CB	Miller, Kamal	183	L	1997	CAN	Portland Timbers FC
51	CB	Pearlman, Adam	185	R	2005	CAN	Toronto FC

		MIDFIELDERS & FORWARDS	HT	S	YR	NAT.	TEAM
30	F	Afrifa, Stephen	180	R	2001	CAN	Sporting Kansas City
22	M / FB	Ahmed, Ali	180	R	2000	CAN	Vanc. Whitecaps FC
9	F	Akinola, Ayo	178	R	2000	CAN	Toronto FC
37	M	Arfield, Scott	178	R	1988	CAN	Charlotte FC
-	M	Biello, Alessandro	184	R	2006	CAN	CF Montréal
64	M	Bombito, Moïse	190	R	2000	CAN	Colorado Rapids
36	W	Cambridge, Brandon	183		2002	CAN	Charlotte FC
29	M	Choinière, Mathieu	173	R	1999	CAN	CF Montréal
8	M	Fraser, Liam	185	R	1998	CAN	FC Dallas
28	W	Johnson, Levonte	178	R	1999	CAN	Vanc. Whitecaps FC
29	M	Kerr, Deandre	180	R	2002	CAN	Toronto FC
7	W	Marshall-Rutty, Jahkeele	170	R	2004	CAN	Toronto FC
83	F	Mbongue, Hugo	180	R	2004	CAN	Toronto FC
14	F	Oluwaseyi, Tani	188		2000	CAN	Minnesota United FC
21	M	Osorio, Jonathan	175	R	1992	CAN	Toronto FC
77	F	Perruzza, Jordan	183	L	2001	CAN	Toronto FC
6	M	Piette, Samuel	171	R	1994	CAN	CF Montréal
13	M	Priso, Ralph	176		2002	CAN	Vanc. Whitecaps FC
7	M / FB	Raposo, Ryan	170	R	1999	CAN	Vanc. Whitecaps FC
19	F	Russell-Rowe, Jacen	184		2002	CAN	Columbus Crew SC
19	M	Saliba, Nathan-Dylan	171		2004	CAN	CF Montréal
14	W	Shaffelburg, Jacob	181	L	1999	CAN	Nashville SC
30	F	Stewart-Baines, Kimani	175	R	2005	CAN	Colorado Rapids
47	M	Thompson, Kosi	180	R	2003	CAN	Toronto FC
28	F / W	Vilsaint, Jules-Anthony	190		2003	CAN	CF Montréal
18	M	Zouhir, Rida	180	R	2003	CAN	CF Montréal

ALL-TIME MLS LEADERS
All MLS matches including regular season and playoffs through 2023

MLS LEADERS	MATCHES
1. De Rosario, Dwayne	366
Johnson, Will	312
Osorio, Jonathan	298+
Teibert, Russell	256
Akindele, Tesho	255
Onstad, Pat	GK 244
Piette, Samuel	162+
Bernier, Patrice	159
Edwards, Raheem	158+
Kaye, Mark-Anthony	155+
Jaković, Dejan	139
Laryea, Richie	136+
Morgan, Ashtone	136
Jazić, Ante	134
Henry, Doneil	121+
Ricketts, Tosaint	119
Miller, Kamal	114+
Hainault, André	114
Aunger, Geoff	113
Chapman, Jay	112+
Crépeau, Maxime	GK 109+
Brault-Guillard, Zachary	109+
Choinière, Mathieu	103

MLS	GOALS SCORED
1. De Rosario, Dwayne	*109
Osorio, Jonathan	50+
Akindele, Tesho	46
Larin, Cyle	43+
Johnson, Will	33
Ricketts, Tosaint	22
Cavallini, Lucas	18+
Bernier, Patrice	17
Akinola, Ayo	15+
Kaye, Mark-Anthony	15+
Jackson-Hamel, Anthony	15
Laryea, Richie	12+
Buchanan, Tajon	12+
Hamilton, Jordan	11

* De Rosario scored 104 goals in MLS regular-season action

MLS	CLEAN SHEETS
1. Onstad, Pat	69
Crépeau, Maxime	27+
St. Clair, Dayne	21+
Sirois, Jonathan	11+
Sutton, Greg	10

2023 CANADIAN SOCCER RESULTS

2023 CANADIAN CHAMPIONSHIP

CANADIAN CHAMPIONSHIP WINNERS : VANCOUVER WHITECAPS FC

1.ROUND CHAMPIONSHIP		HOME TEAM	SCORE	AWAY TEAM	VENUE
2023-04-18	Hamilton, ON	Forge FC Hamilton	W 3-0 L	FC Laval	Tim Hortons (2,117)
2023-04-18	Montréal, QC	CF Montréal	W 2-0 L	Vaughan SC	Saputo (11,069)
2023-04-19	Toronto, ON	Halifax Wanderers FC	L 1-3 W	Atlético Ottawa	York (674)
2023-04-19	Toronto, ON	York United FC	W 1-0 L	Vancouver FC	York (1,272)
2023-04-19	Burnaby, BC	TSS Rovers	W 3-1 L	Winnipeg Valour FC	Swangard (1,869)
2023-04-20	Langford, BC	Pacific FC *	D 1-1 D	Calgary Cavalry FC	Starlight (2,099)

Pacific FC won 5-3 on kicks from the penalty mark against Cavalry FC.

QUARTERFINALS		HOME TEAM	SCORE	AWAY TEAM	VENUE
2023-05-09	Hamilton, ON	Forge FC Hamilton *	D 1-1 D	Atlético Ottawa	Tim Hortons (2,979)

Forge FC Hamilton won 3-2 on kicks from the penalty mark against Atlético Ottawa

2023-05-09	Toronto, ON	Toronto FC	L 1-2 W	CF Montréal	BMO Field (17,726)
2023-05-10	Toronto, ON	York United FC	L 1-4 W	Vancouver Whitecaps FC	York (1,827)
2023-05-10	Langford, BC	Pacific FC	W 2-0 L	TSS Rovers FC	Starlight (2,593)

SEMIFINALS		HOME TEAM	SCORE	AWAY TEAM	VENUE
2023-05-24	Montréal, QC	CF Montréal	W 2-0 L	Forge FC Hamilton	Saputo (10,062)
2023-05-24	Langford, BC	Pacific FC	L 0-3 W	Vancouver Whitecaps FC	Starlight (5,221)

CANADIAN FINAL		HOME TEAM	SCORE	AWAY TEAM	VENUE
2023-06-07	Vancouver, BC	Vancouver Whitecaps FC	W 2-1 L	CF Montréal	BC Place (20,072)

Vancouver Whitecaps FC won the 2023 Canadian Championship and qualified for 2024 Concacaf Champions Cup

2023 CONCACAF CHAMPIONS LEAGUE

ROUND of 16 SERIES		HOME TEAM	SCORE	AWAY TEAM	VENUE
2023-03-08	Vancouver, BC	Vancouver Whitecaps FC	W 5-0 L	RCD España	BC Place (13,644)
2023-03-15	San Pedro Sula, HON	RCD España	W 3-2 L	Vancouver Whitecaps FC	Olímpico Metropolitano

Vancouver Whitecaps FC won the series 7-3 on aggregate

QUARTERFINALS		HOME TEAM	SCORE	AWAY TEAM	VENUE
2023-04-05	Vancouver, BC	Vancouver Whitecaps FC	L 0-3 W	Los Angeles FC	BC Place (11,652)
2023-04-11	Los Angeles, CA, USA	Los Angeles FC	W 3-0 L	Vancouver Whitecaps FC	BMO (18,688)

Los Angeles FC won the series 6-0 on aggregate

2023 CANADIAN PREMIER LEAGUE

STANDINGS	MP	W	D	L	PTS	MATCH-BY-MATCH RESULTS
1. Calgary Cavalry FC	28	16	7	5	55	D D D D W L D W L W W W L W W L W L W W W D W W W W

Cavalry FC won the 2023 Canadian Premier League Shield and qualified for 2024 Concacaf Champions Cup

2. Forge FC Hamilton	28	11	9	8	42	D D W W W D W L D L L L W L W D W W L D D D W D W W L L
3. Halifax Wanderers FC	28	11	9	8	42	D D D D L D L W W D W L W L W W L W D W L D L W L W W
4. Pacific FC	28	11	7	10	40	W D L W W D D W W W W D L L D L W W L L L W D D W L L L
5. York United FC	28	11	5	12	38	L L W L L W W W D W L D L W L D W L D D L W W L L L W W

The top-five teams from the league standings qualified for the Canadian Premier League playoffs

6. Atlético Ottawa	28	10	6	12	36	D D L L W L L W L W L D W W W L W D W W D L L D L L L W
7. Vancouver FC	28	8	5	15	29	L W D D L D D L L L W L L W L L L D L W L L W L W W W L
8. Winnipeg Valour FC	28	6	8	14	26	W D D D L D D D L W L W L L D L L D L W L L L W L L W W L L

2023 CANADIAN PREMIER LEAGUE SHIELD WINNERS : CALGARY CAVALRY FC

2023 CANADA

SEASON	CITY	HOME TEAM	SCORE	AWAY TEAM	VENUE
2023-04-15	Ottawa, ON	Atlético Ottawa	D 1-1 D	HFX Wanderers	TD Place (7,039)
2023-04-15	Hamilton, ON	Forge FC Hamilton	D 2-2 D	Cavalry FC	Tim Hortons (6,892)
2023-04-15	Victoria, BC	Pacific FC	W 1-0 L	Vancouver FC	Starlight (4,825)
2023-04-16	North York, ON	York United	L 0-2 W	Winnipeg Valour FC	York Lions (1,607)
2023-04-22	North York, ON	York United	L 1-2 W	Vancouver FC	York Lions (822)
2023-04-22	Hamilton, ON	Forge FC Hamilton	D 1-1 D	HFX Wanderers	Tim Hortons (3,827)
2023-04-22	Winnipeg, MB	Winnipeg Valour FC	D 1-1 D	Atlético Ottawa	IG Field (3,374)
2023-04-23	Victoria, BC	Pacific FC	D 1-1 D	Cavalry FC	Starlight (2,455)
2023-04-29	Halifax, NS	HFX Wanderers	D 1-1 D	Vancouver FC	Wanderers (6,413)
2023-04-29	Ottawa, ON	Atlético Ottawa	L 0-1 W	York United	TD Place (3,074)
2023-04-30	Calgary, AB	Cavalry FC	D 1-1 D	Winnipeg Valour FC	ATCO Field (4,566)
2023-04-30	Victoria, BC	Pacific FC	L 0-1 W	Forge FC Hamilton	Starlight (3,378)
2023-05-05	North York, ON	York United	L 0-1 W	Forge FC Hamilton	York Lions (1,016)
2023-05-06	Winnipeg, MB	Winnipeg Valour FC	D 0-0 D	HFX Wanderers	IG Field (2,665)
2023-05-06	Ottawa, ON	Atlético Ottawa	L 1-4 W	Pacific FC	TD Place (3,499)
2023-05-07	Langley, BC CAN	Vancouver FC	D 1-1 D	Cavalry FC	Willoughby (6,177)
2023-05-13	Hamilton, ON	Forge FC Hamilton	W 3-2 L	Winnipeg Valour FC	Tim Hortons (4,807)
2023-05-13	Calgary, AB	Cavalry FC	D 2-2 D	HFX Wanderers	ATCO Field (3,546)
2023-05-13	Langley, BC CAN	Vancouver FC	L 0-5 W	Atlético Ottawa	Willoughby (2,800)
2023-05-14	Victoria, BC	Pacific FC	W 4-1 L	York United	Starlight (3,027)
2023-05-20	Hamilton, ON	Forge FC Hamilton	D 0-0 D	Vancouver FC	Tim Hortons (4,378)
2023-05-19	Halifax, NS	HFX Wanderers	L 0-3 W	York United	Wanderers (6,244)
2023-05-20	Winnipeg, MB	Winnipeg Valour FC	D 1-1 D	Pacific FC	IG Field (2,775)
2023-05-21	Calgary, AB	Cavalry FC	W 2-0 L	Atlético Ottawa	ATCO Field (3,500)
2023-05-27	Ottawa, ON	Atlético Ottawa	L 0-1 W	Forge FC Hamilton	TD Place (4,520)
2023-05-27	Victoria, BC	Pacific FC	D 1-1 D	HFX Wanderers	Starlight (2,741)
2023-05-28	North York, ON	York United	W 1-0 L	Cavalry FC	York Lions (1,476)
2023-05-28	Langley, BC CAN	Vancouver FC	D 0-0 D	Winnipeg Valour FC	Willoughby (2,208)
2023-05-31	Hamilton, ON	Forge FC Hamilton	L 1-2 W	York United	Tim Hortons (4,225)
2023-06-02	Langley, BC CAN	Vancouver FC	L 3-6 W	Pacific FC	Willoughby (3,438)
2023-06-03	Calgary, AB	Cavalry FC	D 1-1 D	Forge FC Hamilton	ATCO Field (3,503)
2023-06-03	Ottawa, ON	Atlético Ottawa	W 2-0 L	HFX Wanderers	TD Place (5,058)
2023-06-04	Winnipeg, MB	Winnipeg Valour FC	D 1-1 D	York United	IG Field (3,352)
2023-06-09	North York, ON	York United	W 2-1 L	Atlético Ottawa	York Lions (891)
2023-06-10	Halifax, NS	HFX Wanderers	W 2-0 L	Winnipeg Valour FC	Wanderers (5,524)
2023-06-10	Hamilton, ON	Forge FC Hamilton	L 0-1 W	Pacific FC	Tim Hortons (5,013)
2023-06-11	Calgary, AB	Cavalry FC	W 3-1 L	Vancouver FC	ATCO Field (3,762)
2023-06-16	Winnipeg, MB	Winnipeg Valour FC	W 2-0 L	Forge FC Hamilton	IG Field (3,350)
2023-06-17	Halifax, NS	HFX Wanderers	W 3-1 L	Cavalry FC	Wanderers (6,019)
2023-06-17	Ottawa, ON	Atlético Ottawa	W 1-0 L	Vancouver FC	TD Place (5,194)
2023-06-18	Victoria, BC	Pacific FC	W 1-0 L	York United	Starlight (2,741)
2023-06-20	Langley, BC CAN	Vancouver FC	W 2-0 L	Forge FC Hamilton	Willoughby (2,149)
2023-06-21	North York, ON	York United	D 2-2 D	HFX Wanderers	York Lions (1,013)
2023-06-21	Victoria, BC	Pacific FC	W 1-0 L	Winnipeg Valour FC	Starlight (2,706)
2023-06-24	Calgary, AB	Cavalry FC	W 2-1 L	York United	ATCO Field (4,404)
2023-06-25	Winnipeg, MB	Winnipeg Valour FC	W 1-0 L	Vancouver FC	IG Field (2,208)
2023-06-25	Hamilton, ON	Forge FC Hamilton	W 4-3 L	Atlético Ottawa	Tim Hortons (6,917)
2023-06-30	Halifax, NS	HFX Wanderers	W 2-1 L	Forge FC Hamilton	Wanderers (6,145)
2023-06-30	Victoria, BC	Pacific FC	D 2-2 D	Atlético Ottawa	Starlight (2,591)
2023-07-01	Winnipeg, MB	Winnipeg Valour FC	L 0-2 W	Cavalry FC	IG Field (3,391)
2023-07-02	Langley, BC CAN	Vancouver FC	L 1-2 W	York United	Willoughby (2,482)
2023-07-07	Langley, BC CAN	Vancouver FC	W 2-1 L	HFX Wanderers	Willoughby (2,321)
2023-07-08	Victoria, BC	Pacific FC	L 1-2 W	Cavalry FC	Starlight (2,825)
2023-07-09	Ottawa, ON	Atlético Ottawa	W 2-0 L	Winnipeg Valour FC	TD Place (5,003)
2023-07-09	North York, ON	York United	L 0-4 W	Forge FC Hamilton	York Lions (1,464)
2023-07-11	Halifax, NS	HFX Wanderers	W 2-1 L	Pacific FC	Wanderers (5,255)
2023-07-12	Calgary, AB	Cavalry FC	L 0-2 W	Atlético Ottawa	ATCO Field (3,189)

SEASON	CITY	HOME TEAM		SCORE		AWAY TEAM	VENUE
2023-07-14	North York, ON	York United	D	0-0	D	Pacific FC	York Lions (1,464)
2023-07-15	Calgary, AB	Cavalry FC	W	1-0	L	HFX Wanderers	ATCO Field (3,867)
2023-07-15	Hamilton, ON	Forge FC Hamilton	D	1-1	D	Winnipeg Valour FC	Tim Hortons (5,179)
2023-07-16	Ottawa, ON	Atlético Ottawa	W	3-1	L	Vancouver FC	TD Place (4,016)
2023-07-21	Victoria, BC	Pacific FC	L	0-2	W	Forge FC Hamilton	Starlight (3,311)
2023-07-22	Halifax, NS	HFX Wanderers	W	1-0	L	Atlético Ottawa	Wanderers (5,884)
2023-07-22	Langley, BC CAN	Vancouver FC	L	1-5	W	Cavalry FC	Willoughby (2,239)
2023-07-23	Winnipeg, MB	Winnipeg Valour FC	L	1-2	W	York United	IG Field (3,423)
2023-07-28	Hamilton, ON	Forge FC Hamilton	W	2-0	L	Vancouver FC	Tim Hortons (5,232)
2023-07-29	Winnipeg, MB	Winnipeg Valour FC	L	0-3	W	Pacific FC	IG Field (2,977)
2023-07-29	Ottawa, ON	Atlético Ottawa	W	1-0	L	Cavalry FC	TD Place (5,033)
2023-07-30	North York, ON	York United	L	0-2	W	HFX Wanderers	York Lions (1,490)
2023-08-04	Calgary, AB	Cavalry FC	W	3-0	L	Forge FC Hamilton	ATCO Field (4,106)
2023-08-05	Ottawa, ON	Atlético Ottawa	D	3-3	D	York United	TD Place (5,258)
2023-08-06	Langley, BC CAN	Vancouver FC	D	0-0	D	Winnipeg Valour FC	Willoughby (2,591)
2023-08-07	Halifax, NS	HFX Wanderers	L	1-2	W	Pacific FC	Wanderers (6,254)
2023-08-11	Winnipeg, MB	Winnipeg Valour FC	W	3-2	L	Cavalry FC	IG Field (2,755)
2023-08-12	Halifax, NS	HFX Wanderers	W	3-0	L	Vancouver FC	Wanderers (6,254)
2023-08-12	Hamilton, ON	Forge FC Hamilton	D	3-3	D	York United	Tim Hortons (5,071)
2023-08-13	Victoria, BC	Pacific FC	L	0-1	W	Atlético Ottawa	Starlight (3,356)
2023-08-18	Winnipeg, MB	Winnipeg Valour FC	L	1-3	W	Atlético Ottawa	IG Field (3,317)
2023-08-19	Langley, BC CAN	Vancouver FC	W	3-2	L	Pacific FC	Willoughby (2,363)
2023-08-19	Hamilton, ON	Forge FC Hamilton	D	1-1	D	HFX Wanderers	Tim Hortons (4,824)
2023-08-20	Calgary, AB	Cavalry FC	W	2-1	L	York United	ATCO Field (4,608)
2023-08-25	North York, ON	York United	W	2-1	L	Vancouver FC	York Lions (1,200)
2023-08-26	Halifax, NS	HFX Wanderers	W	3-0	L	Winnipeg Valour FC	Wanderers (4,907)
2023-08-26	Ottawa, ON	Atlético Ottawa	D	0-0	D	Forge FC Hamilton	TD Place (5,211)
2023-08-27	Calgary, AB	Cavalry FC	W	1-0	L	Pacific FC	ATCO Field (4,617)
2023-09-02	Victoria, BC	Pacific FC	W	2-1	L	Winnipeg Valour FC	Starlight (3,286)
2023-09-02	Ottawa, ON	Atlético Ottawa	L	1-2	W	Cavalry FC	TD Place (5,092)
2023-09-03	Langley, BC CAN	Vancouver FC	L	0-3	W	Forge FC Hamilton	Willoughby (2,378)
2023-09-04	Halifax, NS	HFX Wanderers	L	1-2	W	York United	Wanderers (6,254)
2023-09-08	North York, ON	York United	L	1-3	W	Winnipeg Valour FC	York Lions (1,118)
2023-09-08	Victoria, BC	Pacific FC	D	1-1	D	HFX Wanderers	Starlight (3,153)
2023-09-09	Hamilton, ON	Forge FC Hamilton	D	0-0	D	Cavalry FC	Tim Hortons (6,751)
2023-09-09	Langley, BC CAN	Vancouver FC	W	2-1	L	Atlético Ottawa	Willoughby (2,163)
2023-09-12	Halifax, NS	HFX Wanderers	L	1-2	W	Cavalry FC	Wanderers (5,422)
2023-09-13	Ottawa, ON	Atlético Ottawa	D	1-1	D	Pacific FC	TD Place (4,236)
2023-09-18	Halifax, NS	HFX Wanderers	W	3-2	L	Atlético Ottawa	Wanderers (5,132)
2023-09-16	Calgary, AB	Cavalry FC	W	2-1	L	Vancouver FC	ATCO Field (4,990)
2023-09-17	Winnipeg, MB	Winnipeg Valour FC	L	2-3	W	Forge FC Hamilton	IG Field (3,311)
2023-09-17	North York, ON	York United	L	1-4	W	Pacific FC	York Lions (1,151)
2023-09-20	Winnipeg, MB	Winnipeg Valour FC	L	0-1	W	Vancouver FC	IG Field (3,303)
2023-09-23	North York, ON	York United	L	0-1	W	Cavalry FC	York Lions (890)
2023-09-23	Langley, BC CAN	Vancouver FC	W	2-1	L	HFX Wanderers	Willoughby (2,099)
2023-09-23	Hamilton, ON	Forge FC Hamilton	W	3-1	L	Pacific FC	Tim Hortons (5,327)
2023-09-24	Ottawa, ON	Atlético Ottawa	L	0-1	W	Winnipeg Valour FC	TD Place (7,044)
2023-09-29	Calgary, AB	Cavalry FC	W	2-1	L	Winnipeg Valour FC	ATCO Field (3,951)
2023-09-30	Halifax, NS	HFX Wanderers	W	2-1	L	Forge FC Hamilton	Wanderers (6,254)
2023-09-30	Victoria, BC	Pacific FC	L	1-2	W	Vancouver FC	Starlight (4,404)
2023-10-01	North York, ON	York United	W	1-0	L	Atlético Ottawa	York Lions (1,783)
2023-10-06	Winnipeg, MB	Winnipeg Valour FC	L	0-1	W	HFX Wanderers	IG Field (3,317)
2023-10-06	Langley, BC CAN	Vancouver FC	L	1-2	W	York United	Willoughby (1,783)
2023-10-07	Hamilton, ON	Forge FC Hamilton	L	0-1	W	Atlético Ottawa	Tim Hortons (6,013)
2023-10-07	Calgary, AB	Cavalry FC	W	3-0	L	Pacific FC	ATCO Field (4,656)

2023 CPL NORTH STAR CUP WINNERS : FORGE FC HAMILTON

CPL PLAYOFFS		HOME TEAM	SCORE	AWAY TEAM	VENUE
2023-10-11	Langford, BC	Pacific FC	W 1-0 L	York United FC	Starlight (2,780)
2023-10-14	Halifax, NS	Halifax Wanderers FC	L 0-1 W	Pacific FC	Wanderers (6,254)
2023-10-14	Calgary, AB	Cavalry FC	L 1-2 W	Forge FC Hamilton	ATCO (4,385)
2023-10-21	Calgary, AB	Cavalry FC	W 2-1 L	Pacific FC	ATCO (4,066)
CPL CHAMPIONSHIP FINAL		**HOME TEAM**	**SCORE**	**AWAY TEAM**	**VENUE**
2023-10-28	Hamilton, ON	Forge FC Hamilton	W 2-1 L	Cavalry FC	Tim Hortons (13,925)

Forge FC won the 2023 CPL North Star Cup and qualified for 2024 Concacaf Champions Cup

2023 MAJOR LEAGUE SOCCER

WESTERN CONFERENCE   **W-D-L**   **MATCH-BY-MATCH RESULTS FROM THE MLS REGULAR SEASON**
W6. Vancouver Whitecaps FC   12-12-10   L L D D D W W D D W L L W L W D D W L L W W L W W W D W L L D D W D D
The top-nine teams from the Western Conference qualified for the playoffs (including Vancouver)

EASTERN CONFERENCE   **W-D-L**   **MATCH-BY-MATCH RESULTS FROM THE MLS REGULAR SEASON**
The top-nine teams from the Eastern Conference qualified for the playoffs (both Montréal and Toronto missed the playoffs)
E10. CF Montréal   12-5-17   L L L W L L L W W W W L L W D L W W D L L L W W W L L D D L L D W L
E15. Toronto FC   4-10-20   L D D W D D D D L W L L D L W D D D L L L L L L L L W L L L L L L L

SEASON	CITY	HOME TEAM	SCORE	AWAY TEAM	VENUE
2023-02-25	Fort Lauderdale, FL, USA	Inter Miami CF	W 2-0 L	CF Montréal	DRV PNK (17,655)
2023-02-25	Vancouver, BC	Vancouver Whitecaps FC	L 1-2 W	Real Salt Lake	BC Place (19,614)
2023-02-25	Washington, DC, USA	D.C. United	W 3-2 L	Toronto FC	Audi Field (17,397)
2023-03-04	Austin, TX, USA	Austin City FC	W 1-0 L	CF Montréal	Q2 (20,738)
2023-03-04	Atlanta, GA, USA	Atlanta United FC	D 1-1 D	Toronto FC	Mercedes-Benz (42,817)
2023-03-04	San Jose, CA, USA	San Jose Earthquakes	W 2-1 L	Vancouver Whitecaps FC	PayPal (18,000)
2023-03-11	Nashville, TN, USA	Nashville SC	W 2-0 L	CF Montréal	GEODIS (25,958)
2023-03-11	Toronto, ON	Toronto FC	D 1-1 D	Columbus Crew SC	BMO Field (25,796)
2023-03-11	Vancouver, BC	Vancouver Whitecaps FC	D 1-1 D	FC Dallas	BC Place (16,780)
2023-03-18	Toronto, ON	Toronto FC	W 2-0 L	Inter Miami CF	BMO Field (20,701)
2023-03-18	Montréal, QC	CF Montréal	W 3-2 L	Philadelphia Union	Olympique (23,352)
2023-03-18	Carson, CA, USA	Los Angeles Galaxy	D 1-1 D	Vancouver Whitecaps FC	Dignity (23,112)
2023-03-25	San Jose, CA, USA	San Jose Earthquakes	D 0-0 D	Toronto FC	PayPal (12,434)
2023-03-25	St Paul, MN, USA	Minnesota United FC	D 1-1 D	Vancouver Whitecaps FC	Allianz Field (19,609)
2023-04-01	Vancouver, BC	Vancouver Whitecaps FC	W 5-0 L	CF Montréal	BC Place (16,046)
2023-04-01	Toronto, ON	Toronto FC	D 2-2 D	Charlotte FC	BMO Field (22,801)
2023-04-08	Foxborough, MA, USA	New England Revolution	W 4-0 L	CF Montréal	Gillette (18,021)
2023-04-08	Vancouver, BC	Vancouver Whitecaps FC	W 1-0 L	Portland Timbers FC	BC Place (17,029)
2023-04-08	Nashville, TN, USA	Nashville SC	D 0-0 D	Toronto FC	GEODIS (26,999)
2023-04-15	Toronto, ON	Toronto FC	D 2-2 D	Atlanta United FC	BMO Field (27,892)
2023-04-15	Montréal, QC	CF Montréal	L 0-1 W	D.C. United	Saputo (16,039)
2023-04-15	Austin, TX, USA	Austin City FC	D 0-0 D	Vancouver Whitecaps FC	Q2 (20,738)
2023-04-22	Montréal, QC	CF Montréal	W 2-0 L	New York Red Bulls	Saputo (14,021)
2023-04-22	Chester, PA, USA	Philadelphia Union	W 4-2 L	Toronto FC	Subaru (18,533)
2023-04-29	Kansas, KS, USA	Sporting Kansas City	L 0-2 W	CF Montréal	Children's Mercy (18,226)
2023-04-29	Vancouver, BC	Vancouver Whitecaps FC	D 0-0 D	Colorado Rapids	BC Place (14,103)
2023-04-29	Toronto, ON	Toronto FC	W 1-0 L	New York City FC	BMO Field (21,847)
2023-05-06	Vancouver, BC	Vancouver Whitecaps FC	W 3-2 L	Minnesota United FC	BC Place (14,047)
2023-05-06	Toronto, ON	Toronto FC	L 0-2 W	New England Revolution	BMO Field (27,438)
2023-05-06	Montréal, QC	CF Montréal	W 2-0 L	Orlando City SC	Saputo (16,112)
2023-05-13	Montréal, QC	CF Montréal	W 2-0 L	Toronto FC	Saputo (19,619)
2023-05-13	Portland, OR, USA	Portland Timbers FC	W 3-1 L	Vancouver Whitecaps FC	Providence (23,154)
2023-05-17	Cincinnati, OH, USA	FC Cincinnati	W 3-0 L	CF Montréal	TQL (23,461)
2023-05-17	Toronto, ON	Toronto FC	D 0-0 D	New York City FC	BMO Field (22,560)
2023-05-17	Frisco, TX, USA	FC Dallas	W 2-1 L	Vancouver Whitecaps FC	Toyota (15,890)

SEASON	CITY	HOME TEAM	SCORE		AWAY TEAM	VENUE
2023-05-20	Harrison, NJ, USA	New York City FC	W 2-1	L	CF Montréal	Red Bull (13,436)
2023-05-20	Vancouver, BC	Vancouver Whitecaps FC	W 2-0	L	Seattle Sounders FC	BC Place (19,108)
2023-05-20	Austin, TX, USA	Austin City FC	W 1-0	L	Toronto FC	Q2 (20,738)
2023-05-27	Toronto, ON	Toronto FC	W 2-1	L	D.C. United	BMO Field (27,065)
2023-05-27	Montréal, QC	CF Montréal	W 1-0	L	Inter Miami CF	Saputo (19,619)
2023-05-27	St. Louis, MO, USA	St. Louis CITY SC	W 3-1	L	Vancouver Whitecaps FC	CITYPARK (22,423)
2023-05-31	Washington, DC, USA	D.C. United	D 2-2	D	CF Montréal	Audi Field (16,342)
2023-05-31	Toronto, ON	Toronto FC	D 0-0	D	Chicago Fire FC	BMO Field (22,778)
2023-05-31	Vancouver, BC	Vancouver Whitecaps FC	W 6-2	L	Houston Dynamo FC	BC Place (13,232)
2023-06-03	Chester, PA, USA	Philadelphia Union	W 3-0	L	CF Montréal	Subaru (19,245)
2023-06-03	Vancouver, BC	Vancouver Whitecaps FC	D 1-1	D	Sporting Kansas City	BC Place (13,739)
2023-06-03	St Paul, MN, USA	Minnesota United FC	D 1-1	D	Toronto FC	Allianz Field (19,743)
2023-06-10	Vancouver, BC	Vancouver Whitecaps FC	D 1-1	D	FC Cincinnati	BC Place (16,086)
2023-06-10	Montréal, QC	CF Montréal	W 4-0	L	Minnesota United FC	Saputo (17,030)
2023-06-10	Toronto, ON	Toronto FC	D 1-1	D	Nashville SC	BMO Field (27,228)
2023-06-21	Montréal, QC	CF Montréal	W 1-0	L	Nashville SC	Saputo (16,247)
2023-06-21	Cincinnati, OH, USA	FC Cincinnati	W 3-0	L	Toronto FC	TQL (25,513)
2023-06-24	Charlotte, NC, USA	Charlotte FC	D 0-0	D	CF Montréal	Bank of America (18,032)
2023-06-24	Foxborough, MA, USA	New England Revolution	W 2-1	L	Toronto FC	Gillette (24,596)
2023-06-24	Toronto, ON	Los Angeles FC	L 2-3	W	Vancouver Whitecaps FC	BMO (22,133)
2023-07-01	Montréal, QC	CF Montréal	L 0-1	W	New York City FC	Saputo (16,038)
2023-07-01	Toronto, ON	Toronto FC	L 0-1	W	Real Salt Lake	BMO Field (26,694)
2023-07-01	Kansas, KS, USA	Sporting Kansas City	W 3-0	L	Van. Whitecaps FC	Children's Mercy (18,867)
2023-07-04	Orlando, FL, USA	Orlando City SC	W 4-0	L	Toronto FC	Exploria (17,604)
2023-07-08	Montréal, QC	CF Montréal	L 0-1	W	Atlanta United FC	Saputo (19,619)
2023-07-08	Vancouver, BC	Vancouver Whitecaps FC	L 2-3	W	Seattle Sounders FC	BC Place (16,399)
2023-07-08	Toronto, ON	Toronto FC	L 0-1	W	St. Louis CITY SC	BMO Field (26,156)
2023-07-12	Vancouver, BC	Vancouver Whitecaps FC	W 2-1	L	Austin City FC	BC Place (14,995)
2023-07-12	Chicago, IL, USA	Chicago Fire FC	W 3-0	L	CF Montréal	Soldier Field (12,496)
2023-07-15	Montréal, QC	CF Montréal	W 2-0	L	Charlotte FC	Saputo (18,413)
2023-07-15	Vancouver, BC	Vancouver Whitecaps FC	W 4-2	L	Los Angeles Galaxy	BC Place (18,354)
2023-07-15	Chicago, IL, USA	Chicago Fire FC	W 1-0	L	Toronto FC	Soldier Field (18,246)
2023-08-20	Toronto, ON	Toronto FC	L 2-3	W	CF Montréal	BMO Field (27,518)
2023-08-20	Vancouver, BC	Vancouver Whitecaps FC	L 0-1	W	San Jose Earthquakes	BC Place (16,765)
2023-08-26	Montréal, QC	CF Montréal	W 1-0	L	New England Revolution	Saputo (19,619)
2023-08-26	Columbus, OH, USA	Columbus Crew SC	W 2-0	L	Toronto FC	Lower.com (20,548)
2023-08-26	Portland, OR, USA	Portland Timbers FC	L 2-3	W	Vancouver Whitecaps FC	Providence (22,674)
2023-08-30	New York, NY, USA	New York City FC	W 2-0	L	CF Montréal	Yankee (15,273)
2023-08-30	Toronto, ON	Toronto FC	W 3-1	L	Philadelphia Union	BMO Field (25,410)
2023-08-30	Chicago, IL, USA	Chicago Fire FC	L 0-1	W	Vancouver Whitecaps FC	Soldier (9,187)
2023-09-02	Montréal, QC	CF Montréal	L 2-4	W	Columbus Crew SC	Saputo (18,358)
2023-09-02	New York, NY, USA	New York City FC	D 1-1	D	Vancouver Whitecaps FC	Yankee (17,942)
2023-09-16	Montréal, QC	CF Montréal	D 0-0	D	Chicago Fire FC	Saputo (19,619)
2023-09-16	Toronto, ON	Toronto FC	L 1-2	W	Vancouver Whitecaps FC	BMO Field (26,165)
2023-09-20	Montréal, QC	CF Montréal	D 1-1	D	FC Cincinnati	Saputo (13,603)
2023-09-20	Fort Lauderdale, FL, USA	Inter Miami CF	W 4-0	L	Toronto FC	DRV PNK (19,659)
2023-09-20	Houston, TX, USA	Houston Dynamo FC	W 4-1	L	Vancouver Whitecaps FC	Shell Energy (13,866)
2023-09-23	Atlanta, GA, USA	Atlanta United FC	W 4-1	L	CF Montréal	Mercedes-Benz (42,569)
2023-09-23	Harrison, NJ, USA	New York City FC	W 3-0	L	Toronto FC	Red Bull (7,417)
2023-09-23	Sandy, UT, USA	Real Salt Lake	W 2-1	L	Vancouver Whitecaps FC	America First (19,243)
2023-09-27	Commerce City, CO, USA	Colorado Rapids	D 2-2	D	Vancouver Whitecaps FC	Dick's (12,064)
2023-09-30	Orlando, FL, USA	Orlando City SC	W 3-0	L	CF Montréal	Exploria (19,637)
2023-09-30	Vancouver, BC	Vancouver Whitecaps FC	D 2-2	D	D.C. United	BC Place (19,442)
2023-09-30	Toronto, ON	Toronto FC	L 2-3	W	FC Cincinnati	BMO Field (24,658)
2023-10-04	Montréal, QC	CF Montréal	D 1-1	D	Houston Dynamo FC	Saputo (13,509)
2023-10-04	Vancouver, BC	Vancouver Whitecaps FC	W 3-0	L	St. Louis CITY SC	BC Place (13,776)
2023-10-04	Charlotte, NC, USA	Charlotte FC	W 3-0	L	Toronto FC	Bank of America (30,080)
2023-10-07	Montréal, QC	CF Montréal	W 4-1	L	Portland Timbers FC	Saputo (17,559)

2023 CANADA

SEASON	CITY	HOME TEAM	SCORE	AWAY TEAM	VENUE
2023-10-07	Harrison, NJ, USA	New York City FC W	3-0 L	Toronto FC	Red Bull (24,506)
2023-10-07	Seattle, WA, USA	Seattle Sounders FC D	0-0 D	Vancouver Whitecaps FC	Lumen (33,666)
2023-10-21	Columbus, OH, USA	Columbus Crew SC W	2-1 L	CF Montréal	Lower.com (20,526)
2023-10-21	Vancouver, BC	Vancouver Whitecaps FC D	1-1 D	Los Angeles FC	BC Place (25,146)
2023-10-21	Toronto, ON	Toronto FC L	0-2 W	Orlando City SC	BMO Field (27,556)

1.ROUND PLAYOFFS (BEST of THREE)

SEASON	CITY	HOME TEAM	SCORE	AWAY TEAM	VENUE
2023-10-28	Los Angeles, CA, USA	Los Angeles FC W	5-2 L	Vancouer Whitecaps FC	BMO (22,002)
2023-11-05	Vancouver, BC	Vancouver Whitecaps FC L	0-1 W	Los Angeles FC	BC Place (30,204)

Los Angeles FC won the best-of-three playoff series after back-to-back wins

2023 LEAGUES CUP

WEST GROUP 3

SEASON	CITY	HOME TEAM	SCORE	AWAY TEAM	VENUE
2023-07-21	Vancouver, BC	Club León	2-2 (16-15)	Vancouver Whitecaps FC	BC Place (17,391)
2023-07-26	Carson, CA, USA	Los Angeles Galaxy L	0-1 W	Club León	Dignty Health (20,776)
2023-07-30	Carson, CA, USA	Los Angeles Galaxy L	1-2 W	Vancouver Whitecaps FC	Dignty Health (14,787)

West Group 3 standings: Club León 5 points; Vancouver 4 points; Los Angeles 0 points

EAST GROUP 2

SEASON	CITY	HOME TEAM	SCORE	AWAY TEAM	VENUE
2023-07-22	Montréal, QC	CF Montéal	2-2 (4-2)	UNAM Pumas	Stade Saputo (19,619)
2023-07-26	Montréal, QC	CF Montéal L	0-1 W	D.C. United	Stade Saputo (19,619)
2023-07-29	Washington, DC, USA	UNAM Pumas W	2-0 L	D.C. United	Audi Field (14,599)

East Group 2 standings: UNAM Pumas 4 points; D.C. United 3 points; Montréal 2 points

EAST GROUP 3

SEASON	CITY	HOME TEAM	SCORE	AWAY TEAM	VENUE
2023-07-23	New York, NY, USA	New York City FC L	0-1 W	Atlas FC	Citi Field (22,267)
2023-07-26	Harrison, NJ, USA	New York City FC W	5-0 L	Toronto FC	Red Bull Arena (7,417)
2023-07-30	Toronto, ON	Atlas FC W	1-0 L	Toronto FC	BMO Field (24,633)

East Group 3 standings: Atlas FC 6 points; New York 3 points; Toronto 0 points

ROUND of 32 PLAYOFF

SEASON	CITY	HOME TEAM	SCORE	AWAY TEAM	VENUE
2023-08-04	Vancouver, BC	Tigres UANL D	1-1 D	Vancouver Whitecaps FC	BC Place (13,703)

Tigres UANL advanced after they won 5-3 on kicks from the penalty mark

2023 MLS NEXT PRO

WESTERN CONFERENCE   MP W-SW-SL-L   MATCH-BY-MATCH RESULTS
The top-seven teams from the Western Conference qualified for the playoffs (Vancouver missed the playoffs)
W11. Vancouver Whitecaps FC 2   28   8-3-4-13   W SW W L W L W L W W SL SW L W L W L SL L L L SL SW L L L L SL

EASTERN CONFERENCE   MP W-SW-SL-L   MATCH-BY-MATCH RESULTS
The top-seven teams from the Eastern Conference qualified for the playoffs (Toronto missed the playoffs)
E11. Toronto FC II   28   6-3-5-14   L L L SL L W L W L L W SW L SW SL L L SW W W L W SL SL L L SL L

SEASON	CITY	HOME TEAM	SCORE	AWAY TEAM	VENUE
2023-03-26	Burnaby, BC	Van. Whitecaps FC 2 W	2-1 L	Portland Timbers 2	Swangard
2023-03-27	Highland Heights, KY, USA	FC Cincinnati 2 W	4-2 L	Toronto FC II	NKU Soccer
2023-03-31	Bridgeview, IL, USA	Chicago Fire FC II W	2-0 L	Toronto FC II	SeatGeek
2023-04-02	Fullerton, CA, USA	Los Angeles FC 2	1-1 (2-3)	Van. Whitecaps FC 2	Titan
2023-04-09	Arlington, TX, USA	North Texas SC L	1-4 W	Van. Whitecaps FC 2	Choctaw
2023-04-14	Toronto, ON	Toronto FC II L	0-2 W	New York City FC II	York Lions
2023-04-16	Burnaby, BC	Van. Whitecaps FC 2 L	3-4 W	Los Angeles Galaxy II	Swangard
2023-04-23	Chester, PA, USA	Philadelphia Union II	3-3 (5-4)	Toronto FC II	Subaru
2023-04-23	Burnaby, BC	Van. Whitecaps FC 2 W	5-2 L	Minnesota United FC 2	Swangard
2023-04-30	Kissimmee, FL, USA	Orlando City B W	3-2 L	Toronto FC II	Osceola Heritage
2023-04-30	St. Louis, MO, USA	St. Louis CITY 2 W	2-1 L	Van. Whitecaps FC 2	CITYPARK
2023-05-07	Toronto, ON	Toronto FC II W	3-0 L	FC Cincinnati 2	York Lions
2023-05-07	Burnaby, BC	Van. Whitecaps FC 2 W	1-0 L	Houston Dynamo 2	Swangard

SEASON	CITY	HOME TEAM	SCORE	AWAY TEAM	VENUE
2023-05-14	Toronto, ON	Toronto FC II	L 2-3 W	New England Revolution II	York Lions
2023-05-14	Portland, OR, USA	Portland Timbers 2	W 3-1 L	Van. Whitecaps FC 2	Providence
2023-05-21	Toronto, ON	Toronto FC II	W 3-2 L	Chicago Fire FC II	York Lions
2023-05-21	Burnaby, BC	Van. Whitecaps FC 2	W 1-0 L	Tacoma Defiance	Swangard
2023-05-25	New York, NY, USA	New York City FC II	W 3-1 L	Toronto FC II	Belson
2023-05-25	San Jose, CA, USA	San Jose Earthquakes II	L 0-1 W	Van. Whitecaps FC 2	PayPal
2023-05-28	Kennesaw, GA, USA	Atlanta United 2	W 2-0 L	Toronto FC II	Fifth Third Bank
2023-05-28	Carson, CA, USA	Los Angeles Galaxy II	2-2 (4-2)	Van. Whitecaps FC 2	Dignity
2023-06-02	Burnaby, BC	Van. Whitecaps FC 2	1-1 (5-4)	Sporting KC II	Swangard
2023-06-04	Toronto, ON	Toronto FC II	W 3-0 L	Orlando City B	York Lions
2023-06-09	Austin, TX, USA	Austin FC II	W 1-0 L	Van. Whitecaps FC 2	Parmer Field
2023-06-11	Fort Lauderdale, FL, USA	Inter Miami CF II	1-1 (4-5)	Toronto FC II	DRV PNK
2023-06-15	Toronto, ON	Toronto FC II	L 1-2 W	Huntsville City FC	York Lions
2023-06-15	Burnaby, BC	Van. Whitecaps FC 2	W 1-0 L	Real Monarchs	Swangard
2023-06-18	Toronto, ON	Toronto FC II	0-0 (4-3)	Atlanta United 2	York Lions
2023-06-18	Blaine, MN, USA	Minnesota United FC 2	W 2-0 L	Van. Whitecaps FC 2	National Sports
2023-06-22	Burnaby, BC	Van. Whitecaps FC 2	W 1-0 L	Los Angeles FC 2	Swangard
2023-06-23	Foxborough, MA, USA	NE Revolution II	1-1 (4-2)	Toronto FC II	Gillette
2023-06-30	Toronto, ON	Toronto FC II	L 1-2 W	Crown Legacy FC	York Lions
2023-07-02	Lawrence, KS, USA	Sporting KC II	W 7-1 L	Van. Whitecaps FC 2	Rock Chalk
2023-07-07	Toronto, ON	Toronto FC II	L 2-3 W	Columbus Crew 2	York Lions
2023-07-08	Vancouver, BC	Van. Whitecaps FC 2	1-1 (3-4)	Colorado Rapids 2	BC Place
2023-07-12	Toronto, ON	Toronto FC II	1-1 (4-2)	Philadelphia Union II	York Lions
2023-07-15	Vancouver, BC	Van. Whitecaps FC 2	L 0-1 W	Portland Timbers 2	BC Place
2023-07-16	Huntsville, AL, USA	Huntsville City FC	L 1-2 W	Toronto FC II	Joe W. Davis
2023-07-21	Toronto, ON	Toronto FC II	W 6-1 L	Inter Miami CF II	York Lions
2023-07-30	Tukwila, WA, USA	Tacoma Defiance	W 2-1 L	Van. Whitecaps FC 2	Starfire Sports
2023-08-03	Columbus, OH, USA	Columbus Crew 2	W 4-0 L	Toronto FC II	Historic Crew
2023-08-05	Denver, CO, USA	Colorado Rapids 2	W 6-2 L	Van. Whitecaps FC 2	U. Denver
2023-08-09	Montclair, NJ, USA	New York Red Bulls II	L 1-2 W	Toronto FC II	MSU Soccer
2023-08-13	Houston, TX, USA	Houston Dynamo 2	0-0 (3-2)	Van. Whitecaps FC 2	SaberCats
2023-08-18	Toronto, ON	Toronto FC II	0-0 (1-4)	NE Revolution II	York Lions
2023-08-20	Vancouver, BC	Van. Whitecaps FC 2	1-1 (4-3)	Austin FC II	BC Place
2023-08-25	Matthews, NC, USA	Crown Legacy FC	1-1 (3-1)	Toronto FC II	Mecklenburg
2023-08-25	Vancouver, BC	Van. Whitecaps FC 2	L 0-1 W	North Texas SC	BC Place
2023-09-01	Toronto, ON	Toronto FC II	L 0-3 W	New York Red Bulls II	York Lions
2023-09-01	Herriman, UT, USA	Real Monarchs	W 1-0 L	Van. Whitecaps FC 2	Zions Bank
2023-09-08	Chester, PA, USA	Philadelphia Union II	W 5-3 L	Toronto FC II	Subaru
2023-09-09	Vancouver, BC	Van. Whitecaps FC 2	L 0-1 W	St. Louis CITY 2	NDC Vancouver
2023-09-15	New York, NY, USA	New York City FC II	3-3 (4-1)	Toronto FC II	Belson
2023-09-16	Vancouver, BC	Van. Whitecaps FC 2	L 2-5 W	San Jose Earthquakes II	NDC Vancouver
2023-09-24	Toronto, ON	Toronto FC II	L 0-4 W	Crown Legacy FC	York Lions
2023-09-24	Tukwila, WA, USA	Tacoma Defiance	3-3 (5-4)	Van. Whitecaps FC 2	Starline Sports

2023 LEAGUE1 BC

LEAGUE1 BC	MP	W	D	L	PTS	MATCH-BY-MATCH RESULTS
1. Victoria Highlanders FC	14	10	2	2	32	D W W W L W D L W W W W W W

The 2023 League1 BC winners Victoria Highlanders FC qualified for the 2024 Canadian Championship

	MP	W	D	L	PTS	MATCH-BY-MATCH RESULTS
2. Richmond TSS Rovers	14	9	2	3	29	D L W W L W W W D W W W W L
3. Van. Whitecaps FC Academy	14	5	7	2	22	D D W D W L D W D W D W L D
4. Langley Unity FC	14	5	5	4	20	D D L W L W W W L D L D D W

The top-four teams from the league standings qualified for the League1 BC playoffs

	MP	W	D	L	PTS	MATCH-BY-MATCH RESULTS
5. Vancouver Nautsa'mawt FC	14	4	5	5	17	D D L W L W W W L D D L D L W
6. Kamloops Rivers FC	14	4	4	6	16	W D L W L D W L W L D L D
7. North Vancouver Altitude FC	14	2	3	9	9	L D L L D L W L L L D L L W
8. Nanaimo Harbourside FC	14	1	4	9	7	D D W L L D D L L L L L L L

2023 LEAGUE1 BRITISH COLUMBIA WINNERS : VICTORIA HIGHLANDERS FC

SEASON	CITY	HOME TEAM	SCORE	AWAY TEAM	VENUE
2023-04-29	Nanaimo, BC	Harbourside FC	D 1-1 D	Unity FC	Q'unq'inuqwstuxw
2023-04-29	Burnaby, BC	TSS Rovers	D 0-0 D	Nautsa'mawt FC	Swangard
2023-04-30	Kamloops, BC	Rivers FC	W 2-1 L	Altitude FC	Hillside
2023-04-30	Vancouver, BC	Whitecaps FC Academy	D 1-1 D	Victoria Highlanders FC	Thunderbird
2023-05-06	Burnaby, BC	TSS Rovers	L 0-1 W	Victoria Highlanders FC	Swangard
2023-05-06	Vancouver, BC	Nautsa'mawt FC	D 0-0 D	Harbourside FC	Thunderbird
2023-05-07	North Vancouver, BC	Altitude FC	D 1-1 D	Unity FC	Kinsmen
2023-05-07	Nanaimo, BC	Harbourside FC	W 1-0 L	Nautsa'mawt FC	Q'unq'inuqwstuxw
2023-05-07	Vancouver, BC	Whitecaps FC Academy	D 1-1 D	Rivers FC	Thunderbird
2023-05-12	Vancouver, BC	Whitecaps FC Academy	W 4-2 L	Altitude FC	Ken Woods
2023-05-13	Kamloops, BC	Rivers FC	L 0-2 W	Nautsa'mawt FC	MacArthur Island
2023-05-13	Burnaby, BC	TSS Rovers	W 4-0 L	Harbourside FC	Swangard
2023-05-19	Nanaimo, BC	Harbourside FC	L 0-1 W	Victoria Highlanders FC	Q'unq'inuqwstuxw
2023-05-20	Burnaby, BC	TSS Rovers	W 4-0 L	Unity FC	Swangard
2023-05-21	North Vancouver, BC	Altitude FC	L 1-4 W	Rivers FC	Kinsmen
2023-05-22	Vancouver, BC	Nautsa'mawt FC	L 0-5 W	Unity FC	Thunderbird
2023-05-24	Nanaimo, BC	Harbourside FC	D 2-2 D	Whitecaps FC Academy	Q'unq'inuqwstuxw
2023-05-27	Victoria, BC	Victoria Highlanders FC	W 2-1 L	Unity FC	Centennial
2023-05-27	Vancouver, BC	Whitecaps FC Academy	W 1-0 L	TSS Rovers	Ken Woods
2023-05-28	Victoria, BC	Victoria Highlanders FC	L 0-1 W	Nautsa'mawt FC	Centennial
2023-05-28	Langley, BC	Unity FC	W 7-0 L	Rivers FC	Exhibition
2023-05-28	North Vancouver, BC	Altitude FC	D 0-0 D	Harbourside FC	Kinsmen
2023-06-03	Burnaby, BC	TSS Rovers	W 3-1 L	Rivers FC	Swangard
2023-06-03	Vancouver, BC	Nautsa'mawt FC	W 3-2 L	Altitude FC	Thunderbird
2023-06-04	Victoria, BC	Victoria Highlanders FC	W 1-0 L	Whitecaps FC Academy	Centennial
2023-06-04	Langley, BC	Unity FC	W 4-0 L	Harbourside FC	Chase Office
2023-06-07	North Vancouver, BC	Altitude FC	W 3-1 L	Nautsa'mawt FC	Kinsmen
2023-06-10	Kamloops, BC	Rivers FC	D 1-1 D	Victoria Highlanders FC	MacArthur Island
2023-06-11	Langley, BC	Unity FC	W 1-0 L	Victoria Highlanders FC	Chase Office
2023-06-11	Vancouver, BC	Whitecaps FC Academy	D 0-0 D	Nautsa'mawt FC	Ken Woods
2023-06-11	Burnaby, BC	TSS Rovers	W 4-0 L	Altitude FC	Swangard
2023-06-14	Vancouver, BC	Whitecaps FC Academy	W 1-0 L	Unity FC	Ken Woods
2023-06-16	Nanaimo, BC	Harbourside FC	L 0-2 W	Rivers FC	Q'unq'inuqwstuxw
2023-06-17	Victoria, BC	Victoria Highlanders FC	W 3-0 L	Rivers FC	Centennial
2023-06-18	Langley, BC	Unity FC	D 1-1 D	Nautsa'mawt FC	Chase Office
2023-06-18	North Vancouver, BC	Altitude FC	L 1-5 W	TSS Rovers	Kinsmen
2023-06-21	Burnaby, BC	TSS Rovers	D 1-1 D	Whitecaps FC Academy	Swangard
2023-06-24	Langley, BC	Unity FC	L 0-1 W	TSS Rovers	Chase Office
2023-06-24	Vancouver, BC	Nautsa'mawt FC	L 0-2 W	Victoria Highlanders FC	Thunderbird
2023-06-25	North Vancouver, BC	Altitude FC	L 1-2 W	Whitecaps FC Academy	Kinsmen
2023-06-25	Kamloops, BC	Rivers FC	W 3-2 L	Harbourside FC	MacArthur Island
2023-06-30	Kamloops, BC	Rivers FC	L 0-3 W	TSS Rovers	MacArthur Island
2023-07-01	Vancouver, BC	Nautsa'mawt FC	D 1-1 D	Whitecaps FC Academy	Thunderbird
2023-07-02	Victoria, BC	Victoria Highlanders FC	W 1-0 L	Harbourside FC	Centennial
2023-07-02	Langley, BC	Unity FC	D 2-2 D	Altitude FC	Chase Office
2023-07-08	Kamloops, BC	Rivers FC	D 1-1 D	Unity FC	MacArthur Island
2023-07-08	Vancouver, BC	Nautsa'mawt FC	L 0-2 W	TSS Rovers	Thunderbird
2023-07-09	Victoria, BC	Victoria Highlanders FC	W 2-1 L	Altitude FC	Centennial
2023-07-09	Vancouver, BC	Whitecaps FC Academy	W 3-1 L	Harbourside FC	Thunderbird
2023-07-15	Langley, BC	Unity FC	W 2-1 L	Whitecaps FC Academy	Chase Office
2023-07-15	Nanaimo, BC	Harbourside FC	L 2-3 W	TSS Rovers	Q'unq'inuqwstuxw
2023-07-15	Vancouver, BC	Nautsa'mawt FC	W 2-1 L	Rivers FC	Thunderbird
2023-07-16	North Vancouver, BC	Altitude FC	L 1-2 W	Victoria Highlanders FC	Kinsmen
2023-07-22	Victoria, BC	Victoria Highlanders FC	W 3-2 L	TSS Rovers	Centennial
2023-07-23	Kamloops, BC	Rivers FC	D 1-1 D	Whitecaps FC Academy	MacArthur Island
2023-07-23	Nanaimo, BC	Harbourside FC	L 1-2 W	Altitude FC	Q'unq'inuqwstuxw

2023 LEAGUE1 BC PLAYOFF WINNERS : VANCOUVER WHITECAPS FC ACADEMY

SEMIFINALS	HOME TEAM	SCORE	AWAY TEAM	VENUE
2023-07-29 Victoria, BC	Victoria Highlanders FC	W 3-2 L	Unity FC	Centennial
2023-07-29 Vancouver, BC	TSS Rovers	L 0-4 W	Whitecaps FC Academy	Ken Woods
CHAMPIONSHIP FINAL	**HOME TEAM**	**SCORE**	**AWAY TEAM**	**VENUE**
2023-08-05 Vancouver, BC	Victoria Highlanders FC	L 1-2 W	Whitecaps FC Academy	BC Place

2023 LEAGUE1 ALBERTA

LEAGUE1 ALBERTA	MP	W	D	L	PTS	MATCH-BY-MATCH RESULTS
1. Calgary Foothills FC	8	6	2	0	20	D W W W W W W D
2. St. Albert Impact	8	3	2	3	11	L W W D D W L L

The top-two teams from the league standings qualified for the League1 Alberta Championship match

	MP	W	D	L	PTS	MATCH-BY-MATCH RESULTS
3. Edmonton BTB SC	8	3	1	4	10	W W L L L L W D
4. Calgary Cavalry FC U-21	8	2	2	4	8	L D L L D W W L
4. Edmonton Scottish	8	1	3	4	6	D D L D L L W L

SEASON	CITY	HOME TEAM	SCORE	AWAY TEAM	VENUE
2023-05-12	Calgary, AB	Calgary Foothills FC	D 1-1 D	Edmonton Scottish United SC	Macron
2023-05-12	Edmonton, AB	Edmonton BTB SC	W 3-0 L	Calgary Cavalry FC U-21	Taurus
2023-05-26	Edmonton, AB	Edmonton Scottish United SC	D 3-3 D	Calgary Cavalry FC U-21	Hamish Black
2023-05-26	Calgary, AB	Calgary Foothills FC	W 3-0 L	St Albert Impact	Broadview
2023-06-02	Calgary, AB	Calgary Cavalry FC U-21	L 1-2 W	St Albert Impact	Shouldice
2023-06-02	Edmonton, AB	Edmonton Scottish United SC	L 1-2 W	Edmonton BTB SC	Hamish Black
2023-06-09	Calgary, AB	Calgary Cavalry FC U-21	L 0-4 W	Calgary Foothills FC	Macron
2023-06-09	Edmonton, AB	Edmonton BTB SC	L 2-4 W	St Albert Impact	Clarke
2023-06-16	St. Albert, AB	St Albert Impact	D 1-1 D	Edmonton Scottish United SC	Riel 1
2023-06-16	Calgary, AB	Calgary Foothills FC	W 2-1 L	Edmonton BTB SC	Broadview
2023-06-23	St. Albert, AB	St Albert Impact	D 1-1 D	Calgary Cavalry FC U-21	Riel 1
2023-06-23	Edmonton, AB	Edmonton Scottish United SC	L 0-3 W	Calgary Foothills FC	Hamish Black
2023-06-30	Calgary, AB	Calgary Cavalry FC U-21	W 3-1 L	Edmonton BTB SC	Shouldice
2023-07-01	Edmonton, AB	Edmonton Scottish United SC	L 0-1 W	St Albert Impact	Hamish Black
2023-07-07	Edmonton, AB	Edmonton BTB SC	L 0-1 W	Edmonton Scottish United SC	Clarke
2023-07-07	St. Albert, AB	St Albert Impact	L 1-3 W	Calgary Foothills FC	Riel 1
2023-07-16	Calgary, AB	Calgary Cavalry FC U-21	W 2-1 L	Edmonton Scottish United SC	Shouldice
2023-07-21	St. Albert, AB	St Albert Impact	D 0-0 D	Edmonton BTB SC	Riel 1
2023-07-21	Calgary, AB	Calgary Foothills FC	W 2-0 L	Calgary Cavalry FC U-21	Broadview
2023-07-23	Edmonton, AB	Edmonton BTB SC	D 2-2 D	Calgary Foothills FC	Clarke

2023 LEAGUE1 ALBERTA EXHIBITION SERIES : CALGARY FOOTHILLS FC

CHAMPIONSHIP FINAL	HOME TEAM	SCORE	AWAY TEAM	VENUE
2023-07-28 Calgary, AB	Calgary Foothills FC	W 3-0 L	St Albert Impact	Broadview

2023 LEAGUE1 ONTARIO

LEAGUE1 ONTARIO	MP	W	D	L	PTS	MATCH-BY-MATCH RESULTS
1. Scrosoppi FC	20	17	0	3	51	W L W W W W L W W W W W W W W L W W W
2. Simcoe County Rovers FC	20	15	1	4	46	W W L L D W W W L W W W W L W W W W W
3. Vaughan Azzurri	20	14	3	3	45	D W D W W W W W L W W L W D W W W W L
4. Oakville Blue Devils FC	20	12	3	5	39	D W W W D W D W W W W W L W L L W W L L
5. Burlington SC	20	12	3	5	39	W W W L W W L W L L D W W L D D W W W W
6. Guelph United FC	20	11	6	3	39	D D W W W W D W L W W W L W D L D W D W

The top-six teams from the league standings qualified for the League1 Ontario playoffs

#	Team	GP	W	L	D	Pts	Form
7.	Electric City FC	20	11	4	5	37	LWLWWWWLDDDWWWWDLLWW
8.	Alliance United FC	20	9	6	5	33	WDWWDLWWLDWWWDLDWDLL
9.	Sigma FC	20	9	5	6	32	WWDWLWWDDWWLLLLWDWD
10.	North Toronto Nitros	20	9	4	7	31	DLWWWLWDWWWLWLWDLLLD
11.	Hamilton United	20	7	5	8	26	LLDWLDWLDLLWWWWDLWLD
12.	Woodbridge Strikers SC	20	6	8	6	26	LDWWDLWLDDDWLWLWLDDD
13.	FC London	20	6	7	7	25	LLLDDWLLLDDWWDWWDWLD
14.	Darby FC	20	6	5	9	23	WWLLLLLLWDLLDDDWWDLW
15.	Windsor City FC	20	6	2	12	20	WLWLLLDWWLLLWLWLDLLL
16.	St. Catharines Roma	20	6	2	12	20	LWLLLLLWDDLWLWLLWLW
17.	North Mississauga SC	20	5	5	10	20	LDLLWWLDDLLLDLWLLWWD
18.	ProStars FC	20	5	4	11	19	WLWWLWWDDLLDLLDLLLLL
19.	Master's FA	20	4	2	14	14	LLLDLLLLLWLLLDLLWWWL
20.	Unionville Milliken SC	20	1	1	18	4	LLDLLLLLLLLLLLWLLLLL
21.	BVB IA Waterloo	20	1	0	19	3	LLWLLLLLLLLLLLLLLLLL

2023 LEAGUE1 ONTARIO WINNERS : SCROSOPPI FC

SEASON	CITY	HOME TEAM		SCORE		AWAY TEAM	VENUE
2023-04-12	Vaughan, ON	Vaughan SC Azzurri	D	2-2	D	North Toronto Nitros	North Maple
2023-04-14	Mississauga, ON	North Mississauga SC	L	0-3	W	Burlington SC	Mattamy
2023-04-15	Peterborough, ON	Electric City FC	L	0-1	W	Scrosoppi FC	Fleming
2023-04-15	Hamilton, ON	Hamilton United	L	3-5	W	Sigma FC	Tim Hortons
2023-04-15	Scarborough, ON	Alliance United	W	3-0	L	St. Catharines Roma	Birchmount
2023-04-15	Whitby, ON	Darby FC	W	3-0	L	Woodbridge SC Strikers	Whitby Soccer
2023-04-16	Oakville, ON	Oakville Blue Devils	D	2-2	D	Guelph United FC	Sheridan
2023-04-16	Vaughan, ON	ProStars FC	W	2-0	L	Master's FA	Ontario Soccer
2023-04-16	Waterloo, ON	BVB IA Waterloo	L	1-3	W	Simcoe County Rovers FC	RIM
2023-04-16	Vaughan, ON	Unionville Milliken SC	L	0-3	W	Windsor City FC	Ontario Soccer
2023-04-20	Hamilton, ON	Hamilton United	L	1-2	W	Darby FC	McMaster
2023-04-21	Guelph, ON	Guelph United FC	D	0-0	D	Alliance United FC	Gryphon
2023-04-21	Mississauga, ON	North Mississauga SC	D	1-1	D	Woodbridge SC Strikers	Mattamy
2023-04-22	Barrie, ON	Simcoe County Rovers FC	W	6-0	L	Master's FA	J. C. Massie
2023-04-22	Peterborough, ON	Electric City FC	W	2-0	L	North Toronto Nitros	Fleming
2023-04-22	Hamilton, ON	Sigma FC	W	4-1	L	ProStars FC	Tim Hortons
2023-04-22	Vaughan, ON	Scrosoppi FC	L	0-2	W	Vaughan SC Azzurri	Ontario Soccer
2023-04-23	St. Catharines, ON	St. Catharines Roma	W	2-1	L	FC London	Kiwanis
2023-04-23	Burlington, ON	Burlington SC	W	2-0	L	Unionville Milliken SC	Corpus Christi
2023-04-23	Oakville, ON	Oakville Blue Devils	W	4-0	L	Windsor City FC	Sheridan
2023-04-26	Hamilton, ON	Hamilton United	D	0-0	D	Vaughan SC Azzurri	McMaster
2023-04-27	Guelph, ON	Guelph United FC	W	2-0	L	FC London	Gryphon
2023-04-28	Whitby, ON	Darby FC	L	1-2	W	Scrosoppi FC	Whitby Soccer
2023-04-29	Toronto, ON	Master's FA	L	1-2	W	Oakville Blue Devils FC	L'Amoreaux
2023-04-29	Vaughan, ON	Unionville Milliken SC	D	2-2	D	Sigma FC	Ontario Soccer
2023-04-30	Waterloo, ON	BVB IA Waterloo	L	0-6	W	Alliance United FC	RIM
2023-04-30	Burlington, ON	Burlington SC	W	2-0	L	Electric City FC	Corpus Christi
2023-04-30	Windsor, ON	Windsor City FC	W	6-1	L	St. Catharines Roma	St. Clair
2023-04-30	Barrie, ON	Simcoe County Rovers FC	L	1-3	W	Woodbridge SC Strikers	J. C. Massie
2023-05-02	Mississauga, ON	North Mississauga SC	L	0-3	W	North Toronto Nitros	Mattamy
2023-05-03	Vaughan, ON	Woodbridge SC Strikers	W	3-0	L	Unionville Milliken SC	Vaughan Grove
2023-05-05	St. Catharines, ON	St. Catharines Roma	L	0-1	W	BVB IA Waterloo	Brock
2023-05-05	Mississauga, ON	North Mississauga SC	L	2-3	W	Hamilton United	Mattamy
2023-05-06	Toronto, ON	North Toronto Nitros	W	2-1	L	FC London	Downsview
2023-05-06	Mississauga, ON	Sigma FC	W	2-0	L	Simcoe County Rovers FC	Paramount
2023-05-06	Brampton, ON	ProStars FC	W	3-1	L	Unionville Milliken SC	Terry Fox
2023-05-06	Toronto, ON	Master's FA	D	0-0	D	Woodbridge SC Strikers	L'Amoreaux
2023-05-07	Windsor, ON	Windsor City FC	L	0-3	W	Alliance United FC	St. Clair
2023-05-07	Oakville, ON	Oakville Blue Devils	W	3-0	L	Burlington SC	Sheridan
2023-05-07	Vaughan, ON	Vaughan SC Azzurri	W	3-1	L	Darby FC	North Maple

SEASON	CITY	HOME TEAM		SCORE		AWAY TEAM	VENUE
2023-05-09	Peterborough, ON	Electric City FC	W	2-1	L	Sigma FC	Fleming
2023-05-12	Whitby, ON	Darby FC	L	1-2	W	Burlington SC	Whitby Soccer
2023-05-13	Peterborough, ON	Electric City FC	W	2-0	L	Master's FA	Fleming
2023-05-13	Mississauga, ON	St. Catharines Roma	L	3-4	W	Sigma FC	Paramount
2023-05-13	London, ON	FC London	D	1-1	D	Simcoe County Rovers FC	Tricar
2023-05-13	Mississauga, ON	North Mississauga SC	W	2-1	L	Windsor City FC	Mattamy
2023-05-13	Vaughan, ON	Scrosoppi FC	W	4-0	L	Woodbridge SC Strikers	Ontario Soccer
2023-05-14	Toronto, ON	Alliance United	D	0-0	D	Oakville Blue Devils FC	Varsity
2023-05-14	Vaughan, ON	Unionville Milliken SC	L	0-4	W	Guelph United FC	Ontario Soccer
2023-05-14	Waterloo, ON	BVB IA Waterloo	L	2-4	W	ProStars FC	RIM
2023-05-17	Hamilton, ON	Hamilton United	L	1-3	W	North Toronto Nitros	McMaster
2023-05-19	Brampton, ON	ProStars FC	L	0-5	W	Simcoe County Rovers FC	Terry Fox
2023-05-20	Hamilton, ON	Hamilton United	D	1-1	D	FC London	McMaster
2023-05-20	Vaughan, ON	Unionville Milliken SC	L	1-2	W	North Mississauga SC	Ontario Soccer
2023-05-21	Vaughan, ON	Woodbridge SC Strikers	W	3-2	L	BVB IA Waterloo	Vaughan Grove
2023-05-21	Oakville, ON	Oakville Blue Devils	W	5-0	L	Darby FC	Sheridan
2023-05-21	Burlington, ON	Burlington SC	W	2-1	L	Master's FA	Corpus Christi
2023-05-21	Toronto, ON	Alliance United	L	1-2	W	Scrosoppi FC	Varsity
2023-05-21	Windsor, ON	Windsor City FC	L	1-4	W	Sigma FC	St. Clair
2023-05-23	Guelph, ON	Guelph United FC	W	4-3	L	North Toronto Nitros	Centennial
2023-05-24	Vaughan, ON	Unionville Milliken SC	L	0-1	W	Hamilton United	Ontario Soccer
2023-05-26	St. Catharines, ON	St. Catharines Roma	L	1-4	W	Electric City FC	Club Roma
2023-05-26	Mississauga, ON	North Mississauga SC	L	0-4	W	Scrosoppi FC	Mattamy
2023-05-27	Toronto, ON	Master's FA	L	2-3	W	Alliance United FC	L'Amoreaux
2023-05-27	Mississauga, ON	ProStars FC	W	4-0	L	Burlington SC	Mattamy
2023-05-27	Toronto, ON	North Toronto Nitros	W	2-1	L	Darby FC	Downsview
2023-05-27	London, ON	FC London	W	3-1	L	Unionville Milliken SC	Tricar
2023-05-28	Guelph, ON	Guelph United FC	W	6-2	L	BVB IA Waterloo	Centennial
2023-05-28	Barrie, ON	Simcoe County Rovers FC	W	2-1	L	Hamilton United	J. C. Massie
2023-05-28	Oakville, ON	Oakville Blue Devils	D	3-3	D	Sigma FC	Sheridan
2023-05-28	Toronto, ON	Woodbridge SC Strikers	L	0-2	W	Vaughan SC Azzurri	York
2023-05-30	Mississauga, ON	ProStars FC	W	2-0	L	Scrosoppi FC	Mattamy
2023-05-31	Waterloo, ON	BVB IA Waterloo	L	0-5	W	Electric City FC	RIM
2023-06-02	Mississauga, ON	North Mississauga SC	D	1-1	D	Guelph United FC	Mattamy
2023-06-02	St. Catharines, ON	St. Catharines Roma	L	1-2	W	Scrosoppi FC	Club Roma
2023-06-03	London, ON	FC London	L	0-2	W	Oakville Blue Devils FC	Tricar
2023-06-03	Toronto, ON	Alliance United	W	1-0	L	Darby FC	Varsity
2023-06-03	Barrie, ON	Simcoe County Rovers FC	W	2-1	L	Electric City FC	J. C. Massie
2023-06-03	Toronto, ON	North Toronto Nitros	D	1-1	D	Woodbridge SC Strikers	Downsview
2023-06-04	Waterloo, ON	BVB IA Waterloo	L	0-1	W	Burlington SC	RIM
2023-06-04	Windsor, ON	Windsor City FC	D	1-1	D	ProStars FC	St. Clair
2023-06-04	Vaughan, ON	Vaughan SC Azzurri	W	3-1	L	Unionville Milliken SC	North Maple
2023-06-09	Whitby, ON	Darby FC	W	2-1	L	Master's FA	Whitby Soccer
2023-06-10	Peterborough, ON	Electric City FC	D	0-0	D	Hamilton United	Fleming
2023-06-10	Mississauga, ON	Sigma FC	D	2-2	D	North Mississauga SC	Paramount
2023-06-10	Toronto, ON	North Toronto Nitros	W	3-1	L	Unionville Milliken SC	Downsview
2023-06-10	London, ON	FC London	L	1-2	W	Vaughan SC Azzurri	Tricar
2023-06-10	Brampton, ON	ProStars FC	D	1-1	D	Woodbridge SC Strikers	Victoria
2023-06-11	Waterloo, ON	BVB IA Waterloo	L	0-6	W	Oakville Blue Devils FC	RIM
2023-06-11	Burlington, ON	Burlington SC	L	3-5	W	Scrosoppi FC	Corpus Christi
2023-06-11	Windsor, ON	Windsor City FC	W	2-1	L	Simcoe County Rovers FC	St. Clair
2023-06-11	Guelph, ON	Guelph United FC	W	2-1	L	St. Catharines Roma	Centennial
2023-06-13	Vaughan, ON	Vaughan SC Azzurri	W	5-4	L	Alliance United FC	North Maple
2023-06-14	Barrie, ON	Simcoe County Rovers FC	W	4-3	L	Burlington SC	J. C. Massie
2023-06-14	Mississauga, ON	Sigma FC	W	2-0	L	Guelph United FC	Paramount
2023-06-14	St. Catharines, ON	St. Catharines Roma	W	3-2	L	Hamilton United	Club Roma
2023-06-14	Toronto, ON	North Toronto Nitros	W	3-2	L	ProStars FC	Downsview
2023-06-16	St. Catharines, ON	St. Catharines Roma	D	2-2	D	Darby FC	Club Roma
2023-06-17	Vaughan, ON	Scrosoppi FC	W	4-0	L	FC London	Ontario Soccer

2023 CANADA

SEASON	CITY	HOME TEAM		SCORE		AWAY TEAM	VENUE
2023-06-17	Toronto, ON	Master's FA	L	0-1	W	Sigma FC	L'Amoreaux
2023-06-17	Barrie, ON	Simcoe County Rovers FC	W	9-1	L	Unionville Milliken SC	J. C. Massie
2023-06-18	Toronto, ON	Alliance United	D	2-2	D	Electric City FC	Varsity
2023-06-18	Waterloo, ON	BVB IA Waterloo	L	0-8	W	North Toronto Nitros	RIM
2023-06-18	Oakville, ON	Oakville Blue Devils	W	3-2	L	ProStars FC	Sheridan
2023-06-18	Guelph, ON	Guelph United FC	W	1-0	L	Vaughan SC Azzurri	Centennial
2023-06-18	Hamilton, ON	Hamilton United	L	1-2	W	Windsor City FC	McMaster
2023-06-18	Burlington, ON	Burlington SC	D	1-1	D	Woodbridge SC Strikers	Corpus Christi
2023-06-21	Vaughan, ON	Master's FA	W	1-0	L	North Mississauga SC	Ontario Soccer
2023-06-23	Whitby, ON	Darby FC	L	0-1	W	Guelph United FC	Whitby Soccer
2023-06-24	Vaughan, ON	Unionville Milliken SC	L	0-1	W	Oakville Blue Devils FC	Ontario Soccer
2023-06-24	Toronto, ON	North Toronto Nitros	L	2-3	W	Burlington SC	Downsview
2023-06-24	London, ON	FC London	D	2-2	D	Electric City FC	Tricar
2023-06-24	Toronto, ON	Alliance United	W	1-0	L	North Mississauga SC	Varsity
2023-06-24	Brampton, ON	ProStars FC	D	1-1	D	St. Catharines Roma	Victoria
2023-06-24	Vaughan, ON	Scrosoppi FC	W	3-0	L	Windsor City FC	Ontario Soccer
2023-06-25	Vaughan, ON	Vaughan SC Azzurri	W	8-0	L	BVB IA Waterloo	North Maple
2023-06-25	Hamilton, ON	Hamilton United	W	1-0	L	Master's FA	McMaster
2023-06-25	Vaughan, ON	Woodbridge SC Strikers	W	2-1	L	Sigma FC	Vaughan Grove
2023-06-27	Peterborough, ON	Electric City FC	W	1-0	L	Darby FC	Fleming
2023-06-27	Guelph, ON	Guelph United FC	W	3-2	L	Windsor City FC	Centennial
2023-06-30	Mississauga, ON	North Mississauga SC	L	0-1	W	Oakville Blue Devils FC	Mattamy
2023-06-30	Burlington, ON	Burlington SC	W	3-0	L	Sigma FC	Corpus Christi
2023-07-01	Vaughan, ON	Scrosoppi FC	W	1-0	L	Guelph United FC	Ontario Soccer
2023-07-02	Hamilton, ON	Hamilton United	W	8-1	L	BVB IA Waterloo	McMaster
2023-07-02	London, ON	FC London	D	1-1	D	Darby FC	Tricar
2023-07-02	Vaughan, ON	Woodbridge SC Strikers	L	1-4	W	Electric City FC	Vaughan Grove
2023-07-02	Toronto, ON	Master's FA	L	1-3	W	North Toronto Nitros	L'Amoreaux
2023-07-02	Toronto, ON	Alliance United	W	5-0	L	ProStars FC	Varsity
2023-07-02	Barrie, ON	Simcoe County Rovers FC	W	2-0	L	St. Catharines Roma	J. C. Massie
2023-07-02	Vaughan, ON	Vaughan SC Azzurri	W	3-1	L	Windsor City FC	North Maple
2023-07-05	London, ON	FC London	W	3-0	L	BVB IA Waterloo	Tricar
2023-07-05	Oakville, ON	Oakville Blue Devils	L	0-2	W	Woodbridge SC Strikers	Sheridan
2023-07-07	Mississauga, ON	North Mississauga SC	D	2-2	D	Darby FC	Mattamy
2023-07-08	Toronto, ON	North Toronto Nitros	L	1-2	W	Oakville Blue Devils FC	Downsview
2023-07-08	Mississauga, ON	ProStars FC	L	1-5	W	Electric City FC	Paramount
2023-07-08	Toronto, ON	Master's FA	L	0-6	W	Guelph United FC	L'Amoreaux
2023-07-08	Vaughan, ON	Unionville Milliken SC	L	0-4	W	Scrosoppi FC	Ontario Soccer
2023-07-09	Toronto, ON	Sigma FC	L	0-3	W	Alliance United FC	York
2023-07-09	Windsor, ON	Windsor City FC	W	6-2	L	BVB IA Waterloo	St. Clair
2023-07-09	Burlington, ON	Burlington SC	L	2-3	W	FC London	Corpus Christi
2023-07-09	Vaughan, ON	Woodbridge SC Strikers	L	2-3	W	St. Catharines Roma	Vaughan Grove
2023-07-09	Barrie, ON	Simcoe County Rovers FC	W	3-2	L	Vaughan SC Azzurri	J. C. Massie
2023-07-13	Vaughan, ON	Alliance United	D	2-2	D	Burlington SC	Ontario Soccer
2023-07-14	Whitby, ON	Darby FC	D	2-2	D	ProStars FC	Whitby Soccer
2023-07-14	St. Catharines, ON	St. Catharines Roma	L	1-2	W	Vaughan SC Azzurri	Club Roma
2023-07-15	Vaughan, ON	Unionville Milliken SC	W	3-0	L	BVB IA Waterloo	Ontario Soccer
2023-07-15	Toronto, ON	Master's FA	D	0-0	D	FC London	L'Amoreaux
2023-07-15	Peterborough, ON	Electric City FC	W	3-0	L	North Mississauga SC	Fleming
2023-07-15	Vaughan, ON	Scrosoppi FC	W	3-2	L	Simcoe County Rovers FC	Ontario Soccer
2023-07-16	Vaughan, ON	Woodbridge SC Strikers	W	2-0	L	Alliance United FC	Vaughan Grove
2023-07-16	Burlington, ON	Burlington SC	D	1-1	D	Guelph United FC	Corpus Christi
2023-07-16	Oakville, ON	Oakville Blue Devils	L	1-3	W	Hamilton United	Sheridan
2023-07-16	Windsor, ON	Windsor City FC	L	2-3	W	North Toronto Nitros	St. Clair
2023-07-21	St. Catharines, ON	St. Catharines Roma	W	2-1	L	Oakville Blue Devils FC	Club Roma
2023-07-21	Whitby, ON	Darby FC	W	5-0	L	Unionville Milliken SC	Whitby Soccer
2023-07-22	Toronto, ON	North Toronto Nitros	D	2-2	D	Alliance United FC	Downsview
2023-07-22	Hamilton, ON	Hamilton United	W	2-0	L	ProStars FC	McMaster
2023-07-22	Peterborough, ON	Electric City FC	D	0-0	D	Vaughan SC Azzurri	Fleming

SEASON	CITY	HOME TEAM	SCORE	AWAY TEAM	VENUE
2023-07-22	London, ON	FC London W	3-2 L	Woodbridge SC Strikers	Tricar
2023-07-23	Barrie, ON	Simcoe County Rovers FC W	1-0 L	Guelph United FC	J. C. Massie
2023-07-23	Windsor, ON	Windsor City FC W	4-2 L	Master's FA	St. Clair
2023-07-23	Waterloo, ON	BVB IA Waterloo L	0-4 W	North Mississauga SC	RIM
2023-07-23	Vaughan, ON	Scrosoppi FC W	3-2 L	Sigma FC	Ontario Soccer
2023-07-26	Vaughan, ON	Vaughan SC Azzurri W	5-2 L	Sigma FC	North Maple
2023-07-28	St. Catharines, ON	St. Catharines Roma L	0-6 W	Burlington SC	Club Roma
2023-07-28	Mississauga, ON	North Mississauga SC L	1-5 W	Simcoe County Rovers FC	Mattamy
2023-07-29	Vaughan, ON	Unionville Milliken SC L	1-13 W	Alliance United FC	Ontario Soccer
2023-07-29	Mississauga, ON	Sigma FC W	6-1 L	BVB IA Waterloo	Paramount
2023-07-29	Brampton, ON	ProStars FC L	1-2 W	FC London	Victoria
2023-07-29	Toronto, ON	North Toronto Nitros L	1-2 W	Scrosoppi FC	Downsview
2023-07-29	Whitby, ON	Darby FC W	2-0 L	Windsor City FC	Whitby Soccer
2023-07-30	Oakville, ON	Oakville Blue Devils W	3-2 L	Electric City FC	Sheridan
2023-07-30	Vaughan, ON	Vaughan SC Azzurri W	4-0 L	Master's FA	North Maple
2023-08-01	Guelph, ON	Guelph United FC D	2-2 D	Hamilton United	Centennial
2023-08-02	Vaughan, ON	Scrosoppi FC L	0-2 W	Oakville Blue Devils FC	Ontario Soccer
2023-08-05	Mississauga, ON	Sigma FC D	2-2 D	Darby FC	Paramount
2023-08-05	Scarborough, ON	Alliance United D	2-2 D	FC London	Birchmount
2023-08-05	Peterborough, ON	Electric City FC L	0-3 W	Guelph United FC	Fleming
2023-08-05	Vaughan, ON	Unionville Milliken SC L	2-3 W	Master's FA	Ontario Soccer
2023-08-05	Brampton, ON	ProStars FC L	0-4 W	Vaughan SC Azzurri	Victoria
2023-08-06	Burlington, ON	Burlington SC W	3-1 L	Hamilton United	Corpus Christi
2023-08-06	Oakville, ON	Oakville Blue Devils L	2-4 W	Simcoe County Rovers FC	Sheridan
2023-08-06	Vaughan, ON	Woodbridge SC Strikers D	1-1 D	Windsor City FC	Vaughan Grove
2023-08-09	Vaughan, ON	Vaughan SC Azzurri W	1-0 L	North Mississauga SC	North Maple
2023-08-09	Waterloo, ON	BVB IA Waterloo L	0-5 W	Scrosoppi FC	RIM
2023-08-09	Vaughan, ON	Master's FA W	3-1 L	St. Catharines Roma	Ontario Soccer
2023-08-09	London, ON	FC London W	3-2 L	Windsor City FC	Tricar
2023-08-11	Hamilton, ON	Hamilton United W	2-0 L	Alliance United FC	McMaster
2023-08-11	Whitby, ON	Darby FC L	1-2 W	Simcoe County Rovers FC	Whitby Soccer
2023-08-12	Hamilton, ON	Sigma FC W	5-1 L	FC London	Tim Hortons
2023-08-12	Brampton, ON	ProStars FC L	1-7 W	North Mississauga SC	Victoria
2023-08-12	Toronto, ON	North Toronto Nitros L	1-2 W	St. Catharines Roma	Downsview
2023-08-12	Peterborough, ON	Electric City FC W	11-0 L	Unionville Milliken SC	Fleming
2023-08-13	Waterloo, ON	BVB IA Waterloo L	1-4 W	Master's FA	RIM
2023-08-13	Oakville, ON	Oakville Blue Devils L	1-3 W	Vaughan SC Azzurri	Sheridan
2023-08-13	Burlington, ON	Burlington SC W	2-0 L	Windsor City FC	Corpus Christi
2023-08-13	Guelph, ON	Guelph United FC D	2-2 D	Woodbridge SC Strikers	Centennial
2023-08-15	St. Catharines, ON	St. Catharines Roma L	0-1 W	North Mississauga SC	Kiwanis
2023-08-16	Vaughan, ON	Scrosoppi FC W	5-0 L	Hamilton United	Ontario Soccer
2023-08-16	Toronto, ON	North Toronto Nitros L	1-2 W	Simcoe County Rovers FC	Downsview
2023-08-18	St. Catharines, ON	St. Catharines Roma W	3-2 L	Unionville Milliken SC	Club Roma
2023-08-19	Windsor, ON	Windsor City FC L	0-4 W	Electric City FC	St. Clair
2023-08-19	London, ON	FC London D	3-3 D	North Mississauga SC	Tricar
2023-08-19	Mississauga, ON	Sigma FC D	2-2 D	North Toronto Nitros	Paramount
2023-08-19	Toronto, ON	Master's FA L	1-2 W	Scrosoppi FC	L'Amoreaux
2023-08-19	Scarborough, ON	Alliance United L	0-1 W	Simcoe County Rovers FC	Birchmount
2023-08-20	Vaughan, ON	Vaughan SC Azzurri L	1-2 W	Burlington SC	North Maple
2023-08-20	Waterloo, ON	BVB IA Waterloo L	0-6 W	Darby FC	RIM
2023-08-20	Vaughan, ON	Woodbridge SC Strikers D	1-1 D	Hamilton United	Vaughan Grove
2023-08-20	Guelph, ON	Guelph United FC W	3-2 L	ProStars FC	Centennial

2023 LEAGUE1 ONTARIO PLAYOFF WINNERS : SIMCOE COUNTY ROVERS FC

PLAYOFF FIRST ROUND		HOME TEAM	SCORE	AWAY TEAM	VENUE
2023-08-23	Oakville, ON	Oakville Blue Devils W	4-1 L	Burlington SC	Pine Glen
2023-08-23	Vaughan, ON	Vaughan SC Azzurri W	2-0 L	Guelph United	North Maple

PLAYOFF SEMIFINALS		HOME TEAM	SCORE	AWAY TEAM	VENUE
2023-08-26	Vaughan, ON	Scrosoppi FC	W 2-1 L	Oakville Blue Devils FC	Ontario Soccer
2023-08-27	Barrie, ON	Simcoe County Rovers FC	W 3-0 L	Vaughan SC Azzurri	J. C. Massie
CHAMPIONSHIP FINAL		**HOME TEAM**	**SCORE**	**AWAY TEAM**	**VENUE**
2023-09-02	Vaughan, ON	Scrosoppi FC	L 2-4 W	Simcoe County Rovers FC	Ontario Soccer

2023 LEAGUE1 QUÉBEC

LEAGUE1 QUÉBEC	MP	W	D	L	PTS	MATCH-BY-MATCH RESULTS
1. CS Saint-Laurent	22	18	1	3	55	W W W W W W W L W W W W D W W W L W W W W L
The 2023 League1 Québec winners CS St-Laurent qualified for the 2024 Canadian Championship						
2. Royal-Sélect de Beauport	22	13	6	3	45	W W W W W D W L D L D D W W W L W D D W W
3. CS Mont, Royal Outremont	22	12	5	5	41	W W W L W D L W W L W D W D L W W L W W D D
4. FC Laval	22	12	4	6	40	W D W W L L L W W D W W L D W L W W W W L D
5. CF Montréal U-23	22	12	4	6	40	W W L L L D W W W D W W W D L L W W W D W L
6. CS St-Hubert	22	8	6	8	30	L D L D W W D L W W W L W L W D W L L L D D
7. AS Blainville	22	9	3	10	30	L L W D L D W W L W D W W W L W L L L L W
8. CS Longueuil	22	7	5	10	26	L W W W L D L W L L L D L D D L L W W W L D
9. AS Laval	22	7	3	12	24	L L L W W L W L L W D L D L L D W L L W
10. Celtix du Haut-Richelieu	22	5	5	12	20	L L L L W W L L L D D L D L L L W D L W D
11. Ottawa South United	22	5	4	13	19	W L L L L L L L L L W L D D W D W L L L W D
12. CS Lanaudière-Nord	22	0	2	20	2	L L L L L L L L L L L L L L L D D L L L L L

2023 LEAGUE1 QUÉBEC WINNERS : CS SAINT-LAURENT

SEASON	CITY	HOME TEAM	SCORE	AWAY TEAM	VENUE
2023-05-06	Joliette, QC	CS Lanaudière-Nord	L 1-2 W	Ottawa South United	Barthélemy
2023-05-06	Laval, QC	AS Laval	L 0-2 W	FC Laval	Lausanne
2023-05-06	Longueuil, QC	CS Longueuil	L 1-5 W	CS Saint-Laurent	Laurier
2023-05-07	Québec, QC	Royal-Sélect de Beauport	W 2-1 L	AS Blainville	Beauport
2023-05-07	St-Hubert, QC	CS St-Hubert	L 0-1 W	CF Montréal U-23	Rosanne-Laflamme
2023-05-07	Mont-Royal, QC	CS Mont-Royal Outremont	W 2-1 L	Celtix du Haut-Richelieu	TMR
2023-05-13	Montréal, QC	CF Montréal U-23	W 4-0 L	Celtix du Haut-Richelieu	Nutrilait
2023-05-13	Ottawa, ON	Ottawa South United	L 0-1 W	Royal-Sélect de Beauport	Carleton
2023-05-13	Joliette, QC	CS Lanaudière-Nord	L 0-2 W	CS Mont-Royal Outremont	Barthélemy
2023-05-13	Saint-Laurent, QC	CS Saint-Laurent	W 4-0 L	AS Laval	Vanier
2023-05-13	Blainville, QC	AS Blainville	L 0-1 W	CS Longueuil	Blainville
2023-05-14	Laval, QC	FC Laval	D 1-1 D	CS St-Hubert	Montmorency
2023-05-19	St-Hubert, QC	CS St-Hubert	L 0-3 W	CS Saint-Laurent	Rosanne-Laflamme
2023-05-20	St-Jean-sur-Richelieu	Celtix du Haut-Richelieu	L 1-2 W	FC Laval	Pierre-Benoît
2023-05-20	Laval, QC	AS Laval	L 0-3 W	AS Blainville	Lausanne
2023-05-20	Longueuil, QC	CS Longueuil	W 4-0 L	Ottawa South United	Laurier
2023-05-21	Québec, QC	Royal-Sélect de Beauport	W 2-0 L	CS Lanaudière-Nord	Beauport
2023-05-21	Mont-Royal, QC	CS Mont-Royal Outremont	W 2-0 L	CF Montréal U-23	TMR
2023-05-27	Joliette, QC	CS Lanaudière-Nord	L 1-3 W	CS Longueuil	Barthélemy
2023-05-27	Saint-Laurent, QC	CS Saint-Laurent	W 4-0 L	Celtix du Haut-Richelieu	Vanier
2023-05-27	Laval, QC	AS Laval	W 3-1 L	Ottawa South United	Lausanne
2023-05-27	Blainville, QC	AS Blainville	D 0-0 D	CS St-Hubert	Blainville
2023-05-28	Québec, QC	Royal-Sélect de Beauport	W 1-0 L	CS Mont-Royal Outremont	Beauport
2023-05-28	Laval, QC	FC Laval	W 3-0 L	CF Montréal U-23	Montmorency
2023-06-03	Montréal, QC	CF Montréal U-23	L 0-2 W	CS Saint-Laurent	Nutrilait
2023-06-03	Laval, QC	AS Laval	W 3-0 L	CS Lanaudière-Nord	Lausanne
2023-06-03	St-Jean-sur-Richelieu	Celtix du Haut-Richelieu	W 2-1 L	AS Blainville	Pierre-Benoît
2023-06-03	Longueuil, QC	CS Longueuil	L 0-1 W	Royal-Sélect de Beauport	Laurier
2023-06-04	St-Hubert, QC	CS St-Hubert	W 2-1 L	Ottawa South United	Rosanne-Laflamme
2023-06-04	Mont-Royal, QC	CS Mont-Royal Outremont	W 1-0 L	FC Laval	TMR
2023-06-10	Ottawa, ON	Ottawa South United	L 1-4 W	Celtix du Haut-Richelieu	Carleton
2023-06-10	Joliette, QC	CS Lanaudière-Nord	L 2-3 W	CS St-Hubert	Barthélemy

SEASON	CITY	HOME TEAM	SCORE		AWAY TEAM	VENUE
2023-06-10	Saint-Laurent, QC	CS Saint-Laurent	W 6-1	L	FC Laval	Vanier
2023-06-10	Longueuil, QC	CS Longueuil	D 0-0	D	CS Mont-Royal Outremont	Laurier
2023-06-10	Blainville, QC	AS Blainville	D 1-1	D	CF Montréal U-23	Blainville
2023-06-11	Québec, QC	Royal-Sélect de Beauport	W 2-1	L	AS Laval	Beauport
2023-06-17	Montréal, QC	CF Montréal U-23	W 1-0	L	Ottawa South United	Nutrilait
2023-06-17	St-Jean-sur-Richelieu	Celtix du Haut-Richelieu	W 3-1	L	CS Lanaudière-Nord	Pierre-Benoît
2023-06-17	Laval, QC	AS Laval	W 3-1	L	CS Longueuil	Lausanne
2023-06-18	St-Hubert, QC	CS St-Hubert	D 0-0	D	Royal-Sélect de Beauport	Rosanne-Laflamme
2023-06-18	Laval, QC	FC Laval	L 0-2	W	AS Blainville	Montmorency
2023-06-18	Mont-Royal, QC	CS Mont-Royal Outremont	L 0-2	W	CS Saint-Laurent	TMR
2023-06-24	Ottawa, ON	Ottawa South United	L 3-4	W	FC Laval	Carleton
2023-06-24	Laval, QC	AS Laval	L 1-2	W	CS Mont-Royal Outremont	Lausanne
2023-06-24	Longueuil, QC	CS Longueuil	W 3-1	L	CS St-Hubert	Laurier
2023-06-24	Blainville, QC	AS Blainville	W 1-0	L	CS Saint-Laurent	Blainville
2023-06-25	Québec, QC	Royal-Sélect de Beauport	W 4-1	L	Celtix du Haut-Richelieu	Beauport
2023-06-30	St-Hubert, QC	CS St-Hubert	W 2-1	L	AS Laval	Rosanne-Laflamme
2023-07-02	Montréal, QC	CF Montréal U-23	W 1-0	L	Royal-Sélect de Beauport	Nutrilait
2023-07-02	Laval, QC	FC Laval	W 5-1	L	CS Lanaudière-Nord	Montmorency
2023-07-02	Mont-Royal, QC	CS Mont-Royal Outremont	W 3-0	L	AS Blainville	TMR
2023-07-08	Ottawa, ON	Ottawa South United	L 1-3	W	AS Blainville	Carleton
2023-07-08	Joliette, QC	CS Lanaudière-Nord	L 1-5	W	CS Saint-Laurent	Barthélemy
2023-07-08	Laval, QC	AS Laval	W 2-1	L	Celtix du Haut-Richelieu	Lausanne
2023-07-08	Longueuil, QC	CS Longueuil	L 0-2	W	CF Montréal U-23	Laurier
2023-07-09	Québec, QC	Royal-Sélect de Beauport	D 0-0	D	FC Laval	Beauport
2023-07-09	St-Hubert, QC	CS St-Hubert	W 3-1	L	CS Mont-Royal Outremont	Rosanne-Laflamme
2023-07-15	St-Jean-sur-Richelieu	Celtix du Haut-Richelieu	L 2-6	W	CS St-Hubert	Pierre-Benoît
2023-07-15	Saint-Laurent, QC	CS Saint-Laurent	W 5-1	L	Royal-Sélect de Beauport	Vanier
2023-07-16	Montréal, QC	CF Montréal U-23	D 1-1	D	AS Laval	Nutrilait
2023-07-16	Laval, QC	FC Laval	W 4-3	L	CS Longueuil	Roseval
2023-07-16	Mont-Royal, QC	CS Mont-Royal Outremont	W 3-0	L	Ottawa South United	TMR
2023-07-19	Joliette, QC	CS Lanaudière-Nord	L 0-2	W	CF Montréal U-23	Barthélemy
2023-07-22	Blainville, QC	AS Blainville	D 1-1	D	Royal-Sélect de Beauport	Blainville
2023-07-22	Ottawa, ON	Ottawa South United	W 3-1	L	CS Lanaudière-Nord	Carleton
2023-07-22	St-Jean-sur-Richelieu	Celtix du Haut-Richelieu	D 1-1	D	CS Mont-Royal Outremont	Pierre-Benoît
2023-07-22	Saint-Laurent, QC	CS Saint-Laurent	W 1-0	L	CS Longueuil	Vanier
2023-07-23	Montréal, QC	CF Montréal U-23	W 2-1	L	CS St-Hubert	Nutrilait
2023-07-23	Laval, QC	FC Laval	W 3-0	L	AS Laval	Roseval
2023-07-26	Saint-Laurent, QC	CS Saint-Laurent	W 3-0	L	Ottawa South United	Vanier
2023-07-26	St-Jean-sur-Richelieu	Celtix du Haut-Richelieu	D 1-1	D	CS Longueuil	Pierre-Benoît
2023-07-28	St-Hubert, QC	CS St-Hubert	W 3-2	L	FC Laval	Rosanne-Laflamme
2023-07-29	St-Jean-sur-Richelieu	Celtix du Haut-Richelieu	L 1-2	W	CF Montréal U-23	Pierre-Benoît
2023-07-29	Laval, QC	AS Laval	D 3-3	D	CS Saint-Laurent	Lausanne
2023-07-29	Longueuil, QC	CS Longueuil	L 0-2	W	AS Blainville	Laurier
2023-07-30	Québec, QC	Royal-Sélect de Beauport	D 3-3	D	Ottawa South United	Beauport
2023-07-30	Mont-Royal, QC	CS Mont-Royal Outremont	W 3-0	L	CS Lanaudière-Nord	TMR
2023-08-02	Blainville, QC	AS Blainville	W 5-3	L	CS Lanaudière-Nord	Blainville
2023-08-03	Montréal, QC	CF Montréal U-23	D 0-0	D	CS Mont-Royal Outremont	Nutrilait
2023-08-05	Joliette, QC	CS Lanaudière-Nord	L 1-5	W	Royal-Sélect de Beauport	Barthélemy
2023-08-05	Ottawa, ON	Ottawa South United	D 1-1	D	CS Longueuil	Carleton
2023-08-05	Blainville, QC	AS Blainville	W 1-0	L	AS Laval	Blainville
2023-08-05	Saint-Laurent, QC	CS Saint-Laurent	W 2-1	L	CS St-Hubert	Vanier
2023-08-06	Laval, QC	FC Laval	D 3-3	D	Celtix du Haut-Richelieu	Roseval
2023-08-11	St-Hubert, QC	CS St-Hubert	W 2-1	L	AS Blainville	Rosanne-Laflamme
2023-08-12	Montréal, QC	CF Montréal U-23	L 0-2	W	FC Laval	Nutrilait
2023-08-12	Ottawa, ON	Ottawa South United	W 2-1	L	AS Laval	Carleton
2023-08-12	St-Jean-sur-Richelieu	Celtix du Haut-Richelieu	L 1-3	W	CS Saint-Laurent	Pierre-Benoît
2023-08-12	Longueuil, QC	CS Longueuil	D 1-1	D	CS Lanaudière-Nord	Laurier
2023-08-13	Mont-Royal, QC	CS Mont-Royal Outremont	L 3-4	W	Royal-Sélect de Beauport	TMR
2023-08-19	Joliette, QC	CS Lanaudière-Nord	D 0-0	D	AS Laval	Barthélemy

2023 CANADA

SEASON	CITY	HOME TEAM	SCORE	AWAY TEAM	VENUE
2023-08-19	Ottawa, ON	Ottawa South United	D 0-0 D	CS St-Hubert	Carleton
2023-08-19	Blainville, QC	AS Blainville	W 3-1 L	Celtix du Haut-Richelieu	Blainville
2023-08-20	Québec, QC	Royal-Sélect de Beauport	W 2-0 L	CS Longueuil	Beauport
2023-08-20	Saint-Laurent, QC	CS Saint-Laurent	W 2-0 L	CF Montréal U-23	Vanier
2023-08-20	Laval, QC	FC Laval	L 0-4 W	CS Mont-Royal Outremont	Montmorency
2023-08-26	Laval, QC	FC Laval	W 2-0 L	CS Saint-Laurent	Raymond-Millar
2023-08-26	St-Jean-sur-Richelieu	Celtix du Haut-Richelieu	L 0-1 W	Ottawa South United	Pierre-Benoît
2023-08-26	Laval, QC	AS Laval	W 4-1 L	Royal-Sélect de Beauport	Lausanne
2023-08-27	Montréal, QC	CF Montréal U-23	W 3-2 L	AS Blainville	Nutrilait
2023-08-27	St-Hubert, QC	CS St-Hubert	W 3-0 L	CS Lanaudière-Nord	Rosanne-Laflamme
2023-08-27	Mont-Royal, QC	CS Mont-Royal Outremont	W 2-0 L	CS Longueuil	TMR
2023-09-02	Joliette, QC	CS Lanaudière-Nord	L 3-5 W	Celtix du Haut-Richelieu	Barthélemy
2023-09-02	Ottawa, ON	Ottawa South United	L 1-2 W	CF Montréal U-23	Carleton
2023-09-02	Longueuil, QC	CS Longueuil	W 2-1 L	AS Laval	Laurier
2023-09-02	Blainville, QC	AS Blainville	L 0-4 W	FC Laval	Blainville
2023-09-03	Québec, QC	Royal-Sélect de Beauport	W 3-1 L	CS St-Hubert	Beauport
2023-09-03	Montréal, QC	CS Saint-Laurent	W 2-0 L	CS Mont-Royal Outremont	Marie-Victorin
2023-09-09	Montréal, QC	CF Montréal U-23	W 2-0 L	CS Lanaudière-Nord	Nutrilait
2023-09-09	St-Jean-sur-Richelieu	Celtix du Haut-Richelieu	D 2-2 D	Royal-Sélect de Beauport	Pierre-Benoît
2023-09-09	Laval, QC	FC Laval	W 3-1 L	Ottawa South United	Raymond-Millar
2023-09-10	St-Hubert, QC	CS St-Hubert	L 1-4 W	CS Longueuil	Rosanne-Laflamme
2023-09-10	Montréal, QC	CS Saint-Laurent	W 4-3 L	AS Blainville	Marie-Victorin
2023-09-10	Mont-Royal, QC	CS Mont-Royal Outremont	W 1-0 L	AS Laval	TMR
2023-09-16	Québec, QC	Royal-Sélect de Beauport	D 2-2 D	CF Montréal U-23	Beauport
2023-09-16	Joliette, QC	CS Lanaudière-Nord	L 0-3 W	FC Laval	Barthélemy
2023-09-16	Longueuil, QC	CS Longueuil	W 3-0 L	Celtix du Haut-Richelieu	Parc-Laurier
2023-09-16	Laval, QC	AS Laval	W 3-1 L	CS St-Hubert	Lausanne
2023-09-16	Ottawa, ON	Ottawa South United	L 0-6 W	CS Saint-Laurent	Carleton
2023-09-16	Blainville, QC	AS Blainville	L 1-3 W	CS Mont-Royal Outremont	Blainville
2023-09-23	Montréal, QC	CF Montréal U-23	W 3-2 L	CS Longueuil	Nutrilait
2023-09-23	Laval, QC	FC Laval	L 0-4 W	Royal-Sélect de Beauport	Raymond-Millar
2023-09-23	St-Jean-sur-Richelieu	Celtix du Haut-Richelieu	W 3-2 L	AS Laval	Pierre-Benoît
2023-09-23	Blainville, QC	AS Blainville	L 1-3 W	Ottawa South United	Blainville
2023-09-23	Saint-Laurent, QC	CS Saint-Laurent	W 5-1 L	CS Lanaudière-Nord	Saint-Laurent
2023-09-24	Mont-Royal, QC	CS Mont-Royal Outremont	D 1-1 D	CS St-Hubert	TMR
2023-09-30	Québec, QC	Royal-Sélect de Beauport	W 4-1 L	CS Saint-Laurent	Beauport
2023-09-30	Laval, QC	AS Laval	W ? L	CF Montréal U-23	Lausanne
2023-09-30	Ottawa, ON	Ottawa South United	D 1-1 D	CS Mont-Royal Outremont	Carleton
2023-09-30	Joliette, QC	CS Lanaudière-Nord	L 1-4 W	AS Blainville	Barthélemy
2023-09-30	Longueuil, QC	CS Longueuil	D 1-1 D	FC Laval	Laurier
2023-09-30	St-Hubert, QC	CS St-Hubert	D 2-2 D	Celtix du Haut-Richelieu	Rosanne-Laflamme

2023 LEAGUE1 QUÉBEC CUP WINNERS : CS SAINT-LAURENT

CUP FIRST ROUND		HOME TEAM	SCORE	AWAY TEAM	VENUE
2023-10-07	Joliette, QC	CS Lanaudière-Nord	W 4-2 L	Ottawa South United	Barthélemy
2023-10-07	Longueuil, QC	CS Longueuil	L 0-6 W	CS Saint-Laurent	Laurier
2023-10-08	St-Hubert, QC	CS St-Hubert	L 0-2 W	AS Laval	Rosanne-Laflamme
2023-10-08	Mont-Royal, QC	CS Mont-Royal Outremont	W 3-0 L	CF Montréal U-23	TMR
QUARTERFINALS		**HOME TEAM**	**SCORE**	**AWAY TEAM**	**VENUE**
2023-10-14	St-Jean-sur-Richelieu	Celtix du Haut-Richelieu	L 0-2 W	CS Mont-Royal Outremont	Pierre-Benoît
2023-10-14	Laval, QC	FC Laval	D 2-2 D	CS Lanaudière-Nord	Raymond-Millar
2023-10-14	Québec, QC	Royal-Sélect de Beauport	W 5-0 L	AS Laval	Beauport
2023-10-14	Blainville, QC	AS Blainville	L 1-4 W	CS Saint-Laurent	Blainville
SEMIFINALS		**HOME TEAM**	**SCORE**	**AWAY TEAM**	**VENUE**
2023-10-21	Joliette, QC	CS Lanaudière-Nord	L 0-3 W	CS Mont-Royal Outremont	Barthélemy
2023-10-21	Montréal, QC	CS Saint-Laurent	W 4-1 L	Royal-Sélect de Beauport	Vanier
CUP FINAL (FINALE DU COUPE)		**HOME TEAM**	**SCORE**	**AWAY TEAM**	**VENUE**
2023-10-28	Laval, QC	CS Saint-Laurent	W 2-0 L	CS Mont-Royal Outremont	Desjardins

CANADIAN SOCCER'S WHO'S WHO GUIDE TO FOOTBALLERS

Welcome to the 2024 edition of *Canadian Soccer's Who's Who Guide to Footballers*. For the second year in a row, we have compiled a comprehensive list of more than 500 active Canadian men's footballers from across the globe. The guide features an alphabetical list of the most notable professional players, including those that have featured with Canadian clubs in the Canadian Premier League, Major League Soccer and MLS NEXT Pro these past five years.

For each footballer, we have included player vitals, youth clubs, club honours, international "A" highlights, and year-by-year club highlights (including matches played, minutes played and goals scored per competition). The career timelines cover more than 200 different leagues and cup competitions from more than 50 different countries from around the world.

Only Canadian footballers are listed in this section, which means at the time of printing they were eligible to represent Canada at the international level. The list includes Canadians that have played professional football in Canada or been called into National Team (or featured on a Concacaf long list) these past few years. Young prospects from Canada Soccer's youth teams have also been included in the 2024 guide.

From the group of 500 men's footballers, more than 100 of them have represented Canada at the international "A" level, including all 26 who went to the FIFA World Cup in December 2022.

While we have included a big group of players, by no means have we included every pro Canadian player in this publication. We hope to feature a new group of players each season, so we appreciate feedback on new players we should consider or corrections/additions to club statistics or player vitals.

For an in-depth list of Canadian players, we encourage you to follow our friends at Canucks Abroad. For more in-depth player statistics, be sure to follow the teams, leagues and football federations, as well as terrific websites like Transfermarkt and Fbref which offer match-by-match records for many leagues and cup competitions.

To all Canadian players and fans, we wish you all the best for the 2024 season.

CANADIAN SOCCER FOOTBALL ANNUAL

STEPHEN EUSTÁQUIO NAMED THE BEST IN CANADA FOR 2023

Stephen Eustáquio was named Canada Soccer's Player of the Year for the first time in 2023. For his club Porto FC, he won both the Taça da Liga Portuguesa (League Cup) and Taça de Portugal while he also finished second in the 2022-23 league standings.

For country, he helped Canada reach the 2022-23 Concacaf Nations League Finals in June before they were beaten by USA in the confederation championship match.

From January to December 2023 with Porto FC, Eustáquio made 47 appearances and scored five goals across 3,252 minutes in all competitions. In January, he scored the match winner in the 2023 Taça da Liga when FC Porto won 2-0 over Sporting Lisbon. In June, he featured in the 2-0 win over SC Braga when FC Porto won the 2023 Taça de Portugal.

FC Porto finished second in the 2022-23 Primeira Liga just two points back of league winners Benfica. They also reached the Round of 16 in UEFA Champions League before they were knocked out by FC Inter Milan.

In 2023-24 UEFA Champions League, Eustáquio had a goal and an assist in the group phase as FC Porto booked their spot in the Round of 16 once again.

With Canada, Eustáquio had a goal and an assist in six matches during the calendar year. He scored in an away match against Jamaica in the 2023-24 Quarterfinals of Concacaf Nations League.

From 2019 to 2023, Eustáquio has made 34 career international appearances with Canada. He was runner up in voting for Player of the Year honours in 2022 when helped Canada qualify for the men's FIFA World Cup for the first time in 36 years. He also won the Primeira Liga, the Taça de Portugal and Supertaça de Portugal in 2022.

PLAYERS OF THE YEAR
Canadian Soccer's Men's Players of the Year since 1993

PLAYER OF THE YEAR
As voted by media & coaches

2023	Stephen Eustáquio
2022	Alphonso Davies
2021	Alphonso Davies
2020	Alphonso Davies
2019	Jonathan David
2018	Alphonso Davies
2017	Atiba Hutchinson
2016	Atiba Hutchinson
2015	Atiba Hutchinson
2014	Atiba Hutchinson
2013	Will Johnson
2012	Atiba Hutchinson
2011	Dwayne De Rosario
2010	Atiba Hutchinson
2009	Simeon Jackson
2008	Julian de Guzman
2007	Dwayne De Rosario
2006	Dwayne De Rosario
2005	Dwayne De Rosario
2004	Paul Stalteri
2003	Pat Onstad
2002	Jason deVos
2001	Paul Stalteri
2000	Craig Forrest
1999	Jim Brennan
1998	Tomasz Radzinski
1997	Mark Watson
1996	Paul Peschisolido
1995	Alex Bunbury
1994	Craig Forrest
1993	Alex Bunbury

YOUNG PLAYER of the YEAR
As selected by Canada Soccer

2023	Ismaël Koné
2022	Ismaël Koné
2021	Theo Corbeanu
2020	Tajon Buchanan
2019	Jayden Nelson
2018	Derek Cornelius

ABAICHE, YANIS — CF MONTRÉAL U-23
Winger. Born 2004, Montréal, QC, CAN. Youth clubs: CS Longueuil

SEASON	CLUB	NATION	HIGHLIGHTS (MP/MIN)
2022	CS Longueuil	CAN	5th PLSQ (1/19)
2023	CF Montréal U-23	CAN	5th Ligue1 Québec

ABATNEH, NOAH — YORK UNITED FC
Right back. Born 2004, Toronto, ON, CAN. Height 188 cm. Dominant right foot. Youth clubs: Ottawa St. Anthony Futuro Academy, AS Roma (Italy), Savio (Italy), SS Lazio (Italy)

SEASON	CLUB	NATION	HIGHLIGHTS (MP/MIN)
2022-23	FC Lamezia Terme	4.ITA	x- Serie D Girone I (4/89)
	ACD Campodarsego	4.ITA	C4th Serie D Girone C (4/216)
2023	York United FC	1.CAN	5th CPL (12/637); 5th Playoffs (0/0); QF CanChamp (0/0)

ABRAHAM, NATHANIEL — TORONTO FC ACADEMY
Goalkeeper. Born 2007, Toronto, ON, CAN. Height 185 cm. Dominant right foot. Youth clubs: Vaughan SC, Toronto FC Academy

SEASON	CLUB	NATION	HIGHLIGHTS (MP/MIN)
2023	Toronto FC II	CAN-3.US	23rd MLS NEXT Pro (0/0)

ABZI, DIYAEDDINE — ESP / CD LEGANÉS
Left back. Born 1998, Fes, MAR. Grew up Montréal, QC, CAN. Height 185 cm. Dominant left foot. Youth clubs: FS Salaberry
Honours: Futsal Canadian Championship (2017)

SEASON	CLUB	NATION	HIGHLIGHTS (MP/MIN/G)	G
2018	AS Blainville	CAN	1st PLSQ (20/1239/2g); 5th CanChamp (4/244/1g)	3
2019	York9 FC	1.CAN	3rd CPL (24/1815/1g); CanChamp (6/512)	1
2020	York9 FC	1.CAN	5th CPL (5/435)	0
2021	York United FC	1.CAN	4th CPL (25/2217/6g); SF Playoffs (1/90); QF CanChamp (2/180)	6
2022	York United FC	1.CAN	6th CPL (10/837); SF CanChamp (3/270/1g)	1
2022-23	Pau FC	2.FRA	13th Ligue 2 (29/1483/1g); R4 Coupe de France (3/170/1g)	2
2023-24	CD Leganés	2.ESP	Segunda División (current season)	

ACCETTOLA, LUCA — TORONTO FC II
Midfielder. Born 2004, Richmond Hill, ON, CAN. Grew up Vaughan, ON, CAN. Height 168 cm. Youth clubs: Vaughan SC, Toronto FC Academy

SEASON	CLUB	NATION	HIGHLIGHTS (MP/MIN)
2022	Toronto FC II	CAN-3.US	7th MLS NEXT Pro (6/160)
2023	Toronto FC II	CAN-3.US	23rd MLS NEXT Pro (1/11)

ADEKUGBE, ELIJAH — YORK UNITED FC
Midfielder. Born 1996, London, ENG. Grew up Calgary, AB, CAN. Height 174 cm. Dominant left foot. Youth clubs: Manchester City (England), Calgary Foothills SC, Vancouver Whitecaps FC Residency
School: Trinity Western University
Honours: USL PDL Championship (2018)

SEASON	CLUB	NATION	HIGHLIGHTS (MP/MIN/G)	G
2010	Alberta U-14	CAN	3rd Canada Soccer All Stars U-14	
2011	Alberta U-15	CAN	3rd Canada Soccer All Stars U-15	
2012	Alberta U-16	CAN	4th Canada Soccer All Stars U-16	
2015	Calgary Foothills SC	CAN-4.US	USL PDL	
2016	Calgary Foothills SC	CAN-4.US	USL PDL (12/937/2g); 2nd Playoffs (4/390)	2
2017	Calgary Foothills SC	CAN-4.US	Missed season through injury	
2018	Calgary Foothills SC	CAN-4.US	USL PDL (14/1203); 1st Playoffs (4/390)	
2019	Cavalry FC	1.CAN	2nd CPL (19/1575/1g); SF CanChamp (5/337)	1
2020	Cavalry FC	1.CAN	4th CPL (9/636/1g)	1
2021	Cavalry FC	1.CAN	Missed season through injury	
2022	Cavalry FC	1.CAN	3rd CPL (20/812/1g); SF Playoffs (2/157); QF CanChamp (0/0)	1
2023	York United FC	1.CAN	5th CPL (15/562); QF CanChamp (1/90)	

ADEKUGBE, SAMUEL — VANCOUVER WHITECAPS FC
Left back / left midfielder. Born 1995, London, ENG. Grew up Calgary, AB, CAN. Height 178 cm. Dominant right foot.

FOOTBALLERS

Youth clubs: Manchester United (grassroots in England), Sir Bobby Charlton Academy (England), Calgary Foothills SC, Vancouver Whitecaps FC Residency
Honours: Concacaf champion (2021-22), Canadian Championship (2015), Süper Lig (2022-23)

CANADA INTERNATIONAL
1 FIFA World Cup: Group phase at Qatar 2022
1 Concacaf medal: Silver at CNL 2022-23
1st #CANMNT: 2015-09-08 at Belmopán, BLZ (v. BLZ)

SEASON	CLUB	NATION	HIGHLIGHTS (MP/MIN/G)	G
2011	Alberta U-16	CAN	4th Canada Soccer All Stars U-16	
2013	Vancouver Whitecaps FC	1.CAN	13th MLS (1/90)	
2014	Vancouver Whitecaps FC	1.CAN	9th MLS (4/193); Playoffs (0/0)	
2015	Vancouver Whitecaps FC	1.CAN	3rd MLS (9/647); 1st CanChamp (1/17)	
	Vanc. Whitecaps FC 2	CAN-2.US	W11th USL (2/180)	
2015-16	Vancouver Whitecaps FC	Concacaf	16th Champions League (4/277)	
2016	Vancouver Whitecaps FC	1.CAN	16th MLS (2/111); 2nd CanChamp (2/180)	
	Vanc. Whitecaps FC 2	CAN-2.US	W6th USL (4/328)	
2016-17	Brighton & Hove Albion FC	2.ENG	2nd EFL Championship (1/90); 3R EFL Cup (2/180/1g); 4R FA Cup (2/180)	1
2017	IFK Göteborg	1.SWE	10th Allsvenskan (9/698); 2R Svenskan Cup (1/62)	
2018	Vålerenga IF	1.NOR	6th Eliteserien (27/2337); QF NM-Cup (3/185)	
2019	Vålerenga IF	1.NOR	10th Eliteserien (24/1876); 3R NM-Cup (1/73)	
2020	Vålerenga IF	1.NOR	3rd Eliteserien (26/2011)	
2021	Vålerenga IF	1.NOR	x- Eliteserien (12/1080)	
2021-22	Vålerenga IF	UEFA	UEFA Qualifying Europa Conference League (2/164)	
	Hatayspor FC	1.TUR	12th Süper Lig (34/2934); L16 Kupasi (3/250)	
2022-23	Hatayspor FC	1.TUR	x- Süper Lig (18/1368); QF Kupasi (1/90)	
	Galatasaray SK	1.TUR	1st Süper Lig (6/515)	
2023	Vancouver Whitecaps FC	1.CAN	13th MLS (10/408); L16 Playoffs (2/171/1g)	

ADENUGA, IFE — TORONTO FC II
Midfielder. Born 2003. Grew up in Etobicoke, ON, CAN. Height 185. Youth clubs: Toronto FC Academy, Vaughan SC, SC Fortuna Köln (Germany)

SEASON	CLUB	NATION	HIGHLIGHTS (MP/MIN)	
2018	Toronto FC Academy	CAN	4th League1 Ontario (1/9)	
2023	Toronto FC II	CAN-3.US	23rd MLS NEXT Pro (6/365/1g)	1

AFEWORK, THEO — YORK UNITED FC
Winger. Born 2004, Calgary, AB, CAN. Height 181 cm. Youth clubs: Calgary Rangers SC, Calgary Blizzard, Calgary Foothills SC, Vancouver Whitecaps FC Academy, Nürnberg

SEASON	CLUB	NATION	HIGHLIGHTS (MP/MIN)
2023	York United FC	1.CAN	5th CPL (0/0)
	Alliance United FC	CAN	8th League1 Ontario (1/27/1g)

AFRIFA, STEPHEN — USA / SPORTING KANSAS CITY
Forward. Born 2001, Toronto, ON, CAN. Height 180 cm. Dominant right foot. Youth clubs: Woodbridge Strikers SC
School: Florida International University

SEASON	CLUB	NATION	HIGHLIGHTS (MP/MIN/G)	G
2018	Woodbridge Strikers SC	CAN	6th League1 Ontario (2/94)	
2022	One Knoxville SC	4.USA	USL League Two (10/?/6g); SF Playoffs (3/?/2g)	8
2023	Sporting Kansas City	1.USA	15th MLS (3/50); 4R US Cup (1/45); L32 Leagues (0/0)	
	Sporting Kansas City II	3.USA	6th MLS NEXT Pro (8/330/1g)	1

AGYEKUM, J.R. — THOMPSON RIVERS UNIVERSITY
Midfielder. Born 2002, Calgary, AB, CAN. Grew up in Calgary, AB, CAN. Height 178. Dominant right foot. Youth clubs: Calgary West SC, Springbank SC, Vancouver Whitecaps FC Academy
School: Thompson Rivers University

SEASON	CLUB	NATION	HIGHLIGHTS (MP/MIN)
2023	Atlético Ottawa	CAN	x- CPL (0/0)

AHMED, ALI — VANCOUVER WHITECAPS FC

Midfielder / fullback. Born 2000, Toronto, ON, CAN. Height 180 cm. Dominant right foot. Youth clubs: North Toronto SC, Toronto Youth FC, Oromia FC, Belenenses (Portugal), Vancouver Whitecaps FC Academy
Honours: Canadian Championship (2023)

SEASON	CLUB	NATION	HIGHLIGHTS (MP/MIN/G)	G
2022	Vancouver Whitecaps FC	1.CAN	17th MLS (2/54)	
	Vanc. Whitecaps FC 2	CAN-3.US	14th MLS NEXT Pro (15/1184)	
2023	Vancouver Whitecaps FC	Concacaf	QF Champions League (3/177); L32 Leagues Cup (1/10)	
	Vancouver Whitecaps FC	1.CAN	13th MLS (22/1121/2g); L16 Playoffs (2/100); 1st CanChamp (2/91/1g)	3

AIRD, FRASER — CAVALRY FC

Fullback. Born 1995, Scarborough, ON, CAN. Height 173 cm. Dominant right foot. Youth clubs: North Scarborough SC (house league), Pickering SC, Markham SC, Glasgow Rangers FC (youth)
Honours: CPL North Star Shield (2023), Scottish Third Division (2012-13), Scottish League One (2013-14)
1st #CANMNT: 2015-10-13 at Washington, DC, USA (v. GHA)

SEASON	CLUB	NATION	HIGHLIGHTS (MP/MIN/G)	G
2009	Markham Lightning U-14	CAN	2nd U-14 Cup	
2009	Ontario U-14	CAN	1st Canada Soccer All Stars U-14	
2012-13	Rangers FC	4.SCO	1st Third Division (19/740/3g); L16 Cup (2/139); QF Lg.Cup (1/81)	3
2013-14	Rangers FC	3.SCO	1st League One (27/1990/5g); SF Cup (6/347/1g); 1R Lg.Cup (1/74/1g)	7
2014-15	Rangers FC	2.SCO	3rd Championship (13/838/1g); L16 Cup (1/90); SF Lg.Cup (4/264)	1
2015-16	Rangers FC	2.SCO	x- Championship (3/39); L16 Lg.Cup (0/0)	
2016	Vancouver Whitecaps FC	1.CAN	16th MLS (18/1455); 2nd CanChamp (2/180)	
2016-17	Vancouver Whitecaps FC	Concacaf	x- Champions League (4/338)	
	Falkirk FC	2.SCO	2nd Championship (12/584/1g); 4R Cup (1/90)	1
2017-18	Dunfermline Athletic FC	2.SCO	4th Championship (21/971/4g); QF Playoffs (2/180); 4R SFA Cup (0/0)	4
2018-19	Dundee United FC	2.SCO	x- Championship (19/1366/3g); Lg.Cup (3/301)	3
	Queen of the South FC	2.SCO	9th Championship (6/278); Playoffs (2/107); L16 Cup (1/15)	
2019-20	Cove Rangers FC	4.SCO	x- League Two (9/641/3g); 2R SFA Cup (1/90)	3
2020	Valour FC	1.CAN	6th CPL (6/448/1g)	1
2021	FC Edmonton	1.CAN	7th CPL (28/2206/5g); CanChamp (1/29)	5
2022	Cavalry FC	1.CAN	CPL (5/434); Injured missed Playoffs & CanChamp	
2023	Cavalry FC	1.CAN	1st CPL (26/1435/2g); 2nd Playoffs (3/222); CanChamp (1/12)	2

AJAGBE, DAVID — VANCOUVER WHITECAPS FC ACADEMY

Forward. Born Surrey, BC, CAN. Height 178 cm. Dominant right foot. Youth clubs: Athlete Institute FC, Simcoe County Rovers FC, Vancouver Whitecaps FC Academy

SEASON	CLUB	NATION	HIGHLIGHTS (MP/MIN)	
2022	Simcoe County Rovers FC	CAN	5th League1 Ontario (1/9)	
2023	Vanc. Whitecaps FC 2	CAN-3.US	21st MLS NEXT Pro (0/0)	
	Vanc. Whitecaps FC Academy	3.CAN	3rd League1 BC (8/222/1g); 1st Playoffs (1/6)	1

AKINOLA, AYO — TORONTO FC

Forward. Born 2000, Detroit, MI, USA. Grew up Brampton, ON, CAN. Height 178 cm. Dominant right foot. Youth clubs: Brampton East SC, Toronto FC Academy
Honours: Canadian Championship (2018, 2020-22)
1st #CANMNT: 2021-07-15 at Kansas City, KS, USA (v. HAI)

SEASON	CLUB	NATION	HIGHLIGHTS (MP/MIN/G)	G
2016	Toronto FC II	CAN-2.US	E12th USL (10/396/2g)	2
2018	Toronto FC	1.CAN	19th MLS (4/49); 1st CanChamp (2/132/1g)	1
	Toronto FC II	CAN-2.US	E16th USL (16/904/5g)	5
2019	Toronto FC	Concacaf	L16 Champions League (2/96)	
	Toronto FC	1.CAN	9th MLS (8/257/1g); 2nd CanChamp (1/19)	1
	Toronto FC II	CAN-3.US	7th USL League One (8/540/1g)	1
2020	Toronto FC	1.CAN	2nd MLS (15/1060/9g); Playoffs (1/58)	9

FOOTBALLERS

2021	Toronto FC	Concacaf	QF Champions League (2/95)	
	Toronto FC	1.CAN	26th MLS (11/649/3g)	3
2022('20)	Toronto FC	1.CAN	1st CanChamp (1/79)	
2022	Toronto FC	1.CAN	27th MLS (26/1241/2g); 2nd CanChamp (3/145/2g)	4
2023	Toronto FC	1.CAN	x- MLS (14/555); QF CanChamp (1/10)	
	Toronto FC II	CAN-3.US	x- MLS NEXT Pro (1/5)	
	San Jose Earthquakes	1.USA	16th MLS (7/51); MLS Playoffs (0/0); Leagues (1/19)	

AKLIL, LINO — FRA / MONTPELLIER HSC U-19
Left back. Born 2006, Aix-en-Provence, FRA. Height 175 cm. Dominant left foot. Youth clubs: US Puyricard, Luynes Sports, SC Air Bel, Montpellier HSC

ALEMÁN, KEVEN — IDN / PERSIKABO 1973
Attacking midfielder. Born 1994, San José, CRC. Grew up Brampton, ON, CAN. Height 170 cm. Youth clubs: Toronto Spanish League, Club Uruguay Toronto, Toronto FC Academy, Real Valladolid (Spain)
Honours: CRC Primera División Verano (2015-16), CPL Regular Season (2022)
1st #CANMNT: 2013-07-11 at Seattle, WA, USA (v. MEX)

SEASON	CLUB	NATION	HIGHLIGHTS (MP/MIN/G)	G
2010	Ontario U-16	CAN	2nd Canada Soccer All Stars U-16	
2014-15	CS Herediano	Concacaf	SF Champions League (0/0)	
	CS Herediano	1.CRC	2nd Liga Invierno (1/45)	
	Belén FC	1.CRC	12th Liga Verano (18/1151/4g)	4
2015-16	CS Herediano	Concacaf	14th Champions League (0/0)	
	CS Herediano	1.CRC	2nd Liga Invierno (13/709); Playoff (1/44)	
	CS Herediano	1.CRC	1st Liga Verano (4/134/2g); 1st Playoff (0/0)	2
2016-17	Belén FC	1.CRC	9th Liga Invierno (10/328)	
	CD Saprissa	Concacaf	QF Champions League (0/0)	
	CD Saprissa	1.CRC	1st Liga Verano (11/472/1g); 2nd Playoff (4/114)	1
2017-18	CD Saprissa	1.CRC	2nd Liga Invierno (0/0)	
2018	Sacramento Republic	2.USA	W2nd USL (17/866/3g); L16 US Cup (2/124/2g)	5
2019	Sacramento Republic	2.USA	W7th USL (23/1328); QF Playoffs (3/216/1g); 4R US Cup (0/0)	1
2020	FC Edmonton	1.CAN	8th CPL (7/531/1g)	1
2020-21	Guadalupe FC	1.CRC	11th Liga Verano (10/330/1g)	1
2021	Valour FC	1.CAN	5th CPL (24/1388/3g); QF CanChamp (1/90)	3
2022	Atlético Ottawa	1.CAN	1st CPL (23/942/2g); 2nd Playoffs (2/78); R1 CanChamp (1/7)	2
2023-24	Persikabo 1973	1.iDN	Liga 1 (current season)	2

ALEXANDER, BEN — USA / UNIVERSITY OF SOUTH CAROLINA
Goalkeeper. Born 2003, Surrey, BC, CAN. Grew up Chilliwack, BC, CAN. Height 190 cm. Dominant right foot. Youth clubs: Chilliwack FC, Vancouver Whitecaps FC Academy
School: University of South Carolina
Honours: Canadian Championship (2022)

SEASON	CLUB	NATION	HIGHLIGHTS (MP/MIN)
2022	Vancouver Whitecaps FC	1.CAN	17th MLS (0/0); 1st CanChamp (0/0)
	Vanc. Whitecaps FC 2	CAN-3.US	14th MLS NEXT Pro (4/360)
2023	Vanc. Whitecaps FC Academy	3.CAN	3rd League1 BC (10/900)

ALEXANDRE, GUESLY — CF MONTRÉAL U-23
Forward. Born 2005, New York, NY, USA. Dominant right foot.

SEASON	CLUB	NATION	HIGHLIGHTS (MP/MIN/G)	G
2022	CF Montréal U-23	CAN	6th PLSQ (20/874/5g)	5
2023	CF Montréal U-23	CAN	5th Ligue1 Québec	

ALEXANDRE, MEDGY — CF MONTRÉAL U-23
Winger. Born 2004, Miami, FL, USA. Dominant left foot. Youth clubs: Académie de l'Impact de Montréal

SEASON	CLUB	NATION	HIGHLIGHTS (MP/MIN/G)	G
2022	CF Montréal U-23	CAN	6th PLSQ (20/1142/4g)	4
2023	CF Montréal U-23	CAN	5th Ligue1 Québec	

ALI-GAYAPERSAD, ANDRÉ — ESP / CF DAMM
Winger. Born 2008, Brampton, ON, CAN. Height 165 cm. Dominant right foot. Youth clubs: Brampton East SC

ALPHONSE, JEFFERSON   CF MONTRÉAL U-23

Centre back. Born 2003, Anjou, QC, CAN. Height 185 cm. Dominant right foot. Youth clubs: FC Anjou, CS St-Laurent, l'Académie CF Montréal

SEASON	CLUB	NATION	HIGHLIGHTS (MP/MIN)
2022	CF Montréal U-23	CAN	6th PLSQ (12/868)

ALTOBELLI, JULIAN   TORONTO FC II

Midfielder. Born 2002, Toronto, ON, CAN. Grew up Bolton, ON, CAN. Height 178 cm. Youth clubs: Bolton Wanderers, Toronto FC Academy

SEASON	CLUB	NATION	HIGHLIGHTS (MP/MIN/G)	G
2020	York9 FC	1.CAN	5th CPL (0/0)	
2021	Toronto FC II	CAN-3.US	7th USL League One (23/1545/2g)	2
2022	Toronto FC II	CAN-3.US	7th MLS NEXT Pro (21/958/5g); SF Playoffs (2/75)	5
2023	Toronto FC	1.CAN	29th MLS (0/0)	
	Toronto FC II	CAN-3.US	23rd MLS NEXT Pro (25/1260/3g)	3

AMANDA, GLOIRE

Forward. Born 1998, Nyarugusu, TAN. Grew up in Edmonton, AB, CAN. Height 178. Youth clubs: Edmonton Extreme, Edmonton Internazionale, FC Edmonton Academy, Vancouver Whitecaps FC Academy
School: Oregon State University

SEASON	CLUB	NATION	HIGHLIGHTS (MP/MIN/G)	G
2013	Alberta U-15	CAN	Canada Soccer All Stars U-15	
2017	Vancouver Whitecaps FC	1.CAN	SF CanChamp (0/0)	
	Vanc. Whitecaps FC 2	CAN-2.US	W14th United Soccer League (27/1218/3g)	3
2018	Lane United FC	4.USA	USL PDL	
2019	Lane United FC	4.USA	USL League Two	
2021-22	SK Austria Klagenfurt	1.AUT	6th Österreichischen Bundesliga (10/126/1g); QF Pokalen (2/93)	1
2023	Vanc. Whitecaps FC 2	CAN-3.US	21st MLS NEXT Pro (24/1450/3g)	3

AMEDUME, PAUL   PACIFIC FC

Centre back / midfielder. Born 2003, Edmonton, AB, CAN. Height 182 cm. Youth clubs: Edmonton Internazionale SC, St. Nicholas SA, Edmonton BTB Academy, Vancouver Whitecaps FC Academy
Honours: CPL Championship (2021)

SEASON	CLUB	NATION	HIGHLIGHTS (MP/MIN/G)	G
2021	Pacific FC	1.CAN	3rd CPL (1/17); 1st Playoffs (1/1)	
2022	North Texas SC	3.USA	5th MLS NEXT Pro (19/1614/1g)	1
2023	Pacific FC	1.CAN	4th CPL (12/565); 3rd Playoffs (2/91)	
	Nautsa'mawt FC	3.CAN	5th League1 BC (1/90)	

AMLA, DAVID

Centre back. Born 2002, Skjern, DEN. Grew up Granby, QC, CAN. Height 176 cm. Dominant left foot. Youth clubs: B67 Odense (Denmark), 'Académie Impact de Montréal
School: Iowa Western Community College

ANCHOR, MAX   VANCOUVER WHITECAPS FC

Goalkeeper. Born 2004, Surrey, BC, CAN. Grew up North Burnaby, BC, CAN. Height 183 cm. Youth clubs: Coquitlam Metro-Ford SC, Mountain United FC, Vancouver Whitecaps FC Academy

SEASON	CLUB	NATION	HIGHLIGHTS (MP/MIN)
2022	Vancouver Whitecaps FC	1.CAN	17th MLS (1/90)
	Vanc. Whitecaps FC 2	CAN-3.US	14th MLS NEXT Pro (5/450)
2023	Vancouver Whitecaps FC	1.CAN	13th MLS (0/0)
	Vanc. Whitecaps FC 2	CAN-3.US	21st MLS NEXT Pro (14/1260)

ANTINORO, GABRIEL   ATLÉTICO OTTAWA

Midfielder. Born 2004, Brasília, BRA. Grew up Montréal, QC, CAN. Height 15 cm. Youth clubs: CS Mont-Royal Outremont, Académie Impact de Montréal

SEASON	CLUB	NATION	HIGHLIGHTS (MP/MIN)	
2022	CF Montréal U-23	CAN	6th PLSQ (20/1695/4g)	4
2023	Atlético Ottawa	1.CAN	6th CPL (23/720/2g)	2

FOOTBALLERS

ANTONIUK, OWEN — WINDSOR CITY FC
Midfielder. Born 2002, Calgary, AB, CAN. Height 170 cm. Youth clubs: Rosedale Community Association, Calgary Blizzard SC, Calgary Foothills SC, Vancouver Whitecaps FC Academy
Honours: CPL Regular Season (2022)

SEASON	CLUB	NATION	HIGHLIGHTS (MP/MIN/G)	G
2017	Calgary Foothills SC U-15	CAN	2nd U-15 Cup	
2022	Vanc. Whitecaps FC 2	CAN-3.US	x- MLS NEXT Pro (13/477/3g)	3
	Atlético Ottawa	1.CAN	1st CPL (5/166)	
2023	Windsor City FC	1.CAN	15th League1 Ontario (20/1780/13g)	13

ANTONOGLOU, THEMI
Midfielder. Born 2001, Toronto, ON, CAN. Height 178 cm. Youth clubs: West Toronto SC, Toronto FC Academy
Honours: Canadian Championship (2022/'20)

SEASON	CLUB	NATION	HIGHLIGHTS (MP/MIN/G)	G
2018	TFC Academy	CAN	4th League1 Ontario (1/70)	
2019	TFC Academy	CAN-3.US	7th USL League One (2/109)	
2021	Toronto FC II	CAN-3.US	7th USL League One (19/825/3g)	3
2022('20)	Toronto FC	1.CAN	1st CanChamp (0/0)	
2022	Toronto FC	1.CAN	27th MLS (2/39); 2nd CanChamp (0/0)	
	Toronto FC II	CAN-3.US	7th MLS NEXT Pro (20/1738/4g); Playoffs (2/204/2g)	6
2023	Toronto FC	1.CAN	29th MLS (11/478); QF CanChamp (0/0); Leagues (2/20)	1
	Toronto FC II	CAN-3.US	23rd MLS NEXT Pro (15/1304/1g)	

APARICIO, MANUEL
Midfielder. Born 1995, Buenos Aires, ARG. Grew up East York, ON, CAN. Height 168 cm. Dominant right foot. Youth clubs: Los Invincibles in Buenos Aires (Argentina), Toronto FC Academy.
Honours: CPL Championship (2021)
1st #CANMNT: 2014-10-14 at Harrison, NJ, USA (v. COL)

SEASON	CLUB	NATION	HIGHLIGHTS (MP/MIN/G)	G
2014	Wilmington Hammerheads	2.USA	7th USL PRO (19/808/1g)	1
2015	Toronto FC II	CAN-2.US	E11th USL (20/1157)	
2016-17	SD Órdenes	4.ESP	Grupo 1- 20th Tercera División (30/?/4g)	4
2017-18	CD Izarra	3.ESP	Group 2- 16th Segunda División B (20/569)	
2018-19	CD San Roque de Lepe	4.ESP	x- Grupo 10; Tercera División (11/?/1g)	1
2019	York9 FC	1.CAN	3rd CPL (25/2159/2g); CanChamp (6/539)	2
2020	York9 FC	1.CAN	5th CPL (6/529/2g)	2
2021	Pacific FC	1.CAN	3rd CPL (20/1263/3g); Playoffs (2/210); SF CanChamp (3/261/1g)	4
2022	Pacific FC	Concacaf	L16 Concacaf League (4/352)	
	Pacific FC	1.CAN	4th CPL (17/1293/2g); SF Playoffs (2/180)	2
2023	Pacific FC	1.CAN	4th CPL (24/2046/4g); 3rd Playoffs (3/270); SF CanChamp (3/202)	4

APOSTOL, NICOLAS — GRE / ANAGENNISI EPANOMI FC
Midfielder. Born 1999, Surrey, BC, CAN. Height 168 cm. Youth clubs: Guildford Tigers, Vancouver Whitecaps FC Academy
School: University of Connecticut, Oregon State University

SEASON	CLUB	NATION	HIGHLIGHTS (MP/MIN)
2016	Vanc. Whitecaps FC 2	CAN-2.US	W6th USL (1/9)
2017	Vanc. Whitecaps FC 2	CAN-2.US	W14th USL (1/17)
2021	Cavalry FC	1.CAN	2nd CPL (7/301); SF Playoffs (0/0)
2023-24	Anagennisi Epanomi FC	3.GRE	Gamma Ethniki (current season)

ARFIELD, SCOTT — USA / CHARLOTTE FC
Midfielder. Born 1988, Livingston, SCO. Height 178 cm. Youth clubs: Murieston Boys
Honours: Scottish Premiership (2020-21), Scottish Cup (2022), England Championship (2015-16)
1st #CANMNT: 2016-03-25 at Vancouver, BC, CAN (v. MEX)

SEASON	CLUB	NATION	HIGHLIGHTS (MP/MIN/G)	G
2006-07	Falkirk FC	1.SCO	7th Scottish Premier League (0/0)	
2007-08	Falkirk FC	1.SCO	7th Scottish Premier League (35/2715/3g)	3
2008-09	Falkirk FC	1.SCO	10th Scottish Premier League (37/3178/7g); 2nd SFA Cup (3/270/2g); QF Lg.Cup (1/90)	9

SEASON	CLUB	NATION	HIGHLIGHTS (MP/MIN/G)	
2009-10	Falkirk FC	1.SCO	12th SPL (36/3052/3g); R4 SFA Cup (1/90); L16 Lg.Cup (1/90)	3
2010-11	Huddersfield Town FC	3.ENG	3rd League One (40/3085/4g); 2nd Playoffs (2/171); R4 FA Cup (5/242/1g); 2R Lg.Cup (2/146); SF EFL Trophy (4/330/1g)	6
2011-12	Huddersfield Town FC	3.ENG	4th League One (35/2268/2g); 1st Playoffs (2/31); R1 FA Cup (1/33); R2 Lg.Cup (1/90); R2 EFL Trophy (1/7)	2
2012-13	Huddersfield Town FC	2.ENG	19th EFL Championship (21/1018/1g); R5 FA Cup (4/360); R1 Lg.Cup (1/45)	1
2013-14	Burnley FC	2.ENG	2nd EFL Championship (45/3746/8g); R3 FA Cup (1/90); L16 Lg.Cup (3/125/1g)	9
2014-15	Burnley FC	1.ENG	19th FA Premier League (37/3204/2g); R3 FA Cup (2/180); R2 Lg.Cup (1/90)	2
2015-16	Burnley FC	2.ENG	1st EFL Championship (46/3952/8g); R4 FA Cup (2/111); R1 Lg.Cup (1/90)	8
2016-17	Burnley FC	1.ENG	16th FA Premier League (31/2107/1g); R5 FA Cup (3/220); R1 EFL Cup (1/39)	1
2017-18	Burnley FC	1.ENG	7th FA Premier League (18/1335/2g); R3 FA Cup (0/0); R3 EFL Cup (2/162)	2
2018-19	Glasgow Rangers FC	1.SCO	2nd Prem. (29/2334/11g); QF Cup (4/312); SF Lg.Cup (2/87)	11
2019-20	Glasgow Rangers FC	1.SCO	2nd Prem. (26/1961/5g); QF Cup (3/213/3g); 2nd Lg.Cup (3/193)	8
2020-21	Glasgow Rangers FC	1.SCO	1st Prem. (28/1210/4g); QF Cup (2/180); QF Lg.Cup (2/112)	4
2021-22	Glasgow Rangers FC	1.SCO	2nd Prem. (29/1605/4g); 1st Cup (2/126/1g); SF Lg.Cup (3/102/1g)	6
2022-23	Glasgow Rangers FC	1.SCO	2nd Prem. (31/1056/5g); SF Cup (3/78/1g); 2nd Lg.Cup (3/122/2g)	8
2023	Charlotte FC	1.USA	19th MLS (13/403/2g); MLS Playoffs (1/24); QF Leagues (5/334/1g)	3
CONTINENTAL FOOTBALL		UEFA	**HIGHLIGHTS (MP/MIN/G)**	G
2009-10	Falkirk FC	UEFA	UEFA Qualifying Europa League (2/210)	
2018-19	Glasgow Rangers FC	UEFA	Qualifying (6/422); UEFA Europa League (5/450/1g)	1
2019-20	Glasgow Rangers FC	UEFA	Qualifying (7/505/1g); L16 UEFA Europa League (10/609)	1
2020-21	Glasgow Rangers FC	UEFA	Qualifying (3/270/1g); Rof32 UEFA Europa League (10/632/2g)	3
2021-22	Glasgow Rangers FC	UEFA	UEFA Qualifying Champions League (2/160); Qualifying (2/99); 2nd UEFA Europa League (12/434)	
2022-23	Glasgow Rangers FC	UEFA	Qualifying UCL (2/81); UEFA Champions League (4/268/1g)	1

ARTEMENKO, SVYATIK — ELECTRIC CITY FC

Goalkeeper. Born 2000, Odessa, UKR. Grew up Winnipeg, MB, CAN. Height 188 cm. Dominant left foot. Youth clubs: Winnipeg Bonivital SC
School: University of Guelph

SEASON	CLUB	NATION	HIGHLIGHTS (MP/MIN)
2016	Bonivital SC U-16	CAN	2nd U-16 Cup
2017	Winnipeg Bonivital SC U-17	CAN	1st U-17 Cup
	Manitoba U-18	CAN	4th Canada Games (5/400)
2019	Valour FC	1.CAN	6th CPL (0/0)
	WSA Winnipeg	CAN-4.US	USL League Two (2/90)
2021	Guelph United FC	CAN	2nd League1 Ontario (12/1080); 1st Playoffs (2/180)
2022	York United FC	1.CAN	6th CPL (0/0); CanChamp (1/90)
	Guelph United FC	CAN	7th League1 Ontario (13/1125); CanChamp (1/90)
2023	Electric City FC	CAN	7th League1 Ontario (18/1600)

ASSI, JEAN-ANIEL

Winger. Born 2004, Adzopé, CIV. Grew up Montréal, QC, CAN. Height 181 cm. Dominant right foot. Youth clubs: ASM LaSalle, Royal-Sélect de Beauport, Académie de l'Impact de Montréal

SEASON	CLUB	NATION	HIGHLIGHTS (MP/MIN)
2020	Impact de Montréal	Concacaf	QF Champions League (1/7)
2021	CF Montréal	1.CAN	18th MLS (0/0)
2022	Cavalry FC	1.CAN	3rd CPL (19/789); QF CanChamp (2/91)
2023	Atlético Ottawa	1.CAN	6th CPL (26/1743/1g); QF CanChamp (2/172)

ATTARDO, TYLER — FC MANITOBA

Forward. Born 2001, Winnipeg, MB, CAN. Height 185 cm. Youth clubs: FC Northwest Winnipeg, Winnipeg Phoenix

SEASON	CLUB	NATION	HIGHLIGHTS (MP/MIN/G)	G
2014	FC Northwest U-14 Winnipeg	CAN	7th U-14 Cup	
2019	Valour FC	1.CAN	6th CPL (20/999/6g); CanChamp (2/51)	6
2020-21	PO Xylotymbou	2.CYP	12th B Division (28/1374/1g); R1 Cup (1/76)	1
2021-22	US Granville	4.FRA	10th National 2 (14/406/2g)	2
2022-23	Saint-Colomban Locminé	5.FRA	x- National 3 Group Bretagne (10/355/1g)	1
2023	FC Manitoba	CAN-4.US	N-3rd USL League Two	

AWUAH, KWAME

Fullback. Born 1995, Toronto, ON, CAN. Height 173 cm. Youth clubs: Club Uruguay Toronto, Woodbridge Strikers SC, Sigma FC
School: University of Connecticut
Honours: CPL Championship (2019, 2020)

SEASON	CLUB	NATION	HIGHLIGHTS (MP/MIN/G)	G
2011	Ontario U-16	CAN	2nd Canada Soccer All Stars U-16	
2014	Sigma FC	CAN	3rd League1 Ontario	
2016	Sigma FC	CAN	W2nd League1 Ontario (6/510/1g)	1
2017	New York City FC	1.USA	2nd MLS (4/28); QF Playoffs (0/0)	
2018	New York City FC	1.USA	7th MLS (6/143); QF Playoffs (0/0); R4 US Cup (1/90)	
2019	Forge FC Hamilton	Concacaf	L16 Concacaf League (3/269)	
	Forge FC Hamilton	1.CAN	1st CPL (27/1975); CanChamp (2/64)	
2020	Forge FC Hamilton	Concacaf	QF Concacaf League (3/259)	
	Forge FC Hamilton	1.CAN	1st CPL (10/753/1g)	1
2021	Forge FC Hamilton	Concacaf	SF Concacaf League (8/713/1g)	1
	Forge FC Hamilton	1.CAN	1st CPL (24/1997/1g); 2nd Playoffs (2/180); SF CanChamp (1/90)	1
2022	St. Louis CITY 2	3.USA	2nd MLS NEXT Pro (20/1313); 2nd Playoffs (0/0); R3 US Cup (2/48)	
2023	Loudoun United FC	2.USA	x- USL (2/43)	

BADWAL, JEEVAN — VANCOUVER WHITECAPS FC 2

Midfielder. Born 2006, Surrey, BC, CAN. Height 178 cm. Dominant right foot. Youth clubs: Surey FC, Vancouver Whitecaps FC Academy

SEASON	CLUB	NATION	HIGHLIGHTS (MP/MIN)
2019	Vancouver Whitecaps U-13	Concacaf	Concacaf Under-13 Champions League
2023	Vanc. Whitecaps FC 2	CAN-3.US	21st MLS NEXT Pro (8/407)

BAH, ELAGE

Fullback. Born 2004, Ottawa, ON, CAN. Grew up in Ottawa, ON, CAN. Height 170. Youth clubs: Ottawa St. Anthony Futuro Academy

SEASON	CLUB	NATION	HIGHLIGHTS (MP/MIN)	
2022	Vanc. Whitecaps FC 2	CAN-3.US	14th MLS NEXT Pro (19/1074/1g)	1
2023	Vanc. Whitecaps FC 2	CAN-3.US	21st MLS NEXT Pro (26/1861)	

BAHOUS, ZAKARIA — PACIFIC FC

Born 2001, Longueuil, QC, CAN. Height 180 cm. Dominant right foot. Youth clubs: FC Brossard, FC St-Léonard, CS Longueuil
Honours: CPL Regular Season (2022)

SEASON	CLUB	NATION	HIGHLIGHTS (MP/MIN/G)	G
2018	CS Longueuil	CAN	4th PLSQ (1/30)	
2019	CS Longueuil	CAN	8th PLSQ (11/816/1g)	1
2020	CS Longueuil	CAN	5th PLSQ (7/581)	
2021	FC Laval	CAN	4th PLSQ (11/867/2g)	2
2022	Atlético Ottawa	1.CAN	1st CPL (26/1432/1g); 2nd Playoffs (3/168)	1
2023	Atlético Ottawa	1.CAN	x- CPL (12/528/1g); QF CanChamp (2/142)	1
	Pacific FC	1.CAN	4th CPL (4/136); 3rd Playoffs (2/119)	

BAIR, THEO — SCO / MOTHERWELL FC

Forward. Born 1999, Ottawa, ON, CAN. Height 190 cm. Youth clubs: Ottawa Royals SC, Ottawa Capital United, Ottawa West United SC, Vancouver Whitecaps FC Academy
Honours: OBOS-ligaen (2021-22)
1st #CANMNT: 2020-01-7 at Irvine, CA, USA (v. BRB)

SEASON	CLUB	NATION	HIGHLIGHTS (MP/MIN/G)	G
2017	Vanc. Whitecaps FC 2	CAN-2.US	29th USL (0/0)	
2019	Vancouver Whitecaps FC	1.CAN	23rd MLS (17/824/2g); CanChamp (1/90)	2
2020	Vancouver Whitecaps FC	1.CAN	17th MLS (16/446/1g); L16 MLS is Back (1/90)	1
2021	Vancouver Whitecaps FC	1.CAN	x- MLS (4/27)	
	Hamarkameratene	2.NOR	1st OBOS-ligaen (17/966/4g); R3 Cup (1/27)	4
2021-22	St. Johnstone FC	1.SCO	11th Premiership (7/104)	
2022-23	St. Johnstone FC	1.SCO	9th Premiership (27/609/1g); R4 SFA Cup (1/23); Lg.Cup (3/149)	1
2023-24	Motherwell FC	1.SCO	Premiership (current season); SFA Cup (current); Lg.Cup (1/67)	

BALBINOTTI, GABRIEL

Forward. Born 1998, Montréal, QC, CAN. Grew up Porto Alegre, BRA & Montréal, QC, CAN. Height 185 cm. Dominant right foot. Youth clubs: Panamerican School (Brazil), Hudson Saint-Lazare, Lanaudière Centre, Académie Impact Montréal
School: Université du Québec à Trois-Rivières
Honours: CPL Championship (2020)

SEASON	CLUB	NATION	HIGHLIGHTS (MP/MIN/G)	G
2012	Lanaudière Centre U-14	CAN	3rd U-14 Cup	
2012	Québec U-15	CAN	2nd Canada Soccer All Stars U-15	
2018	Ottawa Fury FC	2.USA	E10th USL (2/51); SF CanChamp (0/0)	
2019	FC Lanaudière	CAN	7th PLSQ (10/734/6g)	6
2020	Forge FC Hamilton	Concacaf	QF Concacaf League (0/0)	
2020	Forge FC Hamilton	1.CAN	1st CPL (6/203)	
2021	FC Lanaudière	CAN	9th PLSQ (5/450/3g)	3
2022	Céltix Haut-Richelieu	CAN	10th PLSQ (8/692/4g)	4

BANFI, SAMUEL

Goalkeeper. Born 2003, Montréal, QC, CAN. Grew up in Montréal, QC, CAN. Height 174. Youth clubs: Académie de l'Impact de Montréal
School: Snow College

SEASON	CLUB	NATION	HIGHLIGHTS (MP/MIN)
2022	CF Montréal U-23	CAN	6th PLSQ (4/360)

BARKER, EVAN

Goalkeeper. Born 1997, Winnipeg, MB, CAN. Height 195 cm. Youth clubs: Winnipeg Bonivital SC
School: University of New Brunswick

SEASON	CLUB	NATION	HIGHLIGHTS (MP/MIN)
2010	Winnipeg Bonivital SC U-14	CAN	5th U-14 Cup
2011	Sask'toba U-15	CAN	6th Canada Soccer All Stars U-15
2012	Sask'toba U-15	CAN	3rd Canada Soccer All Stars U-15
2013	Winnipeg Bonivital SC U-16	CAN	6th U-16 Cup
2013	Sask'toba U-16	CAN	Canada Soccer All Stars U-16
2016	WSA Winnipeg	CAN-4.US	USL PDL (7/502)
2017	WSA Winnipeg	CAN-4.US	USL PDL
2018	WSA Winnipeg	CAN-4.US	USL PDL
2022	Valour FC	1.CAN	CanChamp (0/0)

BARRETT, MITCHELL — CAVALRY FC

Goalkeeper. Born 2006. Grew up in Calgary, AB, CAN. Youth clubs: Calgary Foothills SC, Cavalry FC

SEASON	CLUB	NATION	HIGHLIGHTS (MP/MIN)
2022	Alberta U-18	CAN	Bronze at Canada Games (2/160)

BARROW, DÉKWON — TORONTO FC II

Forward. Born 2004. Grew up in .., ON, CAN. Height 185. Youth clubs: Athlete Institute FC, Toronto FC Academy

SEASON	CLUB	NATION	HIGHLIGHTS (MP/MIN)
2023	Toronto FC II	CAN-3.US	23rd MLS NEXT Pro (12/160/2g)

BASKETT, KIERAN

Goalkeeper. Born 2001, Halifax, NS, CAN. Height 190 cm. Dominant left foot. Youth clubs: Halifax City SC
School: College of William & Mary

SEASON	CLUB	NATION	HIGHLIGHTS (MP/MIN)
2015	Halifax City SC U-16	CAN	5th U-16 Cup

FOOTBALLERS

2017	Nova Scotia U-18	CAN	7th Canada Games (4/280)
2021	HFX Wanderers FC	1.CAN	4th CPL (10/900); QF CanChamp (2/180)
2022	HFX Wanderers FC	1.CAN	7th CPL (9/810); QF CanChamp (0/0)
2023	Pacific FC	1.CAN	4th CPL (10/900); 3rd Playoffs (0/0); SF CanChamp (1/90)

BASSONG, ZORHAN

Fullback. Born 1999, Toronto, ON, CAN. Grew up Montréal, QC, CAN. Height 178 cm. Dominant left foot. Youth clubs: CS Longueuil, Royal Excel Mouscron (Belgium), Anderlecht (Belgium), Lille OSC (France)
Honours: Canadian Championship (2021)
1st #CANMNT: 2020-01-10 at Irvine, CA, USA (v. BRB)

SEASON	CLUB	NATION	HIGHLIGHTS (MP/MIN)
2016-17	Lille OSC B	4.FRA	B8th Championnat CFA Groupe B (1/90)
2017-18	Lille OSC B	4.FRA	C11th National 2 Groupe C (16/1221)
2018-19	Lille OSC B	4.FRA	x- National 2 Groupe D (14/811)
	Cercle Brugge KS	2.BEL	13th Championnat (0/0)
2019-20	Cercle Brugge KS	2.BEL	14th Championnat (0/0)
2021	CF Montréal	1.CAN	18th MLS (26/1248); 1st CanChamp (3/210)
2022	CF Montréal	Concacaf	QF Champions League (2/94)
	CF Montréal	1.CAN	3rd MLS (10/181); SF CanChamp (2/135)
	CF Montréal U-23	CAN	6th PLSQ (2/180)
2022-23	FC Argeș	1.ROU	14th Liga I (8/579); Playoffs (2/155)
2023-24	FCV Farul Constanța	1.ROU	x- Liga I (2/115)

BAYIHA, CLÉMENT — YORK UNITED FC

Midfielder. Born 1999, Yaoundé, CMR. Grew up Ste-Thérèse, QC, CAN. Height 174 cm. Youth clubs: Bain de Bretagne, AS Blainville, Académie de l'Impact de Montréal
Honours: Canadian Championship (2019, 2021)

SEASON	CLUB	NATION	HIGHLIGHTS (MP/MIN/G)	G
2018	Impact de Montréal	1.CAN	SF CanChamp (0/0)	
2018	Ottawa Fury FC	2.USA	E10th USL (2/50)	
2019	Impact de Montréal	1.CAN	18th MLS (11/469); 1st CanChamp (5/323)	
2020	Impact de Montréal	1.CAN	18th MLS (4/66); L16 MLS is Back (0/0); Playoffs (0/0)	
2021	CF Montréal	1.CAN	18th MLS (10/281); 1st CanChamp (2/115)	
2022	Hamarkameratene	1.NOR	13th Eliteserien (8/234); R3 Cup (1/45)	
2023	York United FC	1.CAN	5th CPL (27/1533/2g); 5th Playoffs (1/76); QF CanChamp (2/83)	2

BEKKER, KYLE — FORGE FC HAMILTON

Midfielder. Born 1990, Oakville, ON, CAN. Height 178 cm. Dominant right foot. Youth clubs: Oakville SC, Mississauga Dixie SC, Sigma FC
School: Boston College
Honours: CPL Championship (2019, 2020, 2022, 2023), NASL Championship (2017)
1st #CANMNT: 2013-01-26 at Tucson, AZ, USA (v. DEN)

SEASON	CLUB	NATION	HIGHLIGHTS (MP/MIN/G)	G
2004	Oakville SC U-14	CAN	1st Tide U-14 Cup	
2006	Mississauga Dixie Dominators	CAN	1st U-16 Cup	
2013	Toronto FC	1.CAN	17th MLS (9/335); 3rd CanChamp (2/117)	
2014	Toronto FC	1.CAN	13th MLS (20/1117); 2nd CanChamp (4/258)	
2015	FC Dallas	1.USA	x- MLS (8/313); R5 US Cup (1/90)	
	Impact de Montréal	1.CAN	7th MLS (3/165/1g); QF Playoffs (1/13)	1
	FC Montréal	CAN-2.US	E10th USL (1/90)	
2016	Impact de Montréal	1.CAN	11th MLS (18/1139/1g); SF CanChamp (2/157)	1
2017	San Francisco Deltas	2.USA	2nd NASL (28/2030/3g); 1st Playoffs (2/180); R4 US Cup (2/180/1g)	4
2018	North Carolina FC	2.USA	E9th USL (33/2710/7g); R4 US Cup (3/289)	7
2019	Forge FC Hamilton	Concacaf	L16 Concacaf League (4/360)	
	Forge FC Hamilton	1.CAN	1st CPL (28/2444/4g); CanChamp (2/180/1g)	5
2020	Forge FC Hamilton	Concacaf	QF Concacaf League (4/356)	
	Forge FC Hamilton	1.CAN	1st CPL (10/786/3g)	3
2021	Forge FC Hamilton	Concacaf	SF Concacaf League (7/619/2g)	2
	Forge FC Hamilton	1.CAN	1st CPL (26/2027/3g); 2nd Playoffs (2/180); SF CanChamp (2/180)	3
2022('20)	Forge FC Hamilton	1.CAN	2nd CanChamp (1/90)	

2022	Forge FC Hamilton		Concacaf L16 Champions League (2/180)	
	Forge FC Hamilton		1.CAN 2nd CPL (25/2016/2g); 1st Playoffs (2/132); QF CanChamp (1/67)	2
2023	Forge FC Hamilton		1.CAN 2nd CPL (26/2121/3g); 1st Playoffs (2/210/1g); SF CanChamp (2/162/1g)	5

BÉLAND-GOYETTE, LOUIS

Midfielder. Born 1995, Montréal, QC, CAN. Height 178 cm. Youth clubs: ASA Pointe-Claire, Académie de l'Impact de Montréal

SEASON	CLUB	NATION	HIGHLIGHTS (MP/MIN/G)	G
2009	Québec U-14	CAN	2nd Canada Soccer All Stars U-14	
2014	Impact de Montréal	1.CAN	19th MLS (1/15)	
2014-15	Impact de Montréal	Concacaf	2nd Champions League (0/0)	
2015	Impact de Montréal	1.CAN	7th MLS (0/0)	
	FC Montréal	CAN-2.US	E10th USL (15/1024/2g)	2
2016	FC Montréal	CAN-2.US	E14th USL (26/2235/2g)	2
2017	Impact de Montréal	1.CAN	17th MLS (6/293)	
2018	Impact de Montréal	1.CAN	15th MLS (4/109)	
2019	Valour FC	1.CAN	6th CPL (21/1772/1g); CanChamp (2/164)	1
2020	HFX Wanderers FC	1.CAN	2nd CPL (10/652)	
2021-22	Gudja United FC	1.MLT	6th Maltese Premier League (11/973/1g)	1

BELZILE, JEAN-CHRISTOPHE — ACADÉMIE DE CF MONTRÉAL

Goalkeeper. Born 2008. Grew up in Beloeil, QC, CAN. Height 177 cm. Dominant right foot. Youth clubs: Winnipeg Bonivital SC, Colorado Pride SC, Ottawa TFC, Ottawa South United SC, CS St-Hubert, Académie de CF Montréal

BIELLO, ALESSANDRO — CF MONTRÉAL U-23

Midfielder. Born 2006, Montréal, QC, CAN. Height 184 cm. Dominant right foot. Youth clubs: CS St-Léonard, Académie de CF Montréal

SEASON	CLUB	NATION	HIGHLIGHTS (MP/MIN)
2018	Impact de Montréal U-13	Concacaf	Concacaf Under-13 Champions League
2019	Impact de Montréal U-13	Concacaf	Concacaf Under-13 Champions League
2022	CF Montréal U-23	CAN	6th PLSQ (1/45)
2023	CF Montréal U-23	CAN	5th Ligue1 Québec

BINATE, ABDUL

Forward. Born 2003, Abidjan, CIV. Grew up in Montréal, QC, CAN. Height 180. Dominant right foot. Youth clubs: Académie Impact de Montréal

SEASON	CLUB	NATION	HIGHLIGHTS (MP/MIN)	
2022	Pacific FC	1.CAN	4th CPL (0/0)	
2023	Pacific FC	1.CAN	4th CPL (3/35)	
	Nautsa'mawt FC	3.CAN	5th League1 BC (4/294/1g)	1

BELGAY, ALLEN SAYE

Right back & winger. Born 2006, Toronto, ON, CAN. Grew up in Brampton & Barrie, ON, CAN. Height 178. Dominant right foot. Youth clubs: Brampton YSC, Aurora FC, Woodbridge SC, Vaughan SC, Simcoe Rovers FC

SEASON	CLUB	NATION	HIGHLIGHTS (MP/MIN)
2023	Simcoe County Rovers FC	CAN	2nd League1 Ontario (13/945); 1st Playoffs (2/29)

BISKUPSKI, PHILIP — TORONTO FC ACADEMY

Midfielder. Born 2008, Toronto, ON, CAN. Height 173 cm. Dominant left foot. Youth clubs: Erin Mills SC

BOAKYE, GABRIEL

Fullback / midfielder. Born 1998, Richmond Hill, ON, CAN. Height 171 cm. Youth clubs: Oak Ridges SC, Richmond Hill SC, West Toronto SC, Toronto FC Academy, Energie Cottbus (Germany)
Honours: Regionalliga Nordost (2017-18), League1 Ontario (2023)

SEASON	CLUB	NATION	HIGHLIGHTS (MP/MIN)
2015	Toronto FC II	CAN-2.US	E11th USL (9/589)
	TFC Academy	CAN-4.US	USL PDL
2016-17	FC Energie Cottbus	4.GER	Regionalliga
2017-18	FC Energie Cottbus	4.GER	Regionalliga
2018-19	FC Köln II	4.GER	Regionalliga
2019-20	FC Köln II	4.GER	Regionalliga

FOOTBALLERS

2020-21	Lokomotive Leipzig		4.GER	x- Regionalliga
2021	FC Edmonton		1.CAN	7th CPL (7/154)
2023	Turun Palloseura		2.FIN	x- Ykkönen (?); Ykköscup (1/78)
	Simcoe County Rovers FC		CAN	2nd League1 Ontario (3/57); 1st Playoffs (2/48)

BOEHMER, ISAAC — VANCOUVER WHITECAPS FC

Goalkeeper. Born 2001, Penticton, BC, CAN. Grew up Okanagan Falls, BC, CAN. Height 188 cm. Youth clubs: Pinnacles FC, Thompson Okanagan FC, Schalke (Germany), Vancouver Whitecaps FC Academy.
Honours: Canadian Championship (2022), CPL Championship (2021)

SEASON	CLUB	NATION	HIGHLIGHTS (MP/MIN)
2020	Vancouver Whitecaps FC	1.CAN	17th MLS (0/0)
2021	Vancouver Whitecaps FC	1.CAN	12th MLS (0/0)
	Pacific FC	1.CAN	3rd CPL (1/90); 1st Playoffs (0/0); SF CanChamp (0/0)
2022	Vancouver Whitecaps FC	1.CAN	17th MLS (3/225); 1st CanChamp (0/0)
	Vanc. Whitecaps FC 2	CAN-3.US	14th MLS NEXT Pro (10/900)
2023	Vancouver Whitecaps FC	Concacaf	QF Champions League (0/0); L32 Leagues Cup (1/90)
	Vancouver Whitecaps FC	1.CAN	13th MLS (0/0); L16 MLS Playoffs (0/0)
	Vanc. Whitecaps FC 2	CAN-3.US	21st MLS NEXT Pro (9/810)

BOITEAU, LUKA — FRA / US BOULOGNE CÔTE D'OPALE

Born 2006, Sèvres, FRA. Grew up Lille, FRA. Height 174 cm. Dominant right foot. Youth clubs: Lambersart, Lille OSC

BOMBITO, MOÏSE — USA / COLORADO RAPIDS

Centre back / left back. Born 2000, Montréal, QC, CAN. Height 190.5 cm. Youth clubs: CS St-Laurent, CS St-Hubert
School: University of New Hampshire
1 Concacaf medal: Silver at CNL 2022-23

SEASON	CLUB	NATION	HIGHLIGHTS (MP/MIN/G)	G
2014	St-Laurent U-14	CAN	4th U-14 Cup	
2016	St-Laurent U-16	CAN	4th U-16 Cup	
2020	CS Saint-Hubert	CAN	4th PLSQ (7/584/1g)	1
2021	CS Saint-Hubert	CAN	5th PLSQ (6/495/2g)	2
2023	Colorado Rapids	1.USA	28th MLS (11/751); L16 US Cup (1/73); Leagues (2/121)	
	Colorado Rapids 2	3.USA	1st MLS NEXT Pro (4/225)	

BONTIS, DINO — FORGE FC HAMILTON

Goalkeeper. Born 2004, Hamilton, ON, CAN. Grew up Ancaster, ON, CAN. Height 179 cm. Dominant right foot. Youth clubs: Hamilton Sparta, Toronto FC Academy
School: Western University

SEASON	CLUB	NATION	HIGHLIGHTS (MP/MIN)
2017	Toronto FC U-13	Concacaf	Concacaf Under-13 Champions League
2022	Forge FC Hamilton	1.CAN	2nd CPL (0/0)
2022	Sigma FC	CAN	9th League1 Ontario (13/1084)
2023	Sigma FC	CAN	9th League1 Ontario (11/972)

BORGES, TRISTAN — FORGE FC HAMILTON

Forward. Born 1998, Toronto, ON, CAN. Height 170 cm. Dominant left foot. Youth clubs: Vaughan SC (house league), West Toronto SC, Toronto FC Academy, SC Heerenveen (Netherlands)
Honours: CPL Championship (2019, 2022, 2023)
1st #CANMNT: 2020-01-10 at Irvine, CA, USA (v. BRB)

SEASON	CLUB	NATION	HIGHLIGHTS (MP/MIN/G)	G
2015	TFC Academy	CAN	5th League1 Ontario	
2018	Sigma FC	CAN	2nd League1 Ontario (7/605/1g); Playoffs (3/242/1g)	2
2019	Forge FC Hamilton	Concacaf	L16 Concacaf League (4/309)	
	Forge FC Hamilton	1.CAN	1st CPL (27/1974/13g); CanChamp (2/172)	13
2019-20	Oud-Heverlee Leuven	2.BEL	3rd Division 1B Proximus League (4/109)	
2021	Forge FC Hamilton	Concacaf	SF Concacaf League (6/438/1g)	1
	Forge FC Hamilton	1.CAN	1st CPL (24/1384/3g); 2nd Playoffs (2/144); SF CanChamp (2/143)	3
2022('20)	Forge FC Hamilton	1.CAN	2nd CanChamp (1/67/1g)	1
2022	Forge FC Hamilton	Concacaf	L16 Champions League (2/133)	
	Forge FC Hamilton	1.CAN	2nd CPL (23/1807/6g); 1st Playoffs (3/260); QF CanChamp (2/135)	6
2023	Forge FC Hamilton	1.CAN	2nd CPL (26/1294/1g); 1st Playoffs (1/52/1g); SF CanChamp (3/223)	2

BORJAN, MILAN SVK / ŠK SLOVAN BRATISLAVA

Goalkeeper. Born 1987, Knin, YUG. Grew up Hamilton, ON, CAN. Height 195 cm. Youth clubs: Winnipeg Kilcona, Mount Hamilton

Honours: Concacaf champion (2021-22), Bulgaria A Grupa (2015-16), Serbian SuperLiga (2017-18, 2018-19, 2019-20, 2020-21, 2021-22, 2022-23), Serbian Cup (2021, 2022, 2023)

CANADA INTERNATIONAL
1 FIFA World Cup: Group phase at Qatar 2022
1 Concacaf medal: Silver at CNL 2022-23
1st #CANMNT: 2011-02-9 at Larissa, GRE (v. GRE)

SEASON	CLUB	NATION	HIGHLIGHTS (MP/MIN)
2009-10	FK Rad	1.SRB	8th SuperLiga (13/1170)
2010-11	FK Rad	1.SRB	4th SuperLiga (23/2039)
2011-12	Sivasspor	1.TUR	x- Süper Lig (10/876); R3 Kupasi (0/0)
	CS Sporting Vaslui	1.ROU	2nd Liga I (16/1440); SF Cupa (3/270)
2012-13	Sivasspor	1.TUR	12th Süper Lig (29/2583); SF Kupasi (8/750)
2013-14	Sivasspor	1.TUR	5th Süper Lig (4/360); Kupasi (5/510)
2014-15	PFC Ludogrets	1.BUL	x- Grupa A (2/180); Cup (1/90)
2014-15	FK Radnički	1.SRB	9th SuperLiga (15/1350)
2015-16	PFC Ludogrets	1.BUL	1st Grupa A (9/790); L16 Cup (0/0); 2nd Super Cup (0/0)
2016-17	PFC Ludogrets	1.BUL	x- First League (7/630); L16 Cup (2/180)
	Korona Kielce	1.POL	5th Ekstraklasa (14/1260)
2017-18	FK Crvena zvezda	1.SRB	1st SuperLiga (31/2790); QF Kup (3/300)
2018-19	FK Crvena zvezda	1.SRB	1st SuperLiga (28/2486); 2nd Kup (4/360)
2019-20	FK Crvena zvezda	1.SRB	1st SuperLiga (26/2340); SF Kup (2/180)
2020-21	FK Crvena zvezda	1.SRB	1st SuperLiga (32/2835); 1st Kup (3/300)
2021-22	FK Crvena zvezda	1.SRB	1st SuperLiga (30/2700); 1st Kup (4/360)
2022-23	FK Crvena zvezda	1.SRB	1st SuperLiga (33/2970); 1st Kup (4/343)
2023-24	ŠK Slovan Bratislava	1.SVK	liga (current season)

CONTINENTAL FOOTBALL		UEFA	HIGHLIGHTS (MP/MIN)
2014-15	PFC Ludogrets	UEFA	UEFA Champions League (1/90)
2015-16	PFC Ludogrets	UEFA	UEFA Qualifying Champions League (0/0)
2016-17	PFC Ludogrets	UEFA	Qualifying (0/0); UEFA Champions League (1/90)
2017-18	FK Crvena zvezda (Red Star)	UEFA	Qualifying (4/360); Rof32 UEFA Europa League (8/720)
2018-19	FK Crvena zvezda	UEFA	Qualifying (8/750); UEFA Champions League (6/540)
2019-20	FK Crvena zvezda	UEFA	Qualifying (8/750); UEFA Champions League (6/540)
2020-21	FK Crvena zvezda	UEFA	UEFA Qualifying Champions League (3/300)
	FK Crvena zvezda	UEFA	Qualifying (1/90); Rof32 UEFA Europa League (8/720)
2021-22	FK Crvena zvezda	UEFA	UEFA Qualifying Champions League (4/360)
	FK Crvena zvezda	UEFA	Qualifying (2/180); L16 UEFA Europa League (7/630)
2022-23	FK Crvena zvezda	UEFA	Qualifying Champions League (4/360); UEFA Europa League (6/540)
2023-24	ŠK Slovan Bratislava	UEFA	Qualifying Champions League (6/540); UEL Qualifying (2/180) UEFA Europa Conference League

BORJAN, NIKOLA SRB / GRAFICAR BELGRAD

Goalkeeper. Born 2004, Burlington, ON, CAN. Grew up in Burlington, ON, CAN. Dominant right foot. Youth clubs: Hamilton Serbians, FK Crvena zvezda (Serbia), Graficar Belgrad (Serbia)

BORUTSKIE, BRAYDEN

Centre back. Born 2001. Grew up in Bradford, ON, CAN. Height 188. Dominant right foot. Youth clubs: Glen Shields FC, Bradford Eagles, Kleinburg Nobleton, Toronto FC Academy
School: Liberty University, West Virginia University

SEASON	CLUB	NATION	HIGHLIGHTS (MP/MIN)
2018	Toronto FC Academy	CAN	4th League1 Ontario (2/109)
2022	Simcoe County Rovers FC	CAN	5th League1 Ontario (5/114)

BOSSENBERRY, ANTONE TORONTO FC ACADEMY

Midfielder. Born 2008, Kitchener, ON, CAN. Grew up in Toronto, ON, CAN. Height 168 cm. Dominant right foot. Youth clubs: Toronto Brazilian Soccer Academy, Pumitas CU Futbol AC, Boston Bolts Academy, Weston FC Academy, Inter Miami CF Academy, Toronto FC Academy

BOUFFARD, THOMAS CF MONTRÉAL U-23

FOOTBALLERS

Centre back. Born 2005, Montréal, QC, CAN. Grew up in Montréal, QC, CAN. Dominant right foot. Youth clubs: AS St-Lambert, Académie Impact de Montréal

SEASON	CLUB	NATION	HIGHLIGHTS (MP/MIN)
2022	CF Montréal U-23	CAN	6th PLSQ (7/446)
2023	CF Montréal U-23	CAN	5th Ligue1 Québec

BOURGEOIS, MAXIME
Centre back. Born 2002, Granby, QC, CAN. Height 171 cm. Youth clubs: CS Les Cosmos de Granby, Académie de l'Impact de Montréal

BRAULT-GUILLARD, ZACHARY
Fullback. Born 1998, Delmas, HAI. Grew up Montréal, QC, CAN & Lyon, FRA. Height 173 cm. Dominant right foot. Youth clubs: Club Sportif Lagnieu, Ain Sud Foot, Olympique Lyonnais
Honours: Concacaf champion (2021-22), Canadian Championship (2019, 2021)
1st #CANMNT: 2018-10-16 at Toronto, ON, CAN (v. DMA)

SEASON	CLUB	NATION	HIGHLIGHTS (MP/MIN/G)	G
2016-17	Olympique Lyon B	4.FRA	C4th Championnat CFA Groupe C (2/66)	
2017-18	Olympique Lyon B	4.FRA	B11th National 2 Groupe B (15/1242)	
2018-19	Olympique Lyon B	4.FRA	x- National 2 Groupe A (14/1141/1g)	1
2019	Impact de Montréal	1.CAN	18th MLS (13/871); 1st CanChamp (2/180)	
2020	Impact de Montréal	Concacaf	QF Champions League (4/315)	
	Impact de Montréal	1.CAN	18th MLS (21/1789); L16 MLS is Back (1/90); Playoffs (1/90)	
2021	CF Montréal	1.CAN	18th MLS (30/2056/2g); 1st CanChamp (3/172)	2
2022	CF Montréal	Concacaf	QF Champions League (4/123)	
	CF Montréal	1.CAN	3rd MLS (18/619/4g); QF Playoffs (1/11); SF CanChamp (2/104)	4
2023	CF Montréal	1.CAN	20th MLS (24/1307/1g); 2nd CanChamp (4/224/1g); Leagues (2/98)	2

BREZA, SEBASTIAN — CF MONTRÉAL
Goalkeeper. Born 1998, Ottawa, ON, CAN. Grew up Montréal, QC, CAN. Height 196 cm. Dominant right foot. Youth clubs: FS Salaberry, CS Sainte-Julie, Palermo
Honours: Canadian Championship (2021)

SEASON	CLUB	NATION	HIGHLIGHTS (MP/MIN)
2014	Rafales Sainte-Julie U-16	CAN	6th U-16 Cup
2016-17	Palermo FC	1.ITA	Serie A (0/0)
2017-18	SS Monopoli	3.ITA	x- Serie C Girone C (0/0)
	Potenza Calcio	4.ITA	H1st Serie D Girone H (29/2610)
2018-19	Potenza Calcio	3.ITA	C5th Serie C Girone C (8/720)
2019-20	Bologna FC	1.ITA	Serie A (0/0)
	Potenza Calcio	3.ITA	C4th Serie C Girone C (7/630); R2 Coppa Italia (1/1)
2020-21	Bologna FC	1.ITA	Serie A (0/0)
2021	CF Montréal	1.CAN	18th MLS (8/720); 1st CanChamp (3/240)
2022	CF Montréal	Concacaf	QF Champions League (4/360)
	CF Montréal	1.CAN	3rd MLS (23/2070); QF Playoffs (0/0)
2022-23	Carrarese	3.ITA	B4th Serie C Girone B (14/1260); Playoff (1/1)
2023-24	Yverdon Sport FC	1.SUI	x- Super League (5/450); 2R Coupe (2/180)

BRIENZA, EMILIANO
Midfielder. Born 2002, Puerto Vallarta, JA, MEX. Grew up Coquitlam, BC, CAN. Height 180 cm. Youth clubs: Nacional (Mexico), Coquitlam Metro-Ford SC, Vancouver Whitecaps FC Academy

SEASON	CLUB	NATION	HIGHLIGHTS (MP/MIN/G)	G
2022	Vancouver Whitecaps FC	1.CAN	17th MLS (1/2)	
	Vanc. Whitecaps FC 2	CAN-3.US	14th MLS NEXT Pro (21/996/4g)	4

BRYM, CHARLES-ANDREAS — NED / SPARTA ROTTERDAM
Forward. Born 1998, Colombes, FRA. Grew up Saguenay, QC, CAN. Height 182 cm. Youth clubs: CS Jonquière, Académie de l'Impact de Montréal, Gazélec Ajaccio (France), Royal Excel Mouscron (Belgium), SV Zulte Waregem (Belgium)
Honours: Concacaf champion (2021-22)
1st #CANMNT: 2020-01-7 at Irvine, CA, USA (v. BRB)

SEASON	CLUB	NATION	HIGHLIGHTS (MP/MIN/G)	G

MEN'S FOOTBALLERS | 59

2017-18	Lille OSC B	4.FRA	C11th National 2 Groupe C (6/357)	
2018-19	Lille OSC B	4.FRA	D4th National 2 Groupe D (19/1224/10g)	10
2019-20	Belenenses SAD	1.POR	x- Primeira (1/10)	
	Lille OSC B	4.FRA	A14th National 2 Groupe A (5/5/1g)	1
2020-21	Royal Excel Mouscron	2.BEL	18th Championnat (7/198); R6 Beker (1/15)	
2021-22	FC Eindhoven	2.NED	3rd Eerste Division (26/1943); Playoffs (4/325/1g); R1 Beker (1/90)	1
2022-23	Sparta Rotterdam	1.NED	x- Eredivisie (2/9)	
	FC Eindhoven	2.NED	8th Eerste Division (29/2424/11g); Playoffs (2/170); R2 Beker (2/210/1g)	12
2023-24	Sparta Rotterdam	1.NED	Eredivisie (current season); Beker (1/90/1g)	

BUCHANAN, TAJON
ITA / FC INTER MILAN
Winger. Born 1999, Toronto, ON, CAN. Grew up Brampton, ON, CAN. Height 183 cm. Youth clubs: Brampton YSC, Mississauga SC Falcons, Real Colorado (USA)
School: Syracuse University
Honours: Concacaf champion (2021-22), MLS Supporters' Shield (2021), Championnat de Belgique (2021-22), Supercoupe de Belgique (2022), Supercoppa Italiana (2024)

CANADA INTERNATIONAL
1 FIFA World Cup: Group phase at Qatar 2022
1 Concacaf medal: Silver at CNL 2022-23
1st #CANMNT: 2021-06-5 at Bradenton, FL, USA (v. ARU)

SEASON	CLUB	NATION	HIGHLIGHTS (MP/MIN/G)	G
2017	Sigma FC	CAN	W2nd League1 Ontario (2/109/1g)	1
2018	Sigma FC	CAN	2nd League1 Ontario (7/435/2g)	2
2019	New England Revolution	1.USA	14th MLS (10/391); Playoffs (0/0); L16 US Cup (1/37)	
2020	New England Revolution	1.USA	15th MLS (23/1084/2g); L16 MLS is Back (1/67); SF Playoffs (4/277/1g)	3
2021	New England Revolution	1.USA	1st MLS (27/1749/8g); QF Playoffs (1/120/1g)	9
2021-22	Club Brugge KV	1.BEL	2nd Championnat (9/731); Playoff (5/444/1g); SF Beker (1/90)	1
2022-23	Club Brugge KV	UEFA	L16 UEFA Champions League (6/522)	
	Club Brugge KV	1.BEL	4th Championnat (22/1627/1g); Playoff (2/134); L16 Beker (2/180)	1
2023-24	Club Brugge KV	UEFA	Qualifying (5/391/1g); Conference League (3/214)	1
	Club Brugge KV	1.BEL	x- Championnat (12/833/2g); L16 Beker (0/0)	2
	FC Internazionale Milano	1.ITA	Serie A (current season)	

BUNBURY, MATAEO
USA / COLUMBUS CREW 2
Forward. Born 2005, Northfield, MN, USA. Grew up Prior Lake, MN, USA. Height 180 cm. Youth clubs: Lakeville SC, North Oaks SC, TwinStars Academy, Minneapolis United SC, Minnesota United Academy, Sporting Kansas City Academy.

SEASON	CLUB	NATION	HIGHLIGHTS (MP/MIN/G)	G
2021	Sporting Kansas City II	2.USA	E15th USL (7/401)	
2022	Sporting Kansas City II	3.USA	x- MLS NEXT Pro (10/662/4g)	4
2022	Birmingham Legion FC	2.USA	E4th USL (13/206/1g); Playoffs (0/0)	1
2023	Columbus Crew 2	3.USA	5th MLS NEXT Pro (18/839/4g)	4

BUSCHMAN-DORMOND, CARSON
Winger. Born 2002, Vancouver, BC, CAN. Height 188 cm. Dominant left foot.

SEASON	CLUB	NATION	HIGHLIGHTS (MP/MIN/G)	G
2021	Viljandi JK Tulevik	1.EST	x- Meistriliiga (12/1080/2g); SF Cup (2/210)	2
2021-22	FC Zürich	1.SUI	1st Super League (0/0)	
2023	York United FC	CAN	5th CPL (5/61); 5th Playoffs (1/1)	

BUSTOS, MARCO
SWE / IFK VÄRNAMO
Forward. Born 1996, Winnipeg, MB, CAN. Height 167 cm. Dominant left foot. Youth clubs: Garden City Community Centre, FC Northwest Winnipeg, Vancouver Whitecaps FC Residency
Honours: CPL Championship (2021)
1st #CANMNT: 2015-10-13 at Washington, DC, USA (v. GHA)

SEASON	CLUB	NATION	HIGHLIGHTS (MP/MIN/G)	G
2009	Manitoba U-14	CAN	3rd Canada Soccer All Stars U-14	
2010	FC Northwest U-16 Winnipeg	CAN	2nd U-16 Cup	
2010	Manitoba U-14	CAN	5th Canada Soccer All Stars U-14	
2011	Sask'toba U-16	CAN	5th Canada Soccer All Stars U-16	

2014	Vancouver Whitecaps FC	1.CAN	3rd CanChamp (1/64)	
	Vanc. Whitecaps FC U-23	CAN-4.US	USL PDL	
2015	Vancouver Whitecaps FC	1.CAN	3rd MLS (1/29)	
	Vanc. Whitecaps FC 2	CAN-2.US	W11th USL (17/1356/7g)	7
2015-16	Vancouver Whitecaps FC	Concacaf	16th Champions League (4/138)	
2016	Vancouver Whitecaps FC	1.CAN	16th MLS (3/63); 2nd CanChamp (1/58)	
	Vanc. Whitecaps FC 2	CAN-2.US	W6th USL (19/1447/7g); Playoffs (2/179)	7
2016-17	Vancouver Whitecaps FC	Concacaf	SF Champions League (1/26)	
2017	Vancouver Whitecaps FC	1.CAN	SF CanChamp (2/25)	
	Vanc. Whitecaps FC 2	CAN-2.US	W14th USL (21/1813/8g)	
2017-18	CA Zacatepec	2.MEX	6th Ascenso Clausura (5/92); QF Liguilla (1/26); SF Copa MX Clausura (2/123/1g)	1
2018-19	CA Zacatepec	2.MEX	x- Copa MX Apertura (1/55)	1
2018	OKC Energy FC	2.USA	W10th USL (9/485/1g)	1
2019	OKC Energy FC	2.USA	x- USL (7/185)	
	Valour FC	1.CAN	6th CPL (25/2249/7g); CanChamp (2/180/1g)	8
2020	Pacific FC	1.CAN	3rd CPL (10/842/5g)	5
2021	Pacific FC	1.CAN	3rd CPL (17/1352/7g); 1st Playoffs (0/0); SF CanChamp (1/45)	7
2022	Pacific FC	Concacaf	L16 Concacaf League (4/325/1g)	1
	Pacific FC	1.CAN	4th CPL (28/2224/2g); SF Playoffs (2/180); QF CanChamp (1/90)	2
2023	IFK Värnamo	1.SWE	Allsvenskan (8/614/3g); Cupen (1/58)	3

CALDEIRA, MARCUS
Forward. Born 2004, Mississauga, ON, CAN. Height 185 cm. Dominant right foot. Youth clubs: Mississauga SC Falcons, Erin Mills SC, Sigma FC
School: West Virginia University

SEASON	CLUB	NATION	HIGHLIGHTS (MP/MIN/G)	G
2021	Sigma FC	CAN	9th League1 Ontario (10/586/1g)	1
2022	Sigma FC	CAN	9th League1 Ontario (13/987/4g)	1
	Forge FC Hamilton	1.CAN	2nd CPL (3/41); QF CanChamp (1/1)	

CAMARA, MAMADI
Winger. Born 1995, Montréal, QC, CAN. Height 188 cm. Dominant right foot. Youth clubs: CS Longueuil
School: Simon Fraser University

SEASON	CLUB	NATION	HIGHLIGHTS (MP/MIN/G)	G
2009	Québec U-14	CAN	2nd Canada Soccer All Stars U-14	
2011	Longueuil U-16	CAN	2nd U-16 Cup	
2012	Longueuil U-18	CAN	4th U-18 Cup	
2013	Longueuil U-18	CAN	4th U-18 Cup	
2014	CS Longueuil	CAN	1st PLSQ (2/?)	
2015	CS Longueuil	CAN	4th PLSQ (9/?/3g)	3
2017	TSS Rovers FC	CAN-4.US	USL PDL (8/663/2g)	2
2018	Calgary Foothills SC	CAN-4.US	USL PDL (8/347)	
2019	CS Saint-Hubert	CAN	5th PLSQ (4/335/3g)	3
	Surrey Central City Breakers FC	CAN	1st CS National Championships	
2020	Colorado Springs Switchbacks	2.USA	W13th USL (14/352/1g)	1
2021	Celtix du Haut-Richelieu	CAN	3rd PLSQ (10/886/11g)	11
	HFX Wanderers FC	1.CAN	4th CPL (10/434/1g)	1
2022	FC Edmonton	1.CAN	8th CPL (26/2001/4g); CanChamp (1/90)	4

CAMARGO, SERGIO   CAVALRY FC
Midfielder. Born 1994, Cucuta, COL. Grew up Newmarket, ON, CAN. Height 170 cm. Youth clubs: Unionville-Milliken SC, Toronto FC Academy
School: Coastal Carolina University, Syracuse University
Honours: Canadian Championship (2017), CPL North Star Shield (2023), USL PDL Championship (2015, 2018)

SEASON	CLUB	NATION	HIGHLIGHTS (MP/MIN/G)	G
2008	Unionville-Milliken SC U-14 Strikers	CAN	1st U-14 Cup	
2014	K-W United FC	CAN-4.US	USL PDL	
2015	K-W United FC	CAN-4.US	USL PDL; 1st PDL Playoffs	
2016	K-W United FC	CAN-4.US	USL PDL (5/384/4g)	4

2017	Toronto FC	1.CAN	1st CanChamp (0/0)	
	Toronto FC II	CAN-2.US	E15th USL (18/1082/1g)	1
2018	Calgary Foothills SC	CAN-4.US	USL PDL (10/613/4g); 1st PDL Playoffs (2/95)	4
2019	Cavalry FC	1.CAN	2nd CPL (20/1260/6g); SF CanChamp (6/433/2g)	8
2020	Cavalry FC	1.CAN	4th CPL (2/127/1g)	1
2021	Cavalry FC	1.CAN	2nd CPL (22/1237/4g); SF Playoffs (1/76); QF CanChamp (2/115)	4
2022	Cavalry FC	1.CAN	3rd CPL (14/785/2g); QF CanChamp (1/23)	2
2023	Cavalry FC	1.CAN	1st CPL (25/1417/6g); 2nd Playoffs (3/234)	6

CAMBRIDGE, BRANDON — CHARLOTTE FC

Winger. Born 2002, Brooklyn, NY, USA. Grew up Chilliwack, BC, CAN. Height 183 cm. Youth clubs: Fraser Valley, Vancouver Whitecaps FC Academy
School: University of Portland

SEASON	CLUB	NATION	HIGHLIGHTS (MP/MIN/G)	G
2021	PDX FC	4.USA	NW-2nd USL League Two (4/329/1g)	1
2022	PDX FC	4.USA	NW-5th USL League Two (5/351)	
2023	Charlotte FC	1.USA	19th MLS (9/128); L16 Cup (2/118); QF Leagues (2/12)	
	Crown Legacy FC	3.USA	2nd MLS NEXT Pro (9/722/4g); QF Playoffs (1/90)	4

CAMERON, JAMES — VANCOUVER FC

Right back. Born 2005, North Vancouver, BC, CAN. Height 183 cm. Dominant right foot. Youth clubs: North Vancouver FC, Mountain FC, Blaise SA

SEASON	CLUB	NATION	HIGHLIGHTS (MP/MIN/G)	G
2022	British Columbia U-18	CAN	5th Canada Games (4/264/1g)	1
2023	Vancouver FC	1.CAN	7th CPL (19/1504/1g)	1
	Langley Unity FC	3.CAN	4th League1 BC (3/95)	1

CAMPAGNA, CRISTIAN — HALIFAX WANDERERS FC

Centre back. Born 2001, Vancouver, BC, CAN. Grew up Surrey, BC, CAN. Height 180 cm. Dominant left foot. Youth clubs: Surrey United SC, Vancouver Whitecaps FC Academy
School: University at Albany

SEASON	CLUB	NATION	HIGHLIGHTS (MP/MIN)
2015	Surrey United SC U-14	CAN	2nd U-14 Cup
2022	Vanc. Whitecaps FC 2	CAN-3.US	x- MLS NEXT Pro (19/1709)
	HFX Wanderers FC	1.CAN	7th CPL (7/563)
2023	Halifax Wanderers FC	1.CAN	3rd CPL (10/539); CanChamp (1/90)

CAMPAGNA, MATTEO

Centre back. Born 2004, Vancouver, BC, CAN. Grew up Surrey, BC, CAN. Height 188 cm. Dominant right foot. Youth clubs: Surrey United SC, Vancouver Whitecaps FC Academy

SEASON	CLUB	NATION	HIGHLIGHTS (MP/MIN)	
2021	Vancouver Whitecaps FC	1.CAN	12th MLS (0/0)	
2021	York United FC	1.CAN	4th CPL (5/288); SF Playoffs (0/0)	
2022	Vancouver Whitecaps FC	1.CAN	17th MLS (0/0)	
	Vanc. Whitecaps FC 2	CAN-3.US	14th MLS NEXT Pro (16/1181)	
2023	Vancouver Whitecaps FC	Concacaf	QF Champions League (1/3); L32 Leagues Cup (0/0)	
	Vancouver Whitecaps FC	1.CAN	13th MLS (0/0)	
	Vanc. Whitecaps FC 2	CAN-3.US	21st MLS NEXT Pro (13/1145/1g)	1

CAMPBELL, DANTE — VALOUR FC

Midfielder. Born 1999, Etobicoke, ON, CAN. Grew up Brampton, ON, CAN. Height 178 cm. Dominant right foot. Youth clubs: Brampton East SC, Toronto FC Academy

SEASON	CLUB	NATION	HIGHLIGHTS (MP/MIN/G)	G
2016	Toronto FC II	CAN-2.US	E12th USL (1/24)	
	TFC Academy	CAN	W3rd League1 Ontario (18/1139/8g); USL PDL (10/505)	8
2017	Toronto FC II	CAN-2.US	E15th USL (11/412)	
	TFC Academy	CAN	W3rd League1 Ontario (10/737/1g)	1
2018	Toronto FC II	CAN-2.US	E16th USL (22/1759/1g)	1
	TFC Academy	CAN	4th League1 Ontario (2/162)	
2019	Toronto FC	Concacaf	L16 Champions League (0/0)	
	Toronto FC II	CAN-3.US	7th USL League One (15/1289)	

2020	Valour FC	1.CAN	6th CPL (5/228)	
2021	Toronto FC II	CAN-3.US	7th USL League One (20/978)	
2022	LA Galaxy II	2.USA	W11th USL (30/955/1g)	1
2023	Valour FC	1.CAN	8th CPL (25/2165/1g); CanChamp (1/45)	1

CAMPBELL, TERRAN — FORGE FC HAMILTON
Forward. Born 1998, Surrey, BC, CAN. Height 173 cm. Dominant left foot. Youth clubs: South Burnaby Metro SC, Vancouver Whitecaps FC Academy
Honours: CPL Championship (2021, 2022, 2023)

SEASON	CLUB	NATION	HIGHLIGHTS (MP/MIN/G)	G
2015	Vanc. Whitecaps FC 2	CAN-2.US	W11th USL (1/2)	
2016	Vanc. Whitecaps FC 2	CAN-2.US	W6th USL (8/50)	
2017	Vanc. Whitecaps FC 2	CAN-2.US	W14th USL (25/1788/3g)	3
2018	Fresno FC	2.USA	W12th USL (5/47); R4 US Cup (2/187/1g)	1
2019	Pacific FC	1.CAN	5th CPL (28/2332/11g); CanChamp (1/45)	12
2020	Pacific FC	1.CAN	3rd CPL (10/485/1g)	1
2021	Pacific FC	1.CAN	3rd CPL (26/1627/10g); 1st Playoffs (2/210/1g); SF CanChamp (2/157/2g)	13
2022('20)	Forge FC Hamilton	1.CAN	2nd CanChamp (1/90)	
2022	Forge FC Hamilton	Concacaf	L16 Champions League (2/139)	
	Forge FC Hamilton	1.CAN	2nd CPL (27/1414/6g); 1st Playoffs (2/13); QF CanChamp (2/156/1g)	7
2023	Forge FC Hamilton	1.CAN	2nd CPL (28/1918/10g); 1st Playoffs (2/190); SF CanChamp (3/171)	10

CAMPBEAU, MAXWELL
Goalkeeper. Born 2005. Grew up Coquitlam, BC, CAN.
School: University of Toronto

SEASON	CLUB	NATION	HIGHLIGHTS (MP/MIN)
2023	Vanc. Whitecaps FC 2	CAN-3.US	21st MLS NEXT Pro (0/0)

CARDUCCI, MARCO — CAVALRY FC
Goalkeeper. Born 1996, Calgary, AB, CAN. Height 185 cm. Dominant right foot. Youth clubs: Calgary MSB United, Calgary Villains, Vancouver Whitecaps Residency
Honours: Canadian Championship (2015), CPL North Star Shield (2023), USL PDL Championship (2018)

SEASON	CLUB	NATION	HIGHLIGHTS (MP/MIN)
2010	Alberta U-14	CAN	3rd Canada Soccer All Stars U-14
2011	Alberta U-16	CAN	4th Canada Soccer All Stars U-16
2014	Vancouver Whitecaps FC	1.CAN	3rd CanChamp (2/210)
2015	Vancouver Whitecaps FC	1.CAN	1st CanChamp (0/0)
	Vanc. Whitecaps FC 2	CAN-2.US	W11th USL (9/810)
2015-16	Vancouver Whitecaps FC	Concacaf	16th Champions League (0/0)
2016	Vancouver Whitecaps FC	1.CAN	2nd CanChamp (0/0)
	Vanc. Whitecaps FC 2	CAN-2.US	W6th USL (7/630)
2016-17	Vancouver Whitecaps FC	Concacaf	SF Champions League (0/0)
2017	Rio Grande Valley Toros	2.USA	W11th USL (6/540)
2018	Calgary Foothills SC	CAN-4.US	USL PDL (11/945); 1st PDL Playoffs (4/390)
2019	Cavalry FC	1.CAN	2nd CPL (25/2250); SF CanChamp (4/360)
2020	Cavalry FC	1.CAN	4th CPL (9/810)
2021	Cavalry FC	1.CAN	2nd CPL (24/2160); SF Playoffs (1/120); QF CanChamp (1/90)
2022	Cavalry FC	1.CAN	3rd CPL (24/2160); SF Playoffs (2/180); QF CanChamp (2/180)
2023	Cavalry FC	1.CAN	1st CPL (28/2520); 2nd Playoffs (3/300); CanChamp (1/90)

CARLOS, JACOB
Midfielder. Born 2001, Mississauga, ON, CAN. Height 175 cm. Youth clubs: Erin Mills SC, IK Freij (Sweden), Académico de Viseu (Portugal), again Erin Mills SC, Toronto FC Academy
School: Toronto Metropolitan University

SEASON	CLUB	NATION	HIGHLIGHTS (MP/MIN)
2022	Valour FC	1.CAN	5th CPL (12/441); CanChamp (1/9)
2023	North Toronto Nitros	CAN	10th League1 Ontario (4/255/1g)

CARON, RENAUD — CF MONTRÉAL U-23
Winger. Born 2004, LaSalle, QC, CAN. Grew up Saint-Hubert, QC, CAN. Height 172 cm. Youth clubs: CS St-Hubert,

Académie Impact de Montréal

SEASON	CLUB	NATION	HIGHLIGHTS (MP/MIN/G)	G
2022	CF Montréal U-23	CAN	6th PLSQ (12/616/1g)	1
2023	CF Montréal U-23	CAN	5th Ligue1 Québec	

CARTER, AJAHNI   TORONTO FC ACADEMY
Left back. Born 2008, Toronto, ON, CAN. Height 163 cm. Dominant left foot. Youth clubs: Scarborough Timbits, Toronto International Youth FC, Thornhill Bolts, Toronto FC Academy

CASTELLO, SEBASTIAN   FORGE FC HAMILTON
Midfielder. Born 2003, Mississauga, ON, CAN. Height 175 cm. Dominant right foot. Youth clubs: Dixie SC, Oakville SC, RVDL Soccer Academy, Sigma FC

SEASON	CLUB	NATION	HIGHLIGHTS (MP/MIN/G)	G
2021	Sigma FC	CAN	9th League1 Ontario (11/741/1g)	1
	Forge FC Hamilton	Concacaf	SF Concacaf League (0/0)	
	Forge FC Hamilton	1.CAN	1st CPL (6/98/1g); SF CanChamp (0/0)	1
2022('20)	Forge FC Hamilton	1.CAN	2nd CanChamp (0/0)	
2022	Forge FC Hamilton	1.CAN	2nd CPL (6/70); QF CanChamp (1/8)	
2023	Forge FC Hamilton	1.CAN	2nd CPL (2/2)	

CATALANO, GIANLUCA   TORONTO FC II
Goalkeeper. Born 2000, Etobicoke, ON, CAN. Grew up Toronto, ON, CAN. Height 185 cm. Dominant right foot. Youth clubs: Kleinburg Nobleton SC, Toronto FC Academy
School: University of Connecticut

SEASON	CLUB	NATION	HIGHLIGHTS (MP/MIN)
2016	TFC Academy	CAN	W3rd League1 Ontario (9/765)
2017	Toronto FC II	CAN-2.US	E15th USL (0/0)
	TFC Academy	CAN	W3rd League1 Ontario (17/1486)
2018	Toronto FC II	CAN-2.US	E16th USL (5/434)
	TFC Academy	CAN	4th League1 Ontario (2/180)
2019	AC Connecticut	4.USA	USL League Two
2022	York United FC	1.CAN	6th CPL (1/90); SF CanChamp (0/0)
	Vaughan Azzurri	CAN	1st League1 Ontario (8/720); 1st Playoffs (2/180)
2023	Toronto FC II	CAN-3.US	23rd MLS NEXT Pro (3/270)
	Vaughan Azzurri	CAN	3rd League1 Ontario (4/360); CanChamp (1/90)

CATAVOLO, MATTHEW   TORONTO FC II
Midfielder. Born 2003, Montréal, QC, CAN. Grew up Laval, QC, CAN. Height 163 cm. Dominant right foot. Youth clubs: ASTMP St-Michel, Etoile de l'Est Laval, Académie de l'Impact de Montréal

SEASON	CLUB	NATION	HIGHLIGHTS (MP/MIN)
2022	Valour FC	1.CAN	5th CPL (16/424); CanChamp (1/21)
2023	Toronto FC II	CAN-3.US	23rd MLS NEXT Pro (20/1211/1g)

CAVALLINI, LUCAS   MEX / PUEBLA FC
Forward. Born 1992, Toronto, ON, CAN. Grew up Mississauga, ON, CAN. Height 180 cm. Dominant left foot. Youth clubs: Club Uruguay Toronto, Weston SC, North York Hearts SC, Clarkson SC
Honours: Concacaf champion (2021-22), Canadian Championship (2022)

CANADA INTERNATIONAL
1 FIFA World Cup: Group phase at Qatar 2022
1 Concacaf medal: Silver at CNL 2022-23
1st #CANMNT: 2012-08-15 at Lauderhill, FL, USA (v. TRI)

SEASON	CLUB	NATION	HIGHLIGHTS (MP/MIN/G)	G
2012-13	CA Juventud	1.URU	8th Primera División (25/1676/10g)	10
2013-14	Club Nacional	1.URU	2nd Primera División (4/129)	
	CA Fénix	1.URU	9th Primera División (13/783/2g)	2
2014-15	CA Fénix	1.URU	9th Primera División (27/2367/14g)	14
2015-16	CA Fénix	1.URU	9th Primera División (25/2133/7g)	7
2016	CA Fénix	CONMEBOL	Copa Sudamericana (2/171)	
	CA Fénix	1.URU	9th Primera División (11/947/5g)	5
2017	CA Peñarol	CONMEBOL	Copa Libertadores (2/28)	
	CA Peñarol	1.URU	1st Primera División (16/721/6g)	6

				G
2017-18	Puebla FC	1.MEX	15th Liga MX Apertura (9/699/4g); Copa (1/44); 14th Liga MX Clausura (16/1427/8g)	12
2018-19	Puebla FC	1.MEX	12th Liga MX Apertura (17/1530/6g); L16 Copa (1/23); 10th Liga MX Clausura (16/1440/5g); L16 Copa (3/270/1g)	12
2019-20	Puebla FC	1.MEX	18th Liga MX Apertura (12/1213/4g); Copa (1/45)	4
2020	Vancouver Whitecaps FC	1.CAN	17th MLS (18/1457/6g)	6
2021	Vancouver Whitecaps FC	1.CAN	12th MLS (21/1229/3g); Playoffs (1/17)	3
2022	Vancouver Whitecaps FC	1.CAN	17th MLS (24/1519/9g); 1st CanChamp (4/287)	9
	Vanc. Whitecaps FC 2	CAN-3.US	14th MLS NEXT Pro (1/45)	
2022-23	Club Tijuana	1.MEX	15th Liga MX Clausura (12/720/2g)	2
2023-24	Club Tijuana	1.MEX	13th Liga MX Apertura (12/374/1g)	1
	Puebla FC	1.MEX	Liga MX Clausura (current season)	

CEBARA, STEFAN — GIB / EUROPA FC

Centre back. Born 1991, Zadar, CRO. Grew up Calgary, AB & Windsor, ON, CAN. Height 188 cm. Dominant right foot. Youth clubs: Windsor FC Nationals, Riverside Rebels, FK Rad (Croatia)
1st #CANMNT: 2013-03-22 at Doha, QAT (v. JPN)

SEASON	CLUB	NATION	HIGHLIGHTS (MP/MIN/G)	G
2010-11	Zalaegerszegi TE	1.HUN	4th Nemzeti Bajnokság I (2/24); SF Kupa (3/186/1g)	1
2012-13	NK Celje	1.SVN	5th Prva slovenska liga (17/732); SF Pokal (3/175)	
2013-14	NK Celje	UEFA	UEFA Europa League Qualifying (1/45)	
	NK Celje	1.SVN	8th Prva slovenska liga (0/0)	
2014-15	FC ViOn Zlaté Moravce	1.SVK	10th 1. slovenská liga (5/231)	
2015-16	FC ViOn Zlaté Moravce	1.SVK	9th 1. slovenská liga (26/1116/2g); QF Cup (3/125)	2
2017	FK Utenis Utena	1.LTU	6th A Lyga (8/540)	
2017-18	FK Vojvodina	1.SRB	8th SuperLiga (5/131); QF Kup (1/44/1g)	1
2020	Valour FC	1.CAN	6th CPL (6/455)	
2021	Valour FC	1.CAN	5th CPL (26/2186); QF CanChamp (1/70)	
2022	Valour FC	1.CAN	5th CPL (22/1676); CanChamp (1/90)	
2023-24	Europa FC	1.GIB	Gibraltar League (current season)	

CELA, KLAIDI

Centre back. Born 1999, Mississauga, ON, CAN. Height 190 cm. Dominant right foot. Youth clubs: Mississauga SC Falcons, Toronto FC Academy
Honours: CPL Championship (2019, 2020)

SEASON	CLUB	NATION	HIGHLIGHTS (MP/MIN/G)	G
2016	TFC Academy	CAN	USL PDL (11/573); W3rd League1 Ontario (12/822)	
2018	Sigma FC	CAN	2nd League1 Ontario (1/28); 3rd Playoffs (3/270)	
2019	Forge FC Hamilton	Concacaf	Concacaf League (1/1)	
	Forge FC Hamilton	1.CAN	1st CPL (8/326/1g); CanChamp (1/9)	1
2020	Forge FC Hamilton	Concacaf	Missed Concacaf League (injured)	
	Forge FC Hamilton	1.CAN	1st CPL (2/4)	
2021	Forge FC Hamilton	Concacaf	SF Concacaf League (0/0)	
	Forge FC Hamilton	1.CAN	1st CPL (5/199); 2nd Playoffs (1/1); SF CanChamp (0/0)	
	Sigma FC	CAN	9th League1 Ontario (4/360/1g)	1
2022	Toronto FC II	CAN-3.US	7th MLS NEXT Pro (4/300); SF Playoffs (0/0)	
2023	Vaughan Azzurri	CAN	3rd League1 Ontario (2/180); CanChamp (1/90)	
	Valour FC	1.CAN	8th CPL (23/1712/2g)	2

CHANDLER, MATTHEW

Centre back. Born 2000, Toronto, ON, CAN. Height 198 cm. Dominant right foot. Youth clubs: Markham SC
School: St. John's University, University of Wisconsin-Madison

SEASON	CLUB	NATION	HIGHLIGHTS (MP/MIN)
2022	Oakville Blue Devils FC	CAN	2nd League1 Ontario (13/1044)
2023	Valour FC	1.CAN	8th CPL (1/7); CanChamp (1/90)

CHAPMAN, JAY — USA / HARTFORD ATHLETIC

Midfielder. Born 1994, Brampton, ON, CAN. Grew up Campbellford, ON, CAN. Height 183 cm. Youth clubs: Brampton East SC, Ajax SC, Toronto FC Academy
School: Michigan State University
Honours: Canadian Championship (2016, 2017, 2018), MLS Supporters' Shield (2017)

1st #CANMNT: 2017-01-22 at Devonshire Parish, BER (v. BER)

SEASON	CLUB	NATION	HIGHLIGHTS (MP/MIN/G)	G
2010	Ajax Strikers U-16	CAN	1st U-16 Cup	
2010	Ontario U-16	CAN	2nd Canada Soccer All Stars U-16	
2014	K-W United FC	CAN-4.US	USL PDL	
2015	Toronto FC	1.CAN	12th MLS (10/202); 4th CanChamp (1/16)	
	Toronto FC II	CAN-2.US	E11th USL (9/798/2g)	2
2016	Toronto FC	1.CAN	5th MLS (18/780); 1st CanChamp (1/15)	
	Toronto FC II	CAN-2.US	E12th USL (2/139)	
2017	Toronto FC	1.CAN	1st MLS (12/385/1g); 1st CanChamp (1/90/1g)	2
	Toronto FC II	CAN-2.US	E15th USL (3/270)	
2018	Toronto FC	Concacaf	2nd Champions League (1/19)	
	Toronto FC	1.CAN	19th MLS (22/982/3g); 1st CanChamp (4/269); 2nd Campeones (1/90)	3
2019	Toronto FC	Concacaf	L16 Champions League (1/13)	
	Toronto FC	1.CAN	9th MLS (17/522/2g); 2nd CanChamp (0/0)	2
	Toronto FC II	CAN-3.US	7th USL League One (1/90)	
2020	Inter Miami CF	1.USA	19th MLS (8/200); Playoffs (0/0)	
2021	Inter Miami CF	1.USA	20th MLS (25/1185)	
2021-22	Dundee FC	1.SCO	12th Premiership (2/35); QF SFA (0/0)	
2023	Colorado Springs Switchbacks	2.USA	W5th USL (27/1580/1g); L16 Playoffs (1/82)	1

CHEN, LUCA

Born 2007. Grew up in .., BC, CAN. Youth clubs: Coquitlam Metro-Ford SC, Vancouver Whitecaps FC Academy

SEASON	CLUB	NATION	HIGHLIGHTS (MP/MIN)
2023	Vanc. Whitecaps FC 2	CAN-3.US	21st MLS NEXT Pro (0/0)

CHOINIÈRE, DAVID   FORGE FC HAMILTON

Attacking midfielder. Born 1997, Saint-Jean-sur-Richelieu, QC, CAN. Grew up Saint-Alexandre, QC, CAN. Height 163 cm. Dominant right foot. Youth clubs: AS Haut-Richelieu, Académie Impact Montréal
Honours: CPL Championship (2019, 2020, 2022, 2023)

SEASON	CLUB	NATION	HIGHLIGHTS (MP/MIN/G)	G
2012	Québec U-15	CAN	2nd Canada Soccer All Stars U-15	
2016	Impact de Montréal	1.CAN	11th MLS (1/76); SF CanChamp (0/3)	
2016	FC Montréal	CAN-2.US	E14th USL (15/1093/1g)	1
2017	Impact de Montréal	1.CAN	17th MLS (3/34); 2nd CanChamp (1/90/1g)	1
2018	Impact de Montréal	1.CAN	15th MLS (1/12)	
2019	Forge FC Hamilton	Concacaf	L16 Concacaf League (3/131/2g)	2
	Forge FC Hamilton	1.CAN	1st CPL (18/998/2g); CanChamp (2/125)	2
2020	Forge FC Hamilton	Concacaf	QF Concacaf League (4/300/1g)	1
	Forge FC Hamilton	1.CAN	1st CPL (10/511/1g)	
2021	Forge FC Hamilton	Concacaf	SF Concacaf League (8/382/1g)	1
	Forge FC Hamilton	1.CAN	1st CPL (22/1188/4g); 1st Playoffs (1/22); SF CanChamp (2/85/1g)	5
2022('20)	Forge FC Hamilton	1.CAN	2nd CanChamp (1/90)	
2022	Forge FC Hamilton	Concacaf	L16 Champions League (2/133/1g)	1
	Forge FC Hamilton	1.CAN	2nd CPL (26/1675/4g); 1st Playoffs (3/269/2g); QF CanChamp (2/93)	4
2023	Forge FC Hamilton	1.CAN	2nd CPL (15/970/2g); 1st Playoffs (2/20); SF CanChamp (2/155)	2

CHOINIÈRE, MATHIEU   CF MONTRÉAL

Midfielder. Born 1999, Saint-Jean-sur-Richelieu, QC, CAN. Grew up St-Alexandre, QC, CAN. Height 173 cm. Dominant right foot. Youth clubs: AS Haut-Richelieu, Académie Impact Montréal
Honours: Canadian Championship (2019, 2021)
1st #CANMNT: 2023-10-13 at Niigata, JPN (v. JPN)

SEASON	CLUB	NATION	HIGHLIGHTS (MP/MIN/G)	G
2018	Impact de Montréal	1.CAN	15th MLS (5/82); SF CanChamp (1/4)	
2019	Impact de Montréal	1.CAN	18th MLS (17/681); 1st CanChamp (2/156)	
2020	Impact de Montréal	1.CAN	18th MLS (0/0); L16 MLS is Back (0/0)	
2021	CF Montréal	1.CAN	18th MLS (26/1992/2g); 1st CanChamp (1/90)	2
2022	CF Montréal	Concacaf	QF Champions League (2/173)	

	CF Montréal	1.CAN	3rd MLS (26/1384/2g); QF Playoffs (1/10); SF CanChamp (2/107)	2
2023	CF Montréal	1.CAN	20th MLS (28/2436/5g); 2nd CanChamp (4/315); Leagues (2/180/1g)	6
	MLS All-Stars	1.USA	MLS All-Star Game (1/21)	

CHRISTEY, QUENTIN — TORONTO FC ACADEMY
Midfielder. Born 2007, Toronto, ON, CAN. Grew up Milton, ON, CAN. Height 168 cm. Dominant right foot. Youth clubs: Milton YSC, Toronto FC Academy

CHRISTOFFERSEN, NICK
Goalkeeper. Born 2001, Montréal, QC, CAN. Grew up in Toronto, ON, CAN. Height 188. Youth clubs: Westmount SC, North Toronto SC, Toronto FC Academy
School: University of Pennsylvania

SEASON	CLUB	NATION	HIGHLIGHTS (MP/MIN)
2019	Toronto FC II	CAN-3.US	7th USL League One (0/0)

CHUKWU, JOSES — TORONTO FC ACADEMY
Forward. Born 2007, Toronto, ON, CAN. Height 178 cm. Dominant right foot. Youth clubs: Bradford Eagles SC, Toronto FC Academy

CHUKWU, RICHARD — TORONTO FC ACADEMY
Centre back. Born 2008, Toronto, ON, CAN. Height 183 cm. Dominant left foot. Youth clubs: Bradford Eagles SC, Toronto FC Academy

SEASON	CLUB	NATION	HIGHLIGHTS (MP/MIN)
2023	Toronto FC II	CAN-3.US	23rd MLS NEXT Pro (0/0)

CHUNG, KADIN — VANCOUVER FC
Fullback. Born 1998, New Westminster, BC, CAN. Grew up Port Coquitlam, BC, CAN. Height 168 cm. Youth clubs: Coquitlam Metro Ford FC, Vancouver Whitecaps FC Residency
Honours: Canadian Championship (2022/'20), CPL Championship (2021)

SEASON	CLUB	NATION	HIGHLIGHTS (MP/MIN/G)	G
2015	Vanc. Whitecaps FC 2	CAN-2.US	W11th USL (2/101)	
2016	Vanc. Whitecaps FC 2	CAN-2.US	W6th USL (19/1572); Playoffs (3/222)	
2017	Vanc. Whitecaps FC 2	CAN-2.US	W14th USL (24/1809/2g)	2
2017-18	FC Kaiserslautern II	5.GER	Oberliga (8/431)	
2019	Pacific FC	1.CAN	5th CPL (24/2032/1g); CanChamp (1/90)	1
2020	Pacific FC	1.CAN	3rd CPL (9/765); 1st CanChamp (1/25)	
2021	Pacific FC	1.CAN	3rd CPL (24/2069/1g); 1st Playoffs (2/210); SF CanChamp (3/270)	1
2022	Toronto FC	1.CAN	27th MLS (8/451)	
	Toronto FC II	CAN-3.US	7th MLS NEXT Pro (7/372/1g); SF Playoffs (2/7)	1
2023	Vancouver FC	1.CAN	7th CPL (13/1002); CanChamp (1/90)	

CHUNG, LOGAN
Midfielder. Born 2001, New Westminster, BC, CAN. Grew up in Port Coquitlam, BC, CAN. Height 161. Youth clubs: Coquitlam Metro-Ford SC, Vancouver Whitecaps FC Academy
School: University of British Columbia

SEASON	CLUB	NATION	HIGHLIGHTS (MP/MIN)
2023	Nautsa'mawt FC	3.CAN	5th League1 BC (13/578)

CICCARELLI, TAVIO
Forward. Born 2006, Winnipeg, MB, CAN. Height 173. Dominant right foot. Youth clubs: Winnipeg Bonivital SC, Leeds United FC (England), Sheffield United FC (England)

CIMERMANCIC, MARKUS — TORONTO FC II
Midfielder. Born 2004. Grew up in Kitchener, ON, CAN. Height 183. Youth clubs: Kitchener Spirit, Toronto FC Academy

SEASON	CLUB	NATION	HIGHLIGHTS (MP/MIN)
2018	Toronto FC U-13	Concacaf	QF Concacaf Under-13 Champions League
2022	Toronto FC II	CAN-3.US	7th MLS NEXT Pro (13/887); SF Playoffs (2/88)
2023	Toronto FC	1.CAN	29th MLS (0/0)
	Toronto FC II	CAN-3.US	23rd MLS NEXT Pro (21/19/2g)

CLARKE-TOSCZAK, NIKOS
Midfielder. Born 2004, Edmonton, AB, CAN. Grew up in Edmonton, AB, CAN. Youth clubs: Edmonton Warriors SC, FC Lugano (Switzerland), Vancouver Whitecaps FC Academy

Honours: League1 BC (2023)

SEASON	CLUB	NATION	HIGHLIGHTS (MP/MIN)
2022	Vanc. Whitecaps FC Academy	3.CAN	3rd League1 BC
2023	Vanc. Whitecaps FC 2	CAN-3.US	21st MLS NEXT Pro (0/0)
	Vanc. Whitecaps FC Academy	3.CAN	3rd League1 BC (11/850); 1st Playoffs (1/90)

CLOUTIER, LOÏC — CF MONTRÉAL U-23
Centre back. Born 2004, Québec, QC, CAN. Grew up Montréal, QC, CAN. Height 179 cm. Youth clubs: FC Trois Lacs, Académie Impact de Montréal

SEASON	CLUB	NATION	HIGHLIGHTS (MP/MIN)
2022	CF Montréal U-23	CAN	6th PLSQ (12/943)
2023	CF Montréal U-23	CAN	5th Ligue1 Québec

CODINHA, TIAGO
Midfielder. Born 2005, Hilversum, NED. Grew up in Bussum, NED. Height 184. Dominant right foot. Youth clubs: SDO Bussum (Netherlands), BFC Bussum (Netherlands), FC Utrecht (Netherlands), FC Twente / Heracles Acedemie (Netherlands)

COIMBRA, TIAGO — HALIFAX WANDERERS FC
Forward. Born 2004, Fortaleza, BRA. Grew up Vancouver, BC, CAN. Height 188 cm. Dominant right foot. Youth clubs: Escolinha do Flamengo (Brazil), Wesburn FC, Burnaby Metro Selects, Mountain United FC, FC Faly, SE Palmeiras (Brazil)

SEASON	CLUB	NATION	HIGHLIGHTS (MP/MIN/G)	G
2023	Halifax Wanderers FC	1.CAN	3rd CPL (19/837/3g); 4th Playoffs (1/80); CanChamp (1/67)	3

COLYN, SIMON — NED / BV DE GRAAFSCHAP
Midfielder. Born 2002, Langley, BC, CAN. Height 175 cm. Youth clubs: Langley United YSA, Surrey United SC, Vancouver Whitecaps FC Academy, SPAL Primavera (Italy) PSV Eindhoven (Netherlands)

SEASON	CLUB	NATION	HIGHLIGHTS (MP/MIN/G)	G
2015	Surrey United SC U-14	CAN	2nd U-14 Cup	
2018	Vancouver Whitecaps FC	1.CAN	14th MLS (1/5)	
2019	Vancouver Whitecaps FC	1.CAN	23rd MLS (0/0)	
2020	Vancouver Whitecaps FC	1.CAN	L16 MLS is Back (0/0)	
2021	Vancouver Whitecaps FC	1.CAN	12th MLS (0/0)	
2021-22	Jong PSV	2.NED	12th Eerste Division (28/1454/5g)	5
2022-23	Jong PSV	2.NED	14th Eerste Division (36/2381/6g)	6
2023-24	Jong PSV	2.NED	x- Eerste Division (1/11)	
	BV De Graafschap	2.NED	Eerste Division (current season); Beker (2/1/105/1g)	1

COORE, KAIRO — NZL / WESTERN SUBURBS FC
Forward. Born 2001, Ajax, ON, CAN. Grew up Whitby, ON, CAN. Height 185 cm. Youth clubs: Ajax SC, Erin Mills School: Cape Breton University

SEASON	CLUB	NATION	HIGHLIGHTS (MP/MIN/G)	G
2022	FC Edmonton	1.CAN	8th CPL (10/324/2g); CanChamp (1/15)	2

CORBEANU, THEO — ESP / GRANADA CF
Winger. Born 2002, Burlington, ON, CAN. Grew up Hamilton, ON, CAN. Height 190 cm. Youth clubs: Quinndale YS, Mount Hamilton, Hamilton Sparta, Saltfleet, 1v1 Soccer Academy, Givova Soccer Academy, ProStars FC, Global Premier Soccer, Toronto FC Academy, Wolverhampton Wanderers (England)
1st #CANMNT: 2021-03-25 at Orlando, FL, USA (v. BER)

SEASON	CLUB	NATION	HIGHLIGHTS (MP/MIN/G)	G
2018	TFC Academy	CAN	4th League1 Ontario (5/138/2g)	2
2020-21	Wolverhampton Wolves FC	1.ENG	13th FA Premier League (1/8); R5 FA Cup (0/0)	
2021-22	Sheffield Wednesday FC	3.ENG	x- League One (13/680/2g); R1 FA Cup (2/107); R2 EFL Trophy (3/270)	2
	Milton Keynes Dons FC	3.ENG	3rd League One (16/867/1g); SF Playoffs (1/90)	1
2022-23	Blackpool FC	2.ENG	x- EFL Championship (17/842/3g); R1 EFL Cup (1/62)	3
	Arminia Bielefeld	2.GER	16th 2.Bundesliga (13/210)	
2023-24	Grasshopper Club Zürich	1.SUI	x- Super League (16/1021/1g)	1
	Granada CF	1.ESP	La Liga (current season)	

CÓRDOVA, JUAN — YORK UNITED FC
Right back. Born 1995, Los Anges, CHI. Height 166 cm. Dominant right foot. Youth clubs: San Esteban Association (Chile), Unión San Felipe (Chile)

FOOTBALLERS

CANADA INTERNATIONAL
1st #CANMNT: 2017-06-13 at Montréal, QC, CAN (v. CUW)

SEASON	CLUB	NATION	HIGHLIGHTS (MP/MIN)
2014-15	CD Unión San Felipe	2.CHI	Primera B
2015-16	CD Unión San Felipe	2.CHI	Primera B
2016-17	CD Unión San Felipe	2.CHI	Primera B
2017	CD Huachipato	1.CHI	12th Nacional Transicion (7/479)
2018	CD Huachipato	1.CHI	9th Nacional (16/1046)
2019	CD Huachipato	1.CHI	6th Nacional (16/1196)
2020	CD Huachipato	CONMEBOL	R2 Sudamericana (3/270)
	CD Huachipato	1.CHI	8th Nacional (16/1244)
2021	CD Huachipato	CONMEBOL	Sudamericana (7/457)
	CD Huachipato	1.CHI	15th Nacional (23/1610); Promoción (2/10); QF Copa (2/180)
2022	CD Huachipato	1.CHI	12th Nacional (20/1204); SF (2/46)
2023	CD Ñublense	CONMEBOL	Libertadores (4/165); L16 Sudamericana (1/51)
	CD Ñublense	1.CHI	12th Nacional (8/321); R1 Copa (1/90)

CORNELIUS, DEREK — SWE / MALMÖ FF

Centre back. Born 1997, Ajax, ON, CAN. Height 185 cm. Dominant left foot. Youth clubs: Ajax SC (house league), Spartacus SC, Unionville-Milliken SC, VfB Lübeck (Germany).
Honours: Concacaf champion (2021-22), Allsvenskan (2023)

CANADA INTERNATIONAL
1 FIFA World Cup: Group phase at Qatar 2022
1st #CANMNT: 2018-09-9 at Bradenton, FL, USA (v. VIR)

SEASON	CLUB	NATION	HIGHLIGHTS (MP/MIN/G)	G
2015-16	VfB Lübeck	4.GER	x- Regionalliga	
2016-17	VfR Neumünster	4.GER	x- Regionalliga	
	FK Javor Ivanjica	1.SRB	8th SuperLiga (3/218)	
2017-18	FK Javor Ivanjica	1.SRB	15th SuperLiga (22/1855); QF Kup (3/240)	
2018-19	FK Javor Ivanjica	1.SRB	x- SuperLiga (3/270)	
2019	Vancouver Whitecaps FC	1.CAN	23rd MLS (17/1426/1g); CanChamp (1/90)	1
2020	Vancouver Whitecaps FC	1.CAN	17th MLS (13/1011); L16 MLS is Back (1/90)	
2021	Vancouver Whitecaps FC	1.CAN	x- MLS (5/144)	
2021-22	Panetolikos FC	1.GRE	4th Super League 1 (29/2492/2g); QF Kypello (4/360)	2
2022-23	Panetolikos FC	1.GRE	x- Super League 1 (13/1170); R5 Kypello (1/14)	
2023	Malmö FF	1.SWE	1st Allsvenskan (24/2086/3g); QF Cupen (4/390/1g)	4

CORNWALL, MYLES — OTTAWA SOUTH UNITED

Fullback. Born 1998, Ottawa, ON, CAN. Height 182 cm. Youth clubs: Ottawa Royals SC, Ottawa South United SC
School: Walsh University

SEASON	CLUB	NATION	HIGHLIGHTS (MP/MIN/G)	G
2017	Ottawa South United	CAN	E6th League1 Ontario (10/758/1g)	1
2018	Ottawa South United	CAN	14th League1 Ontario (6/540/4g)	4
2019	Ottawa South United	CAN	16th League1 Ontario (1/45)	
2020	Ottawa South United	CAN	2nd PLSQ (7/407)	
2021	Ottawa South United	CAN	10th PLSQ (7/605/1g)	
	Atlético Ottawa	1.CAN	8th CPL (2/58)	
2022	Fort Wayne FC	4.USA	USL League Two	
2023	Ottawa South United	CAN	11th PLSQ	

COSTA, JESSE

Midfielder. Born 2005, Brampton, ON, CAN. Height 188. Dominant right foot. Youth clubs: Brampton YSC, Prostars FC, VfL Wolfsburg (Germany)

COULANGES, JOAQUIM — ACADÉMIE CF MONTRÉAL

Forward. Born 2006, Montréal, QC, CAN. Height 174 cm. Dominant left foot. Youth clubs: CS Les Boucaniers, Académie de CF Montréal

SEASON	CLUB	NATION	HIGHLIGHTS (MP/MIN)
2019	Impact de Montréal U-13	Concacaf	Concacaf Under-13 Champions League

MEN'S FOOTBALLERS | 69

COUPLAND, ANTOINE — VANCOUVER WHITECAPS FC 2

Midfielder. Born 2003, Ottawa, ON, CAN. Grew up Chelsea, QC, CAN. Height 173 cm. Youth clubs: CS des Collines, Ottawa St. Anthony Futuro Academy, HNK Rijeka (Croatia)

SEASON	CLUB	NATION	HIGHLIGHTS (MP/MIN/G)	G
2019	Ottawa Fury FC	2.USA	E8th USL (3/18)	
2020	Atlético Ottawa	1.CAN	7th CPL (3/99)	
2021	Atlético Ottawa	1.CAN	8th CPL (15/513/2g); CanChamp (1/64)	2
2022-23	HNK Rijeka	1.CRO	4th Prva hrvatska liga (0/0)	
2023	Vanc. Whitecaps FC 2	CAN-3.US	21st MLS NEXT Pro (26/2082/2g)	2

COUTURIER, EVAN

Goalkeeper. Born 2001, . Grew up Riverview, NB, CAN. Height 183 cm. Youth clubs: Moncton Codiac SC
School: University of Prince Edward Island

SEASON	CLUB	NATION	HIGHLIGHTS (MP/MIN)
2018	Moncton Codiac SC U-17	CAN	11th U-17 Cup
2020	York9 FC	1.CAN	5th CPL (0/0)

CRAWFORD, TYLER — VANCOUVER FC

Left back. Born 2004, Burlington, ON, CAN. Grew up Tampa, FL, USA. Height 175 cm. Youth clubs: Burlington YSC, Tampa Chargers SC (USA)

SEASON	CLUB	NATION	HIGHLIGHTS (MP/MIN)
2023	Vancouver FC	1.CAN	7th CPL (23/1318); CanChamp (0/0)

CRÉPEAU, MAXIME — USA / PORTLAND TIMBERS FC

Goalkeeper. Born 1994, Greenfield Park, QC, CAN. Grew up Candiac, QC, CAN. Height 185 cm. Dominant right foot.
Youth clubs: LS pour enfants de Candiac, CS Celtix Haut-Richelieu, Académie de l'Impact Montréal
Honours: Concacaf champion (2021-22), MLS Cup (2022), MLS Supporters' Shield (2022), Canadian Championship (2013)
1st #CANMNT: 2016-02-5 at Carson, CA, USA (v. USA)

SEASON	CLUB	NATION	HIGHLIGHTS (MP/MIN)
2008	Québec U-14	CAN	1st Canada Soccer All Stars U-14
2009	Québec U-16	CAN	2nd Canada Soccer All Stars U-16
2010	Québec U-16	CAN	1st Canada Soccer All Stars U-16
2013	Impact de Montréal	1.CAN	11th MLS (0/0); 1st CanChamp (0/0)
2014	Impact de Montréal	1.CAN	19th MLS (0/0)
2014-15	Impact de Montréal	Concacaf	2nd Champions League (0/0)
2015	Impact de Montréal	1.CAN	7th MLS (0/0); 2nd CanChamp (0/0)
	FC Montréal	CAN-2.US	E10th USL (11/990)
2016	Impact de Montréal	1.CAN	11th MLS (0/0)
	FC Montréal	CAN-2.US	E14th USL (19/1710)
2017	Impact de Montréal	1.CAN	17th MLS (3/270); 2nd CanChamp (4/360)
2018	Ottawa Fury FC	2.USA	E10th USL (31/2790); SF CanChamp (4/360)
2019	Vancouver Whitecaps FC	1.CAN	23rd MLS (26/2340); CanChamp (2/180)
2020	Vancouver Whitecaps FC	1.CAN	17th MLS (4/328)
2021	Vancouver Whitecaps FC	1.CAN	12th MLS (27/2430); Playoffs (1/90); CanChamp (1/90)
2022	Los Angeles FC	1.USA	1st MLS (33/2970); 1st Playoffs (3/326); L16 US Cup (2/180)
2023	Los Angeles FC	1.USA	8th MLS (7/630); 2nd MLS Playoffs (5/450); QF Leagues (0/0)

CURIC, ANTONY — TORONTO FC II

Centre back. Born 2001, Toronto, ON, CAN. Grew up in Toronto, ON, CAN. Height 190. Youth clubs: Erin Mills SC, Toronto FC Academy. School: Ryerson University

SEASON	CLUB	NATION	HIGHLIGHTS (MP/MIN)
2021	Toronto FC II	CAN-3.US	7th USL League One (15/867)
2022	Toronto FC II	CAN-3.US	7th MLS NEXT Pro (15/1257); SF Playoffs (2/210)
2023	Toronto FC	1.CAN	29th MLS (1/1)
	Toronto FC II	CAN-3.US	23rd MLS NEXT Pro (19/1601/2g)

DADA-LUKE, OLAKUNLE — PACIFIC FC

Midfielder. Born 2000, Mississauga, ON, CAN. Grew up Toronto, ON, CAN. Height 183 cm. Youth clubs: West Toronto SC, Toronto FC Academy
Honours: CPL Championship (2021)

FOOTBALLERS

SEASON	CLUB	NATION	HIGHLIGHTS (MP/MIN/G)	G
2016	TFC Academy	CAN	W3rd League1 Ontario (1/25)	
2017	TFC Academy	CAN	W3rd League1 Ontario (11/334)	
2018	TFC Academy	CAN	4th League1 Ontario (13/1072/6g)	6
	Toronto FC II	CAN-2.US	E16th USL (5/148)	
2019-20	FC Helsingør	3.DEN	x- 2. division (0/0)	
2021	Pacific FC	1.CAN	3rd CPL (19/894); 1st Playoffs (2/77); SF CanChamp (2/62)	
2022	Pacific FC	Concacaf	L16 Concacaf League (4/346)	
	Pacific FC	1.CAN	4th CPL (23/1782/1g); SF Playoffs (2/165); QF CanChamp (1/90)	1
2023	Pacific FC	1.CAN	4th CPL (27/2149); 3rd Playoffs (2/180); SF CanChamp (3/270)	

DAHER, JOSEPH — TORONTO FC II
Fullback. Born 2004, Ottawa, ON, CAN. Grew up in Ottawa, ON, CAN & Accra, GHA. Height 173. Dominant right foot. Youth clubs: Izzy Sports (Ghana), Ottawa South United, Toronto FC Academy

SEASON	CLUB	NATION	HIGHLIGHTS (MP/MIN/G)	G
2022	Toronto FC II	CAN-3.US	7th MLS NEXT Pro (1/81)	
	Ontario U-18	CAN	Silver at Canada Games (3/129/1g)	1
2023	Toronto FC II	CAN-3.US	23rd MLS NEXT Pro (0/0)	

DANIELS, AIDAN — HALIFAX WANDERERS FC
Midfielder. Born 1998, Markham, ON, CAN. Grew up Ajax, ON, CAN. Height 175 cm. Dominant right foot. Youth clubs: Ajax Azzurri SC, Richmond Hill SC, Toronto FC Academy
Honours: Canadian Championship (2018)

SEASON	CLUB	NATION	HIGHLIGHTS (MP/MIN/G)	G
2014	TFC Academy	CAN	1st League1 Ontario	
2015	TFC Academy	CAN	5th League1 Ontario	
2016	Toronto FC II	CAN-2.US	E12th USL (23/1326/1g)	1
	TFC Academy	CAN-4.US	USL PDL (1/0)	
2017	Toronto FC II	CAN-2.US	E15th USL (16/873)	
	TFC Academy	CAN	W3rd League1 Ontario (4/341)	
2018	Toronto FC	1.CAN	19th MLS (1/12); 1st CanChamp (0/0)	
	Toronto FC II	CAN-2.US	E16th USL (26/1527/2g)	2
2019	Ottawa Fury FC	2.USA	E8th USL (14/166/1g)	1
2020	Colorado Springs Switchbacks	2.USA	W13th USL (16/1279/3g)	3
2021	OKC Energy FC	2.USA	E11th USL (30/1997/3g)	3
2022	HFX Wanderers FC	1.CAN	7th CPL (21/1298/1g); QF CanChamp (2/171/1g)	2
2023	Halifax Wanderers FC	1.CAN	3rd CPL (28/1795/3g); 4th Playoffs (1/90); CanChamp (1/75)	3

DANIELS, WILLIAM — ENG / LEICESTER CITY FC ACADEMY
Left back. Born 2008, St-Hyacinthe, QC, CAN. Grew up in St-Hilaire, QC, CAN. Height 179 cm. Dominant left foot. Youth clubs: CS de la Vallée-du-Richelieu (Beloeil), Académie de l'Impact de Montréal, Burbage Old Boys FC, Boldmere St. Michael's FC, Leicester City FC Academy

DAOUDA, MALICK — CF MONTRÉAL U-23
Midfielder. Born 2004, Montréal, QC, CAN. Grew up Brossard, QC, CAN. Height 183 cm. Youth clubs: AS Brossard, Académie Impact de Montréal

SEASON	CLUB	NATION	HIGHLIGHTS (MP/MIN)
2022	CF Montréal U-23	CAN	6th PLSQ (19/1604)
2023	CF Montréal U-23	CAN	5th Ligue1 Québec

DARWISH, OMAR
Midfielder. Born 2005. Grew up in Ottawa, ON, CAN. Youth clubs: West Ottawa SC

SEASON	CLUB	NATION	HIGHLIGHTS (MP/MIN)
2023	Atlético Ottawa		6th CPL (0/0)
	Ottawa South United		11th Ligue1 Québec

DASOVIC, LUCAS
Centre back. Born 2002, Vancouver, BC, CAN. Grew up in Burnaby, BC, CAN. Height 188. Youth clubs: Mountain United FC, Vancouver Whitecaps FC Academy

SEASON	CLUB	NATION	HIGHLIGHTS (MP/MIN)
2017	Mountain United FC U-15	CAN	5th U-15 Cup
2019	Mountain United FC U-17	CAN	4th U-17 Cup

| 2022 | Vanc. Whitecaps FC 2 | CAN-3.US | 14th MLS NEXT Pro (4/306) | |
| 2023 | Vanc. Whitecaps FC 2 | CAN-3.US | 21st MLS NEXT Pro (13/1103/1g) | |

DAVID, JONATHAN — FRA / LILLE OSC

Forward. Born 2000, Brooklyn, NY, USA. Grew up Ottawa, ON, CAN (Orléans). Height 175 cm. Dominant right foot.
Youth clubs: Ottawa Gloucester Dragons, Ottawa Gloucester SC Hornets, Ottawa Internationals SC
Canada Soccer Player of the Year (2019)
Honours: Concacaf champion (2021-22), Ligue 1 (2020-21), Trophée des Champions (2021)

CANADA INTERNATIONAL
1 FIFA World Cup: Group phase at Qatar 2022
1 Concacaf medal: Silver at CNL 2022-23
1st #CANMNT: 2018-09-9 at Bradenton, FL, USA (v. VIR)

SEASON	CLUB	NATION	HIGHLIGHTS (MP/MIN/G)	G
2017-18	KAA Gent	2.BEL	4th Playoff (0/0)	
2018-19	KAA Gent	2.BEL	5th Cham (23/1336/8g); 5th Playoffs (10/646/4g); 2nd Beker (6/230)	12
2019-20	KAA Gent	2.BEL	2nd Championnat (27/2101/18g); L16 Beker (0/0)	18
2020-21	Lille OSC	1.FRA	1st Ligue 1 (37/2368/13g); L16 Coupe (3/85)	13
2021-22	Lille OSC	1.FRA	10th Ligue 1 (38/2810/15g); R4 Coupe (1/89/1g)	16
2022-23	Lille OSC	1.FRA	5th Ligue 1 (37/3179/24g); L16 Coupe (3/241/2g)	26
2023-24	Lille OSC	1.FRA	Ligue 1 (current season); Coupe (current)	

CONTINENTAL FOOTBALL		UEFA	HIGHLIGHTS (MP/MIN/G)	G
2018-19	KAA Gent	UEFA	UEFA Europa League (4/76/2g)	2
2019-20	KAA Gent	UEFA	Qualifying (6/539/2g); UEFA Europa League (7/620/3g)	5
2020-21	Lille OSC	UEFA	Rof32 UEFA Europa League (8/592)	
2021-22	Lille OSC	UEFA	L16 UEFA Champions League (8/680/3g)	3
2023-24	Lille OSC	UEFA	Qualifying (2/210/1g); Conference League (4/210/1g)	2

DAVIES, ALPHONSO — GER / FC BAYERN MÜNCHEN

Left back & winger. Born 2000, Gomoa Buduburam, GHA. Grew up Edmonton, AB, CAN. Height 183 cm. Dominant left foot. Youth clubs: Edmonton Inter, Edmonton Strikers, St. Nicholas SA, FC Edmonton Academy, Vancouver Whitecaps FC Residency
Canada Soccer Player of the Year (2018, 2020, 2021, 2022)
Concacaf champion (2021-22), FIFA Club World Cup (2020), UEFA Champions League (2019-20), UEFA Super Cup (2020), Bundesliga (2018-19, 2019-20, 2020-21, 2021-22, 2022-23), Pokal (2019, 2020), DFL-Supercup (2020, 2021)

CANADA INTERNATIONAL
1 FIFA World Cup: Group phase at Qatar 2022
1 Concacaf medal: Silver at CNL 2022-23
1st #CANMNT: 2017-06-13 at Montréal, QC, CAN (v. CUW)

SEASON	CLUB	NATION	HIGHLIGHTS (MP/MIN/G)	G
2016	Vancouver Whitecaps FC	1.CAN	16th MLS (8/299); 2nd CanChamp	
	Vanc. Whitecaps FC 2	CAN-2.US	W6th USL (11/677/2g)	2
2017	Vancouver Whitecaps FC	1.CAN	8th MLS (26/1053); QF Playoffs (1/26); SF CanChamp (2/117/2g)	2
2018	Vancouver Whitecaps FC	1.CAN	14th MLS (31/2420/8g); 2nd CanChamp (2/138)	8
	MLS All-Stars	1.USA	MLS All-Star Game (1/29)	
2018-19	FC Bayern München	1.GER	1st Bundesliga (6/74/1g); 1st Pokal (0/0)	1
	FC Bayern München II	4.GER	Regionalliga	
2019-20	FC Bayern München	1.GER	1st Bundesliga (29/2233/3g); 1st Pokal (5/450); 2nd Supercup (1/24)	3
	FC Bayern München II	3.GER	3.Liga (3/253)	
2020-21	FC Bayern München	1.GER	1st Bundesliga (23/1768/1g); 2R Pokal (2/210); 1st Supercup (1/90)	1
2021-22	FC Bayern München	1.GER	1st Bundesliga (22/1743); R2 Pokal (1/55); 1st Supercup (1/90)	
2022-23	FC Bayern München	1.GER	1st Bundesliga (26/2046/1g); QF Pokal (2/109/2g); 1st Supercup (1/90)	3
2023-24	FC Bayern München	1.GER	Bundesliga (current season); Pokal (current)	

CONTINENTAL / GLOBAL		COMPETITION	HIGHLIGHTS (MP/MIN/G)	G
2016-17	Vancouver Whitecaps FC	Concacaf	SF Champions League (7/467/2g)	2
2018-19	FC Bayern München	UEFA	L16 UEFA Champions League (0/0)	
2019-20	FC Bayern München	UEFA	1st UEFA Champions League (8/714)	
2020	FC Bayern München	FIFA	1st FIFA Club World Cup (2/180)	
2020-21	FC Bayern München	UEFA	QF UEFA Champions League (6/320); 1st UEFA Supercup (1/21)	
2021-22	FC Bayern München	UEFA	QF UEFA Champions League (7/478)	

2022-23	FC Bayern München	UEFA	QF UEFA Champions League (9/1203)
2023-24	FC Bayern München	UEFA	UEFA Champions League (current)

DE FOUGEROLLES, LUC — ENG / FULHAM FC

Fullback. Born 2005, London, ENG. Grew up in London, ENG. Height 178. Youth clubs: Battersea Bedhead, Fulham FC

SEASON	CLUB	NATION	HIGHLIGHTS (MP/MIN)
2022-23	Fulham FC U-23	ENG	Premier League 2 (6/382)
2023-24	Fulham FC	1.ENG	Premier League (current season); R4 FA Cup (0/0); SF EFL Cup (1/90)
	Fulham FC U-23	ENG	Premier League 2 (current season)

DE JONG, MARCEL — SURREY BB5 UNITED

Fullback. Born 1986, Newmarket, ON, CAN. Grew up Valkenswaard, NED. Height 175 cm. Dominant left foot. Youth clubs: De Valk, PSV Eindhoven

Honours: US Cup (2015)

1st #CANMNT: 2007-11-20 at Durban, RSA (v. RSA)

SEASON	CLUB	NATION	HIGHLIGHTS (MP/MIN/G)	G
2004-05	Helmond Sport	2.NED	6th Eerste Division; Playoffs	
2005-06	Helmond Sport	2.NED	4th Eerste Division; Playoffs; QF KNVB Beker (0/0)	
2006-07	Roda JC	1.NED	6th Eredivisie (27/1977); QF KNVB Beker	
2007-08	Roda JC	1.NED	9th Eredivisie (25/1891); 2nd KNVB Beker	
2008-09	Roda JC	1.NED	16th Eredivisie (32/2726/1g); QF KNVB Beker (4/401/2g)	3
2009-10	Roda JC	1.NED	9th Eredivisie (31/2721/2g); R2 KNVB Beker (2/98)	2
2010-11	FC Augsburg	1.GER	2nd 2.Bundesliga (27/1969/3g); L16 Pokal (0/0)	3
2011-12	FC Augsburg	1.GER	14th Bundesliga (12/898/1g); L16 Pokal (2/168)	1
2012-13	FC Augsburg	1.GER	15th Bundesliga (20/1270/1g); L16 Pokal (1/90)	1
2013-14	FC Augsburg	1.GER	8th Bundesliga (8/186); L16 Pokal (1/90)	
2014-15	FC Augsburg	1.GER	x- Bundesliga (1/56); R1 Pokal (1/84)	
2015	Sporting Kansas City	1.USA	10th MLS (13/847/1g); Playoffs (0/0); 1st US Cup (1/1)	1
2016	Ottawa Fury FC	2.USA	x- NASL (6/495/2g); SF CanChamp (3/225)	2
	Vancouver Whitecaps FC	1.CAN	16th MLS (7/467)	
2016-17	Vancouver Whitecaps FC	CAN	SF Champions League (4/303)	
2017	Vancouver Whitecaps FC	1.CAN	8th MLS (13/779); QF Playoffs (3/261); SF CanChamp (2/180)	
2018	Vancouver Whitecaps FC	1.CAN	14th MLS (19/1392); 2nd CanChamp (3/270)	
2019	Pacific FC	1.CAN	5th CPL (2/50); CanChamp (0/0)	
2020	Pacific FC	1.CAN	3rd CPL (7/441)	
2022	Surrey BB5 United	CAN	4th CS National Championships (5/..)	
2023	Surrey BB5 United	CAN	7th CS National Championships (3/189)	

DE MONTIGNY, GAËL — ACADÉMIE CF MONTRÉAL

Left back. Born 2006, Montréal, QC, CAN. Height 172 cm. Dominant left foot. Youth clubs: CS Mascouche, Académie de CF Montréal

SEASON	CLUB	NATION	HIGHLIGHTS (MP/MIN)
2019	Impact de Montréal U-13	Concacaf	Concacaf Under-13 Champions League

DE ROSARIO, ADISA — TORONTO FC II

Goalkeeper. Born 2004, San Jose, CA, USA. Grew up Markham, ON, CAN. Height 183 cm. Dominant right foot. Youth clubs: Houston Eclipse (USA), Oakville SC, Ashburn Legends (USA), Vaughan SC, Toronto FC Academy

SEASON	CLUB	NATION	HIGHLIGHTS (MP/MIN)
2022	Toronto FC II	CAN-3.US	7th MLS NEXT Pro (0/0); SF Playoffs (0/0)
	HFX Wanderers FC	1.CAN	7th CPL (1/90)
2023	York United FC	1.CAN	5th CPL (4/360)
	Toronto FC II	CAN-3.US	23rd MLS NEXT Pro (5/450)

DE SÁ, RUBEN — POR / FAMALICÃO

Midfielder. Born 2006, Toronto, ON, CAN. Height 180 cm. Dominant right foot. Youth clubs: Sporting FC Toronto Academy, Vitória SC (Portugal), Famalicão (Portugal)

DE BRIENNE, MATTEO — ATLÉTICO OTTAWA

Winger. Born 2002, Ottawa, ON, CAN. Height 163 cm. Dominant left foot. Youth clubs: Ottawa South United SC, Vancouver Whitecaps FC Academy

School: Carleton University

SEASON	CLUB	NATION	HIGHLIGHTS (MP/MIN/G)	G
2020	Atlético Ottawa	1.CAN	7th CPL (0/0)	
2021	Ottawa South United	CAN	10th PLSQ (1/75)	
2022	Valour FC	1.CAN	5th CPL (22/888/3g); CanChamp (1/9)	3
2023	Valour FC	1.CAN	8th CPL (20/1571/3g); CanChamp (1/1)	3

DEO, SAHIL — VANCOUVER WHITECAPS FC ACADEMY

Fullback. Born 2008, New Westminster, BC, CAN. Grew up in Port Coquitlam, BC, CAN. Height 172 cm. Dominant right foot. Youth clubs: Port Coquitlam Euro-Rite FC, Fraser Valley Premier, Langley United, Vancouver Whitecaps FC Academy

DERRIEN-LAIRET, EWAN — ACADÉMIE CF MONTRÉAL

Goalkeeper. Born 2007, Montréal, QC, CAN. Height 173 cm. Dominant right foot. Youth clubs: CS Les Boucaniers, Académie de CF Montréal

SEASON	CLUB	NATION	HIGHLIGHTS (MP/MIN)
2019	Impact de Montréal U-13	Concacaf	Concacaf Under-13 Champions League

DESJARDINS, AXEL

Goalkeeper. Born 2000, Montréal, QC, CAN. Height 188 cm. Dominant right foot. Youth clubs: Montréal, Spezia (Italy)

SEASON	CLUB	NATION	HIGHLIGHTS (MP/MIN/G)	G
2017-18	AC Spezia	2.ITA	10th Serie B (0/0)	
2018-19	AC Spezia	2.ITA	6th Serie B (0/0)	
2019-20	AC Spezia	2.ITA	3rd Serie B (1/1); Playoff (0/0)	
2020-21	AC Spezia	1.ITA	15th Serie A (0/0)	
	Novara FC	3.ITA	11th Serie C Girone A (4/360)	
2021-22	Novara FC	4.ITA	1st Serie D Girone A (19/1645)	
2022-23	Novara FC	3.ITA	10th Serie C Girone A (17/1494); Playoff (1/90)	
2023-24	Novara FC	3.ITA	Serie C (current season)	

DI CHIARA, JOSEPH — VAUGHAN SC

Midfielder. Born 1992, Toronto, ON, CAN. Grew up Richmond Hill, ON, CAN. Height 185 cm. Dominant right foot. Youth clubs: Glen Shields SC, Spartacus SC, Krylja Sovetov Samara (Russia)

SEASON	CLUB	NATION	HIGHLIGHTS (MP/MIN/G)	G
2011-12	Krylia Sovetov Samara	1.RUS	12th Premier League (5/267)	
2012-13	Kecskeméti TE	1.HUN	7th Nemzeti Bajnokság I (0/0)	
	Torpedo Moscow	2.RUS	14th National League (1/60)	
2014	Vaughan Azzurri	CAN	8th CS National Championships (4/140)	
2015	FC Okzhetpes	1.KAZ	8th Premier League (12/679/1g); QF Kubok (1/120)	1
2016	Vaughan Azzurri	CAN	1st League1 Ontario (11/826/4g)	4
2017	Vaughan Azzurri	CAN	E2nd League1 Ontario (14/1251/8g)	8
2018	Unionville Milliken SC	CAN	8th League1 Ontario (4/360/1g)	1
2018	FK Jonava	1.LTU	8th A Lya (6/463)	
2019	York9 FC	1.CAN	3rd CPL (23/1759/2g); CanChamp (4/214)	2
2020	York9 FC	1.CAN	5th CPL (6/540/3g); QF CanChamp (1/58)	3
2021	Cavalry FC	1.CAN	2nd CPL (24/1444/1g); SF Playoffs (1/75)	1
2022	Cavalry FC	1.CAN	3rd CPL (16/784); SF Playoffs (2/87)	
2023	Vaughan Azzurri	CAN	3rd League1 Ontario (2/82/1g); CanChamp (1/79)	1

DIALLO, OUMAR

Forward. Born 2005, Grew up in Aurora, ON, CAN. Height 184. Dominant right foot. Youth clubs: Aurora FC, Richmond Hill FC, FC Inter Milan (ITA)

SEASON	CLUB	NATION	HIGHLIGHTS (MP/MIN)
2021-22	ASD Cannara	4.ITA	E-17th Serie D (7/?)

DIAS, LUCAS — CAVALRY FC

Attacking midfielder. Born 2003, Toronto, ON, CAN. Grew up Woodbridge, ON, CAN & Lisboa, POR. Height 180 cm. Dominant right foot. Youth clubs: Sporting Toronto, Sporting CP (Portugal)

SEASON	CLUB	NATION	HIGHLIGHTS (MP/MIN)
2021-22	Sporting B	3.POR	B-8th FPF Liga 3 Série B (3/1)
2022-23	Sporting B	3.POR	B-5th FPF Liga 3 Série B (0/0)

FOOTBALLERS

DICLEMENTE, THOMAS — TORONTO FC II
Centre back. Born 2004, Toronto, ON, CAN. Height cm. Youth clubs: Woodbridge Strikers SC, Toronto FC Academy

SEASON	CLUB	NATION	HIGHLIGHTS (MP/MIN)
2022	Ontario U-18	CAN	Silver at Canada Games (4/224)
	Toronto FC II	CAN-3.US	7th MLS NEXT Pro (0/0)
2023	Toronto FC II	CAN-3.US	23rd MLS NEXT Pro (0/0)

DIDIĆ, AMER
Centre back. Born 1994, Zenica, BIH. Grew up Sherwood Park, AB, CAN. Height 193 cm. Dominant right foot. Youth clubs: Sherwood Park SA, Edmonton Southwest United SC, Edmonton Victoria SC
School: Baker University
1st #CANMNT: 2020-01-10 at Irvine, CA, USA (v. BRB)

SEASON	CLUB	NATION	HIGHLIGHTS (MP/MIN/G)	G
2008	Alberta U-14	CAN	5th Canada Soccer All Stars U-14	
2010	Alberta U-16	CAN	3rd Canada Soccer All Stars U-16	
2016	Swope Park Rangers	2.USA	W4th USL (28/1871/1g); 2nd Playoffs (4/390)	1
2016-17	Sporting Kansas City	Concacaf	Champions League (3/270)	
2017	Sporting Kansas City	1.USA	11th MLS (0/0)	
	Swope Park Rangers	2.USA	W4th USL (21/1812/1g); 2nd Playoffs (4/420/1g)	1
2018	Sporting Kansas City	1.USA	3rd MLS (0/0); QF US Cup (1/90)	
	Swope Park Rangers	2.USA	W7th USL (25/2176/1g); Playoffs (2/180)	1
2019	San Antonio FC	2.USA	x- USL (2/180)	
	FC Edmonton	1.CAN	4th CPL (19/1650); CanChamp (1/24)	
2020	FC Edmonton	1.CAN	8th CPL (3/240)	
2021	FC Edmonton	1.CAN	7th CPL (24/2084/3g); CanChamp (1/29)	3
2022	Pacific FC	Concacaf	L16 Concacaf League (4/360)	
	Pacific FC	1.CAN	4th CPL (26/2062/2g); SF Playoffs (2/180); QF CanChamp (1/90/2g)	4
2023	Pacific FC	1.CAN	4th CPL (24/2159/4g); 3rd Playoffs (3/238); SF CanChamp (3/270)	4

DOE, DAVID
Forward. Born 2000, Monrovia, LBR. Grew up Edmonton, AB, CAN. Height 175 cm. Dominant right foot. Youth clubs: McLeod Community League, Edmonton Juventus, FC Edmonton Academy
School: Northern Alberta Institute of Technology

SEASON	CLUB	NATION	HIGHLIGHTS (MP/MIN)
2016	Edmonton Juventus U-16	CAN	1st U-16 Cup
2017	FC Edmonton	2.USA	7th NASL (4/37)
2019	FC Edmonton	1.CAN	4th CPL (7/170); CanChamp (1/45)
2020	FC Edmonton	1.CAN	8th CPL (2/58)
2021	South Bend Lions	4.USA	USL League Two (12/772)

DONER, MOREY — USA / MONTERY BAY FC
Fullback. Born 1994, Collingwood, ON, CAN. Height 173 cm. Dominant right foot. Youth clubs: Collingwood United

SEASON	CLUB	NATION	HIGHLIGHTS (MP/MIN/G)	G
2014	Durham United	CAN	8th League1 Ontario	
2016	Aurora United FC	CAN	E6th League1 Ontario (1/45)	
2017	Aurora FC	CAN	E8th League1 Ontario (5/392)	
2018	Aurora FC	CAN	15th League1 Ontario (16/1440/3g)	3
2019	York9 FC	1.CAN	3rd CPL (25/2250/1g); CanChamp (4/360)	1
2020	York9 FC	1.CAN	5th CPL (7/630)	
2021	HFX Wanderers FC	1.CAN	4th CPL (20/1776); QF CanChamp (1/90)	
2022	Monterey Bay FC	2.USA	W12th USL (34/3046/1g); 2R US Cup (1/45)	1
2023	Monterey Bay FC	2.USA	W11th USL (34/3060/2g); 4R US Cup (3/330)	2

DUHANEY-WALKER, TYR — ATLÉTICO OTTAWA
Centre back. Born 2003, Ottawa, ON, CAN. Grew up in Russell, ON, CAN. Height 188 cm. Dominant right foot. Youth clubs: Ottawa St. Anthony Futuro
School: Acadia University

SEASON	CLUB	NATION	HIGHLIGHTS (MP/MIN)
2023	Atlético Ottawa	1.CAN	6th CPL (5/243); QF CanChamp (0/0)

MEN'S FOOTBALLERS

DUMITRU, ANDREI
Midfielder. Born 2006, Milton, ON, CAN. Grew up Mississauga, ON, CAN. Height 185 cm. Dominant right foot. Youth clubs: Prostars FC, Toronto FC Academy

DUNCAN, MALCOLM   FORGE FC HAMILTON
Fullback. Born 1999, Toronto, ON, CAN. Height 178 cm. Dominant right foot. Youth clubs: Sigma FC
School: Providence College

SEASON	CLUB	NATION	HIGHLIGHTS (MP/MIN)
2016	Sigma FC	CAN	W2nd League1 Ontario (6/480)
2017	Sigma FC	CAN	W2nd League1 Ontario (2/13)
2018	Sigma FC	CAN	2nd League1 Ontario (5/434)
2019	Sigma FC	CAN	5th League1 Ontario (7/537)
2022	Forge FC Hamilton	1.CAN	2nd CPL (2/3)
2023	Forge FC Hamilton	1.CAN	2nd CPL (10/249)
	Sigma FC	CAN	9th League1 Ontario (1/90)

DUNN, JULIAN
Centre back. Born 2000, Toronto, ON, CAN. Grew up Richmond Hill, ON, CAN. Height 188 cm. Youth clubs: Vaughan SC, Brampton SC, Toronto FC Academy

SEASON	CLUB	NATION	HIGHLIGHTS (MP/MIN)
2016	TFC Academy	CAN-4.US	USL PDL (3/37)
2017	Toronto FC II	CAN-2.US	E15th USL (13/1088)
	TFC Academy	CAN	W3rd League1 Ontario (6/540)
2018	Toronto FC	1.CAN	19th MLS (2/105)
	Toronto FC II	CAN-2.US	E16th USL (9/810)
2019	Toronto FC	1.CAN	9th MLS (0/0)
	Toronto FC II	CAN-3.US	7th USL League One (8/585)
2020	Valour FC	1.CAN	6th CPL (7/630)
2021	Toronto FC	1.CAN	26th MLS (1/90); 2nd CanChamp (1/90)
	Toronto FC II	CAN-3.US	7th USL League One (4/360)
2022	Hamarkameratene	1.NOR	13th Eliteserien (4/151); R3 Cup (1/90)

DURRANS, MATTHEW   AUT / SK AUSTRIA KLAGENFURT II
Forward. Born 1998, Vancouver, BC, CAN. Height 183 cm. Dominant right foot. Youth clubs: West Vancouver SC, Mountain United SC, Vancouver Whitecaps FC Academy, TSV 1860 München (Germany), FC Deisenhofen (Germany)

SEASON	CLUB	NATION	HIGHLIGHTS (MP/MIN)	
2017-18	VfR Garching	4.GER	Regionalliga	
2018-19	VfR Garching	4.GER	x- Regionalliga	
	TSV 1860 München II	5.GER	Bayernliga	
2019-20	TSV 1860 München II	5.GER	Bayernliga	
2020-21	TSV 1860 München	3.GER	4th 3.Liga (2/8); R1 Pokal	
	TSV 1860 München II	5.GER	Bayernliga	
2021	FC Edmonton	1.CAN	7th CPL (16/321); CanChamp (1/45)	
2021-22	FC Pipinsried	4.GER	Regionalliga	
2022-23	SK Austria Klagenfurt II	4.AUT	4th Kärntner Liga (9/506/3g)	3

EDWARDS, RAHEEM   CF MONTRÉAL
Midfielder / fullback. Born 1995, Toronto, ON, CAN. Height 172 cm. Dominant left foot. Youth clubs: Erin Mills SC, Toronto FC Academy. School: Sheridan College
Honours: Canadian Championship (2016, 2017), MLS Cup (2017), MLS Supporters' Shield (2017), CCAA (2014)
1st #CANMNT: 2017-06-13 at Montréal, QC, CAN (v. CUW)

SEASON	CLUB	NATION	HIGHLIGHTS (MP/MIN/G)	G
2012	Erin Mills SC U-18 Eagles	CAN	2nd U-18 Cup	
2014	Internacional de Toronto	CAN	League1 Ontario	
	TFC Academy	CAN	1st League1 Ontario	
2015	Toronto FC II	CAN-2.US	E11th USL (21/1283/2g)	2
2016	Toronto FC	1.CAN	5th MLS (1/2); 1st CanChamp (1/4)	
	Toronto FC II	CAN-2.US	E12th USL (20/1510/6g)	6
2017	Toronto FC	1.CAN	1st MLS (21/1058/1g); 1st Playoffs (1/6); 1st CanChamp (3/258)	1
	Toronto FC II	CAN-2.US	E15th USL (1/90)	

FOOTBALLERS

2018	Impact de Montréal	1.CAN	x- MLS (14/808/2g)	2
	Chicago Fire	1.USA	20th MLS (13/916/1g); SF US Cup (1/90)	1
2019	Chicago Fire	1.USA	17th MLS (4/244/1g); 4R US Cup (1/67)	1
2020	Minnesota United FC	1.USA	9th MLS (12/259); SF MLS is Back (3/43); SF Playoffs (0/0)	
2021	Las Vegas Lights FC	2.USA	x- USL (1/65)	
	Los Angeles FC	1.USA	19th MLS (27/1369)	
2022	Los Angeles Galaxy	1.USA	8th MLS (30/2281/1g); QF Playoffs (2/180); QF US Cup (3/226)	1
2023	Los Angeles Galaxy	1.USA	26th MLS (30/1873/2g); QF US Cup (3/114); Leagues (2/89)	2

EGWU, KELSEY — FC LONDON
Centre back. Born 2004. Grew up Sherwood Park, AB, CAN. Height cm. Youth clubs: St. Albert Impact, Edmonton Strikers, Edmonton BtB Academy. School: MacEwan University

SEASON	CLUB	NATION	HIGHLIGHTS (MP/MIN)
2022	Alberta U-18	CAN	Bronze at Canada Games (3/240)
	FC Edmonton	1.CAN	8th CPL (1/90)
2023	Toronto FC II	CAN-3.US	23rd MLS NEXT Pro (0/0)
	FC London	CAN	13th League1 Ontario (20/1346)

ENGBERS, BROGAN
Goalkeeper. Born 1999, Ottawa, ON, CAN. Height 180 cm. Youth clubs: Cumberland United SC, Toronto FC Academy School: Liberty University

SEASON	CLUB	NATION	HIGHLIGHTS (MP/MIN)
2015	TFC Academy	CAN	5th League1 Ontario
2016	TFC Academy	CAN	USL PDL (1/0); W3rd League1 Ontario
2017	TFC Academy	CAN	W3rd League1 Ontario (3/270)
2018	TFC Academy	CAN	4th League1 Ontario (2/180)
2019	Windsor TFC	CAN	13th League1 Ontario (3/180)
2021	Toronto FC II	CAN-3.US	7th USL League One (0/0)
2023	Atlético Ottawa	1.CAN	6th CPL (0/0); QF CanChamp (0/0)

ENNIN, RICHIE — HUN / MTK BUDAPEST FC
Winger. Born 1998, North York, ON, CAN. Grew up in Brampton, ON, CAN. Height 178 cm. Youth clubs: Toronto FC Academy

Honours: A Lyga (2020)

SEASON	CLUB	NATION	HIGHLIGHTS (MP/MIN/G)	G
2015	TFC Academy	CAN	5th League1 Ontario	
2016	Toronto FC II	CAN	26th USL (4/107)	
	TFC Academy	CAN	USL PDL (13/855/1g); W3rd League1 Ontario	1
2017-18	Isola Capo Rizzuto	4.ITA	I-18th Serie D (18/1438)	5
2018-19	US Castrovillari	4.ITA	x- Serie D (12/810/3g)	3
2019	FK Spartaks Jūrmala	1.LTV	5th Virslīga (22/1578/5g)	5
2020	FK Žalgiris	1.LTU	1st A Lyga (11/839/4g); QF Cup (0/0)	4
2020-21	FK Žalgiris	UEFA	Qualifying Europa League (1/9)	
	FC Tom Tomsk	2.RUS	18th National League (19/1611/4g)	4
2021-22	FC Nizhny Novgorod	1.RUS	11th Russian Premier (19/1440/1g); L16 Cup (2/180)	1
2022-23	Honvéd FC	1.HUN	11th Nemzeti Bajnokság I (21/1182/2g); L16 Kupa (2/137)	2
2023-24	MTK Budapest FC	1.HUN	Nemzeti Bajnokság I (current season)	

ESPINAL, EDWIN
Winger. Born 2005. Grew up in Vancouver, BC, CAN. Youth clubs: Blaine SA, Vancouver Whitecaps FC Academy

SEASON	CLUB	NATION	HIGHLIGHTS (MP/MIN)
2023	Vanc. Whitecaps FC 2	CAN-3.US	21st MLS NEXT Pro (3/54)

ESPRIT, TRIVINE — YORK UNITED FC
Midfielder. Born 2002, Scarborough, ON, CAN. Grew up in Scarborough, ON, CAN. Height 170 cm. Youth clubs: North Scarborough SC. School: Ontario Tech

SEASON	CLUB	NATION	HIGHLIGHTS (MP/MIN)
2021	Unionville-Milliken SC	CAN	8th League1 Ontario (9/773)
2022	Simcoe County Rovers FC	CAN	5th League1 Ontario (16/785)
2023	York United FC	1.CAN	5th CPL (11/373); 5th Playoffs (0/0)
	Darby FC	CAN	14th League1 Ontario (7/617)

ESSOUSSI, MEHDI — TORONTO FC II

Midfielder. Born 2001, Tunis, TUN. Grew up Ottawa, ON, CAN. Height 182 cm. Youth clubs: Nepean Hotspurs SC, Ottawa Fury Academy, Ottawa South United, Toronto FC Academy

SEASON	CLUB	NATION	HIGHLIGHTS (MP/MIN/G)	G
2018	TFC Academy	CAN	4th League1 Ontario (13/856/1g)	1
2019	Toronto FC II	CAN-3.US	7th USL League One (6/391)	
2021	Toronto FC II	CAN-3.US	7th USL League One (15/1139)	
2022	Toronto FC	1.CAN	27th MLS (0/0)	
	Toronto FC II	CAN-3.US	7th MLS NEXT Pro (3/82); SF Playoffs (0/0)	
2023	Toronto FC II	CAN-3.US	23rd MLS NEXT Pro (0/0)	
	Alliance United FC	CAN-4.US	8th League1 Ontario (12/980)	

EUSTÁQUIO, STEPHEN — POR / FC PORTO

Midfielder. Born 1996, Leamington, ON, CAN. Height 178 cm. Dominant right foot. Youth clubs: Leamington MS (house league in Canada), GD Os Nazarenos, UD de Leiria, SCU Torreense

Canada Soccer Player of the Year (2023)

Honours: Concacaf champion (2021-22), Primeira (2021-22), Taça de Portugal (2022, 2023), Supertaça de Portugal (2022), Taça da Liga Portuguesa (2023)

CANADA INTERNATIONAL
1 FIFA World Cup: Group phase at Qatar 2022
1 Concacaf medal: Silver at CNL 2022-23
1st #CANMNT: 2019-11-15 at Orlando, FL, USA (v. USA)

SEASON	CLUB	NATION	HIGHLIGHTS (MP/MIN/G)	G
2017-18	Leixões SC	2.POR	x- Primeira (20/1696); R4 Taça (2/210); Taça de Liga (4/351)	
	GD Chaves	1.POR	6th Primeira (13/822)	
2018-19	GD Chaves	1.POR	x- Primeira (16/1407); L16 Taça (3/189); Taça de Liga (3/270/1g)	1
	Cruz Azul FC	1.MEX	4th Liga MX Clausura (1/34); QF Liga MX Liguilla (0/0); Copa 1/79)	
2019-20	Cruz Azul FC	1.MEX	12th Liga MX Apertura (0/0)	
	FC Paços de Ferreira	1.POR	13th Primeira (16/1239); QF Taça (1/90)	
2020-21	FC Paços de Ferreira	1.POR	5th Primeira (32/2805/2g); R4 Taça (2/174); Taça de Liga (1/90)	
2021-22	FC Paços de Ferreira	1.POR	11th Primeira (17/1478) R4 Taça (0/0); Taça de Liga (1/20)	
	FC Porto	1.POR	1st Primeira (8/82); 1st Taça (1/1)	
2022-23	FC Porto	1.POR	2nd Primeira (29/1676/2g); 1st Taça (5/270/1g); 1st Taça de Liga (2/150/2g); 1st Supertaça (1/20)	5
2023-24	FC Porto	1.POR	Primeira (current season); Taça (current); Taça de Liga (current); 1st Supertaça (1/265)	

CONTINENTAL FOOTBALL		UEFA	HIGHLIGHTS (MP/MIN/G)	G
2021-22	FC Paços de Ferreira	UEFA	UEFA Qualifying Europa Conference League (4/347/1g)	1
	FC Porto	UEFA	L16 UEFA Europa League (2/59)	
2022-23	FC Porto	UEFA	L16 UEFA Champions League (7/596/2g)	2
2023-24	FC Porto	UEFA	UEFA Champions League (current season)	

FACCHINERI, GIANFRANCO — WINDSOR CITY FC

Centre back. Born 2002, Windsor, ON, CAN. Height 185 cm. Youth clubs: Windsor Ciociaro SC, Windsor FC Nationals, Vardar SC, Toronto FC Academy, Vancouver Whitecaps FC Academy

School: University of Windsor

SEASON	CLUB	NATION	HIGHLIGHTS (MP/MIN/G)	G
2019	Vancouver Whitecaps FC	1.CAN	23rd MLS (0/0)	
2020	Atlético Ottawa	1.CAN	7th CPL (5/211)	
2021	San Diego Loyal SC	2.USA	W6th USL (6/30)	
2023	Windsor City FC	CAN	15th League1 Ontario (15/1330/2g)	2

FARIA, JORDAN — VALOUR FC

Winger. Born 2000, Brampton, ON, CAN. Height 168 cm. Youth clubs: Brampton YSC, Toronto FC Academy

SEASON	CLUB	NATION	HIGHLIGHTS (MP/MIN/G)	G
2016	TFC Academy	CAN	W3rd League1 Ontario (7/396/1g)	1
2017	TFC Academy	CAN	W3rd League1 Ontario (20/1278/3g)	3
2018	Toronto FC II	CAN-2.US	E16th USL (14/549/1g)	1
	TFC Academy	CAN	4th League1 Ontario (5/413/3g)	3
2019	Toronto FC II	CAN-3.US	7th USL League One (18/864/1g)	1

FOOTBALLERS

SEASON	CLUB	NATION	HIGHLIGHTS (MP/MIN/G)	G
2021	York United FC	1.CAN	4th CPL (12/319/1g); QF CanChamp (1/45)	1
2022	Musan Salama	3.FIN	B11th Kakkosen kausi; Lohko B (20/1776/6g); 4R Cup (2/180)	6
2023	Toronto FC	1.CAN	29th MLS (1/24)	
	Toronto FC II	CAN-3.US	23rd MLS NEXT Pro (23/139/4g)	4

FARSI, MOHAMED — USA / COLUMBUS CREW SC

Fullback. Born 1999, Montréal, QC, CAN. Height 180 cm. Dominant right foot. Youth clubs: CS Boucaniers Montréal, CS Notre-Dame-de-Grâce, CS Panellinios Montréal

Honours: MLS Cup (2023), MLS NEXT Pro Cup (2022), Futsal Canadian Championship (2017)

SEASON	CLUB	NATION	HIGHLIGHTS (MP/MIN/G)	G
2015	Panellinios Montréal FC U-16	CAN	3rd U-16 Cup	
2017	Québec U-18	CAN	Bronze at Canada Games (5/323)	
2018	CS Longueuil	CAN	4th PLSQ (13/1161)	
2019	AS Blainville	CAN	1st PLSQ (9/810)	
2019	AS Blainville	CAN	CanChamp (2/180)	
2019-20	AS Aïn M'lila	1.ALG	8th Ligue 1 d'Algérie (0/0)	
2020	Cavalry FC	1.CAN	4th CPL (10/611/1g)	1
2021	Cavalry FC	1.CAN	2nd CPL (25/2137/1g); SF Playoffs (1/120); QF CanChamp (2/180)	1
2022	Columbus Crew SC	1.USA	16th MLS (7/79)	
	Columbus Crew 2	3.USA	1st MLS NEXT Pro (18/1433/2g); 1st Playoffs (2/164)	2
2023	Columbus Crew SC	1.USA	3rd MLS (31/2158); 1st MLS Cup (5/371); L16 US Cup (3/84/1g); L32 Leagues (3/173)	1

FAYIA, SAAH TBOY

Fullback / forward. Born 2001, Monrovia, LBR. Grew up Edmonton, AB, CAN. Height 175 cm. Youth clubs: Edmonton Strikers, Sherwood Park Phoenix, Vancouver Whitecaps Academy, FC Edmonton Academy

SEASON	CLUB	NATION	HIGHLIGHTS (MP/MIN)
2015	Sherwood Park Phoenix U-14	CAN	4th U-14 Cup
2021	FC Edmonton	1.CAN	7th CPL (10/356); CanChamp (1/12)
2022	FC Edmonton	1.CAN	8th CPL (22/1165); CanChamp (1/75)

FERDINAND, KEESEAN — USA / PORTLAND TIMBERS II

Right back. Born 2003, Montréal, QC, CAN. Height 183 cm. Dominant right foot. Youth clubs: CS Rivière-des-Prairies, CS Panellinios Montréal, Académie de l'Impact de Montréal

SEASON	CLUB	NATION	HIGHLIGHTS (MP/MIN/G)	G
2020	Impact de Montréal	Concacaf	QF Champions League (0/0)	
2021	Atlético Ottawa	1.CAN	8th CPL (17/1056); CanChamp (1/80)	
2022	CF Montréal	1.CAN	3rd MLS (0/0)	
	CF Montréal U-23	CAN	6th PLSQ (17/1518/4g)	4
2023	Portland Timbers II	3.USA	20th MLS NEXT Pro (28/2398)	

FERGUSON, CALUM — SCO / CLACHNACUDDIN FC

Forward. Born 1995, Inverness, SCO. Height 175 cm. Youth clubs: Ross County FC, Inverness Caledonian Thistle

SEASON	CLUB	NATION	HIGHLIGHTS (MP/MIN/G)	G
2012-13	Ross County FC	1.SCO	5th Premier League (0/0)	
2013-14	Montrose FC	4.SCO	6th League Two (4/205)	
2014-15	Inverness Caledonian Thistle FC	1.SCO	3rd Premiership (2/48); 1st SFA Cup (0/0)	
2015-16	Inverness Caledonian Thistle FC	1.SCO	7th Premiership (0/0)	
	Ross County FC	1.SCO	6th Premiership (0/0)	
2016-17	Albion Rovers FC	3.SCO	8th League One (8/302); 4R SFA Cup (2/34/1g); Lg.Cup (4/334)	1
2017-18	Elgin City FC	4.SCO	6th League Two (4/79); 3R SFA Cup (1/25); Lg.Cup (1/33)	
2019	Valour FC	1.CAN	6th CPL (8/343); CanChamp (1/64)	
2019-20	Canterbury United FC	1.NLZ	10th Championship (11/785/2g)	2
2021	Erie Commodores	3.USA	NPSL	
2021-22	Warrenpoint Town FC	1.NIR	12th NIFL Premiership	
2022-23	Brechin City FC	5.SCO	Highland League	

FERNANDEZ, ZACHARY — HALIFAX WANDERERS FC

Fullback / midfielder. Born 2001, Laval, QC, CAN. Grew up Blainville, QC, CAN. Height 158 cm. Dominant right foot. Youth clubs: Académie de CF Montréal

SEASON	CLUB	NATION	HIGHLIGHTS (MP/MIN/G)	G
2021	AS Blainville	CAN	2nd PLSQ (15/1197/3g); CanChamp (1/86)	3
2022	HFX Wanderers FC	1.CAN	7th CPL (24/2100); QF CanChamp (2/180)	
2023	Halifax Wanderers FC	1.CAN	3rd CPL (23/1857/3g); 4th Playoffs (1/90); CanChamp (1/15)	3

FERRARI, MAX — YORK UNITED FC
Midfielder. Born 2000, Newmarket, ON, CAN. Height 172 cm. Dominant right foot. Youth clubs: Newmarket SC, Richmond Hill SC, ANB Futbol, Aurora YSC
School: Humber College

SEASON	CLUB	NATION	HIGHLIGHTS (MP/MIN/G)	G
2017	Aurora FC	CAN	E8th League1 Ontario (6/491)	
2019	Aurora FC	CAN	10th League1 Ontario (15/1199/3g)	3
2020	York9 FC	1.CAN	5th CPL (7/162)	
2021	York United FC	1.CAN	4th CPL (27/2159/2g); SF Playoffs (1/90); QF CanChamp (2/122/1g)	3
2022	York United FC	1.CAN	6th CPL (13/703); SF CanChamp (1/76)	
2023	York United FC	1.CAN	5th CPL (26/1864); 5th Playoffs (1/89); QF CanChamp (2/158)	

FERRARO, RILEY
Forward. Born 2006. Grew up Vancouver, BC, CAN. Youth clubs: Vancouver Whitecaps FC Academy

SEASON	CLUB	NATION	HIGHLIGHTS (MP/MIN)
2019	Vancouver Whitecaps U-13	Concacaf	Concacaf Under-13 Champions League
2023	Vanc. Whitecaps FC Academy	3.CAN	3rd League1 BC (1/16)

FERRAZZO, RILEY — HALIFAX WANDERERS FC
Right back / midfielder. Born 1999, Toronto, ON, CAN. Grew up Richmond Hill, ON, CAN. Height 178 cm. Youth clubs: Vaughan SC, Toronto FC Academy
School: Humber College, Seneca College

SEASON	CLUB	NATION	HIGHLIGHTS (MP/MIN/G)	G
2016	TFC Academy	CAN	W3rd League1 Ontario (20/1624/2g)	2
2017	TFC Academy	CAN	W3rd League1 Ontario (17/1022)	
2018	Vaughan Azzurri	CAN	5th League1 Ontario (3/109)	
2019	Aurora FC	CAN	10th League1 Ontario (15/1335/1g)	1
2021	Vaughan Azzurri	CAN	1st League1 Ontario (7/455/1g)	1
2022	Vaughan Azzurri	CAN	1st League1 Ontario (16/1184/2g); 1st Playoffs (2/158)	2
2023	Halifax Wanderers FC	1.CAN	3rd CPL (22/1198); 4th Playoffs (1/10); CanChamp (1/90)	

FERRIN, MASSIMO — HALIFAX WANDERERS FC
Forward. Born 1998, Mississauga, ON, CAN. Height 178 cm. Youth clubs: Mississauga SC, Vaughan SC
School: University of Alabama at Birmingham, Syracuse University

SEASON	CLUB	NATION	HIGHLIGHTS (MP/MIN/G)	G
2016	Vaughan Azzurri	CAN	1st League1 Ontario (2/100)	
2018	Vaughan Azzurri	CAN	5th League1 Ontario (1/7)	
2019	Vaughan Azzurri	CAN	2nd League1 Ontario (7/552/3g)	3
2020	Loudoun United FC	2.USA	E17th USL (6/269)	
2021	Loudoun United FC	2.USA	E16th USL (15/520)	
2022	Vaughan Azzurri	CAN	1st League1 Ontario (15/1094/23g); 1st Playoffs (2/177/1g)	24
2023	Halifax Wanderers FC	1.CAN	3rd CPL (25/2186/8g); 4th Playoffs (1/90); CanChamp (1/67/1g)	9

FIDALGO, JAMES
Forward. Born 2006. Grew up Maple, ON, CAN. Youth clubs: Toronto FC Academy.

SEASON	CLUB	NATION	HIGHLIGHTS (MP/MIN)
2023	Toronto FC II	CAN-3.US	23rd MLS NEXT Pro (0/0)

FILLION, YANN — HALIFAX WANDERERS FC
Goalkeeper. Born 1996, Ottawa, ON, CAN. Height 193 cm. Youth clubs: Ottawa Gloucester Dragon SC, FC Capital United SC, AS Hull, Académie de l'Impact de Montréal

SEASON	CLUB	NATION	HIGHLIGHTS (MP/MIN)
2015	FC Montréal	CAN-2.US	E10th USL (6/540)
2017	Umeå FC	3.SWE	5th Ettan Norra (17/1520)
2018	Nest-Sotra	2.NOR	x- OBOS-ligaen (1/90); R3 Cup (1/90)
2018-19	FC Aarau	2.SUI	x- Challenge League (0/0); 2R Coupe (0/0)

FOOTBALLERS

2019	Toronto FC II	CAN-3.US	7th USL League One (5/450)
2020	Ekenäs IF	2.FIN	4th Ykkösen kausi (15/1350); Cup (5/450)
2021	AC Oulu	1.FIN	11th Veikkausliiga (21/1845)
2022	IFK Mariehamn	1.FIN	10th Veikkausliiga (9/810); L16 Cup (3/270); Liigacup (2/180)
2023	Halifax Wanderers FC	1.CAN	3rd CPL (28/2520); 4th Playoffs (1/90); CanChamp (1/90)

FIREK, DANIEL
Midfielder. Born 2005. Grew up Mississauga, ON, CAN.
School: University of Akron

SEASON	CLUB	NATION	HIGHLIGHTS (MP/MIN)
2023	Forge FC Hamilton	1.CAN	2nd CPL (0/0)
2023	Sigma FC	CAN	9th League1 Ontario (6/216)

FISK, BEN — VANCOUVER FC
Forward. Born 1993, Vancouver, BC, CAN. Height 178 cm. Dominant left foot. Youth clubs: Boston (USA), Grandview Legion, Vancouver Whitecaps Residency
Honours: CPL North Star Shield (2023), League of Ireland Cup (2018)
1st #CANMNT: 2017-01-22 at Devonshire Parish, BER (v. BER)

SEASON	CLUB	NATION	HIGHLIGHTS (MP/MIN/G)	G
2007	British Columbia U-14	CAN	3rd Canada Soccer All Stars U-14	
2009	British Columbia U-16	CAN	4th Canada Soccer All Stars U-16	
2012	Vanc. Whitecaps FC U-23	CAN-4.US	USL PDL	
2013	Charleston Battery	2.USA	3rd USL PRO (8/280/2g); SF Playoffs (1/5); L16 US Cup (0/0)	2
2014-15	Coruxo FC	3.ESP	Group 1; 8th Segunda División B (24/1031/4g)	4
2016	FC Edmonton	2.USA	3rd NASL (15/881/2g); SF Playoffs (1/22)	2
2017	FC Edmonton	2.USA	7th NASL (29/2176); 5th CanChamp (1/45)	
2018	Derry City FC	NIR-1.IRL	8th Premier Division (12/701/1g); QF FAI Cup (2/154); 1st Lg.Cup (2/165)	1
2018-19	Derry City FC	UEFA	th UEFA Europa League (2/167)	
2019	Pacific FC	1.CAN	5th CPL (24/1663/6g); CanChamp (2/135)	6
2020	Atlético Ottawa	1.CAN	7th CPL (7/598/1g)	1
2021	Cavalry FC	1.CAN	2nd CPL (17/1074/1g); SF Playoffs (1/97); QF CanChamp (2/74/1g)	2
2022	Cavalry FC	1.CAN	3rd CPL (26/1210/1g); SF Playoffs (1/5); QF CanChamp (1/90)	1
2023	Cavalry FC	1.CAN	1st CPL (15/474/1g); 2nd Playoffs (2/12)	1

FONG, AIDAN — VANCOUVER WHITECAPS FC ACADEMY
Fullback. Born 2006, Richmond, BC, CAN. Grew up Vancouver, BC, CAN. Height 175 cm. Dominant right foot. Youth clubs: Killarney YSA, Vancouver Whitecaps FC Academy

SEASON	CLUB	NATION	HIGHLIGHTS (MP/MIN)
2019	Vancouver Whitecaps U-13	Concacaf	Concacaf Under-13 Champions League
2023	Vanc. Whitecaps FC Academy	3.CAN	3rd League1 BC (1/3)

FORTIER, TIM — TORONTO FC ACADEMY
Midfielder. Born 2008, Toronto, ON, CAN. Height 178 cm. Dominant right foot. Youth clubs: Toronto Canada First Academy, Toronto FC Academy

FRANKLIN, KOBE — TORONTO FC
Right back. Born 2003, Toronto, ON, CAN. Height 170 cm. Dominant right foot. Youth clubs: Beach Community SL, Power Soccer, Chicago Fire Academy (USA), Toronto FC Academy

SEASON	CLUB	NATION	HIGHLIGHTS (MP/MIN/G)	G
2018	TFC Academy	CAN	4th League1 Ontario (1/28/1g)	1
2021	Toronto FC II	CAN-3.US	7th USL League One (24/2149/2g)	2
2022	Toronto FC	1.CAN	27th MLS (1/13)	
	Toronto FC II	CAN-3.US	7th MLS NEXT Pro (20/1570/2g); SF Playoffs (2/209)	2
2023	Toronto FC	1.CAN	29th MLS (27/2172); Leagues (1/45); QF CanChamp (1/59)	
	Toronto FC II	CAN-3.US	23rd MLS NEXT Pro (0/0)	

FRASER, LIAM — USA / FC DALLAS
Midfielder. Born 1998, Toronto, ON, CAN. Grew up Vancouver, BC & Toronto, ON, CAN. Height 185 cm. Dominant right foot. Youth clubs: Waterloo MSA, Peace Arch AC, Surrey Guildford, Vancouver Whitecaps FC Residency, Toronto FC Academy. School: Ryerson University

Honours: Concacaf champion (2021-22), Canadian Championship (2018), Campeones Cup (2021)

CANADA INTERNATIONAL
1 FIFA World Cup: Group phase at Qatar 2022
1st #CANMNT: 2019-10-15 at Toronto, ON, CAN (v. USA)

SEASON	CLUB	NATION	HIGHLIGHTS (MP/MIN/G)	G
2015	Toronto FC II	CAN-2.US	E11th USL (10/670)	
	TFC Academy	CAN	5th League1 Ontario; USL PDL	
2016	Toronto FC II	CAN-2.US	E12th USL (22/1462/2g)	2
2017	Toronto FC II	CAN-2.US	E15th USL (20/1576)	
2018	Toronto FC	Concacaf	2nd Champions League (0/0)	
	Toronto FC	1.CAN	19th MLS (10/615); 1st CanChamp (2/180)	
	Toronto FC II	CAN-2.US	E16th USL (10/900)	
2019	Toronto FC	Concacaf	L16 Champions League (0/0)	
	Toronto FC	1.CAN	9th MLS (9/810); 2nd Playoffs (0/0); 2nd CanChamp (2/180)	
	Toronto FC II	CAN-3.US	7th USL League One (2/180)	
2020	Toronto FC	1.CAN	2nd MLS (13/436); L16 MLS is Back (0/0); Playoffs (1/9)	
2021	Toronto FC	Concacaf	QF Champions League (1/15)	
	Toronto FC	1.CAN	26th MLS (1/31)	
	Columbus Crew SC	1.USA	17th MLS (23/1134); 1st Campeones Cup (1/90)	
2021-22	KMSK Deinze	2.BEL	4th Division 1B (10/821)	
2022-23	KMSK Deinze	2.BEL	8th Division 1B (26/1668); L16 Beker (1/41)	
2023	FC Dallas	1.USA	15th MLS (7/368); L16 MLS Playoffs (3/231)	

FRIAS, SANTIAGO

Centre back. Born 2003, Oakville, ON, CAN. Height 193 cm. Youth clubs: Sigma FC
School: University of Akron

SEASON	CLUB	NATION	HIGHLIGHTS (MP/MIN)
2021	Forge FC Hamilton	1.CAN	1st CPL (2/20)
	Sigma FC	CAN	9th League1 Ontario (1/24)
2022	Sigma FC	CAN	9th League1 Ontario (12/1080)

FROESE, KIANZ   GER / FORTUNA DÜSSELDORF

Midfielder. Born 1996, La Habana, CUB. Grew up La Habana, CUB & Winnipeg, MB, CAN. Height 177 cm. Youth clubs: Garden City Community Centre, Portage Trail, Vancouver Whitecaps Residency
Honours: Canadian Championship (2015)
1st #CANMNT: 2015-10-13 at Washington, DC, USA (v. GHA)

SEASON	CLUB	NATION	HIGHLIGHTS (MP/MIN/G)	G
2009	Portage Trail Timberwolves	CAN	5th U-14 Cup	
	Manitoba U-14	CAN	3rd Canada Soccer All Stars U-14	
2010	Manitoba U-14	CAN	5th Canada Soccer All Stars U-14	
2012	Vanc. Whitecaps FC U-23	CAN-4.US	USL PDL	
2014	Vancouver Whitecaps FC	1.CAN	9th MLS (1/45); 3rd CanChamp (1/77)	
	Vanc. Whitecaps FC U-23	CAN-4.US	USL PDL	
2015	Vancouver Whitecaps FC	1.CAN	3rd MLS (9/208/1g); 1st CanChamp (2/176)	1
	Vanc. Whitecaps FC 2	CAN-2.US	W11th USL (6/520/1g)	1
2015-16	Vancouver Whitecaps FC	Concacaf	16th Champions League (4/340/1g)	1
2016	Vancouver Whitecaps FC	1.CAN	16th MLS (5/150); 2nd CanChamp (1/90)	
	Vanc. Whitecaps FC 2	CAN-2.US	W6th USL (13/892/1g); SF Playoffs (3/255/2g)	3
2016-17	Vancouver Whitecaps FC	Concacaf	SF Champions League (1/1)	
	Fortuna Düsseldorf II	4.GER	Regionalliga	
2017-18	Fortuna Düsseldorf	2.GER	1st 2.Bundesliga (0/0)	
	Fortuna Düsseldorf II	4.GER	Regionalliga	
2018-19	Fortuna Düsseldorf II	4.GER	Regionalliga	
2019-20	1. FC Saarbrücken	4.GER	Regionalliga; SF Pokal (5/331)	
2020-21	1. FC Saarbrücken	3.GER	5th 3.Liga (29/1043/2g)	2
2021-22	TSV Havelse	3.GER	19th 3.Liga (31/2633/5g)	5
2022-23	SV Wehen Wiesbaden	3.GER	4th 3.Liga (33/1350/6g); 1st Promotion Playoffs (2/38)	6
2023-24	SV Wehen Wiesbaden	2.GER	2.Bundesliga (current season); Pokal (1/45)	

FOOTBALLERS

FUERST, BRENNEN
Midfielder / centre back. Born 2004. Grew up in Calgary, AB, CAN. Youth clubs: Calgary Blizzard, Vancouver Whitecaps FC Academy
Honours: League1 BC (2023)

SEASON	CLUB	NATION	HIGHLIGHTS (MP/MIN)
2022	Vanc. Whitecaps FC 2	CAN-3.US	14th MLS NEXT Pro (0/0)
	Vanc. Whitecaps FC Academy	3.CAN	3rd League1 BC
2023	Vanc. Whitecaps FC 2	CAN-3.US	21st MLS NEXT Pro (1/90)
	Vanc. Whitecaps FC Academy	3.CAN	3rd League1 BC (11/915); 1st Playoffs (2/178)

FUNG, VICTOR — USA / INTER MIAMI FC ACADEMY
Centre back. Born 2007, Montréal, QC, CAN. Grew up Caracas, VEN & Weston, FL, USA. Height 178 cm. Dominant right foot. Youth clubs: Escuela Campo Alegre (Venezuela), Inter Miami FC Academy

GAGNON-LAPARÉ, JÉRÉMY — HALIFAX WANDERERS FC
Midfielder. Born 1995, Sherbrooke, QC, CAN. Grew up Magog, QC, CAN. Height 180 cm. Dominant left foot. Youth clubs: AS Magog, Académie de l'Impact de Montréal
Honours: Canadian Championship (2004)
1st #CANMNT: 2013-09-8 at Oliva, ESP (v. MTN)

SEASON	CLUB	NATION	HIGHLIGHTS (MP/MIN/G)	G
2009	Québec U-14	CAN	2nd Canada Soccer All Stars U-14	
2011	Québec U-16	CAN	1st Canada Soccer All Stars U-16	
2014	Impact de Montréal	1.CAN	19th MLS (5/270); 1st CanChamp (1/4)	
2014-15	Impact de Montréal		2nd Champions League (2/103)	
2015	Impact de Montréal	1.CAN	7th MLS (2/18); 2nd CanChamp (0/0)	
	FC Montréal	CAN-2.US	E10th USL (16/1301/1g)	1
	Ottawa Fury FC	2.USA	2nd NASL (2/100); 2nd NASL Playoffs (1/18)	
2016	Impact de Montréal	1.CAN	SF CanChamp (1/78)	
	FC Montréal	CAN-2.US	E14th USL (13/1077)	
2016-17	AS Vitré	4.FRA	A6th Championnat CFA Groupe A (13/1118/1g)	1
2017-18	AS Vitré	4.FRA	D11th National 2 Groupe D (24/1889/1g); R2 Coupe (2/180)	1
2018	Ottawa Fury FC	2.USA	E10th USL (11/801); SF CanChamp (1/90)	
2019	Ottawa Fury FC	2.USA	E8th USL (33/2428); SF CanChamp (4/331); Playoffs (1/1)	
2020	Saint Louis FC	2.USA	E8th USL (9/652); QF Playoffs (0/0)	
2021	HFX Wanderers FC	1.CAN	4th CPL (22/1838); QF CanChamp (2/180)	
2022	HFX Wanderers FC	1.CAN	7th CPL (22/1719); QF CanChamp (1/84)	
2023	York United FC	1.CAN	5th CPL (21/1410); 5th Playoffs (1/1); QF CanChamp (1/57)	

GANDER, COLIN
Fullback. Born 2000, Kitchener, ON, CAN. Height 182 cm. Dominant left foot. Youth clubs: Kitchener SC, Toronto FC Academy
School: Missouri State University, University of Guelph

SEASON	CLUB	NATION	HIGHLIGHTS (MP/MIN/G)	G
2017	TFC Academy	CAN	W3rd League1 Ontario (1/12)	
2018	TFC Academy	CAN	4th League1 Ontario (3/270)	
2021	Guelph United FC	CAN	2nd League1 Ontario (4/302/1g)	1
2022	HFX Wanderers FC	1.CAN	7th CPL (15/930); QF CanChamp (2/180)	

GARCIA, RAPHAËL
Fullback. Born 1999, Ottawa, ON, CAN. Height 178 cm. Youth clubs: Ottawa Gloucester Hornets, Académie Impact Montréal
School: Carleton University

SEASON	CLUB	NATION	HIGHLIGHTS (MP/MIN)
2019	Valour FC	1.CAN	6th CPL (16/943)
2020	Valour FC	1.CAN	6th CPL (1/27)

GARDNER, SAMUEL
Centre back. Born 1997, Toronto, ON, CAN. Height 193 cm. Youth clubs: Scarborough Blizzard SC, North Scarborough SC, Power FC
School: Jacksonville University, Grand Canyon University

SEASON	CLUB	NATION	HIGHLIGHTS (MP/MIN/G)	G
2017	K-W United FC	CAN-4.US	USL PDL (1/26)	
2019	Sigma FC	CAN	5th League1 Ontario (8/630/1g); QF Playoffs (1/87)	1
2020	FC Edmonton	1.CAN	8th CPL (2/86)	
2021-22	Cape Town Spurs	2.RSA	14th RSA - National First Division	
2022	Alliance United FC	CAN	3rd League1 Ontario (9/804/1g); SF Playoffs (2/180/1g)	2

GARDNER, THOMAS

Midfielder. Born 1998, Vancouver, BC, CAN. Grew up North Vancouver, BC, CAN. Height 175 cm. Youth clubs: Lynn Valley SA, Vancouver Whitecaps FC Residency
School: University of British Columbia

SEASON	CLUB	NATION	HIGHLIGHTS (MP/MIN/G)	G
2015	Vanc. Whitecaps FC 2	CAN-2.US	W11th USL (3/65)	
2016	Vanc. Whitecaps FC 2	CAN-2.US	W6th USL (16/661); SF Playoffs (2/177)	
2017	Vanc. Whitecaps FC 2	CAN-2.US	W14th USL (21/1408)	
2018	TSS Rovers FC	CAN-4.US	USL PDL (6/470/1g)	1
2021	FC Edmonton	1.CAN	7th CPL (10/487)	
2022	Varsity FC	CAN	League1 BC	

GARNER, JACK — VANCOUVER ISLAND WAVE

Goalkeeper. Born 2005. Grew up in Victoria, BC, CAN. Youth clubs: Victoria Gorge FC, Vancouver Island Wave

SEASON	CLUB	NATION	HIGHLIGHTS (MP/MIN)
2023	Pacific FC	1.CAN	CPL (0/0)

GAVRAN, LUKA — TORONTO FC

Goalkeeper. Born 2000, . Grew up Hamilton, ON, CAN. Height cm. Youth clubs: Hamilton Croatia SC, GNK Dinamo Zagreb (Croatia), GPS Academy
School: St. John's University

SEASON	CLUB	NATION	HIGHLIGHTS (MP/MIN)
2022	Toronto FC	1.CAN	27th MLS (0/0)
	Toronto FC II	CAN-3.US	7th MLS NEXT Pro (18/1620); SF Playoffs (2/210)
2023	Toronto FC	1.CAN	29th MLS (4/360)
	Toronto FC II	CAN-3.US	23rd MLS NEXT Pro (18/1582)

GAZDOV, EMIL — PACIFIC FC

Goalkeeper. Born 2003, Vancouver, BC, CAN. Height 193 cm. Youth clubs: Mountain United FC, Vancouver Whitecaps FC Academy

SEASON	CLUB	NATION	HIGHLIGHTS (MP/MIN)
2022	Pacific FC	Concacaf	L16 Concacaf League (0/0)
2022 zcx	Pacific FC	1.CAN	4th CPL (2/180)
2023	Pacific FC	1.CAN	4th CPL (18/1620); 3rd Playoffs (3/270); SF CanChamp (2/180)

GEE, PARIS — VANCOUVER FC

Fullback. Born 1994, Burnaby, BC, CAN. Height 180 cm. Youth clubs: Burnaby Selects SC, Mountain United SC, Coquitlam Metro-Ford SC, Vancouver Whitecaps FC Academy
School: Simon Fraser University

SEASON	CLUB	NATION	HIGHLIGHTS (MP/MIN/G)	G
2010	British Columbia U-16	CAN	4th Canada Soccer All Stars U-16	
2014-15	NK Rudeš Zagreb	2.CRO	4th Druga hrvatska liga (14/874)	
2015-16	NK Rudeš Zagreb	2.CRO	5th Druga hrvatska liga (21/1662)	
2017	Tulsa Roughnecks	2.USA	W7th USL (20/892); L16 Playoffs (1/90); R4 US Cup (2/113)	
2018	Tulsa Roughnecks	2.USA	W17th USL (33/2711/3g); R2 US Cup (0/0)	3
2019	Saint Louis FC	2.USA	E11th USL (19/1177); QF US Cup (5/459/1g)	1
2020	Saint Louis FC	2.USA	E8th USL (16/1321); QF Playoffs (2/159)	
2021	FC Edmonton	1.CAN	7th CPL (27/2016); CanChamp (0/0)	
2022	York United FC	1.CAN	6th CPL (8/447)	
2023	York United FC	1.CAN	5th CPL (25/2240); 5th Playoffs (1/90); QF CanChamp (2/180)	

GHASEMI, AMIRMAHDI

Forward. Born 2006, .., IRN. Grew up in . Youth clubs: Vancouver Whitecaps FC Academy
Honours: League1 BC (2023)

FOOTBALLERS

SEASON	CLUB	NATION	HIGHLIGHTS (MP/MIN/G)	G
2023	Vanc. Whitecaps FC 2	CAN-3.US	21st MLS NEXT Pro (2/67/1g)	
	Vanc. Whitecaps FC Academy	3.CAN	3rd League1 BC (11/724); 1st Playoffs (2/165/1g)	1

GIANTSOPOULOS, NIKO — YORK UNITED FC

Goalkeeper. Born 1994, Markham, ON, CAN. Height 187 cm. Dominant right foot. Youth clubs: Unionville-Milliken SC, Pickering SC, Ajax Strikers
School: Adrian College, Calvin University

SEASON	CLUB	NATION	HIGHLIGHTS (MP/MIN)
2010	Ajax Strikers U-16	CAN	1st U-16 Cup
2011	Ajax Strikers U-18	CAN	1st U-18 Cup
2014	Durham United	CAN	8th League1 Ontario
2015	Ocala Stampede	4.USA	USL PDL (7/?)
2016	Devonport City	2.AUS	1st Tasmania (21/?), QF Playoffs
2017	Broadmeadow Magic	2.AUS	4th Northern NSW (19/?)
2018	Launceston City	2.AUS	4th Tasmania (21/?)
2019	Cavalry FC	1.CAN	2nd CPL (5/450); SF CanChamp (4/360)
2020	Cavalry FC	1.CAN	4th CPL (1/90)
2021	York United FC	1.CAN	4th CPL (9/710); SF Playoffs (0/0); QF CanChamp (0/0)
2022	York United FC	1.CAN	6th CPL (18/1551); SF CanChamp (3/270)
	Vancouver Whitecaps FC	1.CAN	x- MLS (0/0)
2023	York United FC	1.CAN	5th CPL (22/1980); 5th Playoffs (1/90); QF CanChamp (2/180)

GIRALDO, TOMAS — HALIFAX WANDERERS FC

Midfielder. Born 2003, Medellín, COL. Grew up Montréal, QC, CAN. Height 184 cm. Youth clubs: Instituto Jorge Robledo (Colombia), Braves d'Ahuntsic, FS Salaberry, Académie Impact de Montréal

SEASON	CLUB	NATION	HIGHLIGHTS (MP/MIN/G)	G
2020	Impact de Montréal	Concacaf	QF Champions League (0/0)	
	Impact de Montréal	1.CAN	18th MLS (0/0); Playoffs (0/0)	
2022	CF Montréal	1.CAN	3rd MLS (0/0)	
2023	Halifax Wanderers FC	1.CAN	3rd CPL (19/814/2g)	2

GODIN, ÉTIENNE — ACADÉMIE CF MONTRÉAL

Centre back. Born 2006, Lebanon, NH, USA. Grew up Montréal, QC, CAN. Height 184.5 cm. Dominant right foot. Youth clubs: CS Mont-Royal Outremont, Académie de CF Montréal

SEASON	CLUB	NATION	HIGHLIGHTS (MP/MIN)
2019	Impact de Montréal U-13	Concacaf	Concacaf Under-13 Champions League

GODINHO, MARCUS — POL / KORONA KIELCE

Fullback. Born 1997, Toronto, ON, CAN. Height 178 cm. Dominant right foot. Youth clubs: North York Azzurri Hearts, Kleinburg Nobelton SC, Woodbridge SC, Toronto FC Academy
Honours: Canadian Championship (2022)
1st #CANMNT: 2018-03-24 at San Pedro del Pinatar, ESP (v. NZL)

SEASON	CLUB	NATION	HIGHLIGHTS (MP/MIN/G)	G
2011	KNSC Red Lions U-14	CAN	1st U-14 Cup	
2014	TFC Academy	CAN	1st League1 Ontario	
2015	Toronto FC II	CAN-2.US	E11th USL (7/356)	
2016	Vaughan Azzurri	CAN	1st League1 Ontario (2/180)	
2016-17	Heart of Midlothian FC	UEFA	UEFA Qualifying Europa League (0/0)	
	Heart of Midlothian FC	1.SCO	L16 SFA Cup (0/0)	
2017-18	Berwick Rangers FC	4.SCO	x- League Two (7/604); R3 SFA Cup (0/0)	
	Heart of Midlothian FC	1.SCO	6th Premiership (5/420); QF SFA Cup (1/90)	
2018-19	Heart of Midlothian FC	1.SCO	6th Premiership (12/917/1g); 2nd SFA Cup (2/180)	1
2019-20	FSV Zwickau	3.GER	16th 3.Liga (25/1846)	
2020-21	FSV Zwickau	3.GER	10th 3.Liga (5/292)	
2021	Vancouver Whitecaps FC	1.CAN	12th MLS (4/114); Playoffs (1/65)	
2022	Vancouver Whitecaps FC	1.CAN	17th MLS (23/1018); 1st CanChamp (3/114)	
	Vanc. Whitecaps FC 2	CAN-3.US	14th MLS NEXT Pro (0/0)	
2022-23	Korona Kielce	1.POL	13th Ekstraklasa (15/601/1g)	1
2023-24	Korona Kielce	1.POL	Ekstraklasa (current season); Puchar (current)	

GOLDSON, ISAIAH   TORONTO FC II
Goalkeeper. Born 2005, Oakville, ON, CAN. Grew up in Oakville, ON, CAN. Height 183. Youth clubs: Oakville SC, Vaughan, SC, Toronto FC Academy

SEASON	CLUB	NATION	HIGHLIGHTS (MP/MIN)
2022	Toronto FC II	CAN-3.US	7th MLS NEXT Pro (0/0)
2023	Toronto FC II	CAN-3.US	23rd MLS NEXT Pro (0/0)

GORDON, JOSHUA   TORONTO FC II
Right back. Born 2005, Ajax, ON, CAN. Grew up Toronto, ON, CAN. Height 175 cm. Youth clubs: Scarborough National Malvern SC, Toronto FC Academy

SEASON	CLUB	NATION	HIGHLIGHTS (MP/MIN)
2018	Toronto FC U-13	Concacaf	QF Concacaf Under-13 Champions League
2022	Toronto FC II	CAN-3.US	7th MLS NEXT Pro (4/47)
2023	Toronto FC II	CAN-3.US	23rd MLS NEXT Pro (0/0)

GOULBOURNE, ROHAN   TORONTO FC II
Left back. Born 2002, Brampton, ON, CAN. Height 172 cm. Youth clubs: Kinder Soccer, Woodbridge SC, TFC Acamdey

SEASON	CLUB	NATION	HIGHLIGHTS (MP/MIN)
2018	TFC Academy	CAN	4th League1 Ontario (1/28)
2021	Toronto FC II	CAN-3.US	7th USL League One (22/1238)
2022	Toronto FC II	CAN-3.US	7th MLS NEXT Pro (22/1793); SF Playoffs (2/210)
2023	Toronto FC II	CAN-3.US	23rd MLS NEXT Pro (1/89)

GRECO-TAYLOR, CHRISTIAN
Midfielder. Born 2005, Calgary, AB, CAN. Grew up in Calgary, AB, CAN. Height 175. Youth clubs: Calgary Foothills SC, Vancouver Whitecaps FC Academy

SEASON	CLUB	NATION	HIGHLIGHTS (MP/MIN)
2022	Vanc. Whitecaps FC 2	CAN-3.US	14th MLS NEXT Pro (0/0)
2023	Vanc. Whitecaps FC 2	CAN-3.US	21st MLS NEXT Pro (21/1063)

GUARDIERO, SIMON   SIGMA FC
Centre back. Born 2006, Guelph, ON, CAN. Height 185 cm. Dominant Bight foot. Youth clubs: Guelph SC, Sigma

SEASON	CLUB	NATION	HIGHLIGHTS (MP/MIN)
2023	Sigma FC	CAN	9th League1 Ontario (6/323)

GUTIÉRREZ, CRISTIÁN   TORONTO FC II
Fullback. Born 1997, Greenfield Park, QC, CAN. Grew up Santiago, CHI. Height 182 cm. Dominant left foot. Youth clubs: Escuela CSD Colo-Colo, Colo Colo
Honours: Concacaf champion (2021-22), Canadian Championship (2022)

SEASON	CLUB	NATION	HIGHLIGHTS (MP/MIN/G)	G
2015-16	CSD Colo Colo	1.CHI	1st Nacional Apertura (11/924); 2nd Clausura (7/569)	
2016	CSD Colo Colo	CONMEBOL	Copa Libertadores (0/0)	
2016-17	CSD Colo Colo	1.CHI	5th Nacional Apertura (3/207)	
	Club Unión Española	1.CHI	5th Nacional Clausura (5/450)	
2017	CD Huachipato	1.CHI	12th Nacional Transicion (7/419)	
2018	CD Huachipato	1.CHI	9th Nacional (7/630)	
2019	CSD Colo Colo	1.CHI	2nd Nacional (6/502); QF Copa (3/183)	
2020	Vancouver Whitecaps FC	1.CAN	17th MLS (12/665); L16 MLS is Back (1/90)	
2021	Vancouver Whitecaps FC	1.CAN	12th MLS (19/1546)	
2022	Vancouver Whitecaps FC	1.CAN	17th MLS (11/613); 1st CanChamp (1/90)	
	Vanc. Whitecaps FC 2	CAN-3.US	14th MLS NEXT Pro (3/180)	
2023	Vancouver Whitecaps FC	1.CAN	29th MLS (6/244)	
	Vanc. Whitecaps FC 2	CAN-3.US	23rd MLS NEXT Pro (3/163)	

GUTIÉRREZ ZUÑIGA, DIEGO   CAVALRY FC
Fullback & midfielder. Born 1997, Greenfield Park, QC, CAN. Grew up Santiago, CHI. Height 178 cm. Dominant right foot. Youth clubs: Escuela CSD Colo-Colo, CD Palestino

SEASON	CLUB	NATION	HIGHLIGHTS (MP/MIN)
2015-16	CD Palestino	1.CHI	4th Nacional Apertura (1/34); 4th Clausura (0/0)
2016-17	CD Palestino	1.CHI	14th Nacional Clausura (2/90)

FOOTBALLERS

2017	CD Palestino	CONMEBOL	Copa Sudamericana (3/199)
	CD Palestino	1.CHI	15th Nacional Transicion (1/11)
2018	CD Palestino	1.CHI	13th Nacional (1/56)
2019	Valour FC	1.CAN	6th CPL (23/1605); CanChamp (1/90)
2020	Valour FC	1.CAN	6th CPL (7/489)
2021	AC Barnechea	2.CHI	15th Primera B de Chile (12/552)
2022	Valour FC	1.CAN	CanChamp (1/81)
2023	Valour FC	1.CAN	8th CPL (25/2113/4g); CanChamp (1/45)

HABER, MARCUS — CAM / PREAH KHAN REACH SVAY RIENG

Forward. Born 1989, Vancouver, BC, CAN. Height 192 cm. Dominant right foot. Youth clubs: Dunbar SA, Vancouver Selects, FC Groningen (Netherlands)
1st #CANMNT: 2010-10-8 at Kyiv, UKR (v. UKR)

SEASON	CLUB	NATION	HIGHLIGHTS (MP/MIN/G)	G
2005	Vancouver Selects	CAN	1st U-16 Cup	
2005	British Columbia U-16	CAN	1st Canada Soccer All Stars U-16	
2009	Vancouver Whitecaps FC	CAN-2.US	7th USL First Division (30/1978/8g); 2nd CanChamp (3/258/1g)	9
2009-10	Exeter City FC	3.ENG	x- League One (5/239)	
2010	Vancouver Whitecaps	1.CAN	x- USSF2 (11/872/1g); 2nd CanChamp (4/301/1g)	2
2010-11	St. Johnstone FC	1.SCO	8th Premier (11/467/1g); QF Lg.Cup (3/72/1g)	2
2011-12	St. Johnstone FC	1.SCO	6th Premier (31/1549/2g); L16 Cup (2/117); L16 Lg.Cup (1/20)	2
2012-13	Stevenage FC	3.ENG	18th League One (42/3012/7g); R1 FA Cup (1/90); R1 Lg.Cup (2/174); R1 EFL Trophy (1/45)	7
2013-14	Notts County FC	3.ENG	x- League One (11/572/2g); L16 EFL Trophy (0/0)	2
	Stevenage FC	3.ENG	24th League One (3/107); R4 FA Cup (1/78); R2 Lg.Cup (1/18)	
2014-15	Crewe Alexandra FC	3.ENG	20th League One (36/2272/7g); R1 FA Cup (1/90); R2 Lg.Cup (2/54/1g)	8
2015-16	Crewe Alexandra FC	3.ENG	24th League One (40/3101/9g); R1 FA Cup (1/90); R1 Lg.Cup (1/63); 2R EFL Trophy (1/90/1g)	10
2016-17	Dundee FC	1.SCO	10th Premiership (27/2350/9g); R4 SFA Cup (1/90)	9
2017-18	Dundee FC	1.SCO	9th Premiership (11/748/2g); L16 SFA Cup (0/0); QF Lg.Cup (2/117)	2
2018-19	Falkirk FC	2.SCO	10th Championship (15/618); Lg.Cup (1/30)	
2019	Pacific FC	1.CAN	5th CPL (13/704/3g); CanChamp (2/180/1g)	4
2020	Cavalry FC	1.CAN	4th CPL (9/508/2g)	2
2021	Visakha FC	1.CAM	3rd C-League (17/?/17g)	17
2022	PKR Svay Rieng	1.CAM	2nd Cambodian Premier (27/?/25g)	25
2023-24	PKR Svay Rieng	1.CAM	Cambodian Premier (current season)	

HABIBULLAH, KAMRON

Winger. Born 2003, Tashkent, UZB. Grew up Vancouver, BC, CAN. Height 173 cm. Dominant right foot. Youth clubs: South Burnaby Metro SC, Mountain United FC, Cliff Avenue FC, Vancouver Whitecaps FC Academy

SEASON	CLUB	NATION	HIGHLIGHTS (MP/MIN/G)	G
2021	Vancouver Whitecaps FC	1.CAN	12th MLS (3/34)	
2022	Vancouver Whitecaps FC	1.CAN	17th MLS (0/0)	
	Pacific FC	Concacaf	L16 Concacaf League (0/0)	
	Pacific FC	1.CAN	4th CPL (14/519); SF Playoffs (2/139); QF CanChamp (0/0)	
2023	Vancouver Whitecaps FC	CAN	QF Champions League (0/0)	
	Vancouver Whitecaps FC	1.CAN	13th MLS (0/0)	
	Vanc. Whitecaps FC 2	CAN-3.US	21st MLS NEXT Pro (18/1320/4g)	4

HABUSH, ABDULLAH — CF MONTRÉAL U-23

Midfielder. Born 2003, Dubai, UAE. Grew up in Montréal, QC, CAN. Height 178 cm. Dominant right foot. Youth clubs: West Ottawa SC, AC Fiorentina Ottawa

SEASON	CLUB	NATION	HIGHLIGHTS (MP/MIN)
2023	CF Montréal U-23	CAN	5th Ligue1 Québec

HALLEY, IJAH — SIMCOE COUNTY ROVERS FC

Forward. Born 2001, Brampton, ON, CAN. Height 180 cm. Youth clubs: Woodbridge Strikers SC, Erin Mills SC, Toronto FC Academy
Honours: League1 Ontario (2023)

MEN'S FOOTBALLERS | 87

SEASON	CLUB	NATION	HIGHLIGHTS (MP/MIN/G)	G
2020	York9 FC	1.CAN	5th CPL (4/159)	
2021	York United FC	1.CAN	4th CPL (14/381); SF Playoffs (1/34); QF CanChamp (1/3)	
2022	Scrosoppi FC	CAN	12th League1 Ontario (12/787/3g)	3
2023	Simcoe County Rovers FC	CAN	2nd League1 Ontario (17/1264/4g); 1st Playoffs (2/112)	4

HAMILTON, JORDAN — FORGE FC HAMILTON

Forward. Born 1996, Scarborough, ON, CAN. Height 185 cm. Dominant left foot. Youth clubs: North Scarborough SC, Ajax SC, Toronto FC Academy
Honours: Canadian Championship (2016, 2017, 2018), MLS Cup (2017), MLS Supporters' Shield (2017), CPL Championship (2022, 2023)
1st #CANMNT: 2014-10-14 at Harrison, NJ, USA (v. COL)

SEASON	CLUB	NATION	HIGHLIGHTS (MP/MIN/G)	G
2009	Markham Lightning U-14	CAN	2nd U-14 Cup	
2009	Ontario U-14	CAN	1st Canada Soccer All Stars U-14	
2010	Ontario U-14	CAN	2nd Canada Soccer All Stars U-14	
2011	Ontario U-16	CAN	2nd Canada Soccer All Stars U-16	
2012	Ontario U-16	CAN	1st Canada Soccer All Stars U-16	
2014	Toronto FC	1.CAN	13th MLS (1/1)	
	Wilmington Hammerheads	2.USA	7th USL PRO (11/459/5g)	5
2014-15	CD Trofense	2.POR	24th Primeira (4/69); R2 Taça da Liga (2/132)	
2015	Toronto FC	1.CAN	12th MLS (2/13); 4th CanChamp (0/0)	
	Toronto FC II	CAN-2.US	E11th USL (20/1387/3g)	3
2016	Toronto FC	1.CAN	5th MLS (14/911/3g); 1st CanChamp (4/185/2g)	5
	Toronto FC II	CAN-2.US	E12th USL (4/272)	
2017	Toronto FC	1.CAN	1st MLS (8/142/2g); 1st CanChamp (3/197)	2
	Toronto FC II	CAN-2.US	E15th USL (9/733/5g)	5
2018	Toronto FC	Concacaf	2nd Champions League (3/44)	
	Toronto FC	1.CAN	19th MLS (14/862/2g); 1st CanChamp (2/48/1g)	3
	Toronto FC II	CAN-2.US	E16th USL (10/739/8g)	8
2019	Toronto FC	Concacaf	L16 Champions League (1/90/1g)	1
	Toronto FC	1.CAN	x- MLS (14/623/4g)	4
	Toronto FC II	CAN-3.US	x- USL League One (1/90/1g)	1
	Columbus Crew SC	1.USA	20th MLS (4/56)	
2020	Columbus Crew SC	1.USA	4th MLS (2/13); L16 MLS is Back (0/0); 1st Playoffs (0/0)	
2021	Indy Eleven	2.USA	E12th USL (18/895/5g)	5
2022	Sligo Rovers FC	1.IRL	x- Premier Division (13/651/2g)	2
	Forge FC Hamilton	1.CAN	2nd CPL (10/305/1g); 1st Playoffs (2/7)	1
2023	Forge FC Hamilton	1.CAN	2nd CPL (17/602/4g); 1st Playoffs (2/36); SF CanChamp (3/73)	4

HANSON, JOE

Forward. Born 2003, Whitehorse, YT, CAN. Grew up in Whitehorse, YT, CAN. Height 193. Youth clubs: Whitehorse Yukon Strikers, Whitehorse Yukon Selects, Total Soccer Excellence Academy, Vancouver Island Wave, Crossfire Premier

SEASON	CLUB	NATION	HIGHLIGHTS (MP/MIN/G)	G
2016	Yukon Strikers U-14	CAN	10th U-14 Cup	
2017	Whitehorse Yukon Selects FC U-15	CAN	11th U-15 Cup	
2018	Whitehorse Yukon Selects FC	CAN	7th U-15 Cup	
2022	Vanc. Whitecaps FC 2	CAN-3.US	14th MLS NEXT Pro (17/442/3g)	3
2023	Vanc. Whitecaps FC 2	CAN-3.US	21st MLS NEXT Pro (20/778)	

HARMS, MICHAEL — CAVALRY FC

Fullback & centre back. Born 2005, Calgary, AB, CAN. Dominant right foot. Youth clubs: Calgary Foothills SC
Honours: CPL North Star Shield (2023)

SEASON	CLUB	NATION	HIGHLIGHTS (MP/MIN)
2019	Calgary Foothills FC U-15	CAN	2nd U-15 Cup
2022	Alberta U-18	CAN	Bronze at Canada Games (3/240)
2023	Cavalry FC	1.CAN	1st CPL (3/114)

HARRIS, DAYONN — USA / NEW MEXICO UNITED

Midfielder & forward. Born 1997, Brampton, ON, CAN. Height 168 cm. Youth clubs: Brampton East SC, Woodbridge Strikers SC, Vaughan SC

School: Penn State University, University of Connecticut

SEASON	CLUB	NATION	HIGHLIGHTS (MP/MIN/G)	G
2012	Ontario U-15	CAN	1st Canada Soccer All Stars U-15	
2013	Ontario U-18	CAN	Bronze at Canada Games (4/277)	
2015	Vaughan Azzurri	CAN	3rd League1 Ontario	
2016	Vaughan Azzurri	CAN	1st League1 Ontario (2/67/2g)	2
2017	Vaughan Azzurri	CAN	E2nd League1 Ontario (2/88)	
2018	Vaughan Azzurri	CAN	5th League1 Ontario (2/41/1g)	1
2019	Vaughan Azzurri	CAN	2nd League1 Ontario (2/111)	
	Vaughan Azzurri	CAN	CanChamp (2/29)	
2020	Real Monarchs	2.USA	W14th USL (14/913)	
2021	Tampa Bay Rowdies	2.USA	E1st USL (17/662); 2nd Playoffs (3/108)	
2022	Tampa Bay Rowdies	2.USA	E3rd USL (26/948/5g); SF Playoffs (3/130); R3 US Cup (2/160)	5
2023	Tampa Bay Rowdies	2.USA	E2nd USL (28/1349/1g); R3 US Cup (2/90)	1

HARTILL, JASON — TORONTO FC II
Midfielder. Born 2004. Grew up in .., ON, CAN. Height 175. Dominant left foot. Youth clubs: West Ottawa SC, Toronto FC Academy

SEASON	CLUB	NATION	HIGHLIGHTS (MP/MIN)
2022	Ontario U-18	CAN	Silver at Canada Games (4/279)
2023	Toronto FC II	CAN-3.US	23rd MLS NEXT Pro (0/0)

HASAL, THOMAS — VANCOUVER WHITECAPS FC
Goalkeeper. Born 1999, Cambridge, ON, CAN. Grew up Saskatoon, SK, CAN. Height 193 cm. Youth clubs: Ottawa, Saskatoon Aurora SC, Whitecaps Saskatchewan, Vancouver Whitecaps FC Academy
Honours: Canadian Championship (2023)

SEASON	CLUB	NATION	HIGHLIGHTS (MP/MIN)
2019	Vancouver Whitecaps FC	1.CAN	23rd MLS (0/0)
2020	Vancouver Whitecaps FC	1.CAN	17th MLS (9/753); L16 MLS is Back (1/90)
2021	Vancouver Whitecaps FC	1.CAN	12th MLS (7/630); Playoffs (0/0); CanChamp (0/0)
2022	Vancouver Whitecaps FC	1.CAN	17th MLS (17/1510)
	Vanc. Whitecaps FC 2	CAN-3.US	14th MLS NEXT Pro (3/270)
2023	Vancouver Whitecaps FC	Concacaf	QF Champions League (2/180); L32 Leagues Cup (0/0)
2023	Vancouver Whitecaps FC	1.CAN	13th MLS (1/90); 1st CanChamp (0/0)
	Vanc. Whitecaps FC 2	CAN-3.US	21st MLS NEXT Pro (4/337)

HAWORTH, CARL
Retired at the end of the 2023 season
Right midfielder & right back. Born 1989, Southport, ENG. Grew up Barrie, ON, CAN. Height 173 cm. Dominant right foot. Youth clubs: Barrie SC
School: Niagara University
Honours: CPL Regular Season (2022), USL PDL Championship (2012)
1st #CANMNT: 2016-11-11 at Cheonan, KOR (v. KOR)

SEASON	CLUB	NATION	HIGHLIGHTS (MP/MIN/G)	G
2009	Forest City London	CAN-4.US	USL PDL; PDL Playoffs	
2010	Forest City London	CAN-4.US	USL PDL; PDL Playoffs	
2011	Forest City London	CAN-4.US	USL PDL; PDL Playoffs	
2012	Forest City London	CAN-4.US	USL PDL; 1st PDL Playoffs	
2013	Ottawa Fury SC	CAN-4.US	USL PDL	
2014	Ottawa Fury FC	2.USA	8th NASL (24/1534/2g); 5th CanChamp (2/122)	2
2015	Ottawa Fury FC	2.USA	2nd NASL (25/1655/2g); 2nd NASL Playoffs; 5th CanChamp (2/100)	2
2016	Ottawa Fury FC	2.USA	10th NASL (27/2135/7g); SF CanChamp (4/348/1g)	8
2017	Ottawa Fury FC	2.USA	E10th USL (21/1504/2g)	2
2018	Ottawa Fury FC	2.USA	E10th USL (30/2279/3g); SF CanChamp (2/180/1g)	4
2019	Ottawa Fury FC	2.USA	E8th USL (33/2882/10g); Playoffs (1/90); SF CanChamp (4/331)	10
2020	Indy Eleven	2.USA	E9th USL (11/927/1g)	1
2021	Indy Eleven	2.USA	E12th USL (4/54)	
2022	Atlético Ottawa	1.CAN	1st CPL (23/1257); 2nd Playoffs (3/222); CanChamp (1/34)	
2023	Atlético Ottawa	1.CAN	6th CPL (17/647/3g)	3

HAYNES, BENJAMIN — CF MONTRÉAL U-23

Winger & fullback. Born 2004, Montréal, QC, CAN. Grew up in Montréal, QC, CAN. Height 168. Youth clubs: St-Lazare Hudson

SEASON	CLUB	NATION	HIGHLIGHTS (MP/MIN/G)	G
2022	Québec U-18	CAN	Gold at Canada Games (4/271/1g)	1
2023	CF Montréal U-23	CAN	5th Ligue1 Québec	

HAYNES, JORDAN — VALOUR FC

Left back & midfielder. Born 1996, Peterborough, ON, CAN. Height 178 cm. Dominant left foot. Youth clubs: Cavan Maple Leaf, Peterborough City, Whitby Iroquois, Ajax Thunder, Toronto FC Academy, Vancouver Whitecaps Residency
School: University of British Columbia
Honours: CPL Championship (2021)

SEASON	CLUB	NATION	HIGHLIGHTS (MP/MIN/G)	G
2010	Ontario U-14	CAN	2nd Canada Soccer All Stars U-14	
2011	Ontario U-15	CAN	2nd Canada Soccer All Stars U-15	
2014	Vancouver Whitecaps FC	1.CAN	3rd CanChamp (0/0)	
2014	Vanc. Whitecaps FC U-23	CAN-4.US	USL PDL	
2015	Vanc. Whitecaps FC 2	CAN-2.US	W11th USL (16/1197)	
2016	Vanc. Whitecaps FC 2	CAN-2.US	W6th USL (14/432/1g)	1
2017	OKC Energy U-23	4.USA	R2 US Cup (1/65)	
	Vaughan Azzurri	CAN	E2nd League1 Ontario (6/510)	
2018	Calgary Foothills SC	CAN-4.US	USL PDL (12/898)	
2019	TSS Rovers FC	CAN-4.US	USL League Two (14/1086)	
2020	Pacific FC	1.CAN	3rd CPL (8/467)	
2021	Pacific FC	1.CAN	3rd CPL (24/1729); 1st Playoffs (2/209); SF CanChamp (3/241)	
2022	Pacific FC	Concacaf	L16 Concacaf League (0/0)	
	Pacific FC	1.CAN	4th CPL (16/889)	
2023	Valour FC	1.CAN	8th CPL (14/902)	

HEARD, JOSHUA — PACIFIC FC

Winger. Born 1994, Cardiff, WAL. Grew up Victoria, BC, CAN. Height 175 cm. Youth clubs: Lakehill SA, Victoria Metro
School: University of Washington
Honours: CPL Championship (2021)

SEASON	CLUB	NATION	HIGHLIGHTS (MP/MIN/G)	G
2011	Victoria Highlanders	CAN-4.US	USL PDL	
2012	Victoria Highlanders	CAN-4.US	USL PDL	
2013	Victoria Highlanders	CAN-4.US	USL PDL	
2014	Puget Sound Gunners	4.USA	USL PDL	
2016	Bethlehem Steel FC	2.USA	E11th USL (22/917/2g)	2
2017	Bethlehem Steel FC	2.USA	E8th USL (15/266); Playoffs (1/16)	
2018	Real Monarchs	2.USA	W4th USL (24/1463/1g); Playoffs (0/0)	1
2019	Real Monarchs	2.USA	W4th USL (14/975/2g)	2
2019-20	FC Pinzgau Saalfelden	4.GER	x- Regionalliga	
2020	Pacific FC	1.CAN	3rd CPL (5/218/1g)	1
2021	Pacific FC	1.CAN	3rd CPL (24/1478/4g); 1st Playoffs (2/146); SF CanChamp (3/240)	4
2022	Pacific FC	Concacaf	L16 Concacaf League (4/360/2g)	2
	Pacific FC	1.CAN	4th CPL (25/1933/6g); SF Playoffs (2/170); QF CanChamp (1/90)	6
2023	Pacific FC	1.CAN	4th CPL (25/1717/4g); 3rd Playoffs (2/146); SF CanChamp (3/248/1g)	5

HÉBERT, MATISSE — CF MONTRÉAL U-23

Goalkeeper. Born 2004, Saint-Eustache, QC, CAN. Grew up in . Youth clubs: Académie de CF Montréal

SEASON	CLUB	NATION	HIGHLIGHTS (MP/MIN)
2023	CF Montréal U-23	CAN	5th Ligue1 Québec

HENNESSY, MICHAEL

Forward. Born 2005, Burnaby, BC, CAN. Grew up in Burnaby, BC, CAN. Youth clubs: Mountain United FC, Vancouver Whitecaps FC Academy

SEASON	CLUB	NATION	HIGHLIGHTS (MP/MIN)	
2023	Vanc. Whitecaps FC 2	CAN-3.US	21st MLS NEXT Pro (0/0)	
	Vanc. Whitecaps FC Academy	3.CAN	3rd League1 BC (13/864/7g)	7

FOOTBALLERS

HENRY, DONEIL

Centre back. Born 1993, North York, ON, CAN. Grew up Brampton, ON, CAN. Height 183 cm. Dominant right foot. Youth clubs: Brampton YSC, Royal Orchard Middle School, North Mississauga SC, Toronto FC Academy, Fletchers Meadow High SChool
Honours: Concacaf champion (2021-22), Canadian Championship (2010, 2011, 2012)
1st #CANMNT: 2012-08-15 at Lauderhill, FL, USA (v. TRI)

SEASON	CLUB	NATION	HIGHLIGHTS (MP/MIN/G)	G
2006	Brampton Blast U-14	CAN	1st Tide U-14 Cup	
2009	Ontario U-18	CAN	Bronze at Canada Games (5/405)	
2010	Toronto FC	1.CAN	11th MLS (1/1); 1st CanChamp (1/90)	
2011	Toronto FC	1.CAN	16th MLS (10/503); 1st CanChamp (1/3)	
2012	Toronto FC	1.CAN	19th MLS (18/1139/1g); 1st CanChamp (4/360)	1
2013	Toronto FC	1.CAN	17th MLS (20/1651); 3rd CanChamp (2/180/1g)	1
2014	Toronto FC	1.CAN	13th MLS (21/1802/1g); 2nd CanChamp (4/390/2g)	3
2014-15	West Ham United FC	1.ENG	R5 FA Cup (0/0)	
	Blackburn Rovers FC	2.ENG	9th EFL Championship (3/250); 6R FA Cup (0/0)	
2015-16	Blackburn Rovers FC	2.ENG	x- EFL Championship (1/3)	
	West Ham United FC	1.ENG	7th FA Premier League (0/0); 6R FA Cup (0/0)	
2016-17	AC Horsens	1.DEN	x- Superliga (4/132)	
2018	Ottawa Fury FC	2.USA	E10th USL (3/270)	
	Vancouver Whitecaps FC	1.CAN	14th MLS (14/1260); 2nd CanChamp (3/270)	
2019	Vancouver Whitecaps FC	1.CAN	23rd MLS (25/2123/4g); CanChamp (2/180)	4
2020	Suwon Samsung Bluewings	1.KOR	8th K-League (20/1719/1g); QF KFA Cup (2/210)	1
2021	Suwon Samsung Bluewings	1.KOR	6th K-League (21/1622/2g); QF KFA Cup (1/90)	2
2022	Los Angeles FC	1.USA	x- MLS (5/133); L16 US Cup (1/45)	
	Toronto FC	1.CAN	27th MLS (7/140); 2nd CanChamp (1/8)	
2023	Minnesota United FC	1.USA	x- MLS (0/0)	
	Minnesota United FC 2	3.USA	x- MLS NEXT Pro (1/72)	
	Halifax Wanderers FC	1.CAN	3rd CPL (13/410); 4th Playoffs (1/10)	

CONTINENTAL FOOTBALL		COMPETITION	HIGHLIGHTS (MP/MIN)
2010-11	Toronto FC	Concacaf	9th Champions League (2/120)
2011-12	Toronto FC	Concacaf	4th Champions League (7/437)
2012-13	Toronto FC	Concacaf	Champions League (2/83)
2015-16	West Ham United FC	UEFA	UEFA Europa League (1/90)
2020	Suwon Samsung Bluewings	AFC	QF AFC Champions League (1/90)

HENRY, MAËL — CAVALRY FC

Midfielder. Born 2004, Montréal, QC, CAN. Height 178 cm. Dominant right foot. Youth clubs: CS Les Boucaniers Montréal, FS Salaberry, Académie de CF Montréal
Honours: CPL North Star Shield (2023)

SEASON	CLUB	NATION	HIGHLIGHTS (MP/MIN/G)	G
2022	CF Montréal U-23	CAN	6th PLSQ (13/1062/5g)	5
2023	Vancouver FC	1.CAN	x- CPL (3/121)	
	Cavalry FC	1.CAN	1st CPL (12/559/2g); 2nd Playoffs (3/49)	2

HENRY, TRISTON — FORGE FC HAMILTON

Goalkeeper. Born 1993, Scarborough, ON, CAN. Height 183 cm. Dominant right foot. Youth clubs: Wexford SC, Toronto Lynx. School: Herkimer Community College, University of Connecticut, Quinnipiac University
Honours: CPL Championship (2019, 2020, 2022, 2023)

SEASON	CLUB	NATION	HIGHLIGHTS (MP/MIN)
2013	Toronto Lynx	CAN-4.US	USL PDL
2014	Toronto Lynx	CAN-4.US	USL PDL
2016	Sigma FC	CAN	W2nd League1 Ontario
2017	Sigma FC	CAN	W2nd League1 Ontario (20/1789)
2018	Sigma FC	CAN	2nd League1 Ontario (16/1440)
	Sigma FC	CAN	3rd League1 Ontario Playoffs (3/270)
2019	Forge FC Hamilton	Concacaf	L16 Concacaf League (4/360)
	Forge FC Hamilton	1.CAN	1st CPL (22/1980); CanChamp (1/90)
2020	Forge FC Hamilton	Concacaf	QF Concacaf League (4/360)
	Forge FC Hamilton	1.CAN	1st CPL (9/810)

2021	Forge FC Hamilton	Concacaf	SF Concacaf League (8/720)	
	Forge FC Hamilton	1.CAN	1st CPL (22/1980); 2nd Playoffs (2/180); SF CanChamp (2/180)	
2022('20)	Forge FC Hamilton	1.CAN	2nd CanChamp (1/90)	
2022	Forge FC Hamilton	Concacaf	L16 Champions League (2/180)	
	Forge FC Hamilton	1.CAN	2nd CPL (27/2430); 1st Playoffs (3/270); QF CanChamp (2/180)	
2023	Forge FC Hamilton	1.CAN	2nd CPL (27/2400); 1st Playoffs (2/210); SF CanChamp (3/270)	

HERNÁNDEZ, JOSÉ

Forward. Born 2000, Edmonton, AB, CAN. Height 178 cm. Youth clubs: Edmonton Internazionale, Edmonton Juventus, FC Edmonton Academy, Vancouver Whitecaps FC Residency

SEASON	CLUB	NATION	HIGHLIGHTS (MP/MIN/G)	G
2019	Pacific FC	1.CAN	5th CPL (19/653/1g); CanChamp (1/29)	1
2020	Cavalry FC	1.CAN	4th CPL (3/103)	
2021	Cavalry FC	1.CAN	2nd CPL (17/413); QF CanChamp (2/95)	
2022	Rivers FC	3.CAN	7th League1 BC	

HIEBERT, KYLE   USA / ST. LOUIS CITY SC

Centre back & midfielder. Born 1997, Winnipeg, MB, CAN. Grew up La Salle, MB, CAN. Height 178 cm. Youth clubs: Linden Woods SC, WSA Winnipeg. School: Missouri State University
1st #CANMNT: 2023-03-28 at Toronto, ON, CAN (v. HON)

SEASON	CLUB	NATION	HIGHLIGHTS (MP/MIN/G)	G
2000	Manitoba U-15	CAN	7th Canada Soccer All Stars U-15	
2001	Manitoba U-17	CAN	7th All Stars U-17 Showcase	
2002	Manitoba U-17	CAN	6th All Stars U-17 Showcase	
2012	Sask'toba U-15	CAN	3rd Canada Soccer All Stars U-15	
2013	Sask'toba U-16	CAN	th Canada Soccer All Stars U-16	
2016	WSA Winnipeg	CAN-4.US	USL PDL (7/463)	
2017	WSA Winnipeg	CAN-4.US	USL PDL (12/945)	
2022	St. Louis CITY 2	3.USA	2nd MLS NEXT Pro (24/2156/3g); 2nd Playoffs (3/270); R3 US Cup (2/210)	3
2023	St. Louis CITY SC	1.USA	4th MLS (27/2128/2g); L16 MLS Playoffs (2/121); R4 US Cup (1/90); L16 Leagues (1/90)	2

HIGAZY, IBRAHIM   ESP / RAYO VALLECANO

Forward. Born 2006, Ottawa, ON, CAN. Grew up Ottawa & Toronto, ON, CAN, London, ENG & Madrid, ESP. Height 176 cm. Dominant right foot. Youth clubs: Ottawa Futuro Soccer Academy, MK Dons (England), Rayo Vallecano (Spain)

HIGGINS, NYAL   VAUGHAN SC

Centre back. Born 1998, Ajax, ON, CAN. Height 185 cm. Dominant right foot. Youth clubs: Ajax SC, Vaughan SC
School: Oakland University, Syracuse University

SEASON	CLUB	NATION	HIGHLIGHTS (MP/MIN/G)	G
2013	Ontario U-15	CAN	th Canada Soccer All Stars U-15	
2016	Vaughan Azzurri	CAN	1st League1 Ontario (5/365)	
2017	Michigan Bucks	4.USA	PDL; L16 Playoffs; R3 US Cup	
2018	Vaughan Azzurri	CAN	5th League1 Ontario (3/238)	
2020	Nyköpings BIS	3.SWE	16th Ettan Norra (17/1484/1g); R2 Cupen (1/90)	1
2021	Toronto FC II	CAN-3.US	x- USL League One (9/511)	
	Atlético Ottawa	1.CAN	8th CPL (8/458)	
2022	FC Edmonton	1.CAN	8th CPL (24/2082); CanChamp (1/90)	
2023	Vaughan Azzurri	CAN	3rd League1 Ontario (18/1497); SF Playoffs (2/180); CanChamp (1/73)	

HIMARAS, ELEIAS   YORK UNITED FC

Goalkeeper. Born 2002, London, ON, CAN. Height 184 cm. Youth clubs: London NorWest Optimist SC, London Alliance FC, London Portuguese, Toronto FC Academy

SEASON	CLUB	NATION	HIGHLIGHTS (MP/MIN)
2018	TFC Academy	CAN	4th League1 Ontario (1/90)
2021	York United FC	1.CAN	4th CPL (0/0)
	FC London	CAN	4th League1 Ontario (10/900)
2022	York United FC	1.CAN	6th CPL (10/879)
	Electric City FC	CAN	10th League1 Ontario (3/270)
2023	York United FC	1.CAN	5th CPL (2/180); 5th Playoffs (0/0); QF CanChamp (0/0)

FOOTBALLERS

HOILETT, JUNIOR
Winger. Born 1990, Brampton, ON, CAN. Height 174 cm. Dominant right foot. Youth clubs: Brampton YSC, Toronto CS Azzurri, Oakville SC, Blackburn Rovers FC (England)
Honours: Concacaf champion (2021-22)

CANADA INTERNATIONAL
1 FIFA World Cup: Group phase at Qatar 2022
1 Concacaf medal: Silver at CNL 2022-23
1st #CANMNT: 2015-10-13 at Washington, DC, USA (v. GHA)

SEASON	CLUB	NATION	HIGHLIGHTS (MP/MIN/G)	G
2007-08	SC Paderborn	2.GER	17th 2.Bundesliga (13/565)	1
2008-09	FC St. Pauli	2.GER	8th 2.Bundesliga (26/1609/6g); R1 Pokal (1/3)	6
2009-10	Blackburn Rovers FC	1.ENG	10th Premier League (23/942); R3 FA Cup (0/0); SF Lg.Cup (4/320/1g)	1
2010-11	Blackburn Rovers FC	1.ENG	15th FA Premier League (24/1495/5g); R4 FA Cup (2/180/1g); R3 Lg.Cup (2/168)	6
2011-12	Blackburn Rovers FC	1.ENG	19th FA Premier League (34/2954/7g); R3 FA Cup (0/0); QF Lg.Cup (3/141)	7
2012-13	Queens Park Rangers	1.ENG	20th FA Premier League (26/1448/2g); R4 FA Cup (0/0); R3 Lg.Cup (2/150/1g)	3
2013-14	Queens Park Rangers	2.ENG	4th EFL Championship (35/2096/4g); 1st Playoff (3/298); R3 FA Cup (0/0); R2 Lg.Cup (1/90)	4
2014-15	Queens Park Rangers	1.ENG	20th FA Premier League (22/878); R3 FA Cup (1/45); R2 Lg.Cup (1/90)	
2015-16	Queens Park Rangers	2.ENG	12th EFL Championship (29/1996/6g); R3 FA Cup (0/0); R2 Lg.Cup (1/87)	6
2016-17	Cardiff City FC	WAL-2.ENG	12th EFL Championship (33/2421/2g)	2
2017-18	Cardiff City FC	WAL-2.ENG	2nd EFL Championship (46/3808/9g); R4 FA Cup (3/193/2g); R2 Lg.Cup (1/33)	11
2018-19	Cardiff City FC	WAL-1.ENG	18th FA Premier League (32/2142/3g); R3 FA Cup (1/1); R2 Lg.Cup (0/0)	3
2019-20	Cardiff City FC	WAL-2.ENG	5th EFL Championship (41/2479/7g); SF Playoffs (2/115); R4 FA Cup (1/12); R2 Lg.Cup (1/90)	7
2020-21	Cardiff City FC	WAL-2.ENG	8th EFL Championship (21/1168/2g); R3 FA Cup (1/27); R1 Lg.Cup (1/90)	2
2021-22	Reading FC	2.ENG	18th EFL Championship (27/1731/3g); R3 FA Cup (0/0)	3
2022-23	Reading FC	2.ENG	22nd EFL Championship (34/2563/1g); R4 FA Cup (1/69); R1 Lg.Cup (0/0)	1
2023	Vancouver Whitecaps FC	1.CAN	13th MLS (7/231); L16 MLS Playoffs (2/88)	

HOJABRPOUR, ALESSANDRO — FORGE FC HAMILTON
Midfielder. Born 2000, Vancouver, BC, CAN. Height 181 cm. Dominant right foot. Youth clubs: Vancouver Italian Canadian SF, Coquitlam Metro-Ford SC, Vancouver Whitecaps FC Residency, Lokomotiv Plovdiv (Bulgaria)
Honours: CPL Championship (2021, 2022, 2023)

SEASON	CLUB	NATION	HIGHLIGHTS (MP/MIN/G)	G
2019	Pacific FC	1.CAN	5th CPL (22/1731); CanChamp (2/163)	
2020	Pacific FC	1.CAN	3rd CPL (10/389)	
2021	Pacific FC	1.CAN	3rd CPL (24/1696/1g); 1st Playoffs (2/203/1g); SF CanChamp (3/270)	2
2022('20)	Forge FC Hamilton	1.CAN	2nd CanChamp (1/90)	
2022	Forge FC Hamilton	Concacaf	L16 Champions League (2/95)	
	Forge FC Hamilton	1.CAN	2nd CPL (26/2076/2g); 1st Playoffs (3/270/1g); QF CanChamp (2/180)	3
2023	Forge FC Hamilton	1.CAN	2nd CPL (22/1417); 1st Playoffs (2/193); SF CanChamp (3/172)	

HOLLIDAY, JOSEPH
Goalkeeper. Born 2005, Edmonton, AB, CAN. Height 178 cm. Youth clubs: FC Edmonton Academy
Honours: CPL North Star Shield (2023)

SEASON	CLUB	NATION	HIGHLIGHTS (MP/MIN)
2021	FC Edmonton	1.CAN	CanChamp (0/0)
2022	FC Edmonton	1.CAN	8th CPL (1/1)
2023	Cavalry FC	1.CAN	1st CPL (0/0); 2nd Playoffs (0/0)

HUGO, AIDAN
Midfielder. Born 2004. Grew up Toronto, ON, CAN. Height 175cm. Dominant left foot. Youth clubs: North Toronto SC, Toronto FC Academy

SEASON	CLUB	NATION	HIGHLIGHTS (MP/MIN/G)	G
2021	North Toronto Nitros	CAN	14th League1 Ontario (10/775/2g)	2
2022	York United FC	1.CAN	SF CanChamp (0/0)	
	North Toronto Nitros	CAN	4th League1 Ontario (7/174); QF Playoffs (1/4)	
2023	Simcoe County Rovers FC	CAN	x- League1 Ontario (2/28)	
	Woodbridge Strikers SC	CAN	12th League1 Ontario (10/787/4g)	4

HUNDAL, SHAAN   VALOUR FC
Forward. Born 1999, Brampton, ON, CAN. Height 183 cm. Dominant right foot. Youth clubs: Caledon SC, ANB Futbol, Mississauga SC, Brampton YSC, Toronto FC Academy

SEASON	CLUB	NATION	HIGHLIGHTS (MP/MIN/G)	G
2016	Toronto FC II	CAN-2.US	E12th USL (27/1700/6g); USL PDL (1/0)	6
2017	Toronto FC II	CAN-2.US	E15th USL (22/1531/7g)	7
2018	Toronto FC II	CAN-2.US	E16th USL (24/1083/2g)	2
	TFC Academy	CAN	4th League1 Ontario (2/164/4g)	4
2019	Ottawa Fury FC	2.USA	x- USL (1/5)	
	Toronto FC II	CAN-3.US	7th USL League One (11/264/2g)	2
2020	Valour FC	1.CAN	6th CPL (6/238)	
2021	Fort Lauderdale CF	3.USA	10th USL League One (27/1875/11g)	11
2022	Inter Miami CF	1.USA	12th MLS (0/0)	
2022 zc	Inter Miami CF II	3.USA	11th MLS NEXT Pro (21/1276/6g)	6
2023	Vancouver FC	1.CAN	7th CPL (28/1854/6g); CanChamp (1/45)	6

HUTCHINSON, ATIBA
Retired after the 2022-23 season

Midfielder. Born 1983, North York, ON, CAN. Grew up Brampton, ON, CAN. Height 185.5 cm. Youth clubs: Brampton YSC, Woodbridge SC

6x Canada Soccer Player of the Year (2010, 2012, 2014, 2015, 2016, 2017)

Honours: Concacaf champion (2021-22), Danish Superliga (2005-06, 2006-07, 2008-09, 2009-10), DBU Pokalen (2009), KNVB Beker (2012), flickr.g (2015-16, 2016-17, 2020-21), Türkiye Kupası (2021), Türkiye Süper Kupası (2022)

CANADA INTERNATIONAL
1 FIFA World Cup: Group phase at Qatar 2022
1 Concacaf medal: Silver at CNL 2022-23
1st #CANMNT: 2003-01-18 at Fort Lauderdale, FL, USA (v. USA)

DOMESTIC FOOTBALL		NATION	HIGHLIGHTS (MP/MIN/G)	G
1998	Ontario U-15	CAN	1st Canada Soccer All Stars U-15	
1998	Brampton YSC Blades U-15	CAN	4th JVC U-15 Cup	
2002	Toronto Lynx	2.USA	13th USL A-League (4/?)	
	York Region Shooters	CAN	Canadian Professional Soccer League	
2003	Östers IF	1.SWE	13th Allsvenskan (24/?/6g)	6
2004	Helsingborgs IF	1.SWE	10th Allsvenskan (24/?)	
2005	Helsingborgs IF	1.SWE	6th Allsvenskan (24/?/6g)	6
2005-06	FC København	1.DEN	1st Superliga (13/1170/1g); QF Pokalen (1/120)	1
2006-07	FC København	1.DEN	1st Superliga (32/2760/3g); 2nd Pokal (0/0)	3
2007-08	FC København	1.DEN	3rd Superliga (31/2453/8g); SF Pokal (1/120)	8
2008-09	FC København	1.DEN	1st Superliga (33/2955/6g); 1st Pokal (3/209)	6
2009-10	FC København	1.DEN	1st Superliga (30/2680/3g); L16 (2/135)	3
2010-11	PSV Eindhoven	1.NED	3rd Eredivisie (33/2895/2g); QF KNVB Beker (4/320)	2
2011-12	PSV Eindhoven	1.NED	3rd Eredivisie (14/1145); 1st KNVB Beker (3/188)	
2012-13	PSV Eindhoven	1.NED	2nd Eredivisie (33/2941/2g); 2nd KNVB Beker (4/360); 1st Cruijff Schaal (1/90)	2
2013-14	Beşiktaş JK	1.TUR	3rd Süper Lig (30/2626/1g); 4R Kupasi (1/90)	1
2014-15	Beşiktaş JK	1.TUR	3rd Süper Lig (30/2496/2g); L16 Kupasi (3/238)	2
2015-16	Beşiktaş JK	1.TUR	1st Süper Lig (34/3004/2g); QF Kupasi (3/270)	2
2016-17	Beşiktaş JK	1.TUR	1st Süper Lig (28/2366/1g); L16 Kupasi (1/90); 2nd Süper (1/120)	1
2017-18	Beşiktaş JK	1.TUR	4th Süper Lig (25/2103/2g); SF Kupasi (1/40); 2nd Süper (1/90)	2
2018-19	Beşiktaş JK	1.TUR	3rd Süper Lig (27/2250/4g)	4

2019-20	Beşiktaş JK	1.TUR	3rd Süper Lig (30/2585/6g); L16 Kupasi (1/13)	6
2020-21	Beşiktaş JK	1.TUR	1st Süper Lig (36/2939/4g); 1st Kupasi (3/241)	4
2021-22	Beşiktaş JK	1.TUR	6th Süper Lig (25/1261/1g); QF Kupasi (3/234/1g); 1st Süper (1/120/1g)	3
2022-23	Beşiktaş JK	1.TUR	3rd Süper Lig (5/78/1g); L16 Kupasi (3/116)	1

CONTINENTAL FOOTBALL	COMPETITION	HIGHLIGHTS (MP/MIN/G)	G
2006-07	FC København	UEFA	Qualifying (4/360); UEFA Champions League (6/540/1g)	1
2007-08	FC København	UEFA	Qualifying Champions League (4/390/1g); UEFA Cup (6/547)	1
2008-09	FC København	UEFA	Qualifying (4/315/2g); UEFA Cup (8/701)	2
2009-10	FC København	UEFA	Qualifying Champions League (4/360); UEFA Europa League (8/720)	
2010-11	PSV Eindhoven	UEFA	Qualifying (2/171); QF UEFA Europa League (11/990)	
2011-12	PSV Eindhoven	UEFA	UEFA Europa League (4/297)	
2012-13	PSV Eindhoven	UEFA	UEFA Europa League (6/540)	
2013-14	Beşiktaş JK	UEFA	UEFA Europa League (2/180)	
2014-15	Beşiktaş JK	UEFA	Qualifying Champions League (3/270); UEFA Europa League (7/643)	
2015-16	Beşiktaş JK	UEFA	UEFA Europa League (6/540)	
2016-17	Beşiktaş JK	UEFA	UEFA Champions League (6/540); QF UEFA Europa League (5/480/1g)	1
2017-18	Beşiktaş JK	UEFA	L16 UEFA Champions League (7/563)	
2018-19	Beşiktaş JK	UEFA	UEFA Europa League (0/0)	
2019-20	Beşiktaş JK	UEFA	UEFA Europa League (inc. Qualifying) (1/16)	
2020-21	Beşiktaş JK	UEFA	Qualifying Champions League (1/?); UEL Qualifying (0/0)	
2021-22	Beşiktaş JK	UEFA	UEFA Champions League (4/156)	

IAMARINO, DAMIAN

Fullback. Born 2002, Daytona Beach, FL, USA. Grew up Port Orange, FL, USA. Height 180 cm. Youth clubs: Port Orange YMCA, Orlando City Academy, Chievo Verano (Italy), Potenza (Italy)

SEASON	CLUB	NATION	HIGHLIGHTS (MP/MIN)
2022-23	GC Arconatese	4.ITA	B4th Serie D Girone B (0/0)

IGBINOBARO, PHILIP — TORONTO FC ACADEMY

Midfielder. Born 2006, Benin City, NGA. Grew up in Toronto, ON, CAN. Height 183 cm. Dominant right foot. Youth clubs: Glen Shields, Toronto FC Academy

ILIADIS, COSTA — CF MONTRÉAL U-23

Winger. Born 2005, Toronto, ON, CAN. Grew up in . Youth clubs: GC Ilioupoli FC

SEASON	CLUB	NATION	HIGHLIGHTS (MP/MIN)
2023	CF Montréal U-23	CAN	5th Ligue1 Québec

INCE, EVAN — ALTITUDE FC

Goalkeeper. Born 2000, North Vancouver, BC, CAN. Grew up in North Vancouver, BC, CAN. Height 188. Youth clubs: Lynn Valley Fusion, Vancouver Whitecaps FC Academy
School: University of Massachusetts Amherst, California Baptist University

INGHAM, NATHAN — ATLÉTICO OTTAWA

Goalkeeper. Born 1993, Newmarket, ON, CAN. Grew up Keswick, ON, CAN. Height 188 cm. Dominant right foot. Youth clubs: Markham SC
School: Florida Gulf Coast University
Honours: CPL Regular Season (2022), USL PDL Championship (2015, 2018)

SEASON	CLUB	NATION	HIGHLIGHTS (MP/MIN)
2009	Ajax U-16 Gunners	CAN	3rd U-16 Cup
2014	K-W United FC	CAN-4.US	USL PDL
2015	K-W United FC	CAN-4.US	USL PDL
2016	FC Edmonton	CAN-2.US	3rd NASL (0/0); SF Playoffs (0/0); 5th CanChamp (0/0)
	Toronto FC II	CAN-2.US	E12th USL (2/116)
2017	FC Edmonton	2.USA	7th NASL (8/674); 5th CanChamp (0/0)
2018	Calgary Foothills SC	CAN-4.US	USL PDL (7/315); 1st PDL Playoffs
	Pittsburgh Riverhounds SC	2.USA	E3rd USL (0/0); Playoffs (0/0)
2019	York9 FC	1.CAN	3rd CPL (26/2340); CanChamp (6/540)
2020	York9 FC	1.CAN	5th CPL (6/540)
2021	York United FC	1.CAN	4th CPL (21/1810); SF Playoffs (1/90); QF CanChamp (2/180)

| 2022 | Atlético Ottawa | | 1.CAN | 1st CPL (25/2247); 2nd Playoffs (3/270); CanChamp (1/90) |
| 2023 | Atlético Ottawa | | 1.CAN | 6th CPL (22/1980); QF CanChamp (1/90) |

IRVING, CALLUM   VANCOUVER FC

Goalkeeper. Born 1993, Vancouver, BC, CAN. Height 183 cm. Dominant right foot. Youth clubs: Marpole SC, Vancouver Selects, Vancouver Whitecaps FC Residency
School: University of Kentucky
Honours: CPL Championship (2021)
1st #CANMNT: 2017-01-22 at Devonshire Parish, BER (v. BER)

SEASON	CLUB	NATION	HIGHLIGHTS (MP/MIN)
2009	British Columbia U-16	CAN	4th Canada Soccer All Stars U-16
2011	Vanc. Whitecaps Residency	CAN-4.US	USL PDL
2012	Vanc. Whitecaps FC U-23	CAN-4.US	USL PDL
2016	Houston Dynamo FC	1.USA	19th MLS (0/0)
	Rio Grande Valley Toros	2.USA	W2nd USL (14/1243)
2017	Ottawa Fury FC	2.USA	E10th USL (32/2880); SF CanChamp (4/360)
2018	Ottawa Fury FC	2.USA	E10th USL (2/180)
2019	Ottawa Fury FC	2.USA	E8th USL (32/2910); Playoffs (1/120); SF CanChamp (4/360)
2020	Pacific FC	1.CAN	3rd CPL (6/540)
2021	Pacific FC	1.CAN	3rd CPL (25/2236); 1st Playoffs (2/210); SF CanChamp (3/270)
2022	Pacific FC	Concacaf	L16 Concacaf League (4/360)
	Pacific FC	1.CAN	4th CPL (26/2340); SF Playoffs (2/180); QF CanChamp (1/90)
2023	Vancouver FC	1.CAN	7th CPL (27/2430); CanChamp (1/90)

IVANISEVIC, JOVAN   TORONTO FC II

Midfielder. Born 2005. Grew up in .., ON, CAN. Youth clubs: London Alliance FC, Toronto FC Academy

SEASON	CLUB	NATION	HIGHLIGHTS (MP/MIN)
2022	Ontario U-18	CAN	Silver at Canada Games (4/58)
2023	Toronto FC II	CAN-3.US	23rd MLS NEXT Pro (1/5)

JACKSON, SIMEON

Forward. Born 1987, Kingston, JAM. Grew up in Mississauga, ON, CAN. Height 172 cm. Youth clubs: Clarkson SC (house league), Sunoco, ASPIRE Academy, Dulwich Hamlet (England)
1st #CANMNT: 2009-05-30 at Larnaka, CYP (v. CYP)

SEASON	CLUB	NATION	HIGHLIGHTS (MP/MIN/G)	G
2002	Ontario U-15	CAN	2nd Canada Soccer All Stars U-15	
2004-05	Rushden & Diamonds FC	4.ENG	22nd League Two (2/37)	
2005-06	Rushden & Diamonds FC	4.ENG	24th League Two (14/805/5g)	5
2006-07	Rushden & Diamonds FC	ENG	12th Conference League (?/20g); R2 FA Cup (0/0)	20
2007-08	Gillingham FC	3.ENG	22nd League One (18/1262/4g)	4
2008-09	Gillingham FC	4.ENG	5th League Two (41/3340/17g); 1st Playoffs (3/246/3g); R3 FA Cup (3/270/1g); R2 EFL Trophy (1/75)	21
2009-10	Gillingham FC	3.ENG	21st League One (42/3183/14g); R3 FA Cup (3/270); R2 Lg.Cup (2/180/2g); R1 EFL Trophy (1/23/1g)	16
2010-11	Norwich City FC	2.ENG	2nd EFL Championship (39/1835/13g); R3 FA Cup (1/18); R2 Lg.Cup (1/90)	13
2011-12	Norwich City FC	1.ENG	12th FA Premier League (22/940/3g); 5R FA Cup (3/158/2g); R2 Lg.Cup (1/90)	5
2012-13	Norwich City FC	1.ENG	11th FA Premier League (13/401/1g); 4R FA Cup (2/180/1g); QF Lg.Cup (4/82/1g)	3
2013-14	Eintracht Braunschweig	1.GER	x- Bundesliga (9/475); R1 Pokal (1/35)	
	Millwall FC	2.ENG	19th EFL Championship (14/529/2g)	2
2014-15	Coventry City FC	3.ENG	17th League One (28/1228/3g); R1 FA Cup (1/90); QF EFL Trophy (1/90)	3
2015-16	Barnsley FC	3.ENG	x- League One (9/156); R1 FA Cup (0/0)	
	Blackburn Rovers FC	2.ENG	16th EFL Championship (17/454/2g); 5R FA Cup (2/121)	2
2016-17	Walsall FC	3.ENG	14th League One (38/2244/7g); R1 FA Cup (1/90); R1 Lg.Cup (1/120); R1 EFL Trophy (1/90)	7
2017-18	Walsall FC	3.ENG	x- League One (8/204); 1R FA Cup (0/0); 1R Lg.Cup (1/14)	
	Grimsby Town FC	4.ENG	18th League Two (5/221/1g)	1

FOOTBALLERS

2018-19	St. Mirren FC	1.SCO	11th Scottish Premiership (30/2125/6g); L16 SFA Cup (2/134)	6
2019-20	Kilmarnock FC	1.SCO	x- Scottish Premiership (4/154)	
	Stevenage FC	4.ENG	23rd League Two (4/169); QF EFL Trophy (1/34)	
2020-21	Chelsmford City FC	5.ENG	x- National League South (2/?/1g)	1
	King's Lynn Town	5.ENG	21st National League	
2021-22	Chelsmford City FC	5.ENG	19th National League South	
2022-23	Chelsmford City FC	5.ENG	5th National League South	

JAKOVIĆ, DEJAN

Centre back. Born 1985, Karlovac, CRO. Grew up Etobicoke, ON, CAN. Height 187.5 cm. Youth clubs: Rexdale SC, Glen Shields FC, Dixie SC. School: University Alabama-Birmingham
Honours: MLS Supporters' Shield (2019), US Cup (2013)
1st #CANMNT: 2008-01-30 at Fort-de-France, MTQ (v. MTQ)

SEASON	CLUB	NATION	HIGHLIGHTS (MP/MIN/G)	G
2002	Ontario U-17	CAN	2nd All Stars U-17 Showcase	
2008-09	FK Crvena zvezda	UEFA	Qualifying UEFA Cup (2/147)	
	FK Crvena zvezda	1.SRB	3rd SuperLiga (3/270)	
2009	D.C. United	1.USA	10th MLS (23/2070); 2nd US Cup (1/90)	
2009-10	D.C. United	Concacaf	9th Champions League (4/179)	
2010	D.C. United	1.USA	16th MLS (19/1624); SF US Cup (2/210)	
2011	D.C. United	1.USA	13th MLS (15/1324)	
2012	D.C. United	1.USA	3rd MLS (23/1861/1g); SF Playoffs (4/360)	1
2013	D.C. United	1.USA	19th MLS (18/1575); 1st US Cup (2/180)	
2014	S-Pulse Shimizu	1.JPN	15th JPN - J.League (25/2161); SF JFA Cup (4/390); Lg.Cup (5/450)	
2015	S-Pulse Shimizu	1.JPN	17th JPN - J.League (16/1373); 2R JFA Cup (0/0); Lg.Cup (1/90)	
2016	S-Pulse Shimizu	2.JPN	2nd JPN - J2 League (1/90); 4R JFA Cup (1/90)	
2017	New York Cosmos	2.USA	4th NASL (22/1980/1g); 2nd Playoffs (2/210); R2 US Open (1/45)	1
2018	Los Angeles FC	1.USA	5th MLS (15/1147); Playoffs (0/0); SF US Cup (3/152)	
2019	Los Angeles FC	1.USA	1st MLS (3/181); SF Playoffs (1/16)	
	Las Vegas Lights FC	2.USA	W13th USL (4/360)	
2020	Los Angeles FC	Concacaf	2nd Champions League (2/180)	
	Los Angeles FC	1.USA	12th MLS (16/1075/1g); QF MLS is Back (2/180); Playoffs (0/0)	1
2021	Forge FC Hamilton	1.CAN	1st CPL (5/403)	

JAMES, MANJREKAR   CRC / LD ALAJUELENSE

Centre back. Born 1993, Roseau, DMA. Grew up North York, ON, CAN. Height 191 cm. Dominant right foot. Youth clubs: North York Hearts Azzurri, Siga FC, Pécsi MFC (Hungary)
School: Colo Colo
Honours: CPL Championship (2023), Danish Superliga (2019-20), DBU Pokalen (2019)
1st #CANMNT: 2015-01-16 at Orlando, FL, USA (v. ISL)

SEASON	CLUB	NATION	HIGHLIGHTS (MP/MIN/G)	G
2014-15	Pécsi MFC	1.HUN	11th Nemzeti Bajnokság I (16/1192/1g); QF Kupa (3/63)	1
2015-16	Diósgyőr VTK	1.HUN	9th Nemzeti Bajnokság I (17/928)	
2016-17	Vasas SC	1.HUN	3rd Nemzeti Bajnokság I (11/526); 2nd Kupa (6/409/2g)	2
2017-18	Vasas SC	1.HUN	12th Nemzeti Bajnokság I (28/2260/2g); 2R Kupa (2/102)	2
2018-19	FC Fredericia	2.DEN	x- 1. division (17/1530/1g); R3 DBU Pokalen (3/283)	1
2018-19	FC Midtjylland	1.DEN	2nd Superliga (5/450); 1st DBU Pokalen (3/283)	
2019-20	FC Midtjylland	UEFA	UEFA Europa League (0/0)	
2019-20	FC Midtjylland	1.DEN	1st Superliga (5/277); R3 DBU Pokalen (1/90)	
2020-21	FC Midtjylland	UEFA	Qualifying (0/0); UEFA Champions League (1/90)	
2020-21	FC Midtjylland	1.DEN	x- Superliga (4/360); Rog16 DBU Pokalen (1/90)	
2020-21	Lamia FC	1.GRE	11th Super League (7/176); QF Kypello (2/91/1g)	1
2021-22	Vejle BK	1.DEN	11th Superliga (13/1042); QF DBU Pokalen (3/254)	
2022-23	Chornomorets Odesa	1.UKR	x- Liha (13/1125/1g)	1
2023	Forge FC Hamilton	1.CAN	2nd CPL (26/2340); 1st Playoffs (2/174); SF CanChamp (3/270)	
2023-24	LD Alajuelense	1.CRC	Liga Verano (current season)	

JAMES, RYAN

Left back & midfielder. Born 1994, Mississauga, ON, CAN. Height 173 cm. Youth clubs: Dixie SC, TFC Academy
School: Bowling Green State University

SEASON	CLUB	NATION	HIGHLIGHTS (MP/MIN/G)	G
2008	Ontario U-14	CAN	2nd Canada Soccer All Stars U-14	
2010	Ontario U-16	CAN	2nd Canada Soccer All Stars U-16	
2015	TFC Academy	CAN-4.US	USL PDL	
2016	Rochester Rhinos	2.USA	E4th USL (27/2074/1g); QF Playoffs (2/183)	1
2017	Rochester Rhinos	2.USA	E4th USL (30/2620); QF Playoffs (2/210); R4 US Cup (1/69)	
2018	Nashville SC	2.USA	E8th USL (16/1013); Playoffs (0/0); L16 US Cup (3/197)	
2019	Pittsburgh Riverhounds SC	2.USA	E1st USL (34/2833); QF Playoffs (2/196); R4 US Cup (2/180)	
2020	Pittsburgh Riverhounds SC	2.USA	E3rd USL (16/1355/5g); L16 Playoffs (1/90)	5
2021	Birmingham Legion FC	2.USA	E3rd USL (32/2408); QF Playoffs (1/26)	
2022	Birmingham Legion FC	2.USA	E4th USL (27/1176/1g); R3 US Cup (1/45)	1
2023	Halifax Wanderers FC	1.CAN	3rd CPL (6/394); CanChamp (0/0)	

JAMSHIDI, KOUROSH
Forward. Born 2006, Toronto, ON, CAN. Height 188. Dominant right foot. Youth clubs: Wexford SC, Markham SC, North Toronto SC

SEASON	CLUB	NATION	HIGHLIGHTS (MP/MIN)
2023	Langley Unity FC	3.CAN	4th League1 BC (2/17)

JENSEN, NOAH — FORGE FC HAMILTON
Midfielder & centre back. Born 1999, Markham, ON, CAN. Grew up Courtice, ON, CAN. Height 178 cm. Dominant right foot. Youth clubs: Darlington SC
School: Oakland University
Honours: CPL Championship (2022, 2023)

SEASON	CLUB	NATION	HIGHLIGHTS (MP/MIN/G)	G
2016	Sigma FC	CAN	W2nd League1 Ontario (7/397)	
2017	Sigma FC	CAN	W2nd League1 Ontario (2/73)	
2018	Sigma FC	CAN	2nd League1 Ontario (3/158)	
2019	Sigma FC	CAN	5th League1 Ontario (14/1079/1g)	1
2021	Flint City Bucks	4.USA	USL League Two (14/?/2g)	2
2022('20)	Forge FC Hamilton	1.CAN	2nd CanChamp (0/0)	
2022	Forge FC Hamilton	Concacaf	L16 Champions League (1/21)	
	Forge FC Hamilton	1.CAN	2nd CPL (22/700/3g); 1st Playoffs (1/71); QF CanChamp (2/34)	3
2023	Forge FC Hamilton	1.CAN	2nd CPL (21/945/1g); 1st Playoffs (2/137); SF CanChamp (3/94/2g)	3

JIMOH, SHOLA — TORONTO FC ACADEMY
Winger. Born 2008, Newcastle-Upon-Tyne, ENG. Grew up in Brampton, ON, CAN. Height 163 cm. Dominant left foot. Youth clubs: Brampton East SC, Toronto Dutch Connections, TFC Academy

JOHN-WENTWORTH, KAHLIL
Fullback. Born 2001. Grew up in Ajax, ON, CAN. Height 178. Dominant left foot. Youth clubs: Notre Dame Catholic Secondary School

SEASON	CLUB	NATION	HIGHLIGHTS (MP/MIN/G)	G
2021	Vaughan Azzurri	CAN	1st League1 Ontario (1/20); SF Playoffs (2/180)	
2022	Simcoe County Rovers FC	CAN	5th League1 Ontario (19/1140/1g)	1

JOHNSON, LEVONTE — VANCOUVER WHITECAPS FC
Forward. Born 1999, Brampton, ON, CAN. Height 178 cm. Youth clubs: Botelho ST, Brampton YSC
School: Eastern Florida State College, Salt Lake Community College, Seattle Univrersity, Syracuse University
Honours: Canadian Championship (2023)

SEASON	CLUB	NATION	HIGHLIGHTS (MP/MIN/G)	G
2016	Master's FA	CAN	E8th League1 Ontario (15/709/1g)	1
2017	Master's FA	CAN	E5th League1 Ontario (1/25)	
2023	Vancouver Whitecaps FC	Concacaf	QF Champions League (0/0); L32 Leagues Cup (2/59)	
	Vancouver Whitecaps FC	1.CAN	13th MLS (7/199); L16 MLS Playoffs (1/9); 1st CanChamp (2/90/1g)	1
	Vancouver Whitecaps FC	CAN-3.US	21st MLS NEXT Pro (15/1168/7g)	7

JOHNSON, MALIK — USA / COLORADO SPRINGS SWITCHBACKS FC
Forward. Born 1998, Toronto, ON, CAN. Grew up Brampton, ON, CAN. Height 173 cm. Youth clubs: Brampton East SA, Toronto FC Academy
Honours: Canadian Championship (2016, 2018)

FOOTBALLERS

SEASON	CLUB	NATION	HIGHLIGHTS (MP/MIN/G)	G
2012	Ontario U-15	CAN	1st Canada Soccer All Stars U-15	
2015	Toronto FC II	CAN-2.US	E11th USL (7/392)	
	TFC Academy	CAN-4.US	USL PDL	
2016	Toronto FC	1.CAN	1st CanChamp (1/10)	
	Toronto FC II	CAN-2.US	E12th USL (21/1101/4g)	4
2017	Toronto FC II	CAN-2.US	E15th USL (19/1000/1g)	1
	TFC Academy	CAN	W3rd League1 Ontario (3/222/1g)	1
2018	Toronto FC	1.CAN	1st CanChamp (1/67)	
	Toronto FC II	CAN-2.US	E16th USL (28/1610/2g)	2
2019	Tampa Bay Rowdies	2.USA	E5th USL (23/1641/3g); L16 Playoffs (0/0); R3 US Cup (1/16)	3
2020	Tampa Bay Rowdies	2.USA	E4th USL (10/494/2g); SF Playoffs (3/55)	2
2021	Real Monarchs	2.USA	W14th USL (31/2216/1g)	1
2022	Colorado Springs Switchbacks	2.USA	W3rd USL (18/1369/1g); R2 Playoffs (1/74)	1

JOHNSTON, ALISTAIR — SCO / CELTIC FC

Right back. Born 1998, North Vancouver, BC, CAN. Grew up Aurora, ON, CAN. Height 180 cm. Dominant right foot.
Youth clubs: Lakeshore SC, Aurora YSC, Richmond Hill SC, ANB Futbol, Vaughan SC
School: Wake Forest University
Honours: Concacaf champion (2022), Scottish Premiership (2022-23), Scottish Cup (2023), Scottish Lg.Cup (2023)

CANADA INTERNATIONAL
1 FIFA World Cup: Group phase at Qatar 2022
1 Concacaf medal: Silver at CNL 2022-23
1st #CANMNT: 2021-03-25 at Orlando, FL, USA (v. BER)

SEASON	CLUB	NATION	HIGHLIGHTS (MP/MIN/G)	G
2015	Vaughan Azzurri	CAN	3rd League1 Ontario	
2016	Vaughan Azzurri	CAN	1st League1 Ontario (1/90)	
2017	Vaughan Azzurri	CAN	E2nd League1 Ontario (5/435)	
2018	Vaughan Azzurri	CAN	5th League1 Ontario (1/89)	
2019	Vaughan Azzurri	CAN	2nd League1 Ontario (6/433/1g)	1
	Vaughan Azzurri	CAN	CanChamp (2/179)	
2020	Nashville SC	1.USA	14th MLS (18/1365); QF Playoffs (3/315)	
2021	Nashville SC	1.USA	7th MLS (26/2144/1g); QF Playoffs (2/210)	1
2022	CF Montréal	Concacaf	QF Champions League (3/195)	
	CF Montréal	1.CAN	3rd MLS (33/2648/4g); QF Playoffs (2/180); SF CanChamp (1/90)	4
2022-23	Glasgow Celtic FC	1.SCO	1st Premiership (14/1233/1g); 1st Cup (5/414); 1st Lg.Cup (1/90)	1
2023-24	Glasgow Celtic FC	UEFA	UEFA Champions League (6/540)	
	Glasgow Celtic FC	1.SCO	Premiership (current season); SFA Cup (current)	

JOHNSTON, ISAIAH — USA / HUNTSVILLE CITY FC

Right back. Born 2001, Mississauga, ON, CAN. Grew up Georgetown & Milton, ON, CAN. Height 173 cm. Dominant right foot. Youth clubs: Georgetown SC, The Future SA, Milton YSC

SEASON	CLUB	NATION	HIGHLIGHTS (MP/MIN/G)	G
2017	Woodbridge Strikers SC	CAN	2nd League1 Ontario (5/212/1g)	1
2018	Woodbridge Strikers SC	CAN	6th League1 Ontario (7/292); 2nd Playoffs (3/124)	
2019	Woodbridge Strikers SC	CAN	8th League1 Ontario (12/966/1g)	1
2020	York9 FC	1.CAN	5th CPL (3/20)	
2021	York United FC	1.CAN	4th CPL (25/1987/3g); SF Playoffs (1/90); QF CanChamp (2/166)	3
2022	York United FC	1.CAN	6th CPL (19/1438); SF CanChamp (3/203/1g)	1
2023	Huntsville City FC	3.USA	17th MLS NEXT Pro (20/1348/3g)	

JOHNSTON, MALCOLM

Midfielder. Born 2001. Grew up in Aurora, ON, CAN. Height 183. Youth clubs: Vaughan SC, Vancouver Whitecaps FC Academy. School: University of Maryland

SEASON	CLUB	NATION	HIGHLIGHTS (MP/MIN)
2018	Vaughan Azzurri	CAN	5th League1 Ontario (1/45); 1st Playoffs (1/90)
2019	Vaughan Azzurri	CAN	2nd League1 Ontario (1/1)
2023	Vanc. Whitecaps FC 2	CAN-3.US	21st MLS NEXT Pro (17/999/2g)

JONES, ISHMAËL — CF MONTRÉAL U-23
Born 2004. Grew up in Montréal, QC, CAN. Height 173.

SEASON	CLUB	NATION	HIGHLIGHTS (MP/MIN/G)	G
2022	Québec U-18	CAN	Gold at Canada Games (4/244/1g)	1
2023	CF Montréal U-23	CAN	5th Ligue1 Québec	

JUDELSON, DYLAN — USA / ORLANDO CITY SC ACADEMY
Midfielder. Born 2008, Darien, CT, USA. Grew up in Weston, CT & Winter Park, FL, USA. Height 180 cm. Dominant right foot. Youth clubs: Darien SA, Everton America CT, Beachside SC, FC Westchester, Orlando City SC Academy

KACHER, MASTANABAL
Midfielder. Born 1995, Azazga, ALG. Grew up Anjou, QC, CAN. Height 183 cm. Youth clubs: Académie de l'Impact de Montréal

SEASON	CLUB	NATION	HIGHLIGHTS (MP/MIN/G)	G
2013	Québec U-18	CAN	Gold at Canada Games (5/252)	
2015	FC Montréal	CAN-2.US	E10th USL (14/577)	
2016	FC Montréal	CAN-2.US	E14th USL (21/1206/2g)	2
2017	Colorado Springs Switchbacks	2.USA	W9th USL (32/2674/7g)	7
2018	Real Monarchs	2.USA	W4th USL (23/1339/3g); Playoffs (1/90)	3
2019	Real Monarchs	2.USA	x- USL (14/734/1g)	1
	Saint Louis FC	2.USA	E11th USL (15/635)	
2020	Valour FC	1.CAN	6th CPL (6/357/1g); QF CanChamp (1/20)	1
2021	Valour FC	1.CAN	5th CPL (11/305)	
2022	FC Edmonton	1.CAN	8th CPL (23/870/1g); CanChamp (0/0)	1

KAISER, DANIEL
Centre back. Born 2000, Calgary, AB, CAN. Height 183 cm. Youth clubs: Calgary NSD SC, Calgary Foothills SC, Vancouver Whitecaps FC Academy
School: University of British Columbia

SEASON	CLUB	NATION	HIGHLIGHTS (MP/MIN)	
2004	Edmonton Mill Woods SC U-16 Warriors	CAN		8th U-16 Cup
2013	Calgary Foothills U-14	CAN	2nd U-14 Cup	
2014	Calgary Foothills U-14	CAN	3rd U-14 Cup	
2019	Calgary Foothills SC	CAN-4.US	USL League Two (6/159)	
2021	Cavalry FC	1.CAN	2nd CPL (11/492)	
2023	Nautsa'mawt FC	3.CAN	5th League1 BC (10/826/3g)	3

KAISER, MARKUS
Centre back. Born 2002, Calgary, AB, CAN. Height 170 cm. Youth clubs: Willow Ridge - Carburn SC, Calgary Foothills SC. School: University of British Columbia

SEASON	CLUB	NATION	HIGHLIGHTS (MP/MIN)
2017	Calgary Foothills SC U-15	CAN	2nd U-15 Cup
2018	Calgary Foothills FC U-17	CAN	5th U-17 Cup
2019	Calgary Foothills FC U-17	CAN	1st U-17 Cup
2022	Cavalry FC	1.CAN	3rd CPL (6/69)

KALONGO, CHRISTOPHER — FORGE FC HAMILTON
Goalkeeper. Born 2002, Toronto, ON, CAN. Grew up Oakville, ON, CAN. Height 184 cm. Dominant right foot. Youth clubs: Oakville SC, Milton YSC, Sigma FC
Honours: CPL Championship (2022, 2023)

SEASON	CLUB	NATION	HIGHLIGHTS (MP/MIN)
2022('20)	Forge FC Hamilton	1.CAN	2nd CanChamp (0/0)
2021	Forge FC Hamilton	Concacaf	SF Concacaf League (0/0)
	Forge FC Hamilton	1.CAN	SF CanChamp (0/0)
	Sigma FC	CAN	9th League1 Ontario (10/817)
2022	Forge FC Hamilton	1.CAN	2nd CPL (1/90); 1st Playoffs (0/0); QF CanChamp (0/0)1
2023	Forge FC Hamilton	1.CAN	2nd CPL (2/120); 1st Playoffs (0/0); SF CanChamp (0/0)

KAMDEM, BRADLEY — CAVALRY FC
Left back. Born 1994, Paris. FRA. Grew up Calgary, AB, CAN. Height 184 cm. Dominant left foot. Youth clubs: Calgary Chinooks SC

FOOTBALLERS

Schools: Huntington University, University of Nevada, Las Vegas
Honours: CPL North Star Shield (2023)

SEASON	CLUB	NATION	HIGHLIGHTS (MP/MIN)	
2015	Calgary Foothills SC	CAN-4.US	USL PDL	
2016	Rochester Rhinos	2.USA	E4th USL (25/1722); QF Playoffs (2/210); R3 Cup (1/90)	
2017	Rochester Rhinos	2.USA	E4th USL (24/1725/1g); R4 US Cup (2/141)	1
2018	Fresno FC	2.USA	W12th USL (20/1745); R4 Cup (2/210)	
2019	Saint Louis FC	2.USA	E11th USL (19/1450)	
2020	Atlanta United 2	2.USA	E15th USL (1/90)	
2021	Atlanta United 2	2.USA	E13th USL (28/2139)	
2022-23	Valletta FC	1.MLT	8th Maltese Premier League (20/1685); L16 Cup (2/180)	
2023	Cavalry FC	1.CAN	1st CPL (22/1947); 2nd Playoffs (3/276)	

KANE, KHADIM   FORGE FC HAMILTON
Midfielder. Born 2005, .., SEN. Grew up St-Laurent, QC, CAN. Height 190 cm. Dominant right foot. Youth clubs: Académie de CF Montréal

SEASON	CLUB	NATION	HIGHLIGHTS (MP/MIN)	G
2022	CF Montréal U-23	CAN	6th PLSQ (8/350/1g)	1
2023	Forge FC Hamilton	1.CAN	2nd CPL (16/518); SF CanChamp (0/0)	
	Sigma FC	CAN	9th League1 Ontario (2/167)	

KANE, MOUHAMADOU   VANCOUVER FC
Born 2003, Mbaké, SEN. Grew up Montréal, QC, CAN. Height 183 cm. Dominant right foot. Youth clubs: FS Salaberry, Académie Impact de Montréal

SEASON	CLUB	NATION	HIGHLIGHTS (MP/MIN)
2022	FC Edmonton	1.CAN	x- CPL (7/76)
	York United FC	1.CAN	6th CPL (11/291); SF CanChamp (2/16)
2023	Vancouver FC	1.CAN	7th CPL (8/157)

KANG, ALBERT
Midfielder. Born 2001. Grew up in Saskatoon, SK & Vancouver, BC, CAN. Height 178. Dominant right foot. Youth clubs: Saskatoon Lakewood Atletico, Coquitlam Metro-Ford SC, Vancouver Whitecaps FC Academy
School: Loyola University Maryland

SEASON	CLUB	NATION	HIGHLIGHTS (MP/MIN/G)	G
2015	Saskatoon Lakewood U-14 Atletico	CAN	6th U-14 Cup	
2018	Coquitlam Metro-Ford SC U-17	CAN	1st U-17 Cup	
2021	Long Island Rough Riders	4.USA	USL League Two (9/679/1g)	1
2022	Long Island Rough Riders	4.USA	th USL League Two (13/969)	

KANG, ETHAN   TORONTO FC II
Midfielder & fullback. Born 2005. Grew up in .., ON, CAN. Height 173. Youth clubs: FC Emery, Toronto FC Academy

SEASON	CLUB	NATION	HIGHLIGHTS (MP/MIN)
2018	Toronto FC U-13	CAN	QF Concacaf Under-13 Champions League
2022	Ontario U-18	CAN	Silver at Canada Games (4/281)
2023	Toronto FC II	CAN-3.US	23rd MLS NEXT Pro (2/69)

KANTOR, STEFAN   TORONTO FC ACADEMY
Centre back. Born 2008, Burlington, ON, CAN. Grew up in Stoney Creek, ON, CAN. Height 188 cm. Dominant left foot. Youth clubs: Hamilton Serbians, Toronto FC Academy

KANTOROWICZ, DOMINIC   TORONTO FC ACADEMY
Goalkeeper. Born 2008, Mississauga, ON, CAN. Grew up in Caledon, ON, CAN. Height 183 cm. Dominant right foot. Youth clubs: Brampton Elite SA, Toronto FC Academy

KARAJOVANOVIC, STEFAN   NZL / NAPIER CITY ROVERS FC
Midfielder. Born 1999, Gatineau, QC, CAN. Height 175 cm. Youth clubs: AS Hull, Académie de l'Impact de Montréal, Ottawa Fury Academy
School: Carleton University

SEASON	CLUB	NATION	HIGHLIGHTS (MP/MIN/G)	G
2016	Ottawa Fury FC Reserves	CAN	7th PLSQ (5/?)	
2017	FC Gatineau	CAN	7th PLSQ (2/154/2g)	2

2018	FC Gateneau	CAN	3rd PLSQ (12/984/14g)	14
2019	AS Blainville	CAN	1st PLSQ (12/792/5g); CanChamp (1/22)	5
2020	Ottawa South United	CAN	2nd PLSQ (6/501/7g)	7
2021	HFX Wanderers FC	1.CAN	4th CPL (26/1506/1g); QF CanChamp (2/31)	1
2022	Toronto FC II	CAN-3.US	7th MLS NEXT Pro (19/785/2g)	2
2023	Napier City FC	NZL	Central League (12/?/7g)	7

KAYE, MARK-ANTHONY   USA / NEW ENGLAND REVOLUTION

Midfielder. Born 1994, Toronto, ON, CAN. Height 185 cm. Youth clubs: Wexford SC, Ajax SC, Glen Shields SC, Toronto FC Academy
School: York University
Honours: Concacaf champion (2021-22), MLS Supporters' Shield (2019), USL Cup (2017)

CANADA INTERNATIONAL
1 FIFA World Cup: Group phase at Qatar 2022
1st #CANMNT: 2017-06-13 at Montréal, QC, CAN (v. CUW)

SEASON	CLUB	NATION	HIGHLIGHTS (MP/MIN/G)	G
2014	TFC Academy	CAN	1st League1 Ontario	
	Wilmington Hammerheads	2.USA	7th USL PRO (7/518/2g); QF Playoffs (1/74)	2
2015	Toronto FC II	CAN-2.US	E11th USL (22/1661)	
2016	Louisville City FC	2.USA	E2nd USL (24/1452/1g); SF Playoffs (2/112); R3 US Cup	1
2017	Louisville City FC	2.USA	E1st USL (19/1008/4g); 1st Playoffs (4/180); R3 US Cup (2/117/1g)	5
2018	Los Angeles FC	1.USA	5th MLS (20/1582/2g); Playoffs (0/0); SF US Cup (2/103)	2
2019	Los Angeles FC	1.USA	1st MLS (31/2501/4g); SF Playoffs (1/45); QF US Cup (1/90)	4
	MLS All-Stars	1.USA	MLS All-Star Game (1/45)	
2020	Los Angeles FC	Concacaf	2nd Champions League (5/422)	
	Los Angeles FC	1.USA	12th MLS (16/1095/3g); QF MLS is Back (2/145); Playoffs (1/90)	3
2021	Los Angeles FC	1.USA	19th MLS (10/758)	
	Colorado Rapids	1.USA	2nd MLS (15/1104); QF Playoffs (1/83)	
2022	Colorado Rapids	Concacaf	L16 Champions League (2/169)	
	Colorado Rapids	1.USA	18th MLS (17/1286/3g); R4 US Cup (1/45)	3
	Toronto FC	1.CAN	27th MLS (8/622)	
2023	Toronto FC	1.CAN	x- MLS (21/1843/2g); QF CanChamp (1/90)	2
	New England Revolution	1.USA	6th MLS (10/783); L16 MLS Playoffs (2/90); L16 Leagues (4/289)	

KENNEDY, SCOTT   AUT / WOLFSBERGER AC

Centre back. Born 1997, Calgary, AB, CAN. Height 193 cm. Dominant left foot. Youth clubs: Calgary West, Calgary Chinook United
Honours: Concacaf champion (2021-22)
1 Concacaf medal: Silver at CNL 2022-23
1st #CANMNT: 2021-06-8 at Bridgeview, IL, USA (v. SUR)

SEASON	CLUB	NATION	HIGHLIGHTS (MP/MIN/G)	G
2015-16	SB Chiemgau Traunstein	6.GER	8th Landesliga Bayern Südost (31/?/2g)	2
2016-17	FC Amberg	5.GER	10th Bayernliga (11/?/1g)	1
2017-18	SV Grödig	3.AUT	Regionalliga (24/?/4g); R2 Pokal (2/240)	4
2018-19	SK Austria Klagenfurt	2.AUT	7th 2.Liga (29/2550/3g); R2 Pokal (2/180)	3
2019-20	SK Austria Klagenfurt	2.AUT	2nd 2.Liga (9/671)	
2020-21	SSV Jahn Regensburg	2.GER	14th 2.Bundesliga (22/1378); QF Pokal (3/204/1g)	1
2021-22	SSV Jahn Regensburg	2.GER	15th 2.Bundesliga (23/1730/2g); R2 Pokal (1/90)	2
2022-23	SSV Jahn Regensburg	2.GER	17th 2.Bundesliga (23/1181); R2 Pokal (1/41)	
2023-24	Wolfsberger AC	1.AUT	Österreichischen Bundesliga (current season); L16 OFB Cup (2/1/98)	

KERR, DEANDRE   TORONTO FC

Forward. Born 2002, Toronto, ON, CAN. Height 180 cm. Dominant right foot. Youth clubs: Ajax Azzurri SC, Ajax FC, United FA, Whitby Iroquois SC
School: Syracuse University
Honours: Canadian Championship (2022/'20)

SEASON	CLUB	NATION	HIGHLIGHTS (MP/MIN/G)	G
2022('20)	Toronto FC	1.CAN	1st CanChamp (1/90)	
2022	Toronto FC	1.CAN	27th MLS (26/1301/3g); 2nd CanChamp (1/45)	3
2023	Toronto FC	1.CAN	29th MLS (23/1225/5g); QF CanChamp (1/31); Leagues (2/135)	5

FOOTBALLERS

KERR, STERLING
Goalkeeper. Born 2000, Calgary, AB, CAN. Height cm. Youth clubs: Calgary South West United
School: Mount Royal University
Honours: CPL North Star Shield (2023)

SEASON	CLUB	NATION	HIGHLIGHTS (MP/MIN)
2023	Cavalry FC	1.CAN	1st CPL (0/0); 2nd Playoffs (0/0); CanChamp (0/0)

KHAN, KEVIN — NED / FEYENOORD ACADEMY
Midfielder. Born 2008, Toronto, ON, CAN. Grew up in Woodbridge, ON, CAN. Height 170 cm. Dominant right foot. Youth clubs: Brampton YSC, Vaughan SC, Toronto Lion Kings FC, Atlético Canadians FC, Toronto Dutch Connections FC, Feyenoord Academy

KIBATO, KEMBO — CAN / VANCOUVER FC
Midfielder & winger. Born 2000, . Grew up Toronto, ON, CAN. Height 176 cm. Dominant left foot. Youth clubs: North Toronto SC, Toronto FC Academy

SEASON	CLUB	NATION	HIGHLIGHTS (MP/MIN/G)	G
2016	North Toronto Nitros	CAN	E3rd League1 Ontario (2/34)	
2017	North Toronto Nitros	CAN	E4th League1 Ontario (19/1234/4g)	4
	Ontario U-18	CAN	Gold at Canada Games (5/291)	
2018	TFC Academy	CAN	4th League1 Ontario (8/420)	
2019-20	FC Helsingør	3.DEN	x- 2. division (0/0)	
2020	Rio Grande Valley Toros	2.USA	W16th USL (12/776/1g)	1
2021	FC Tulsa	2.USA	E8th USL (29/1469/2g); L16 (1/55)	2
2022	FC Tulsa	2.USA	E8th USL (28/1647); R3 US Cup (2/99)	
2023	Hartford Athletic FC	2.USA	E12th USL (19/1056); R3 US Cup (0/0)	

KLUKOWSKI, ANTONI — POL / POGOŃ SZCZECIN II
Winger. Born 2007, Lille, FRA. Grew up Warsaw, POL & Palma Mallorca, ESP. Height 184 cm. Dominant left foot. Youth clubs: Escola Varovia (Spain), RCD Mallorca (Spain), CD Atletico Baleares (Spain), Polonia Warszawa (Poland), Legia Warszawa (Poland)

SEASON	CLUB	NATION	HIGHLIGHTS (MP/MIN/G)	G
2023-24	Pogoń Szczecin II	4.POL	3.liga (current season)	

KNIGHT-LEBEL, JAMIE — ENG / BRISTOL CITY FC U-18
Centre back. Born 2004, Montréal, QC, CAN. Grew up Bristol, ENG. Height 188 cm. Dominant right foot. Youth clubs: Stapleton AFC, Frenchay Lions, Longwell Green FC, South Gloucestershire FC, Southampton FC, Bristol City FC

KOBZA, ERYK — CAVALRY FC
Centre back. Born 2001, Vancouver, BC, CAN. Grew up in North Vancouver, BC, CAN. Height 169. Youth clubs: North Vancouver SC, Mountain United FC, Vancouver Whitecaps FC Residency
School: University of Calgary
Honours: CPL North Star Shield (2023)

SEASON	CLUB	NATION	HIGHLIGHTS (MP/MIN)
2023	Cavalry FC	1.CAN	1st CPL (26/2068/2g); 2nd Playoffs (3/300)

KONÉ, AMADOU — FORGE FC HAMILTON
Winger. Born 2005. Grew up in Ottawa, ON, CAN. Height 190. Dominant right foot. Youth clubs: West Ottawa SC
School: Carleton University

KONÉ, ISMAËL — ENG / WATFORD FC
Midfielder. Born 2002, Abidjan, CIV. Grew up Montréal, QC, CAN. Height 188 cm. Dominant right foot. Youth clubs: AS Notre-Dame-de-Grâce, CS Saint-Laurent
Honours: Concacaf champion (2021-22)

CANADA INTERNATIONAL
1 FIFA World Cup: Group phase at Qatar 2022
1 Concacaf medal: Silver at CNL 2022-23
1st #CANMNT: 2022-03-24 at San José, CRC (v. CRC)

SEASON	CLUB	NATION	HIGHLIGHTS (MP/MIN/G)	G
2019	CS St-Laurent U-17	CAN	3rd U-17 Cup	
2022	CF Montréal	Concacaf	QF Champions League (3/236/1g)	1
2022	CF Montréal	1.CAN	3rd MLS (26/1587/2g); QF Playoffs (2/159/1g); SF CanChamp (1/90)	3

MEN'S FOOTBALLERS | 103

2022-23	Watford FC	2.ENG	11th EFL Championship (16/1020); R3 FA Cup (1/90)	
2023-24	Watford FC	2.ENG	EFL Championship (current season); FA Cup (current); EFL Cup (1/29)	

KOUADIO, MARC — USA / MONTVERDE ACADEMY

Goalkeeper. Born 2002, Montréal, QC, CAN. Height 183 cm. Youth clubs: FC Trois Lacs, AS Pierrefonds, Montverde Academy (USA)
School: University of Dayton

KOWAL, MAKSYM — GER / GREIFSWALDER FC

Forward. Born 1991, . Grew up Mississauga, ON, CAN. Height 182 cm. Youth clubs: USC Karpaty, Erin Mills SC
School: University of Buffalo

SEASON	CLUB	NATION	HIGHLIGHTS (MP/MIN/G)	G
2012	Des Moines Menace	4.USA	PDL; R2 US Cup	
2013	Toronto Lynx	CAN-4.US	PDL	
2015-16	Raków Częstochowa	3.POL	x- 2.liga (13/337/2g)	2
	Olimpia Zambrów	3.POL	14th 2.liga (13/634/1g); Puchar (1/76)	1
2016-17	ŁKS Łódź	4.POL	2nd 3.liga (25/665/4g)	4
2017-18	Tasman United	1.NLZ	6th Championship (18/1233/6g)	6
2018-19	Canterbury United	1.NLZ	3rd Championship (16/1334/6g); SF Playoffs (1/84)	6
2019	Vaughan Azzurri	CAN	CanChamp (2/115)	
	Vaughan Azzurri	CAN	2nd League1 Ontario (14/980/14g); QF Playoffs (2/180/2g)	16
2020	Atlético Ottawa	1.CAN	7th CPL (3/53)	
2020-21	Germania Halberstadt	4.GER	Regionalliga	
2021-22	Germania Halberstadt	4.GER	Regionalliga	
2022-23	Werder Bremen II	4.GER	Regionalliga	
	Greifswalder FC	4.GER	Regionalliga	

KOZLOVSKIY, SERGEI — ACADÉMIE DE CF MONTRÉAL

Centre back. Born 2008, Montréal, QC, CAN. Height 180 cm. Dominant left foot. Youth clubs: AS Dynamo Montréal, CS Longueuil, CF Montréal

KRATT, RONAN — GER / WERDER BREMEN II

Forward. Born 2003, Burlington, VT, USA. Grew up Ottawa, ON, CAN. Height 178 cm. Youth clubs: Ottawa South United SC, Barca Residency Academy, SSV Ulm 1846 (Germany)

SEASON	CLUB	NATION	HIGHLIGHTS (MP/MIN/G)	G
2020	Ottawa South United	CAN	2nd PLSQ (6/181/1g)	1
2022	York United FC	1.CAN	6th CPL (14/858/2g)	2

LAJEUNESSE, ERIC

Centre back. Born 2003, Ottawa, ON, CAN. Height 188 cm. Youth clubs: Ottawa St. Anthony Futuro, Vancouver Whitecaps FC Academy
School: University of British Columbia

SEASON	CLUB	NATION	HIGHLIGHTS (MP/MIN)
2022	Whitecaps FC	3.CAN	3rd League1 BC
2023	Pacific FC	1.CAN	4th CPL (6/455); SF CanChamp (1/67)
	Nautsa'mawt FC	3.CAN	5th League1 BC (4/303)

LAMOTHE, PIERRE

Midfielder. Born 1997, Greenfield Park, QC, CAN. Grew up Longueuil, QC, CAN. Height 173 cm. Dominant right foot.
Youth clubs: CS Longueuil, Académie de l'Impact Montréal
School: Université de Montréal
Honours: U-Sport Championship (2018)

SEASON	CLUB	NATION	HIGHLIGHTS (MP/MIN/G)	G
2012	Québec U-15	CAN	2nd Canada Soccer All Stars U-15	
2016	FC Montréal	CAN-2.US	E14th USL (4/55)	
2017	CS Longueuil	CAN	3rd PLSQ (9/689)	
2018	CS Longueuil	CAN	4th PLSQ (10/787)	
2019	CS Longueuil	CAN	8th PLSQ (9/756)	
2020	AS Blainville	CAN	1st PLSQ (1/90)	
2021	HFX Wanderers FC	1.CAN	4th CPL (24/1234/1g); QF CanChamp (2/88)	1
2022	HFX Wanderers FC	1.CAN	7th CPL (21/1500/2g); QF CanChamp (1/64)	2
2023	Pacific FC	1.CAN	x- CPL (6/196); SF CanChamp (1/13)	

LANDICHO-CORREIA, MATTEO — TORONTO FC ACADEMY

Forward & winger. Born 2006, Windsor, ON, CAN. Height 180 cm. Dominant right foot. Youth clubs: Windsor SC, Windsor Wheels, Belle River SC, Tecumseh SC, Vardar, Toronto FC Academy

LANGWA, NDZEMDZELA

Midfielder. Born 1998, Ottawa, ON, CAN. Height 173 cm. Youth clubs: Goulbourn SC, Ottawa South United SC, Toronto FC Academy, Ottawa Fury FC Academy, Vancouver Whitecaps FC Residency

SEASON	CLUB	NATION	HIGHLIGHTS (MP/MIN/G)	G
2015	Ottawa Fury FC	CAN	5th PLSQ (5/?/1g)	1
2017-18	US Triestina	3.ITA	x- Serie C Girone B (2/?); R2 Coppa Italia (0/0)	
2017-18	US Palmese	4.ITA	l14th Serie D Girone I (13/?/2g)	2
2018-19	UD Socuéllamos	4.ESP	1st Tercera División Grupo 18	
2019	HFX Wanderers FC	1.CAN	7th CPL (19/1282); CanChamp (5/376)	
2021-22	VfB Straubing	6.GER	Landesliga Bayern Mitte	
2022-23	SV Donaustauf	5.GER	Bayernliga Nord	

LARIN, CYLE — ESP / RCD MALLORCA

Forward. Born 1995, Brampton, ON, CAN. Height 188 cm. Youth clubs: Brampton YSC, Sigma FC
School: University of Connecticut
Honours: Concacaf champion (2021-22), Türkiye Süper Lig (2020-21), Türkiye Kupası (2021), Türkiye Süper Kupası (2022), Supercoupe de Belgique (2022)

CANADA INTERNATIONAL
1 FIFA World Cup: Group phase at Qatar 2022
1 Concacaf medal: Silver at CNL 2022-23
1st #CANMNT: 2014-05-23 at Ritzing, AUT (v. BUL)

SEASON	CLUB	NATION	HIGHLIGHTS (MP/MIN/G)	G
2014	Sigma FC	CAN	3rd League1 Ontario	
2015	Orlando City SC	1.USA	14th MLS (27/1906/17g); QF US Cup (1/90/1g)	18
2016	Orlando City SC	1.USA	15th MLS (32/2455/14g); L16 US Cup (1/34)	14
	MLS All-Stars	1.USA	MLS All-Star Game (1/13)	
2017	Orlando City SC	1.USA	18th MLS (28/2169/12g); R1 US Cup (0/0)	12
2017-18	Beşiktaş JK	1.TUR	4th Süper Lig (4/154/4g); SF Kupasi (0/0)	4
2018-19	Beşiktaş JK	UEFA	UEFA Europa League (10/714/3g)	3
	Beşiktaş JK	1.TUR	3rd Süper Lig (12/310/1g)	1
2019-20	SV Zulte Waregem	2.BEL	9th Championnat (29/2494/7g); SF Beker (4/345/2g)	9
2020-21	Beşiktaş JK	UEFA	UEFA Qualifying Champions League (1/1/1g)	1
	Beşiktaş JK	UEFA	UEFA Europa League Qualifying (1/56)	
	Beşiktaş JK	1.TUR	1st Süper Lig (38/2886/19g); 1st Kupasi (5/326/3g)	22
2021-22	Beşiktaş JK	1.TUR	6th Süper Lig (29/1758/7g); QF Kupasi (1/79); 1st Süper (1/79)	7
	Beşiktaş JK	UEFA	UEFA Champions League (5/354/1g)	1
2022-23	Club Brugge KV	UEFA	L16 UEFA Champions League (1/11)	
	Club Brugge KV	2.BEL	x- Championnat (9/192/1g); L16 Beker (2/137); 1st Supercup (1/24)	1
	Real Valladolid CF	1.ESP	18th La Liga (19/1469/8g)	8
2023-24	RCD Mallorca	1.ESP	La Liga (current season); Copa (current)	

LARYEA, RICHIE — ENG / NOTTINGHAM FOREST FC

Fullback. Born 1995, Toronto, ON, CAN. Height 175 cm. Dominant right foot. Youth clubs: Club Uruguay Toronto, Sigma FC. School: University of Akron
Honours: Concacaf champion (2021-22)

CANADA INTERNATIONAL
1 FIFA World Cup: Group phase at Qatar 2022
1 Concacaf medal: Silver at CNL 2022-23
1st #CANMNT: 2019-09-7 at Toronto, ON, CAN (v. CUB)

SEASON	CLUB	NATION	HIGHLIGHTS (MP/MIN/G)	G
2014	Sigma FC	CAN	3rd League1 Ontario	
2015	Sigma FC	CAN	4th League1 Ontario	
2016	Orlando City SC	1.USA	15th MLS (0/0); L16 US Cup (0/0)	
	Orlando City B	2.USA	E8th USL (23/1587); Playoffs (0/0)	
2017	Orlando City SC	1.USA	18th MLS (12/250)	
	Orlando City B	2.USA	E9th USL (12/995/3g)	3

2018	Orlando City SC	1.USA	22nd MLS (9/253); QF US Cup (0/0)	
2019	Toronto FC	1.CAN	9th MLS (20/1468/1g); 2nd Playoffs (4/109/1g); 2nd CanChamp (4/331)	2
2020	Toronto FC	1.CAN	2nd MLS (20/1398/4g); L16 MLS is Back (1/75); Playoffs (1/112)	4
2021	Toronto FC	1.CAN	26th MLS (27/2294/3g); 2nd CanChamp (3/270)	3
	Toronto FC	Concacaf	QF Champions League (3/270)	
2021-22	Nottingham Forest FC	2.ENG	4th EFL Championship (5/117); 1st Playoffs (0/0); QF FA Cup (0/0)	
2022	Toronto FC	1.CAN	27th MLS (10/865)	
2023	Toronto FC	1.CAN	x- MLS (18/1611/2g); QF CanChamp (1/90)	2
	Vancouver Whitecaps FC	1.CAN	13th MLS (12/953/1g); L16 Playoffs (2/146)	1

LEBEL-KNIGHT, JAMIE   ENG / BRISTOL CITY FC

Centre back. Born 2004, Montréal, QC, CAN. Grew up Bristol, ENG. Height 188 cm. Youth clubs: Stapleton AFC, Frenchay Lions, Longwell Green FC, South Gloucestershire FC, Southampton FC, Bristol City FC

SEASON	CLUB	NATION	HIGHLIGHTS (MP/MIN)
2023-24	Bristol City FC	2.ENG	EFL Championship (current season); FA Cup (current); EFL Cup (0/0)

LE BOURHIS, YOHAN

Midfielder & centre back. Born 2000, Montréal, QC, CAN. Height 186 cm. Youth clubs: CS Mont-Royal Outremont, Académie Impact Montréal

SEASON	CLUB	NATION	HIGHLIGHTS (MP/MIN/G)	G
2019	AS Blainville	CAN	1st PLSQ (3/189)	
	Valour FC	1.CAN	6th CPL (8/720)	
2020	Valour FC	1.CAN	6th CPL (1/90/1g)	1

LEE, CHRIS

Fullback. Born 2001, North Vancouver, BC, CAN. Grew up West Vancouver, BC, CAN. Height 180 cm. Youth clubs: West Vancouver SC, Mountain United FC, Vancouver Whitecaps FC Academy
School: University of British Columbia

SEASON	CLUB	NATION	HIGHLIGHTS (MP/MIN)
2021	Pacific FC	1.CAN	3rd CPL (3/237)
2022	Vancouver Whitecaps FC	1.CAN	17th MLS (0/0)
	Vanc. Whitecaps FC 2	CAN-3.US	14th MLS NEXT Pro (11/578)
2023	Nautsa'mawt FC	3.CAN	5th League1 BC (11/829)

LEE, DURAN

Centre back. Born 1995, Toronto, ON, CAN. Height cm. Dominant left foot. Youth clubs: Brampton YSC, Toronto FC Academy
School: Western Texas College, Dodge City Community College, University of Connecticut, University of Massachussets Lowell

SEASON	CLUB	NATION	HIGHLIGHTS (MP/MIN/G)	G
2016	Sigma FC	CAN	W2nd League1 Ontario (5/397)	
2017	Sigma FC	CAN	W2nd League1 Ontario (5/369/1g)	1
2018	Sigma FC	CAN	2nd League1 Ontario (11/671)	
	Sigma FC	CAN	3rd League1 Ontario Playoffs (3/147)	
2019	HFX Wanderers FC	1.CAN	7th CPL (8/678)	
	Vaughan Azzurri	CAN	2nd League1 Ontario (9/735/1g); CanChamp (2/180)	1
2020	FC Edmonton	1.CAN	8th CPL (2/120)	
2021	Pacific FC	CAN	Missed season through injury	
2023	Des Moines Menace	4.USA	USL League Two (current season); R2 (1/45)	
	North Mississauga SC	CAN	17th League1 Ontario (1/45)	

LEFEVRE, MARIO

Midfielder. Born 2006, Victoria, BC, CAN. Grew up Edmonton, AB, CAN. Height 184 cm. Youth clubs: Calgary Foothills SC

SEASON	CLUB	NATION	HIGHLIGHTS (MP/MIN)
2023	Vanc. Whitecaps FC 2	CAN-3.US	21st MLS NEXT Pro (0/0)

LEUTWILER, JAYSON   ENG / PORT VALE FC

Goalkeeper. Born 1989, Neuchâtel, SUI. Height 195 cm. Dominant right foot. Youth clubs: FC Cornaux, Neuchâtel Xamax, FC Basel

FOOTBALLERS

Honours: Concacaf champion (2021-22), Swiss Super League (2007-08)
1st #CANMNT: 2016-11-11 at Cheonan, KOR (v. KOR)

SEASON	CLUB	NATION	HIGHLIGHTS (MP/MIN)
2007-08	FC Basel	UEFA	UEFA Cup (0/0)
	FC Basel	1.SUI	1st Super League (0/0)
2008-09	FC Basel	UEFA	UEFA Qualifying Champions League (0/0)
	FC Basel	1.SUI	3rd Super League (0/0); SF Coupe (0/0)
2009-10	Yverdon-Sport FC	2.SUI	9th Challenge League (30/2700); R2 Coupe (1/90)
2010-11	FC Wohlen	2.SUI	Challenge League (15/1350); L16 Coupe (3/300)
2012-13	Middlesbrough FC	2.ENG	16th EFL Championship (0/0); R5 FA Cup (0/0); QF Lg.Cup (1/90)
2013-14	Middlesbrough FC	2.ENG	12th EFL Championship (3/148); R3 FA Cup (0/0); R1 Lg.Cup (1/90)
2014-15	Shrewsbury Town FC	4.ENG	2nd League Two (46/4125); R2 FA Cup (3/251); L16 Lg.Cup (4/360); R1 EFL Trophy (1/90)
2015-16	Shrewsbury Town FC	3.ENG	20th League One (29/2610); R5 FA Cup (4/315); R2 Lg.Cup (2/210); R2 EFL Trophy (2/180)
2016-17	Shrewsbury Town FC	3.ENG	18th League One (43/3870); R2 FA Cup (3/270); R2 Lg.Cup (2/180); EFL Trophy (1/90)
2017-18	Blackburn Rovers FC	3.ENG	2nd League One (1/90); R3 FA Cup (4/360); R2 Lg.Cup (0/0)
2018-19	Blackburn Rovers FC	2.ENG	15th EFL Championship (5/450); R3 FA Cup (0/0); R3 Lg.Cup (0/0)
2019-20	Blackburn Rovers FC	2.ENG	11th EFL Championship (0/0); R3 FA Cup (1/90); R2 Lg.Cup (2/180)
2020-21	Fleetwood Town FC	3.ENG	15th League One (16/1440); R1 FA Cup (1/90); R3 Lg.Cup (0/0); R3 EFL Trophy (1/90)
2021-22	Oldham Athletic AFC	4.ENG	23rd League Two (22/1980); R1 FA Cup (2/180); R3 Lg.Cup (1/90); L16 EFL Trophy (4/360)
2022-23	Oldham Athletic AFC	5.ENG	12th National League (0/0); R1 FA Cup (1/90)
2023-24	Port Vale FC	5.ENG	League One (current season); 2R FA Cup (0/0); QF Lg.Cup (0/0); 2R EFL Trophy (4/360)

LEVIS, BRETT — USA / DETROIT CITY FC

Fullback & midfielder. Born 1993, Saskatoon, SK, CAN. Height 173 cm. Dominant left foot. Youth clubs: Saskatoon United, AC Pumas
School: University of Saskatchewan

SEASON	CLUB	NATION	HIGHLIGHTS (MP/MIN/G)	G
2007	Saskatchewan U-14	CAN	7th Canada Soccer All Stars U-14	
2009	Saskatchewan U-16	CAN	6th Canada Soccer All Stars U-16	
2009	Saskatchewan U-18	CAN	10th Canada Games (4/390)	
2010	AC Pumas	CAN	7th Sony U-18 Cup (4/?/5g)	5
2013	Victoria Highlanders	CAN-4.US	USL PDL	
2014	Vanc. Whitecaps FC U-23	CAN-4.US	USL PDL	
2015	Vanc. Whitecaps FC 2	CAN-2.US	W11th USL (20/1094/4g)	4
2016	Vancouver Whitecaps FC	1.CAN	16th MLS (1/6)	
	Vanc. Whitecaps FC 2	CAN-2.US	W6th USL (24/1966/4g); SF Playoffs (3/270)	4
2016-17	Vancouver Whitecaps FC	Concacaf	SF Champions League (4/266)	
2017	Vanc. Whitecaps FC 2	CAN-2.US	W14th USL (5/239)	
	Vancouver Whitecaps FC	1.CAN	8th MLS (0/0)	
2018	Vancouver Whitecaps FC	1.CAN	14th MLS (14/960); 2nd CanChamp (1/73)	
2019	Vancouver Whitecaps FC	1.CAN	23rd MLS (9/330); CanChamp (0/0)	
2020	Valour FC	1.CAN	6th CPL (5/381)	
2021	Valour FC	1.CAN	5th CPL (16/960/1g); QF CanChamp (1/89)	1
2022	Valour FC	1.CAN	5th CPL (22/1926/2g); CanChamp (1/69)	2
2023	FC Tulsa	2.USA	x- USL (8/502); R2 US Cup (1/4)	
	Detroit City FC	2.USA	E8th USL (15/728)	

LOMANGINO, DANTE

Midfielder. Born 2005, . Grew up Toronto, ON, CAN. Height 192 cm. Dominant right foot. Youth clubs: Glen Shields SC, Toronto FC Academy

SEASON	CLUB	NATION	HIGHLIGHTS (MP/MIN)
2022	York United FC	1.CAN	6th CPL (0/0); SF CanChamp (0/0)

LONDONO, TYLER

Midfielder. Born 2006, Toronto, ON, CAN. Grew up Aurora & Toronto, ON, CAN. Height 175 cm. Dominant right foot. Youth clubs: Driftwood Spanish SL, Woodbridge Strikers SC, FC Emery, TFC Academy.

SEASON	CLUB	NATION	HIGHLIGHTS (MP/MIN)
2023	Toronto FC II	CAN-3.US	23rd MLS NEXT Pro (0/0)

LÓPEZ, SANTIAGO

Forward. Born 2005, Morelia, MI, MEX, Grew up in Morelia, MI, MEX & Oakville, ON, CAN. Height 180. Dominant right foot. Youth clubs: Oakville SC, Pumas UNAM (MEX)

LOTURI, VICTOR   SCO / ROSS COUNTY FC

Midfielder. Born 2001, Ottawa, ON, CAN. Grew up Calgary, AB, CAN. Height 178 cm. Dominant right foot. Youth clubs: Calgary Northside SC, Calgary Foothills SC

School: Mount Royal University

1 Concacaf medal: Silver at CNL 2022-23

SEASON	CLUB	NATION	HIGHLIGHTS (MP/MIN/G)	G
2017	Calgary Northside U-17 Hurricanes	CAN	7th U-17 Cup	
2019	Cavalry FC	1.CAN	2nd CPL (2/137); SF CanChamp (2/81)	
2021	Cavalry FC	1.CAN	2nd CPL (27/1625/2g); SF Playoffs (1/120); QF CanChamp (1/90)	2
2022	Cavalry FC	1.CAN	3rd CPL (10/769); QF CanChamp (2/113)	
2022-23	Ross County FC	1.SCO	11th Premiership (27/1724); 1st Playoffs (2/160); R4 SFA Cup (1/74); L16 Lg.Cup (3/144/1g)	1
2023-24	Ross County FC	1.SCO	Premiership (current season); 4R SFA Cup (1/90); QF Lg.Cup (5/251)	

LOUGHREY, CALE   HALIFAX WANDERERS FC

Centre back. Born 2001, Ajax, ON, CAN. Height 190 cm. Dominant left foot. Youth clubs: Richmond Hill SC, Whitby FC, Unionville-Milliken SC

School: Seneca College, University of Alabama at Birmingham

SEASON	CLUB	NATION	HIGHLIGHTS (MP/MIN/G)	G
2018	Darby FC	CAN	9th League1 Ontario (7/407)	
	Darby FC	CAN	5th League1 Ontario Playoffs (1/90)	
2019	Unionville Milliken SC	CAN	12th League1 Ontario (13/1170)	1g
2022	Forge FC Hamilton	Concacaf	L16 Champions League (1/11)	
	FC Edmonton	1.CAN	8th CPL (24/1297); CanChamp (1/85)	
2023	Halifax Wanderers FC	1.CAN	3rd CPL (24/2145); 4th Playoffs (1/80); CanChamp (0/0)	

MAAN, BAJ

Goalkeeper. Born 2000, . Grew up Brampton, ON, CAN. Height 190 cm. Youth clubs: Rexdale SC, Brampton East SC, Sigma FC

School: North Kentucky University

Honours: CPL Championship (2020), League1 Ontario (2023)

SEASON	CLUB	NATION	HIGHLIGHTS (MP/MIN)
2019	Forge FC Hamilton	1.CAN	CanChamp (0/0)
	Sigma FC	CAN	5th League1 Ontario (7/630)
2020	Forge FC Hamilton	Concacaf	QF Concacaf League (0/0)
	Forge FC Hamilton	1.CAN	1st CPL (1/90)
	Forge FC Hamilton	Concacaf	SF Concacaf League (0/0)
2021	Forge FC Hamilton	1.CAN	1st CPL (6/540); 2nd Playoffs (0/0); SF CanChamp (0/0)
2022	Forge FC Hamilton	Concacaf	L16 Champions League (0/0)
	Toronto FC II	CAN-3.US	7th MLS NEXT Pro (0/0)
2023	Toronto FC II	CAN-3.US	23rd MLS NEXT Pro (0/0)
	Simcoe County Rovers FC	CAN	2nd League1 Ontario (19/1665); 1st Playoffs (2/180)

MACKENZIE, LIAM   VANCOUVER WHITECAPS FC ACADEMY

Midfielder. Born 2007, Comox, BC, CAN. Height 180 cm. Dominant right foot. Youth clubs: Comox Valley United SC, Vancouver Whitecaps FC Academy

SEASON	CLUB	NATION	HIGHLIGHTS (MP/MIN)
2023	Vanc. Whitecaps Academy	CAN-3.US	21st MLS NEXT Pro (1/13)

MACNAUGHTON, LUKAS   USA / NASHVILLE SC

Centre back. Born 1995, New York City, NY, USA. Grew up Brussels, BEL. Height 188 cm. Dominant right foot. Youth

FOOTBALLERS

clubs: Genval, Rosières-Rixensart
School: University of Toronto
Honours: Canadian Championship (2022/'20), CPL Championship (2021)
1st #CANMNT: 2022-11-11 at Isa Town, BHR (v. BHR)

SEASON	CLUB	NATION	HIGHLIGHTS (MP/MIN/G)	G
2016	North Toronto Nitros	CAN	E3rd League1 Ontario (5/315/2g)	2
2017	North Toronto Nitros	CAN	E4th League1 Ontario (4/315/2g)	2
2018	Alliance United FC	CAN	7th League1 Ontario (8/402)	
	Alliance United FC	CAN	6th League1 Ontario Playoffs (2/177)	
2019	Pacific FC	1.CAN	5th CPL (20/1705/2g); CanChamp (2/180)	2
2020	Pacific FC	1.CAN	3rd CPL (8/720/1g)	1
2021	Pacific FC	1.CAN	3rd CPL (25/2250/2g); Playoffs (1/90); SF CanChamp (3/270)	2
2022('20)	Toronto FC	1.CAN	1st CanChamp (1/89)	
2022	Toronto FC	1.CAN	27th MLS (25/1789); 2nd CanChamp (2/172/1g)	1
2023	Toronto FC	1.CAN	x- MLS (3/180)	
	Nashville SC	1.USA	12th MLS (14/1077/1g); L16 MLS Playoffs (2/96); L16 US Cup (1/45); 2nd Leagues (7/538)	1

MAHESHE, OUSMAN

Forward & midfielder. Born 2002, Kinshasa, COD. Grew up Edmonton, AB, CAN. Height 175 cm. Dominant right foot. Youth clubs: South Claireview Cobras, Edmonton Xtreme FC, Edmonton Victoria SC, St .Albert Impact, FC Edmonton Academy
School: North Alberta Institute of Technology, MacEwan University

SEASON	CLUB	NATION	HIGHLIGHTS (MP/MIN)
2016	St. Albert Impact U-14	CAN	4th U-14 Cup
2022	FC Edmonton	1.CAN	8th CPL (1/8)

MANN, JOVEN

Midfielder. Born 2004. Grew up in Surrey, BC, CAN. Height 183. Dominant right foot. Youth clubs: Surrey United SC, Vancouver Whitecaps FC Academy
Honours: League1 BC (2023)

SEASON	CLUB	NATION	HIGHLIGHTS (MP/MIN/G)	G
2022	Vanc. Whitecaps FC 2	CAN-3.US	14th MLS NEXT Pro (0/0)	
	Vanc. Whitecaps FC Academy	3.CAN	3rd League1 BC	
2023	Vanc. Whitecaps FC 2	CAN-3.US	21st MLS NEXT Pro (0/0)	
	Vanc. Whitecaps FC Academy	3.CAN	3rd League1 BC (12/904/1g); 1st Playoffs (2/164/1g)	1

MANNELLA, CHRIS — VAUGHAN SC

Born 1994, Toronto, ON, CAN. Height 180 cm. Dominant right foot. Youth clubs: West End United, Islington, Spartacus SC, Toronto FC Academy
Honours: CPL Regular Season (2022)
1st #CANMNT: 2015-01-16 at Orlando, FL, USA (v. ISL)

SEASON	CLUB	NATION	HIGHLIGHTS (MP/MIN/G)	G
2008	Ontario U-14	CAN	2nd Canada Soccer All Stars U-14	
2014	TFC Academy	CAN	1st League1 Ontario	
2015	Toronto FC	1.CAN	4th CanChamp (0/0)	
	Toronto FC II	CAN-2.US	E11th USL (16/1295/1g)	1
2016	Toronto FC II	CAN-2.US	E12th USL (22/1562)	
2018	Ottawa Fury FC	2.USA	E10th USL (29/1956); SF CanChamp (4/266)	
2019	Ottawa Fury FC	2.USA	E8th USL (31/2189); Playoffs (1/79); SF CanChamp (4/300)	
2020	York9 FC	1.CAN	5th CPL (2/100)	
2021	Atlético Ottawa	1.CAN	8th CPL (19/959)	
2022	Atlético Ottawa	1.CAN	1st CPL (6/89); 2nd Playoffs (0/0)	
2023	Vaughan Azzurri	CAN	3rd League1 Ontario (1/71); CanChamp (1/73)	

MARKOVIC, NIKOLA — CF MONTRÉAL U-23

Centre back. Born 2004, Gatineau, QC, CAN. Grew up in Gatineau, QC, CAN. Height 192. Youth clubs: CS Collines

SEASON	CLUB	NATION	HIGHLIGHTS (MP/MIN)
2022	Québec U-18	CAN	Gold at Canada Games (4/281)
2023	CF Montréal U-23	CAN	5th Ligue1 Québec

MARMOLEJO, EMMANUEL

Goalkeeper. Born 2007. Grew up Mississauga, ON, CAN. Height 182 cm. Dominant right foot. Youth clubs: Sigma FC

SEASON	CLUB	NATION	HIGHLIGHTS (MP/MIN)
2023	Forge FC Hamilton	1.CAN	2nd CPL (0/0); SF CanChamp (0/0)

MARSHALL-RUTTY, JAHKEELE — TORONTO FC

Fullback & midfielder. Born 2004, Brampton, ON, CAN. Height 170 cm. Youth clubs: Brampton East SC, Toronto FC Academy

SEASON	CLUB	NATION	HIGHLIGHTS (MP/MIN/G)	G
2019	Toronto FC II	CAN-3.US	7th USL League One (3/10)	
2020	Toronto FC	1.CAN	2nd MLS (1/18); 2nd CanChamp (1/29)	
2021	Toronto FC	Concacaf	QF Champions League (0/0)	
	Toronto FC	1.CAN	26th MLS (11/421)	
	Toronto FC II	CAN-3.US	7th USL League One (7/500/1g)	1
2022	Toronto FC	1.CAN	27th MLS (17/613); 2nd CanChamp (1/17)	
2023	Toronto FC	1.CAN	29th MLS (22/1146); QF CanChamp (1/68); Leagues (2/109)	
	Toronto FC II	CAN-3.US	23rd MLS NEXT Pro (3/260/1g)	1

MARTIN, ALEXIS — CF MONTRÉAL U-23

Goalkeeper. Born 2006, Laval, QC, CAN. Grew up in Laval, QC, CAN. Height 198. Dominant right foot. Youth clubs: CS Les Étoiles de L'Est, AS Laval

SEASON	CLUB	NATION	HIGHLIGHTS (MP/MIN)
2023	CF Montréal U-23	CAN	5th Ligue1 Québec

MARTIN-PEREUX, KADIN — YORK UNITED FC

Fullback. Born 2002, Victoria, BC, CAN. Height 183 cm. Dominant left foot.

SEASON	CLUB	NATION	HIGHLIGHTS (MP/MIN)
2023	York United FC	CAN	5th CPL (5/228); 5th Playoffs (1/89)

MARVASTI, SAMI

Midfielder. Grew up in .., BC, CAN. Youth clubs: Saanish Fusion FC, Vancouver Island Wave

SEASON	CLUB	NATION	HIGHLIGHTS (MP/MIN)
2023	Pacific FC	CAN	4th CPL (0/0)

MASI, SIMONE

Centre back. Born 2002, Burnaby, BC, CAN. Grew up in Burnaby, BC, CAN. Height 188. Youth clubs: Mountain United FC, Vancouver Whitecaps FC Academy
School: Simon Fraser University

SEASON	CLUB	NATION	HIGHLIGHTS (MP/MIN/G)	G
2017	Mountain United FC U-15	CAN	5th U-15 Cup	
2022	Vanc. Whitecaps FC 2	CAN-3.US	14th MLS NEXT Pro (19/1449/1g)	1
2023	Vanc. Whitecaps FC 2	CAN-3.US	21st MLS NEXT Pro (7/586)	

MATHE, IMMANUEL — VANCOUVER WHITECAPS FC ACADEMY

Centre back. Born 2006, Burnaby, BC, CAN. Height 189 cm. Dominant right foot. Youth clubs: Cliff Avenue United, Vancouver Whitecaps FC Academy

SEASON	CLUB	NATION	HIGHLIGHTS (MP/MIN)
2023	Vanc. Whitecaps FC Academy	3.CAN	3rd League1 BC (1/25)

MAVAKALA, DAVID — CF MONTRÉAL U-23

Right back. Born 2006, Kinshasa, COD. Grew up in Moncton, NB, CAN. Height 168. Dominant right foot. Youth clubs: Moncton Codiac, Académie de CF Montréal

SEASON	CLUB	NATION	HIGHLIGHTS (MP/MIN/G)	G
2022	CF Montréal U-23	CAN	6th PLSQ (9/734/2g)	2
2023	CF Montréal U-23	CAN	5th Ligue1 Québec	

MAWOKO, KUNDAI — TORONTO FC II

Right back. Born 2005, Toronto, ON, CAN. Grew up in Whitby, ON, CAN. Height 178. Youth clubs: Oshawa Turul SC, DeRo United FA, Toronto FC Academy

SEASON	CLUB	NATION	HIGHLIGHTS (MP/MIN)
2018	Toronto FC U-13	CAN	QF Concacaf Under-13 Champions League

FOOTBALLERS

2022	Toronto FC II	CAN-3.US	7th MLS NEXT Pro (5/291)
2023	Toronto FC II	CAN-3.US	23rd MLS NEXT Pro (3/34)

MAZZAFERRO, SALVATORE — USA / AUSTIN FC II

Centre back & left back. Born 2001. Grew up in Toronto, ON, CAN. Height 185. Youth clubs: Toronto Epic FC, Toronto FC Academy
School: University of South Florida

SEASON	CLUB	NATION	HIGHLIGHTS (MP/MIN)
2015	Epic FC Toronto U-14	CAN	1st U-14 Cup
2018	Toronto FC Academy	CAN	4th League1 Ontario (8/374)

MBONGUE, HUGO — TORONTO FC

Forward. Born 2004, Toronto, ON, CAN. Height 180 cm. Dominant right foot. Youth clubs: Cherry Beach Recreation Centre, Clairlea Westview SC, North Toronto SC, Toronto FC Academy

SEASON	CLUB	NATION	HIGHLIGHTS (MP/MIN/G)	G
2021	Toronto FC II	CAN-3.US	7th USL League One (10/105)	
2022	Toronto FC	1.CAN	27th MLS (1/22)	
	Toronto FC II	CAN-3.US	7th MLS NEXT Pro (16/1147/4g); SF Playoffs (2/155/1g)	5
2023	Toronto FC	1.CAN	29th MLS (11/255); Leagues (2/53)	
	Toronto FC II	CAN-3.US	23rd MLS NEXT Pro (15/101/5g)	5

MCGILL, TOM — ENG / BRIGHTON & HOVE ALBION

Goalkeeper. Born 2000, Belleville, ON, CAN. Grew up Haywards Heath, ENG. Height 185 cm. Dominant right foot. Youth clubs: Cuckfield Cosmos, Brighton & Hove Albion FC
1 Concacaf medal: Silver at CNL 2022-23

SEASON	CLUB	NATION	HIGHLIGHTS (MP/MIN)
2019-20	Crawley Town FC	4.ENG	13th League Two (0/0)
2020-21	Crawley Town FC	4.ENG	x- League Two (1/35); R3 FA Cup (1/64); R1 Lg.Cup (1/90); EFL Trophy (2/180)
	Brighton & Hove Albion FC	1.ENG	16th FA Premier League (0/0)
2021-22	Brighton & Hove Albion FC	1.ENG	9th FA Premier League (0/0); R4 FA Cup (0/0); R4 Lg.Cup (0/0)
2022-23	Brighton & Hove Albion FC	1.ENG	6th FA Premier League (0/0); SF FA Cup (0/0); R4 Lg.Cup (0/0)
	Brighton & Hove Albion FC U-21	ENG	Premier League 2 (5/450)
2023-24	Brighton & Hove Albion FC	UEFA	UEFA Europa League (0/0)
	Brighton & Hove Albion FC U-21	ENG	Premier League 2 (current season)

MCGRAW, ZAC — USA / PORTLAND TIMBERS FC

Centre back. Born 1997, . Grew up Torrence, CA, USA. Height 193 cm. Youth clubs: FC Golden State Force

SEASON	CLUB	NATION	HIGHLIGHTS (MP/MIN/G)	G
2020	Portland Timbers FC	1.USA	8th MLS (0/0); 1st MLS is Back (0/0); Playoffs (0/0)	
2021	Portland Timbers FC	Concacaf	QF Champions League (1/7)	
	Portland Timbers FC	1.USA	5th MLS (11/275); 2nd Playoffs (0/0)	
2022	Portland Timbers FC	1.USA	15th MLS (22/1068/1g); R4 US Cup (1/90)	1
2023	Portland Timbers FC	1.USA	18th MLS (28/2423/1g); L32 Leagues (3/270)	1
	Portland Timbers 2	3.USA	MLS NEXT Pro (4/330/2g)	2

MCKENDRY, BEN

Midfielder & centre back. Born 1993, Vancouver, BC, CAN. Height 180 cm. Dominant right foot. Youth clubs: Grandview Legion, Vancouver Whitecaps FC Residency
School: University of New Mexico
Honours: Canadian Championship (2015), CPL Regular Season (2022)
1st #CANMNT: 2017-01-22 at Devonshire Parish, BER (v. BER)

SEASON	CLUB	NATION	HIGHLIGHTS (MP/MIN/G)	G
2007	British Columbia U-14	CAN	3rd Canada Soccer All Stars U-14	
2009	British Columbia U-16	CAN	4th Canada Soccer All Stars U-16	
2012	Vanc. Whitecaps FC U-23	CAN-4.US	USL PDL	
2015	Vancouver Whitecaps FC	1.CAN	1st CanChamp (0/0)	
	Vanc. Whitecaps FC 2	CAN-2.US	W11th USL (21/1618/2g)	2
2016	Vancouver Whitecaps FC	1.CAN	16th MLS (0/0); 2nd CanChamp (2/162)	
	Vanc. Whitecaps FC 2	CAN-2.US	W6th USL (20/1436/2g)	2
2016-17	Vancouver Whitecaps FC	Concacaf	SF Champions League (2/116)	

2017	Vanc. Whitecaps FC 2	CAN-2.US	W14th USL (14/1203/2g)	2
	Vancouver Whitecaps FC	1.CAN	8th MLS (1/90); SF CanChamp (2/158)	
	FC Edmonton	2.USA	7th NASL (15/1050)	
2018	Turun Palloseura	1.FIN	11th Veikkausliiga (28/2300)	
2019	Nyköpings BIS	3.SWE	8th Ettan Norra	
2020	Atlético Ottawa	1.CAN	7th CPL (7/409)	
2021	Atlético Ottawa	1.CAN	8th CPL (25/2132/1g)	1
2022	Atlético Ottawa	1.CAN	1st CPL (25/1166); 2nd Playoffs (2/27); CanChamp (1/7)	

MEDEIROS, MATTHEW — TORONTO FC II

Centre back. Born 2003, Toronto, ON, CAN. Grew up in Toronto, ON, CAN. Height 190. Dominant right foot. Youth clubs: Toronto FC Academy

SEASON	CLUB	NATION	HIGHLIGHTS (MP/MIN)
2022	Toronto FC II	CAN-3.US	7th MLS NEXT Pro (4/288)
2023	Toronto FC II	CAN-3.US	23rd MLS NEXT Pro (9/481)

MEILLEUR-GIGUÈRE, THOMAS — PACIFIC FC

Centre back. Born 1997, Repentigny, QC, CAN. Grew up L'Assomption, QC, CAN. Height 185 cm. Dominant right foot. Youth clubs: CS L'Assomption, Académie de l'Impact Montréal
Honours: CPL Championship (2021)

SEASON	CLUB	NATION	HIGHLIGHTS (MP/MIN/G)	G
2012	FC L'Assomption	CAN	2nd PLSQ (1/?)	
	Québec U-15	CAN	2nd Canada Soccer All Stars U-15	
2013	Québec U-16	CAN	Canada Soccer All Stars U-16	
2016	FC Montréal	CAN-2.US	E14th USL (21/1832/2g)	2
2017	Ottawa Fury FC	2.USA	E10th USL (4/59); SF CanChamp (0/0)	
2018	Ottawa Fury FC	2.USA	E10th USL (27/2399); SF CanChamp (4/360)	
2019	Ottawa Fury FC	2.USA	E8th USL (31/2608/1g); Playoffs (1/120); SF CanChamp (4/360)	1
2020	Pacific FC	1.CAN	3rd CPL (10/900)	
2021	Pacific FC	1.CAN	3rd CPL (8/535); 1st Playoffs (2/210); SF CanChamp (2/19)	
2022	Pacific FC	Concacaf	L16 Concacaf League (4/360)	
	Pacific FC	1.CAN	4th CPL (27/2175); SF Playoffs (2/180/1g); QF CanChamp (1/90)	1
2023	Pacific FC	1.CAN	4th CPL (26/2339/4g); 3rd Playoffs (3/270); SF CanChamp (2/180)	4

MELVIN, SEAN — PACIFIC FC

Goalkeeper. Born 1994, Victoria, BC, CAN. Height 193 cm. Dominant right foot. Youth clubs: Gordon Head SA, Victoria United Metro, Vancouver Whitecaps FC Residency
School: University of North Carolina Wilmington
Honours: CPL Regular Season (2022)
1st #CANMNT: 2017-01-22 at Devonshire Parish, BER (v. BER)

SEASON	CLUB	NATION	HIGHLIGHTS (MP/MIN)
2008	British Columbia U-14	CAN	4th Canada Soccer All Stars U-14
2010	British Columbia U-16	CAN	4th Canada Soccer All Stars U-16
2011	Vanc. Whitecaps Residency	CAN-4.US	USL PDL
2012	Vanc. Whitecaps FC U-23	CAN-4.US	USL PDL
2015	Calgary Foothills SC	CAN-4.US	USL PDL
2016	Vanc. Whitecaps FC 2	CAN-2.US	W6th USL (8/720)
2017	Vancouver Whitecaps FC	1.CAN	SF CanChamp (0/0)
	Vanc. Whitecaps FC 2	CAN-2.US	W14th USL (13/1170)
2018	Vancouver Whitecaps FC	1.CAN	14th MLS (0/0); 2nd CanChamp (0/0)
2019	Vancouver Whitecaps FC	1.CAN	23rd MLS (0/0)
2020	Colorado Springs Switchbacks	2.USA	W13th USL (11/990)
2021	Colo. Springs Switchbacks FC	2.USA	W5th USL (24/2160); Playoffs (1/90)
2022	Atlético Ottawa	1.CAN	1st CPL (4/273); 2nd Playoffs (0/0); CanChamp (0/0)
2023	Atlético Ottawa	1.CAN	6th CPL (6/540); QF CanChamp (1/90)

MERCURE, JAEDEN — AUS / LAUNCESTON UNITED SC

Forward. Born 2003. Grew up in Ottawa, ON, CAN. Height 180 cm. Youth clubs: Ottawa South United SC, Vancouver Whitecaps FC Academy

SEASON	CLUB	NATION	HIGHLIGHTS (MP/MIN/G)	G
2019	Ottawa South United	CAN	16th League1 Ontario (1/90)	

2021	Ottawa South United	CAN	10th PLSQ (7/538/1g)	1
	Atlético Ottawa	1.CAN	8th CPL (5/58)	
2022	Ottawa South United	CAN	12th PLSQ (16/1315/3g)	3

METCALFE, PATRICK — NOR / FREDRIKSTAD

Midfielder. Born 1998, Richmond, BC, CAN. Height 183 cm. Dominant right foot. Youth clubs: Richmond FC, Fusion FC, Vancouver Whitecaps FC Academy
School: University of British Columbia

SEASON	CLUB	NATION	HIGHLIGHTS (MP/MIN/G)	G
2017	Vanc. Whitecaps FC 2	CAN-2.US	W14th USL (4/222)	
2018	TSS Rovers FC	CAN-4.US	USL PDL (10/487)	
2020	Vancouver Whitecaps FC	1.CAN	17th MLS (7/204); L16 MLS is Back (0/0)	
2021	Vancouver Whitecaps FC	1.CAN	12th MLS (13/361); CanChamp (1/89)	
2022	Fredrikstad FK	2.NOR	10th OBOS-ligaen (23/929/1g); L16 Cup (2/180)	1
2023	Fredrikstad FK	2.NOR	1st OBOS-ligaen (30/2360/1g); R3 Cup (3/193)	1

MICHEL, DIEU-MERCI — POR / VITÓRIA GUIMARÃES SC B

Left winger. Born 2004, Montréal, QC, CAN. Grew up in Edmonton, AB, CAN. Height 191. Dominant right foot. Youth clubs: Edmonton BTB Academy, Vancouver Whitecaps FC Academy, Vitória Guimarães SC (Portugal)

SEASON	CLUB	NATION	HIGHLIGHTS (MP/MIN)
2019	St. Albert Impact U-15	CAN	1st U-15 Cup

MICHEL, JUDWELLIN — CF MONTRÉAL U-23

Goalkeeper. Born 2004, Port-au-Prince, HAI. Grew up in Montréal, QC, CAN. Youth clubs: CS St-Laurent, CS Montréal-Nord

SEASON	CLUB	NATION	HIGHLIGHTS (MP/MIN)
2022	Québec U-18	CAN	Gold at Canada Games (4/281)
2023	CF Montréal U-23	CAN	5th Ligue1 Québec

MILLAR, LIAM — ENG / PRESTON NORTH END FC

Winger. Born 1999, Toronto, ON, CAN. Grew up Brampton, ON, CAN. Height 176 cm. Dominant right foot. Youth clubs: Brampton YSC, North Mississauga SC, Burlington YSC, Fulham FC (England), Liverpool FC (England)
Honours: Concacaf champion (2021-22)

CANADA INTERNATIONAL
1 FIFA World Cup: Group phase at Qatar 2022
1st #CANMNT: 2018-03-24 at San Pedro del Pinatar, ESP (v. NZL)

SEASON	CLUB	NATION	HIGHLIGHTS (MP/MIN/G)	G
2018-19	Kilmarnock FC	1.SCO	3rd Premiership (13/296/1g); L16 SFA Cup (1/6)	1
2019-20	Liverpool FC	1.ENG	R5 FA Cup (1/82)	
	Kilmarnock FC	1.SCO	8th Premiership (20/1207/1g); QF Lg.Cup (2/115)	1
2020-21	Charlton Athletic FC	3.ENG	7th League One (27/1976/3g); EFL Trophy (3/270/2g)	5
2021-22	FC Basel	UEFA	Qualifying (4/119); L16 UEFA Conference League (8/502/2g)	2
	FC Basel	1.SUI	2nd Super League (31/2024/7g); L16 Coupe (3/201/1g)	8
2022-23	FC Basel	UEFA	Qualifying (6/457/1g); SF UEFA Conference League (10/441)	1
	FC Basel	1.SUI	5th Super League (26/1448); SF Coupe (4/190)	
2023-24	FC Basel	UEFA	Qualifying Conference League (1/78)	
	FC Basel	1.SUI	x- Super League (4/294)	
	Preston North End FC	2.ENG	Championship (current season); FA Cup (1/90)	

MILLER, KAMAL — USA / PORTLAND TIMBERS FC

Centre back. Born 1997, Scarborough, ON, CAN. Height 183 cm. Dominant left foot. Youth clubs: Scarborough Malvern SC, North Scarborough SC, Vaughan SC
School: Syracuse University
Honours: Concacaf champion (2021-22), Canadian Championship (2021), Leagues (2023)

CANADA INTERNATIONAL
1 FIFA World Cup: Group phase at Qatar 2022
1 Concacaf medal: Silver at CNL 2022-23
1st #CANMNT: 2019-06-23 at Charlotte, NC, USA (v. CUB)

SEASON	CLUB	NATION	HIGHLIGHTS (MP/MIN/G)	G
2012	Ontario U-15	CAN	1st Canada Soccer All Stars U-15	

2013	Vaughan Azzuri U-16	CAN	2nd U-16 Cup
	Ontario U-18	CAN	Bronze at Canada Games (5/450/1g) 1
	Ontario U-16	CAN	Canada Soccer All Stars U-16
2014	Vaughan Azzurri	CAN	4th League1 Ontario
	Vaughan Azzurri	CAN	4th League1 Ontario
2015	Vaughan Azzurri	CAN	3rd League1 Ontario
2016	K-W United FC	CAN-4.US	USL PDL (12/980)
2017	K-W United FC	CAN-4.US	USL PDL (11/880/2g) 2
2019	Orlando City SC	1.USA	22nd MLS (16/1350)
2020	Orlando City SC	1.USA	5th MLS (12/805); 2nd MLS is Back (0/0); QF Playoffs (2/120)
2021	CF Montréal	1.CAN	18th MLS (27/2377/1g); 1st CanChamp (1/90) 1
2022	CF Montréal	Concacaf	QF Champions League (4/302)
	CF Montréal	1.CAN	3rd MLS (27/2298/2g); QF Playoffs (2/180) 2
	MLS All-Stars	1.USA	MLS All-Star Game (1/?)
2023	CF Montréal	1.CAN	x- MLS (6/477)
	Inter Miami CF	1.USA	27th MLS (22/1845); US Cup (current); 1st Leagues (7/614)

MILOSEVIC, ALEXANDER — VANCOUVER WHITECAPS FC ACADEMY

Goalkeeper. Grew up in .., BC, CAN. Youth clubs: Mountain United FC, Vancouver Whitecaps FC Academy

SEASON	CLUB	NATION	HIGHLIGHTS (MP/MIN)
2023	Vanc. Whitecaps FC 2	CAN-3.US	21st MLS NEXT Pro (0/0)

MOHAMMED, TERIQUE — USA / LEXINGTON SC

Fullback & forward. Born 2000, Toronto, ON, CAN. Grew up Scarborough, ON, CAN. Height 175 cm. Youth clubs: Scarborough Blizzards, Unionville-Milliken SC, Toronto FC Academy

SEASON	CLUB	NATION	HIGHLIGHTS (MP/MIN/G)	G
2016	TFC Academy	CAN	W3rd League1 Ontario (2/63)	
2017	TFC Academy	CAN	W3rd League1 Ontario (4/160)	
2018	Toronto FC II	CAN-2.US	E16th USL (10/651)	
	TFC Academy	CAN	4th League1 Ontario (7/502/2g)	2
2019	Toronto FC II	CAN-3.US	7th USL League One (20/1495/2g)	2
2020	FC Edmonton	1.CAN	8th CPL (5/304)	
2021	York United FC	1.CAN	4th CPL (9/761)	
	Dundalk FC	1.IRL	6th Premier Division (0/0)	
2022	FC Edmonton	1.CAN	8th CPL (22/797); CanChamp (0/0)	
2023	Lexington SC	3.USA	9th USL League One (22/1738); R2 US Cup (1/74)	

MOHSEN, MONTI

Left midfielder & fullback. Born 2000, Ottawa, ON, CAN. Height 175 cm. Dominant left foot. Youth clubs: Ottawa St. Anthony SC, Ottawa Gloucester Hornets, Ottawa South United, Ottawa Internationals SC
Honours: CPL Championship (2019, 2020)

SEASON	CLUB	NATION	HIGHLIGHTS (MP/MIN/G)	G
2017	Ontario U-18	CAN	Gold at Canada Games (5/386/3g)	3
2018	Ottawa Fury FC	CAN-2.US	E10th USL (1/45)	
	Ottawa Fury FC	2.CAN	SF CanChamp (0/0)	
2019	Forge FC Hamilton	Concacaf	Concacaf League (0/0)	
	Forge FC Hamilton	1.CAN	1st CPL (9/363/1g); CanChamp (0/0)	1
2020	Forge FC Hamilton	Concacaf	Concacaf League (1/11)	
	Forge FC Hamilton	1.CAN	1st CPL (3/207)	
2021	Forge FC Hamilton	Concacaf	Concacaf League (0/0)	
	Forge FC Hamilton	1.CAN	1st CPL (8/230)	
2022-23	"Shabab Al-Khalil SC	" 1.PLE	West Bank Premier League	

MONTGOMERY, CALLUM — CAVALRY FC

Centre back. Born 1998, Nanaimo, BC, CAN. Height 190 cm. Youth clubs: Nanaimo SA, Vancouver Island Wave
School: UNC Charlotte
Honous: CPL North Star Shield (2023), USL League One (2019)

SEASON	CLUB	NATION	HIGHLIGHTS (MP/MIN/G)	G
2016	Victoria Highlanders FC	CAN-4.US	USL PDL (12/1080/1g)	1
2017	Victoria Highlanders FC	CAN-4.US	USL PDL (3/189/1g)	1
2018	Victoria Highlanders FC	CAN-4.US	USL PDL (10/882/2g)	2

FOOTBALLERS

SEASON	CLUB	NATION	HIGHLIGHTS (MP/MIN/G)	G
2019	FC Dallas	1.USA	13th MLS (0/0); Playoffs (0/0); L16 US Cup (0/0)	
	North Texas SC	2.USA	1st USL (20/1778/3g); 1st Playoffs (2/180)	3
2020	FC Dallas	1.USA	11th MLS (0/0); QF Playoffs (0/0)	
	San Antonio FC	2.USA	W3rd USL (9/808/2g)	2
2021	San Diego Loyal SC	2.USA	W6th USL (17/1013/1g); Playoffs (1/80)	1
2022	Minnesota United FC	1.USA	11th MLS (0/0)	
	Minnesota United 2	3.USA	12th MLS NEXT Pro (8/556)	
2023	Cavalry FC	1.CAN	1st CPL (11/656); 2nd Playoffs (2/34); CanChamp (1/90)	

MORANO, ANTHONY
Forward. Born 2006.

SEASON	CLUB	NATION	HIGHLIGHTS (MP/MIN/G)	G
2023	York United FC	1.CAN	5th CPL (0/0)	1
2023	North Mississauga SC	CAN	17th League1 Ontario (11/691/3g)	1

MORGAN, ASHTONE
Retired from active play in July 2023
Left back. Born 1991, Toronto, ON, CAN. Height 175 cm. Dominant left foot. Youth clubs: West End United, Toronto FC Academy
Honours: Canadian Championship (2012, 2016, 2017, 2018), MLS Supporters' Shield (2017), CPL Championship (2022)
1st #CANMNT: 2011-10-7 at Gros Islet, LCA (v. LCA)

SEASON	CLUB	NATION	HIGHLIGHTS (MP/MIN/G)	G
2005	Ontario U-14	CAN	1st Canada Soccer All Stars U-14	
2007	Ontario U-16	CAN	2nd Canada Soccer All Stars U-16	
2009	Ontario U-18	CAN	Bronze at Canada Games (5/405)	
2011	Toronto FC	1.CAN	16th MLS (14/903)	
2012	Toronto FC	1.CAN	19th MLS (30/2528); 1st CanChamp (4/360)	
2013	Toronto FC	1.CAN	17th MLS (22/1805); 3rd CanChamp (2/180)	
2014	Toronto FC	1.CAN	13th MLS (3/168); 2nd CanChamp (2/169)	
2015	Toronto FC	1.CAN	12th MLS (19/1554); Playoffs (0/0); 4th CanChamp (1/90)	
	Toronto FC II	CAN-2.US	E11th USL (1/90)	
2016	Toronto FC	1.CAN	5th MLS (7/157); 1st CanChamp (2/180)	
	Toronto FC II	CAN-2.US	E12th USL (1/61)	
2017	Toronto FC	1.CAN	1st MLS (5/283/1g); 1st CanChamp (1/22)	1
	Toronto FC II	CAN-2.US	E15th USL (7/554/1g)	1
2018	Toronto FC	1.CAN	19th MLS (18/1009); 1st CanChamp (4/279); 2nd Campeones (0/0)	
	Toronto FC II	CAN-2.US	E16th USL (1/63)	
2019	Toronto FC	1.CAN	9th MLS (9/308/1g); 2nd CanChamp (3/135)	1
	Toronto FC II	CAN-3.US	7th USL League One (1/45)	
2020	Real Salt Lake	1.USA	21st MLS (0/0); L16 MLS is Back (0/0)	
	Real Monarchs	2.USA	W14th USL (1/90)	
2021	Real Salt Lake	1.USA	13th MLS (8/371); SF Playoffs (1/15)	
	Real Monarchs	2.USA	W14th USL (4/360)	
2022('20)	Forge FC Hamilton	1.CAN	2nd CanChamp (1/84)	
2022	Forge FC Hamilton	1.CAN	2nd CPL (20/1339/1g); 1st Playoffs (3/233); QF CanChamp (1/64)	1
2023	Forge FC Hamilton	1.CAN	x- CPL (11/339); SF CanChamp (3/166)	

CONCACAF		NATION	HIGHLIGHTS (MP/MIN/G)	G
2010-11	Toronto FC	Concacaf	Champions League (1/90)	
2011-12	Toronto FC	Concacaf	SF Champions League (12/922)	
2012-13	Toronto FC	Concacaf	Champions League (4/360)	
2018	Toronto FC	Concacaf	2nd Champions League (4/337/1g)	1
2019	Toronto FC	Concacaf	L16 Champions League (1/57)	
2022	Forge FC Hamilton	Concacaf	L16 Champions League (2/169)	

MORGAN, MYLES — TORONTO FC II
Midfielder. Born 2005. Grew up in .., ON, CAN. Height 175. Youth clubs: DeRo TFC, Toronto FC Academy

SEASON	CLUB	NATION	HIGHLIGHTS (MP/MIN/G)	G
2022	Ontario U-18	CAN	Silver at Canada Games (4/158/2g)	2
2023	Toronto FC II	CAN-3.US	23rd MLS NEXT Pro (9/313/2g)	

MORRISON, BLAKE — CAVALRY FC
Goalkeeper. Born 2008. Grew up in Calgary, AB, CAN. Youth clubs: Cavalry FC

MUKUMBILWA, GEORGES — PACIFIC FC
Fullback & winger. Born 1999, Goma, COD. Grew up Winnipeg, MB, CAN. Height 180 cm. Dominant right foot. Youth clubs: Portage Trail SC, Vancouver Whitecaps FC Residency

SEASON	CLUB	NATION	HIGHLIGHTS (MP/MIN)
2019	Vancouver Whitecaps FC	1.CAN	23rd MLS (1/9)
2020	Vancouver Whitecaps FC	1.CAN	17th MLS (0/0)
2022	Pacific FC	Concacaf	L16 Concacaf League (2/180)
	Pacific FC	1.CAN	4th CPL (17/891); SF Playoffs (1/10); QF CanChamp (0/0)
2023	Pacific FC	1.CAN	4th CPL (21/1506); 3rd Playoffs (3/270); SF CanChamp (3/206)

MULLINGS, O'VONTE — USA / NEW YORK RED BULLS
Forward. Born 2000, ... Grew up Toronto, ON, CAN. Height 175 cm. Youth clubs: FC Durham Academy, Northview Heights Secondary School
School: Florida Gulf Coast University

SEASON	CLUB	NATION	HIGHLIGHTS (MP/MIN/G)	G
2019	Seattle Sounders U-23	4.USA	USL League Two	
2022	New York Red Bulls 2	2.USA	E14th USL (31/2660/1g)	1
2023	New York Red Bulls	1.USA	17th MLS (2/43); L16 (1/40)	
	New York Red Bulls 2	3.USA	7th MLS NEXT Pro (23/1805/4g)	4

MURASIRANWA, DARLINGTON — VALOUR FC
Goalkeeper. Born 2001, Harare, ZIM. Grew up Cape Town, RSA & Edmonton, AB, CAN. Height 178 cm. Youth clubs: Cape Town Barca Juniors (South Africa), Hazeldean Community, Edmonton Victoria SC, FC Edmonton Academy, Vancouver Whitecaps Residency
School: University of Guelph

SEASON	CLUB	NATION	HIGHLIGHTS (MP/MIN)
2021	FC Edmonton	1.CAN	7th CPL (5/431); CanChamp (1/90)
2022	FC Edmonton	1.CAN	8th CPL (8/675); CanChamp (0/0)
2023	Winnipeg Valour FC	1.CAN	8th CPL (2/180)
	FC London	CAN	13th League1 Ontario (16/1431)

MYRONIUK, NIKO
Midfielder. Born 2005, Calgary, AB, CAN. Height 180 cm. Dominant right foot. Youth clubs: Calgary South West United SC, Calgary Blizzards SC, Vancouver Whitecaps FC Academy

SEASON	CLUB	NATION	HIGHLIGHTS (MP/MIN)
2022	Alberta U-18	CAN	Bronze at Canada Games (3/221)
2023	Cavalry FC	1.CAN	1st CPL (1/3); CanChamp (1/57)

MZOUGHI, ESKANDER
Right back. Born 2003, Montréal, QC, CAN. Grew up . Height 175 cm. Dominant right foot. Youth clubs: CS Phénix des Rivières, OH Leuven (Belgium)

SEASON	CLUB	NATION	HIGHLIGHTS (MP/MIN)
2023	Valour FC	1.CAN	8th CPL (14/516); CanChamp (1/90)

N'DIAYE, ANTOINE — ACADÉMIE CF MONTRÉAL
Midfielder. Born 2006, Montréal, QC, CAN. Grew up Longueuil, QC, CAN. Height 183 cm. Dominant right foot. Youth clubs: CS Longueuil, Académie CF Montréal

SEASON	CLUB	NATION	HIGHLIGHTS (MP/MIN)
2019	Impact de Montréal U-13	Concacaf	Concacaf Under-13 Champions League

NANCO, CHRIS
Midfielder. Born 1995, North York, ON, CAN. Grew up Brampton, ON, CAN. Height 163 cm. Dominant right foot. Youth clubs: Malton, Brampton YSC, Sigma FC
School: Syracuse University
Honours: CPL Championship (2019, 2020)

SEASON	CLUB	NATION	HIGHLIGHTS (MP/MIN/G)	G
2014	Sigma FC	CAN	3rd League1 Ontario	
2016	Sigma FC	CAN	W2nd League1 Ontario (9/757/1g)	1

FOOTBALLERS

2017	Bethlehem Steel FC	2.USA	E8th USL (27/1619/4g); Playoffs (1/66)	4
2018	Bethlehem Steel FC	2.USA	E6th USL (30/1184/5g); QF Playoffs (2/155)	5
2019	Forge FC Hamilton	Concacaf	L16 Concacaf League (2/162/1g)	1
	Forge FC Hamilton	1.CAN	1st CPL (26/1496/4g); CanChamp (1/8)	4
2020	Forge FC Hamilton	Concacaf	QF Concacaf League (2/74)	
	Forge FC Hamilton	1.CAN	1st CPL (5/222/2g)	2
2021	Forge FC Hamilton	Concacaf	QF Concacaf League (5/86)	
	Forge FC Hamilton	1.CAN	1st CPL (18/805/2g); 2nd Playoffs (1/8)	2
2022	Forge FC Hamilton	Concacaf	L16 Champions League (2/47)	
	Forge FC Hamilton	1.CAN	2nd CPL (8/209); QF CanChamp (1/79)	
2023	Des Moines Menace	4.USA	USL League Two	

NDAKALA, JOSHUÉ — VANCOUVER WHITECAPS FC 2
Centre back. Born 2004, Montréal, QC, CAN. Grew up in Edmonton, AB, CAN. Height 183. Youth clubs: AS Pierrefonds, Edmonton Strikers, Edmonton St. Nicholas Soccer Academy, Edmonton BTB Academy, Vancouver Whitecaps FC Academy

SEASON	CLUB	NATION	HIGHLIGHTS (MP/MIN)
2022	Vanc. Whitecaps FC 2	CAN-3.US	14th MLS NEXT Pro (8/390)
2023	Vanc. Whitecaps FC 2	CAN-3.US	21st MLS NEXT Pro (12/1054/1g)
	Vanc. Whitecaps FC Academy	CAN	League1 BC (2/180)

NDIAYE, MOUHAMED — FORGE FC HAMILTON
Midfielder. Grew up in Trois-Rivières, QC, CAN.
School: Université du Québec à Trois-Rivières

NELSON, JAYDEN — NOR / ROSENBORG BK
Winger. Born 2002, Toronto, ON, CAN. Grew up Brampton, ON, CAN. Height 170 cm. Youth clubs: Brampton YSC, Atletico Toronto, Toronto FC Academy
Honours: Canadian Championship (2022/'20)
1st #CANMNT: 2020-01-7 at Irvine, CA, USA (v. BRB)

SEASON	CLUB	NATION	HIGHLIGHTS (MP/MIN/G)	G
2017	TFC Academy	CAN	W3rd League1 Ontario (1/17)	
2018	TFC Academy	CAN	4th League1 Ontario (7/185/1g)	1
2019	Toronto FC II	CAN-3.US	7th USL League One (14/645)	
2020	Toronto FC	1.CAN	2nd MLS (7/141); L16 MLS is Back (1/57)	
2021	Toronto FC II	CAN-3.US	7th USL League One (8/686/3g)	3
	Toronto FC	1.CAN	26th MLS (7/247)	
2022('20)	Toronto FC	1.CAN	1st CanChamp (1/45)	
2022	Toronto FC	1.CAN	27th MLS (31/1982/1g); 2nd CanChamp (3/258)	1
2023	Rosenborg BK	1.NOR	9th Eliteserien (24/1466/4g); R2 Cup (2/101)	4
2023-24	Rosenborg BK	UEFA	Qualifying UEFA Conference League (3/269/2g)	2

NGONGANG, FARREL — CF MONTRÉAL U-23
Forward. Born 2005, Douala, CMR. Grew up in .., QC, CAN.

SEASON	CLUB	NATION	HIGHLIGHTS (MP/MIN)
2023	CF Montréal U-23	CAN	5th Ligue1 Québec

NIMICK, DAN — HALIFAX WANDERERS FC
Centre back. Born 2000, Happy Valley-Goose Bay, NL, CAN. Grew up in Harrogate, ENG. Height 188 cm. Dominant right foot. Youth clubs: Beckwithshaw Saints FC, Pannal Ash FC, Leeds United FC, Harrogate Town
School: Western Michigan University

SEASON	CLUB	NATION	HIGHLIGHTS (MP/MIN)	
2023	Halifax Wanderers FC	1.CAN	3rd CPL (27/2430/6g); 4th Playoffs (1/90); CanChamp (1/90)	6

NOGUEIRA, MATTHEW
Goalkeeper. Born 1998, Toronto, ON, CAN. Height 186 cm. Youth clubs: Sporting Toronto, Benfica (Portugal), Toronto FC Academy, Gil Vicente FC (Portugal)

SEASON	CLUB	NATION	HIGHLIGHTS (MP/MIN)
2016-17	Gil Vicente FC	2.POR	13th Primeira (0/0)
2017-18	CD Fátima	3.POR	x- Campeonato Serie C
	RD Águeda	3.POR	C5th Campeonato Serie C

2018-19	CS Marítimo	1.POR	11th Primeira (0/0); Taça da Liga (1/90)
	CS Marítimo B	3.POR	B9th Campeonato Serie B
2019-20	CS Marítimo B	3.POR	A8th Campeonato Serie A
2020-21	CS Marítimo B	3.POR	C4th Campeonato Serie A
2022	York United FC	1.CAN	x- CPL (0/0)

NORMAN, DAVID   VANCOUVER FC

Centre back & midfielder. Born 1998, New Westminster, BC, CAN. Grew up Coquitlam, BC, CAN. Height 185 cm. Dominant left foot. Youth clubs: Coquitlam Metro Ford SC, Vancouver Whitecaps FC Residency, FSV Mainz (Germany)
School: Oregon State University
Honours: FAI Cup (2023)

SEASON	CLUB	NATION	HIGHLIGHTS (MP/MIN/G)	G
2017	Vancouver Whitecaps FC	1.CAN	SF CanChamp (0/0)	
	Vanc. Whitecaps FC 2	CAN-2.US	W14th USL (26/2057/1g)	1
2018	Vancouver Whitecaps FC	1.CAN	2nd CanChamp (1/71)	
2018-19	Queen of the South FC	2.SCO	9th Championship (10/550); R3 SFA Cup (1/72)	
2019	Pacific FC	1.CAN	5th CPL (8/595)	
2021	Cavalry FC	1.CAN	2nd CPL (23/1759/1g); SF Playoffs (1/45); QF CanChamp (2/180)	1
2022	Cavalry FC	1.CAN	3rd CPL (19/966); SF Playoffs (2/110); QF CanChamp (1/1)	
2022-23	Northampton Town FC	4.ENG	3rd League Two (6/304/1g)	1
2023	St. Patrick's FC	1.IRL	3rd Premier Division (5/587); 1st FAI Cup (3/270)	

NOUAJAA, NASSIM

Centre back. Born 2004, Québec, QC, CAN. Height 185 cm. Youth clubs: Olympique de Cap-Rouge St-Augustin, Caravelles Ste-Foy-Sillery, Académie de l'Impact de Montréal

SEASON	CLUB	NATION	HIGHLIGHTS (MP/MIN)
2022	HFX Wanderers FC	1.CAN	7th CPL (0/0)

NOVAK, ANTHONY

Forward. Born 1994, Toronto, ON, CAN. Grew up Pickering, ON, CAN. Height 178 cm. Dominant right foot. Youth clubs: Pickering SC, Wexford SC, Glen Shields SC, Toronto Lynx
School: Lake Erie College
Honours: CPL Championship (2019, 2020)

SEASON	CLUB	NATION	HIGHLIGHTS (MP/MIN/G)	G
2012	Toronto Lynx	CAN-4.US	USL PDL	
2013	Toronto Lynx	CAN-4.US	USL PDL	
2014	Toronto Lynx	CAN-4.US	USL PDL	
2015	Oakville Blue Devils FC	CAN	1st League1 Ontario	
2016	Oakville Blue Devils FC	CAN	W6th League1 Ontario (2/110)	
2017	Oakville Blue Devils FC	CAN	1st League1 Ontario (21/1572/10g)	10
2018	Oakville Blue Devils FC	CAN	3rd League1 Ontario (16/1205/18g); 4th Playoffs (2/180)	18
	Oakville Blue Devils FC	CAN	6th CanChamp (2/135/1g)	1
2019	Forge FC Hamilton	Concacaf	L16 Concacaf League (4/273)	
	Forge FC Hamilton	1.CAN	1st CPL (18/1113/6g)	6
2020	Forge FC Hamilton	Concacaf	QF Concacaf League (4/81/1g)	1
2020 zcx	Forge FC Hamilton	1.CAN	1st CPL (8/368/2g)	2
2021	Cavalry FC	1.CAN	2nd CPL (24/1311/4g); SF Playoffs (1/9); QF CanChamp (2/108)	4
2022	Cavalry FC	CAN	Missed season through injury	
2023	Valour FC	1.CAN	8th CPL (23/943/1g); CanChamp (1/90/1g)	2

N'SA, CHRISNOVIC   USA / HUNTSVILLE CITY FC

Right back & centre back. Born 1999, Montréal, QC, CAN. Height 180 cm. Dominant right foot. Youth clubs: ARS Concordia, CS Panellinios Montréal, l'Académie de l'Impact de Montréal

SEASON	CLUB	NATION	HIGHLIGHTS (MP/MIN/G)	G
2013	Panellinios Montréal FC U-14	CAN	1st U-14 Cup	
2015	Panellinios Montréal FC U-16	CAN	3rd U-16 Cup	
2018	CS Longueuil U-15	CAN	4th PLSQ (3/224)	
2019	HFX Wanderers FC	1.CAN	7th CPL (18/1217); CanChamp (3/196)	
2020	HFX Wanderers FC	1.CAN	2nd CPL (8/646)	
2021	York United FC	1.CAN	4th CPL (25/2183/1g); SF Playoffs (1/90); QF CanChamp (2/180)	1

FOOTBALLERS

2022	York United FC	1.CAN	6th CPL (27/2423/2g); SF CanChamp (3/270)	2
2023	Nashville SC	1.USA	L16 US Cup (0/0)	
	Huntsville City FC	3.USA	17th MLS NEXT Pro (25/2032/2g)	2

N'SA, FÉLIX
Centre back. Born 2003, Montréal, QC, CAN. Height 180 cm. Youth clubs: CS Panellinios Montréal

SEASON	CLUB	NATION	HIGHLIGHTS (MP/MIN)
2021	York United FC	1.CAN	4th CPL (1/81)
2022	FC Edmonton	1.CAN	8th CPL (1/1)

NSÉKÉ, NOAH   CF MONTRÉAL U-23
Forward. Born 2003. Grew up in Montréal, QC, CAN. Height 183.

SEASON	CLUB	NATION	HIGHLIGHTS (MP/MIN)
2022	CS Mont-Royal Outremont	CAN	4th PLSQ (1/9
2023	CF Montréal U-23	CAN	5th Ligue1 Québec

NTEZIRYAYO, JOSH   ACADÉMIE DE CF MONTRÉAL
Right back. Born 2008, Terrebonne, QC, CAN. Height 183 cm. Dominant right foot. Youth clubs: AS Mascouche

O'BRIEN, ALEXANDER   TORONTO FC ACADEMY
Goalkeeper. Born 2006, Toronto, ON, CAN. Height 189 cm. Dominant right foot. Youth clubs: North Toronto SC, Vaughan SC, Toronto FC Academy

OKELLO, NOBLE   USA / ATLANTA UNITED 2
Midfielder. Born 2000, Toronto, ON, CAN. Height 193 cm. Youth clubs: North York Hearts Azzurri, Mooredale SC, Toronto FC Academy
1st #CANMNT: 2020-01-7 at Irvine, CA, USA (v. BRB)

SEASON	CLUB	NATION	HIGHLIGHTS (MP/MIN/G)	G
2016	TFC Academy	CAN	W3rd League1 Ontario (1/46)	
2017	Toronto FC II	CAN-2.US	E15th USL (1/19)	
	TFC Academy	CAN	W3rd League1 Ontario (13/955/1g)	1
2018	Toronto FC II	CAN-2.US	E16th USL (22/1437)	
	TFC Academy	CAN	4th League1 Ontario (2/180)	
2019	Toronto FC	1.CAN	2nd CanChamp (1/45)	
	Toronto FC II	CAN-3.US	7th USL League One (19/1448)	
2020	Toronto FC	1.CAN	2nd MLS (1/22); L16 MLS is Back (0/0)	
2020-21	HB Køge	2.DEN	x- 1. division (12/766/1g); R3 Pokalen (2/161)	1
2021	Toronto FC	Concacaf	QF Champions League (3/133)	
	Toronto FC II	CAN-3.US	7th USL League One (3/243/1g)	1
	Toronto FC	1.CAN	26th MLS (14/854/1g); 2nd CanChamp (3/171/1g)	2
2022	Toronto FC	1.CAN	27th MLS (8/349)	
2023	New England Revolution II	3.USA	4th MLS NEXT Pro (10/485/1g)	1

OLATOYE, SOJI
Midfielder. Born 1999, . Grew up Brampton, ON, CAN. Height 180 cm. Dominant right foot. Youth clubs: Sigma FC
School: La Salle University, York University

SEASON	CLUB	NATION	HIGHLIGHTS (MP/MIN/G)	G
2016	Sigma FC	CAN	W2nd League1 Ontario (7/500/2g)	2
2019	Sigma FC	CAN	5th League1 Ontario (1/5)	
	Sigma FC	CAN	QF League1 Ontario Playoffs (1/14)	
2021	Sigma FC	CAN	9th League1 Ontario (5/183)	
2022	York United FC	1.CAN	6th CPL (0/0)	
	Sigma FC	CAN	9th League1 Ontario (17/1343/3g)	3
2023	Vaughan Azzurri	CAN	3rd League1 Ontario (9/360); SF Playoffs (2/165/1g)	1

OLATUNJI, RIMI
Goalkeeper. Born 2005. Grew up in .., ON, CAN. Youth clubs: Glen Shields FC, Toronto FC Academy

SEASON	CLUB	NATION	HIGHLIGHTS (MP/MIN/G)	G
2018	Toronto FC U-13	CAN	QF Concacaf Under-13 Champions League	
2022	Ontario U-18	CAN	Silver at Canada Games (4/318/1g)	1
2023	Forge FC Hamilton	1.CAN	x- CPL (0/0)	
	Sigma FC	CAN	9th League1 Ontario (9/738)	

OLGUIN, LUCAS   TORONTO FC II
Midfielder. Born 2001, Toronto, ON, CAN. Grew up in Brampton, ON, CAN. Height 183. Youth clubs: Toronto FC Academy
School: Providence College

SEASON	CLUB	NATION	HIGHLIGHTS (MP/MIN)
2018	Toronto FC Academy	CAN	4th League1 Ontario (1/0)
2023	Toronto FC II	CAN-3.US	23rd MLS NEXT Pro (24/1802)

OMAR, MOHAMED
Midfielder. Born 1999, . Grew up Toronto, ON, CAN. Height 190 cm. Dominant left foot. Youth clubs: Black Rock FC, Toronto FC Academy
School: University of Notre Dame

SEASON	CLUB	NATION	HIGHLIGHTS (MP/MIN)
2018	TFC Academy	CAN	4th League1 Ontario (3/225)
2019	Chicago FC United	4.USA	USL League Two
2022	HFX Wanderers FC	1.CAN	7th CPL (15/1006); QF CanChamp (1/96)
2023	Halifax Wanderers FC	1.CAN	3rd CPL (25/1468); 4th Playoffs (1/90); CanChamp (1/90)

OMEONGA, JÉRÉMIE
Left winger. Born 2002, Kinshasa, COD. Grew up Longueuil, QC, CAN. Height 174 cm. Youth clubs: CS Longueuil, Académie Impact de Montréal

SEASON	CLUB	NATION	HIGHLIGHTS (MP/MIN/G)	G
2017	CS Longueuil U-15	CAN	1st U-15 Cup	
2022	CF Montréal U-23	CAN	6th PSLQ (21/1523/6g)	6

OMEZE, CHIMERE   TORONTO FC ACADEMY
Centre back. Born 2006, Toronto, ON, CAN. Height 180 cm. Dominant right foot. Youth clubs: Brampton East SC, Toronto FC Academy

SEASON	CLUB	NATION	HIGHLIGHTS (MP/MIN)
2023	Toronto FC II	CAN	23rd MLS NEXT Pro (1/15)

OMORENIYE, WILLIAM
Midfielder. Born 2004, Calgary, AB, CAN. Grew up in Calgary, AB, CAN. Youth clubs: Calgary Foothills SC
School: University of Calgary

SEASON	CLUB	NATION	HIGHLIGHTS (MP/MIN)
2019	Calgary Foothills FC U-15	CAN	2nd U-15 Cup
2022	Alberta U-18	CAN	Bronze at Canada Games (3/211)
2023	Cavalry FC	CAN	x- CPL (0/0)

OMRANI, SHYON   POR / CLUBE OLÍMPICO MONTIJO
Attacking midfielder. Born 2003, Mississauga, ON, CAN. Height 178 cm. Dominant right foot. Youth clubs: Erin Mills SC, North Mississauga SC, Rush Canada SA, Brampton Elite SA, CD Pinhalnovense (Portugal), Vitória Setúbal (Portugal)

SEASON	CLUB	NATION	HIGHLIGHTS (MP/MIN)
2022-23	Clube Olímpico Montijo	4.POR	Seniores 1ª Divisão; R2 Taça (1/75)

ONGARO, EASTON
Forward. Born 1998, Edmonton, AB, CAN. Height 198 cm. Dominant left foot. Youth clubs: Edmonton Internazionale
School: University of Alberta

SEASON	CLUB	NATION	HIGHLIGHTS (MP/MIN/G)	G
2011	Edmonton Internazionale U-14	CAN	2nd U-14 Cup	
2016	Edmonton Green & Gold	CAN	5th CS National Championships (5/450/2g)	2
2019	FC Edmonton	1.CAN	4th CPL (21/1167/10g); CanChamp (1/21)	10
2020	FC Edmonton	1.CAN	8th CPL (7/479/3g)	3
2020-21	Vendsyssel FF	2.DEN	10th 1. division (7/435/2g); DBU Pokalen (1/90)	2
2021	FC Edmonton	1.CAN	7th CPL (27/1920/12g); CanChamp (1/90)	12
2021-22	AFC UTA Arad	1.ROU	11th Liga I (6/141/1g)	1
2022	Vancouver Whitecaps FC	1.CAN	17th MLS (1/45)	
	Vanc. Whitecaps FC 2	CAN-3.US	14th MLS NEXT Pro (7/422/3g)	3
2023	Pacific FC	1.CAN	4th CPL (26/1028/5g); 3rd Playoffs (3/229); SF CanChamp (3/173/1g)	6
2023-24	Novara FC	3.ITA	Serie C (current season)	

OSORIO, JONATHAN   TORONTO FC

Midfielder. Born 1992, Toronto, ON, CAN. Grew up Brampton, ON, CAN. Height 175 cm. Youth clubs: Toronto Futsal League, Brampton YSC, Clarkson Sheridan, Club Nacional (Uruguay)
Honours: Concacaf champion (2021-22), Canadian Championship (2016, 2017, 2018), MLS Cup (2017), MLS Supporters' Shield (2017)

CANADA INTERNATIONAL
1 FIFA World Cup: Group phase at Qatar 2022
1 Concacaf medal: Silver at CNL 2022-23
1st #CANMNT: 2013-05-28 at Edmonton, AB, CAN (v. CRC)

SEASON	CLUB	NATION	HIGHLIGHTS (MP/MIN/G)	G
2006	Brampton Blast U-14	CAN	1st Tide U-14 Cup	
2013	Toronto FC	1.CAN	17th MLS (28/1697/5g); 3rd CanChamp (2/164)	5
2014	Toronto FC	1.CAN	13th MLS (27/2039/3g); 2nd CanChamp (2/142)	3
2015	Toronto FC	1.CAN	12th MLS (29/2235/1g); Playoffs (1/70); 4th CanChamp (2/171)	1
2016	Toronto FC	1.CAN	5th MLS (30/2440/2g); 2nd Playoffs (6/405/2g); 1st CanChamp (4/356/2g)	6
2017	Toronto FC	1.CAN	1st MLS (27/1060/2g); 1st Playoffs (5/305); 1st CanChamp (4/287)	2
2018	Toronto FC	1.CAN	19th MLS (30/2603/10g); 1st CanChamp (4/279/3g); 2nd Campeones Cup (1/90)	13
2019	Toronto FC	1.CAN	9th MLS (24/1756/5g); 2nd Playoffs (4/377/2g); 2nd CanChamp (4/256)	7
2020	Toronto FC	1.CAN	2nd MLS (17/1408/1g); L16 MLS is Back (1/33); Playoffs (1/120)	1
2021	Toronto FC	1.CAN	26th MLS (24/1653/4g); 2nd CanChamp (3/267/1g)	5
2022	Toronto FC	1.CAN	27th MLS (23/1690/9g); 2nd CanChamp (3/163/1g)	10
2023	Toronto FC	1.CAN	29th MLS (21/1877/4g); QF CanChamp (0/0); Leagues (2/90)	4

CONTINENTAL FOOTBALL		COMPETITION	HIGHLIGHTS (MP/MIN/G)	G
2018	Toronto FC	Concacaf	2nd Champions League (8/717/4g)	4
2019	Toronto FC	Concacaf	L16 Champions League (2/166)	
2021	Toronto FC	Concacaf	QF Champions League (2/104/1g)	1

OUIMETTE, KARL W.   ATLÉTICO OTTAWA

Centre back & right back. Born 1992, Repentigny, QC, CAN. Grew up Terrebonne, QC, CAN. Height 183 cm. Dominant right foot. Youth clubs: CS Terrebonne, Conquérants Laval, Académie de l'Impact de Montréal
Honours: Canadian Championship (2013, 2014), MLS Supporters' Shield (2015), NASL Championship (2017)
1st #CANMNT: 2013-11-19 at Celje, SVN (v. SVN)

SEASON	CLUB	NATION	HIGHLIGHTS (MP/MIN/G)	G
2008	CS Conquérants de Laval	CAN	5th U-16 Cup	
	Québec U-16	CAN	1st Canada Soccer All Stars U-16	
2009	Québec U-18		Gold at Canada Games (5/450)	
2012	Impact de Montréal	1.CAN	12th MLS (2/66)	
2013	Impact de Montréal	1.CAN	11th MLS (7/547/1g); 1st CanChamp (1/90)	1
2013-14	Impact de Montréal	Concacaf	Champions League (1/90)	
2014	Impact de Montréal	1.CAN	19th MLS (11/834); 1st CanChamp (4/360)	
2014-15	Impact de Montréal	Concacaf	x- Champions League (2/161)	
2015	New York Red Bulls	1.USA	1st MLS (11/711); QF Playoffs (0/0); QF US Cup (0/0)	
	New York Red Bulls 2	2.USA	E4th USL (5/437)	
2016	New York Red Bulls	1.USA	x- MLS (7/582)	
	New York Red Bulls 2	2.USA	x- USL (1/85)	
2016	Jacksonville Armada	2.USA	11th NASL (7/529)	
2017	San Francisco Deltas	2.USA	2nd NASL (23/2013); 1st Playoffs (2/180); R4 US Cup (1/90)	
2018	Indy Eleven	2.USA	E7th USL (31/2749/3g); Playoffs (1/90); R2 US Cup (1/90)	3
2019	Indy Eleven	2.USA	E3rd USL (27/2405/2g); SF Playoffs (3/300/1g); R3 US Cup (1/90)	3
2020	Indy Eleven	2.USA	E9th USL (15/1350)	
2021	Indy Eleven	2.USA	E12th USL (25/1717/2g)	2
2022	Indy Eleven	2.USA	x- USL (2/91); R2 US Cup (1/90)	
	Detroit City FC	2.USA	E7th USL (15/1238); Playoffs (0/0)	
2023	Atlético Ottawa	1.CAN	6th CPL (26/2192); QF CanChamp (2/180)	

OWOLABI-BELEWU, MALIK — FORGE FC HAMILTON
Centre back. Born 2002, London, ENG. Grew up London, ENG & London, ON, CAN. Height 190 cm. Dominant left foot. Youth clubs: Junior Red Spartans, London Youth Whitecaps, Toronto FC Academy, SPAL (Italy)
Honours: CPL Championship (2022, 2023)

SEASON	CLUB	NATION	HIGHLIGHTS (MP/MIN/G)	G
2020-21	SPAL	2.ITA	9th Serie B (10/708)	
2022('20)	Forge FC Hamilton	1.CAN	2nd CanChamp (1/90)	
2022	Forge FC Hamilton	1.CAN	2nd CPL (18/1061/1g); 1st Playoffs (3/104); QF CanChamp (1/68)	1
2023	Forge FC Hamilton	1.CAN	2nd CPL (16/809); 1st Playoffs (2/23); SF CanChamp (1/14)	

OXNER, CHRISTIAN
Goalkeeper. Born 1996, Halifax, NS, CAN. Height 182 cm. Dominant right foot. Youth clubs: Halifax Dunbrack SC
School: Saint Mary's University
Honours: Canada Soccer National Championships (2017)

SEASON	CLUB	NATION	HIGHLIGHTS (MP/MIN)
2010	Nova Scotia U-14	CAN	7th Canada Soccer All Stars U-14
2012	Atlantic U-16	CAN	5th Canada Soccer All Stars U-16
2016	Western Halifax FC	CAN	12th CS National Championships (3/270)
2017	Western Halifax FC	CAN	1st CS National Championships (5/450)
2018	Western Halifax FC	CAN	7th CS National Championships
2019	HFX Wanderers FC	1.CAN	7th CPL (18/1489); CanChamp (3/270)
2020	HFX Wanderers FC	1.CAN	2nd CPL (6/540)
2021	HFX Wanderers FC	1.CAN	4th CPL (18/1620); QF CanChamp (0/0)
2022	HFX Wanderers FC	1.CAN	7th CPL (18/1620); QF CanChamp (2/180)

OYEGUNLE, OLUWASEUN
Centre back. Born 2002, Toronto, ON, CAN. Grew up Brampton, ON, CAN. Height 188 cm. Youth clubs: Brampton East SC, Sigma FC
School: Syracuse University

SEASON	CLUB	NATION	HIGHLIGHTS (MP/MIN)
2016	Brampton East U-14 Blades	CAN	1st U-14 Cup
2018	Sigma FC	CAN	2nd League1 Ontario (5/141)
2019	Forge FC Hamilton	1.CAN	1st CPL (1/38)
	Sigma FC	CAN	5th League1 Ontario (12/967); QF Playoffs (1/90)
2022	Sigma FC	CAN	9th League1 Ontario (14/1260)
2023	Sigma FC	CAN	9th League1 Ontario (5/300)

OZIMEC, LUCAS — CZE / DINAMO ZAGREB
Forward. Born 2006, Mississauga, ON, CAN. Grew up Oakville, ON, CAN. Height 178 cm. Dominant left foot. Youth clubs: Oakville SC, Toronto FC Academy

SEASON	CLUB	NATION	HIGHLIGHTS (MP/MIN/G)	G
2022	Ontario U-18	CAN	Silver at Canada Games (4/191/1g)	

PACIUS, WOOBENS — FORGE FC HAMILTON
Forward. Born 2001, Montréal, QC, CAN. Grew up Terrebonne, QC, CAN. Height 190 cm. Dominant right foot. Youth clubs: FC L'Assomption, Académie de l'Impact de Montréal,
Honours: CPL Championship (2022, 2023)

SEASON	CLUB	NATION	HIGHLIGHTS (MP/MIN/G)	G
2021	Forge FC Hamilton	Concacaf	SF Concacaf League (6/204)	
	Forge FC Hamilton	1.CAN	1st CPL (18/1003/6g); 2nd Playoffs (2/104/1g); SF CanChamp (1/69/1g)	8
2022('20)	Forge FC Hamilton	1.CAN	2nd CanChamp (1/23)	
2022	Forge FC Hamilton	Concacaf	L16 Champions League (2/41)	
	Forge FC Hamilton	1.CAN	2nd CPL (27/1686/10g); 1st Playoffs (3/246/2g); QF CanChamp (2/34/1g)	13
2023	Forge FC Hamilton	1.CAN	2nd CPL (28/1403/10g); 1st Playoffs (0/0); SF CanChamp (3/248/1g)	11

PANAIT, DANIEL — ACADÉMIE DE CF MONTRÉAL
Centre back. Born 2008, Montréal, QC, CAN. Grew up in Laval, QC, CAN. Height 185 cm. Dominant right foot. Youth clubs: CS Fabrose Laval

FOOTBALLERS

PANTALEO, ADAMO — TORONTO FC II
Fullback & winger. Born 2005. Grew up in Toronto, ON CAN. Height 178. Dominant right foot. Youth clubs: Toronto FC Academy

SEASON	CLUB	NATION	HIGHLIGHTS (MP/MIN)
2018	Toronto FC U-13	CAN	QF Concacaf Under-13 Champions League
2022	Vaughan Azzurri	CAN	1st League1 Ontario (4/40)
2023	Toronto FC II	CAN-3.US	23rd MLS NEXT Pro (3/158)

PANTEMIS, JAMES — USA / PORTLAND TIMBERS FC
Goalkeeper. Born 1997, Montréal, QC, CAN. Grew up Kirkland, QC, CAN. Height 185 cm. Youth clubs: AS Pierrefonds, Lakeshore SC, Académie de l'Impact de Montréal
Honours: Concacaf champion (2021-22), Canadian Championship (2019, 2021)

CANADA INTERNATIONAL
1 FIFA World Cup: Group phase at Qatar 2022

SEASON	CLUB	NATION	HIGHLIGHTS (MP/MIN)
2012	Québec U-15	CAN	2nd Canada Soccer All Stars U-15
2013	Québec U-16	CAN	th Canada Soccer All Stars U-16
2016	FC Montréal	CAN-2.US	E14th USL (2/180)
2018	Impact de Montréal	1.CAN	SF CanChamp (0/0)
2019	Impact de Montréal	1.CAN	1st CanChamp (2/180)
2020	Impact de Montréal	Concacaf	QF Champions League (0/0)
	Impact de Montréal	1.CAN	18th MLS (3/270); Playoffs (0/0)
	Valour FC	1.CAN	6th CPL (7/630)
2021	CF Montréal	1.CAN	18th MLS (18/1620); 1st CanChamp (0/0)
2022	CF Montréal	1.CAN	3rd MLS (11/990); QF Playoffs (2/180); SF CanChamp (2/180)
	CF Montréal	Concacaf	QF Champions League (0/0)
2023	CF Montréal	1.CAN	20th MLS (2/173); 2nd CanChamp (0/0); Leagues (0/0)
	CF Montréal U-23	CAN	5th Ligue1 Québec

PARK, COHEN
Goalkeeper. Born 2005, North Vancouver, BC, CAN. Grew up in North Vancouver, BC, CAN. Youth clubs: Mountain United FC, Vancouver Whitecaps FC Academy
Honours: League1 BC (2023)

SEASON	CLUB	NATION	HIGHLIGHTS (MP/MIN)
2022	Vanc. Whitecaps FC 2	CAN-3.US	14th MLS NEXT Pro (1/90)
2023	Vanc. Whitecaps FC 2	CAN-3.US	21st MLS NEXT Pro (2/111)
	Vanc. Whitecaps FC Academy	3.CAN	3rd League1 BC (1/90); 1st Playoffs (2/180)

PASHER, TYLER — USA / BIRMINGHAM LEGION FC
Forward. Born 1994, Elmira, ON, CAN. Height 175 cm. Youth clubs: Woolwich SA, Newcastle United FC (England), Toronto FC Academy
1st #CANMNT: 2021-07-15 at Kansas City, KS, USA (v. HAI)

SEASON	CLUB	NATION	HIGHLIGHTS (MP/MIN/G)	G
2008	Ontario U-14	CAN	2nd Canada Soccer All Stars U-14	
2013	PS Kemi	3.FIN	P1st Kakkosen Pohjoislohko; 2nd Playoffs; L16 Cup	
2014	Lansing United	3.USA	NPSL (10/?/3g); Playoffs	3
2015	Pittsburgh Riverhounds	2.USA	E5th USL (21/1061/2g); 2nd Playofs (4/390); R4 US Cup (2/133)	2
2016-17	Sporting Kansas City	Concacaf	15th Champions League (1/90)	
2017	Sporting Kansas City	1.USA	11th MLS (1/45)	
	Swope Park Rangers	2.USA	W4th USL (24/1870); 2nd Playoffs (3/208)	
2018	Indy Eleven	2.USA	E7th USL (10/729/1g)	1
2019	Indy Eleven	2.USA	E3rd USL (32/2155/11g); SF Playoffs (3/291/2g); R3 US Cup (2/180)	13
2020	Indy Eleven	2.USA	E9th USL (15/1208/10g)	10
2021	Houston Dynamo FC	1.USA	25th MLS (19/844/4g)	4
2022	Houston Dynamo FC	1.USA	x- MLS (17/622/2g); L16 US Cup (3/41)	2
	New York Red Bulls	1.USA	6th MLS (0/0)	
2023	Birmingham Legion FC	2.USA	E7th USL (20/1279/4g); QF Playoffs (2/174); QF US Cup (4/252/1g)	5

PATON, BEN — SCO / ROSS COUNTY FC
Midfielder. Born 2000, Kitchener, ON, CAN. Height 170 cm. Youth clubs: Kitchener SC, Brampton YSC, Blackburn FC (England)

SEASON	CLUB	NATION	HIGHLIGHTS (MP/MIN)
2021-22	Ross County FC	1.SCO	6th Premiership (10/624); R4 SFA Cup (1/90)
2022-23	Ross County FC	1.SCO	11th Premiership (7/227); R4 SFA Cup (0/0); L16 Lg.Cup (4/227)

PATON, HARRY — SCO / MOTHERWELL FC
Midfielder. Born 1998, Kitchener, ON, CAN. Height cm. Youth clubs: Kitchener SC, Fulham FC (England), Heart of Midlothian (Scotland)
1st #CANMNT: 2023-10-13 at Niigata, JPN (v. JPN)

SEASON	CLUB	NATION	HIGHLIGHTS (MP/MIN/G)	G
2013	Ontario U-15	CAN	Canada Soccer All Stars U-15	
2016-17	Heart of Midlothian FC	2.SCO	5th Championship (0/0)	
2017-18	Stenhousemuir FC	4.SCO	4th League Two (15/1278/5g); 1st Playoffs (4/358); R3 SFA Cup; Lg.Cup	5
2018-19	Stenhousemuir FC	3.SCO	x- League One (13/982/1g); SFA Cup (1/90)	1
	Ross County FC	2.SCO	1st Championship (4/109); R2 Lg.Cup (1/1)	
2019-20	Ross County FC	1.SCO	10th Premiership (19/1054); R4 Cup (1/57); L16 Lg.Cup (3/191/1g)	1
2020-21	Ross County FC	1.SCO	10th Premiership (32/2106/1g); R3 SFA Cup; QF Lg.Cup (5/405/1g)	2
2021-22	Ross County FC	1.SCO	6th Premiership (31/1950); R4 SFA Cup (1/4); Lg.Cup (0/0)	
2022-23	Motherwell FC	1.SCO	7th Premiership (7/246); L16 SFA Cup (0/0)	
2023-24	Motherwell FC	1.SCO	Premiership (current season); SFA Cup (current); Lg.Cup (4/92)	

PAVELA, IVAN
Goalkeeper. Born 2005, Georgetown, ON, CAN. Height 193 cm. Youth clubs: ProStars FC

SEASON	CLUB	NATION	HIGHLIGHTS (MP/MIN)
2021	ProStars FC	CAN	10th League1 Ontario (5/360)
2022	ProStars FC	CAN	6th League1 Ontario (1/25)
2023	York United FC	1.CAN	5th CPL (0/0); QF CanChamp (0/0)
	ProStars FC	CAN	18th League1 Ontario (5/270)

PEARLMAN, ADAM — TORONTO FC II
Centre back. Born 2005, Johannesburg, RSA. Grew up Thornhill, ON, CAN. Height 6'1 cm. Dominant right foot. Youth clubs: Highland Parks FC (South Africa), Glen Shields SC, Future SA, Toronto FC Academy

SEASON	CLUB	NATION	HIGHLIGHTS (MP/MIN)
2018	Toronto FC U-13	Concacaf	QF Concacaf Under-13 Champions League
2022	Toronto FC	1.CAN	27th MLS (0/0)
	Toronto FC II	CAN-3.US	7th MLS NEXT Pro (20/1791)
2023	Toronto FC	1.CAN	29th MLS (1/6)
	Toronto FC II	CAN-3.US	23rd MLS NEXT Pro (26/2233)

PECILE, DAMIANO — ITA / VIS PESARO
Midfielder. Born 2002, Vancouver, BC, CAN. Grew up Burnaby, BC, CAN. Height 183 cm. Youth clubs: Cliff Avenue United, Vancouver Whitecaps FC Academy, Venezia (Italy)

SEASON	CLUB	NATION	HIGHLIGHTS (MP/MIN)
2020	Vancouver Whitecaps FC	1.CAN	L16 MLS is Back (MLS) (0/0)
	Vancouver Whitecaps FC	1.CAN	17th MLS (1/1)
2021-22	Venezia FC	1.ITA	20th Serie A (0/0)
2022-23	Venezia FC	2.ITA	R1 Coppa Italia (1/90)
2023	Kotkan Työväen Palloilijat	1.FIN	Veikkausliiga (12/563); QF Kuppi (4/234/2g); Liigacup (3/157)
2023-24	Vis Pesaro	3.ITA	Serie C Girona B (current season)

PELLEGRINO, GABRIEL — ITA / SÜDTIROL
Midfielder. Born 2004, Toronto, ON, CAN. Height 178 cm. Dominant right foot. Youth clubs: Woodbridge SC, Toronto FC Academy, SC Freiburg (Germany)

SEASON	CLUB	NATION	HIGHLIGHTS (MP/MIN)	
2021-22	SC Freiburg II	3.GER	12th 3.Liga (0/0)	
2022-23	SC Freiburg II	3.GER	2nd 3.Liga (0/0)	
2023-24	SC Freiburg II	3.GER	3.Liga (7/267/1g)	1
	FC Südtirol	2.ITA	Serie B (current season)	

FOOTBALLERS

PEPPLE, ARIBIM — SCO / INVERNESS CALEDONIAN THISTLE FC
Forward. Born 2002, Kettering, ENG. Grew up Calgary, AB, CAN. Height 183 cm. Dominant right foot. Youth clubs: Oadby Owls (England), Calgary Eastside Memorial FC, Calgary Foothills SC, Getafe CF (Spain)

SEASON	CLUB	NATION	HIGHLIGHTS (MP/MIN/G)	G
2017	Calgary Foothills SC U-15	CAN	2nd U-15 Cup	
2018	Calgary Foothills FC U-17	CAN	5th U-17 Cup	
2019	Calgary Foothills SC	CAN-4.US	USL League Two (11/500/3g)	3
	Cavalry FC	1.CAN	2nd CPL (8/61); SF CanChamp (1/11)	
2020	Cavalry FC	1.CAN	4th CPL (6/74)	
2022	Cavalry FC	1.CAN	3rd CPL (7/419/6g); QF CanChamp (1/13)	6
2022-23	Grimsby Town FC	4.ENG	x- League Two (11/213); R2 Lg.Cup (2/124); R2 EFL Trophy (2/109)	
	Luton Town FC	2.ENG	3rd Championship (0/0); R4 FA Cup (0/0)	
2023-24	Bromley FC	5.ENG	x- National League (6/310); FA Cup (0/0)	

PERRUZZA, JORDAN — TORONTO FC
Forward. Born 2001, Vaughan, ON, CAN. Height 183 cm. Dominant left foot. Youth clubs: Vaughan SC, Empoli FC (Italy), Toronto FC Academy
Honours: Canadian Championship (2022/'20)

SEASON	CLUB	NATION	HIGHLIGHTS (MP/MIN/G)	G
2018	Toronto FC II	CAN-2.US	E16th USL (4/129/2g)	2
2019	Toronto FC II	CAN-3.US	7th USL League One (24/1809/15g)	15
2020	San Antonio FC	2.USA	W3rd USL (5/289/3g); Playoffs (1/88)	3
2021	Toronto FC	Concacaf	QF Champions League (1/30)	
	Toronto FC	1.CAN	26th MLS (5/137/1g); 2nd CanChamp (1/12)	1
	Toronto FC II	CAN-3.US	7th USL League One (2/106)	
	San Antonio FC	2.USA	W4th USL (6/158/1g)	1
2022('20)	Toronto FC	1.CAN	1st CanChamp (1/11)	
2022	Toronto FC	1.CAN	27th MLS (13/223); 2nd CanChamp (3/81)	
	Toronto FC II	CAN-3.US	7th MLS NEXT Pro (9/579/2g); SF Playoffs (2/135)	2
2023	Toronto FC	1.CAN	x- MLS (5/122); Leagues (1/45)	
	Toronto FC II	CAN-3.US	x- MLS NEXT Pro (1/60)	
	Halifax Wanderers FC	1.CAN	3rd CPL (10/563/2g); 4th Playoffs (1/32)	2

PETRASSO, LUCA — ITA / US TRIESTINA
Midfielder. Born 2000, Toronto, ON, CAN. Grew up Woodbridge, ON, CAN. Height 173 cm. Dominant left foot. Youth clubs: Kleinburg Nobleton SC, Toronto FC Academy
Honours: Canadian Championship (2022/'20)

SEASON	CLUB	NATION	HIGHLIGHTS (MP/MIN/G)	G
2016	TFC Academy	CAN	W3rd League1 Ontario (4/146)	
2017	TFC Academy	CAN	W3rd League1 Ontario (14/837/7g)	7
2018	Toronto FC II	CAN-2.US	E16th USL (9/446/2g)	2
	TFC Academy	CAN	4th League1 Ontario (2/180/2g)	2
2019	Toronto FC II	CAN-3.US	7th USL League One (26/1813/2g)	2
2021	Toronto FC II	CAN-3.US	7th USL League One (28/2386/1g)	1
2022('20)	Toronto FC	1.CAN	1st CanChamp (1/65)	
2022	Toronto FC	1.CAN	27th MLS (23/1684); 2nd CanChamp (3/172)	
2023	Orlando City SC	Concacaf	L16 Concacaf Championship League (2/149)	
	Orlando City SC	1.USA	2nd MLS (12/430); QF MLS Playoffs (0/0); L32 Leagues (0/0)	
	Orlando City B	3.USA	12th MLS NEXT Pro (1/59)	
2023-24	US Triestina	3.ITA	Serie C (current season)	

PETRASSO, MICHAEL
Winger & fullback. Born 1995, Toronto, ON, CAN. Grew up Woodbridge, ON, CAN. Height 168 cm. Dominant right foot. Youth clubs: Kleinburg Nobleton SC, Toronto FC Academy, Queens Park Rangers FC (England)
1st #CANMNT: 2016-06-3 at Rohrbach an der Lafnitz, AUT (v. AZE)

SEASON	CLUB	NATION	HIGHLIGHTS (MP/MIN/G)	G
2009	Ontario U-14	CAN	1st Canada Soccer All Stars U-14	
2013-14	Oldham Athletic AFC	3.ENG	x- League One (11/730/1g); R3 FA Cup (3/213); EFL Trophy (1/81)	1
2013-14	Coventry City FC	3.ENG	x- League One (7/534/1g)	1
2013-14	Queens Park Rangers	2.ENG	4th EFL Championship (1/14)	

MEN'S FOOTBALLERS | 125

2014-15	Leyton Orient FC	3.ENG	x- League One (3/155); R3 Lg.Cup (1/62)		
2014-15	Notts County FC	3.ENG	21st League One (8/479/3g); R1 FA Cup (2/180); QF EFL Trophy (2/165)		3
2014-15	Queens Park Rangers	1.ENG	20th FA Premier League (0/0)		
2015-16	Queens Park Rangers	2.ENG	12th EFL Championship (8/228); R3 FA Cup (1/29)		
2016-17	Queens Park Rangers	2.ENG	18th EFL Championship (2/60)		
2017-18	Queens Park Rangers	2.ENG	x- EFL Championship (0/0); R2 Lg.Cup (1/16)		
2018	Impact de Montréal	1.CAN	15th MLS (14/782); SF CanChamp (2/128)		
2019	Valour FC	1.CAN	6th CPL (18/1301/6g); CanChamp (2/135)		6
2020	York9 FC	1.CAN	x- CPL (3/128)		
2020-21	Barnet FC	5.ENG	22nd National League (28/1659/8g); R2 FA Cup (2/157)		8
2021	York United FC	1.CAN	4th CPL (21/1462/2g); SF Playoffs (1/56/1g); QF CanChamp (2/139)	3	
2022	York United FC	1.CAN	6th CPL (13/437)		
2023	York United FC	1.CAN	x- CPL (14/305)		
2023-24	Maidstone United FC	5.ENG	x- National League South (11/500)		

PIEPGRASS, MAX
Midfielder. Born 2004, Calgary, AB, CAN. Height 178 cm. Youth clubs: Calgary Foothills SC
School: Cape Breton University

SEASON	CLUB	NATION	HIGHLIGHTS (MP/MIN)
2019	Calgary Foothills FC U-15	CAN	2nd U-15 Cup
2021	Cavalry FC	1.CAN	2nd CPL (2/22); QF CanChamp (1/7)

PIETTE, SAMUEL   CF MONTRÉAL
Midfielder. Born 1994, Le Gardeur, QC, CAN. Height 171.5 cm. Dominant right foot. Youth clubs: Lionceaux de le Gardeur, Olympiques de Repentigny, FC Boisbriand, FC Metz (France), Fortuna Düsseldorf (Germany)
Honours: Concacaf champion (2021-22), Canadian Championship (2019, 2021)

CANADA INTERNATIONAL
1 FIFA World Cup: Group phase at Qatar 2022
1st #CANMNT: 2012-06-3 at Toronto, ON, CAN (v. USA)

SEASON	CLUB	NATION	HIGHLIGHTS (MP/MIN/G)	G
2008	Québec U-14	CAN	1st Canada Soccer All Stars U-14	
2009	Québec U-16	CAN	2nd Canada Soccer All Stars U-16	
2010	Québec U-16	CAN	1st Canada Soccer All Stars U-16	
2012-13	Fortuna Düsseldorf II	4.GER	Regionalliga	
2013-14	Fortuna Düsseldorf	2.GER	6th 2.Bundesliga (2/14)	
	Fortuna Düsseldorf II	4.GER	Regionalliga	
2015-16	Racing Ferrol	3.ESP	x- Segunda División B Group 1 (14/540)	
2016-17	Racing Ferrol	3.ESP	13th Segunda División B Group 1 (32/2840)	
2017	Impact de Montréal	1.CAN	17th MLS (11/960)	
2018	Impact de Montréal	1.CAN	15th MLS (34/3000); SF CanChamp (2/180)	
2019	Impact de Montréal	1.CAN	18th MLS (25/2220); 1st CanChamp (4/355)	
2020	Impact de Montréal	Concacaf	QF Champions League (4/353)	
	Impact de Montréal	1.CAN	18th MLS (22/1943/1g); L16 MLS is Back (1/87)	1
2021	CF Montréal	1.CAN	18th MLS (25/1714/1g); 1st CanChamp (3/191)	1
2022	CF Montréal	Concacaf	QF Champions League (0/0)	
	CF Montréal	1.CAN	3rd MLS (26/1486); QF Playoffs (2/144); SF CanChamp (2/157)	
2023	CF Montréal	1.CAN	20th MLS (16/1098); Leagues (1/77)	

POKU, KWASI   FORGE FC HAMILTON
Midfielder. Born 2003, Brampton, ON, CAN. Height 188 cm. Dominant left foot. Youth clubs: Brampton East SC, Woodbridge SC, Unionville-Milliken SC, Toronto FC Academy
Honours: CPL Championship (2022, 2023)

SEASON	CLUB	NATION	HIGHLIGHTS (MP/MIN/G)	G
2021	Toronto FC II	CAN-3.US	7th USL League One (1/7)	
2022('20)	Forge FC Hamilton	1.CAN	2nd CanChamp (1/6)	
2022	Forge FC Hamilton	Concacaf	L16 Champions League (2/75)	
	Forge FC Hamilton	1.CAN	2nd CPL (19/1066/1g); 1st Playoffs (1/1); QF CanChamp (2/116)	1
2023	Forge FC Hamilton	1.CAN	2nd CPL (21/1337/2g); 1st Playoffs (2/114); SF CanChamp (1/25)	2
	Sigma FC	CAN	9th League1 Ontario (1/90)	

POLISI, MARCELLO — VALOUR FC

Midfielder. Born 1997, Burnaby, BC, CAN. Grew up Coquitlam, BC, CAN. Height 173 cm. Dominant right foot. Youth clubs: Coquitlam Metro-Ford SC, Vancouver Whitecaps FC Residency
School: Simon Fraser University

SEASON	CLUB	NATION	HIGHLIGHTS (MP/MIN)
2017	TSS Rovers FC	CAN-4.US	USL PDL (5/390)
2018	TSS Rovers FC	CAN-4.US	USL PDL (14/1067)
2019	TSS Rovers FC	CAN-4.US	USL League Two (3/270)
2021	HFX Wanderers FC	1.CAN	4th CPL (15/1013); QF CanChamp (2/180)
2022	HFX Wanderers FC	1.CAN	7th CPL (17/1045); QF CanChamp (2/116)
2023	Valour FC	1.CAN	8th CPL (22/1912/1g)

POLISI, MATTEO — GRE / ANAGENNISI EPANOMI FC

Midfielder. Born 1998, Coquitlam, BC, CAN. Height 178 cm. Dominant right foot. Youth clubs: Coquitlam Metro-Ford SC, Vancouver Whitecaps FC Residency
School: Simon Fraser University
Honours: CPL Championship (2021)

SEASON	CLUB	NATION	HIGHLIGHTS (MP/MIN/G)	G
2013	British Columbia U-15	CAN	Canada Soccer All Stars U-15	
2014	Coquitlam SC U-16	CAN	1st U-16 Cup	
2017	TSS Rovers FC	CAN-4.US	USL PDL (12/766/3g)	3
2018	TSS Rovers FC	CAN-4.US	USL PDL (14/1056/2g)	2
2019	TSS Rovers FC	CAN-4.US	USL League Two (13/1060/6g)	6
2021	Pacific FC	1.CAN	3rd CPL (21/728/3g); 1st Playoffs (1/18); SF CanChamp (0/0)	3
2022	Pacific FC	Concacaf	L16 Concacaf League (2/13)	
	Pacific FC	1.CAN	4th CPL (15/383); SF Playoffs (0/0); QF CanChamp (0/0)	
2023	TSS Rovers FC	3.CAN	2nd League1 BC (8/523/1g); SF Playoffs (1/35); QF CanChamp (2/180)	1
2023-24	Anagennisi Epanomi FC	3.GRE	Gamma Ethniki (current season)	

POP, ERIK — GER / KARLSRUHER FC

Forward. Born 2006, Mississauga, ON, CAN. Height 186 cm. Dominant right foot. Youth clubs: ProStars FC, Karlsruher FC (Germany)

PORTER, KYLE — SCROSOPPI FC

Fullback. Born 1990, Toronto, ON, CAN. Grew up Mississauga, ON, CAN. Height 183 cm. Dominant right foot. Youth clubs: North Mississauga SC, Mississauga SC Falcons, Vancouver Whitecaps FC Residency, FC Energie Cottbus (Germany)
Honours: US Cup (2013)
1st #CANMNT: 2013-01-26 at Tucson, AZ, USA (v. DEN)

SEASON	CLUB	NATION	HIGHLIGHTS (MP/MIN/G)	G
2004	Ontario U-14	CAN	3rd Canada Soccer All Stars U-14	
2006	Ontario U-16	CAN	4th Canada Soccer All Stars U-16	
2008	Vanc. Whitecaps Residency	CAN-4.US	USL PDL	
2008-09	FC Energie Cottbus II	4.GER	Regionalliga	
2009-10	FC Energie Cottbus II	5.GER	1st NOFV-Oberliga Nordost	
2010	Vancouver Whitecaps	CAN	5th USSF2 (1/33)	
2011	FC Edmonton	2.USA	5th NASL (24/1684/7g); SF Playoffs (4/143); 4th CanChamp (2/180)	7
2012	FC Edmonton	2.USA	8th NASL (24/1810/5g); QF Playoffs (1/30); 4th CanChamp (2/111)	5
2013	D.C. United	1.USA	19th MLS (27/1594/3g); 1st US Cup (3/234)	3
2014	D.C. United	1.USA	3rd MLS (5/65); QF Playoffs (0/0)	
	Richmond Kickers	2.USA	4th USL PRO (6/538/4g); SF Playoffs (1/76)	4
2014-15	D.C. United	Concacaf	x- Champions League (4/327)	
2015	Atlanta Silverbacks	2.USA	8th NASL (29/2315/2g); R4 US Cup (2/173)	2
2016	Ottawa Fury FC	2.USA	10th NASL (15/966); SF CanChamp (3/127)	
	Ottawa Fury FC Reserves	CAN	7th PLSQ (3/?)	
2017	Tampa Bay Rowdies	2.USA	E3rd USL (11/861); US Cup (1/90)	
2018	Ottawa Fury FC	2.USA	x- USL (8/560); SF CanChamp (0/0)	
	Tampa Bay Rowdies	2.USA	E12th USL (5/360)	
2019	York9 FC	1.CAN	3rd CPL (25/1917/2g); CanChamp (6/520)	2

	2020	York9 FC		1.CAN	5th CPL (6/369/1g)	1
	2021	FC Edmonton		1.CAN	7th CPL (19/652/1g); CanChamp (1/45)	1
	2022	Oakville Blue Devils FC		CAN	2nd League1 Ontario (19/1482/5g); 2nd Playoffs (2/135)	5
	2023	Scrosoppi FC		CAN	1st League1 Ontario (6/96)	

PRISO, RALPH   USA / COLORADO RAPIDS

Midfielder. Born 2002, Toronto, ON, CAN. Height 176 cm. Youth clubs: Clairlea Westview SC, North Toronto SC, Toronto FC Academy
Honours: Canadian Championship (2022/'20)

SEASON	CLUB	NATION	HIGHLIGHTS (MP/MIN/G)	G
2018	TFC Academy	CAN	4th League1 Ontario (6/199/1g)	1
2019	Toronto FC II	CAN-3.US	7th USL League One (5/354)	
2020	Toronto FC	1.CAN	2nd MLS (4/158); Playoffs (1/19)	
2021	Toronto FC	Concacaf	QF Champions League (4/225)	
	Toronto FC	1.CAN	26th MLS (11/575/1g)	1
	Toronto FC II	CAN-3.US	7th USL League One (3/269)	
2022('20)	Toronto FC	1.CAN	1st CanChamp (1/1)	
2022	Toronto FC	1.CAN	x- MLS (10/274/1g); 2nd CanChamp (2/107)	1
	Toronto FC II	CAN-3.US	x- MLS NEXT Pro (1/90)	
	Colorado Rapids	1.USA	18th MLS (6/190)	
	Colorado Rapids 2	3.USA	17th MLS NEXT Pro (3/256)	
2023	Colorado Rapids	1.USA	28th MLS (26/1028); L16 US Cup (2/169); Leagues (2/94)	
	Colorado Rapids 2	3.USA	1st MLS NEXT Pro (1/77)	

PUSZTAHEGYI, MARKUS

Centre back. Born 2004, Kitchener, ON, CAN. Height 180 cm. Youth clubs: Kitchener SC, Toronto FC Academy

RAPOSO, RYAN   VANCOUVER WHITECAPS FC

Midfielder & fullback. Born 1999, Hamilton, ON, CAN. Height 170 cm. Dominant right foot. Youth clubs: Mount Hamilton YSC, Toronto FC Academy, Burlington YSC, Vaughan SC. School: Syracuse University
Honours: Canadian Championship (2022, 2023)

SEASON	CLUB	NATION	HIGHLIGHTS (MP/MIN/G)	G
2017	Vaughan Azzurri	CAN	E2nd League1 Ontario (10/601/9g)	9
	Ontario U-18	CAN	Gold at Canada Games (5/373/1g)	1
2018	Vaughan Azzurri	CAN	5th League1 Ontario (4/220)	
2019	Vaughan Azzurri	CAN	2nd League1 Ontario (10/686/4g)	4
	Vaughan Azzurri	CAN	CanChamp (2/165/1g)	1
2020	Vancouver Whitecaps FC	1.CAN	17th MLS (15/375); L16 MLS is Back (0/0)	
2021	Vancouver Whitecaps FC	1.CAN	12th MLS (21/372); Playoffs (0/0); CanChamp (1/45)	
2022	Vancouver Whitecaps FC	1.CAN	17th MLS (30/1440/2g); 1st CanChamp (4/268/1g)	3
2023	Vancouver Whitecaps FC	Concacaf	QF Champions League (4/293/1g); L32 Leagues Cup (2/180)	1
	Vancouver Whitecaps FC	1.CAN	13th MLS (26/1335); L16 Playoffs (1/34); 1st CanChamp (3/213)	

REA, SEAN

Midfielder. Born 2002, Montréal, QC, CAN. Height 170 cm. Dominant right foot. Youth clubs: FC St-Léonard, Académie de l'Impact de Montréal

SEASON	CLUB	NATION	HIGHLIGHTS (MP/MIN/G)	G
2020	Impact de Montréal	Concacaf	QF Champions League (0/0)	
2021	Valour FC	1.CAN	5th CPL (23/1176/1g); QF CanChamp (2/96/1g)	2
2022	CF Montréal	1.CAN	3rd MLS (0/0)	
2022	Valour FC	1.CAN	5th CPL (27/2273/5g); CanChamp (1/90)	5
2023	CF Montréal	1.CAN	20th MLS (15/744); 2nd CanChamp (3/174/1g)	1

READ, TRYSTAN   VANCOUVER WHITECAPS FC ACADEMY

Goalkeeper. Born 2007, Delta, BC, CAN. Height 185 cm. Dominant right foot. Youth clubs: South Delta United SC, Vancouver Whitecaps FC Academy

SEASON	CLUB	NATION	HIGHLIGHTS (MP/MIN)
2023	Vanc. Whitecaps FC 2	CAN	21st MLS NEXT Pro (0/0)

RECORD-WRIGHT, KEMARI   TORONTO FC ACADEMY

Forward. Born 2008, Toronto, ON, CAN. Height 180 cm. Dominant right foot. Youth clubs: Unionville-Milliken SC, Toronto FC Academy

FOOTBALLERS

REID, ADONIJAH — PACIFIC FC
Forward. Born 1999-08-13, Brampton, ON, CAN. Height 168 cm. Dominant right foot. Youth clubs: Caledon SC, ANB Futbol, David Suzuki Secondary School

SEASON	CLUB	NATION	HIGHLIGHTS (MP/MIN/G)	G
2015	ANB Futbol	CAN	6th League1 Ontario	
2017	Ottawa Fury FC	2.USA	E10th USL (12/582/1g)	1
2018	Ottawa Fury FC	2.USA	E10th USL (29/1810/4g); SF CanChamp (4/224)	4
2018-19	Le Havre AC B	4.FRA	C16 Championnat CFA Groupe C (4/227)	
2021	Miami FC	2.USA	E6th USL (29/1008/6g); Playoffs (1/20)	6
2022	Miami FC	2.USA	E6th USL (23/750/3g); Playoffs (1/15); R3 US Cup (2/94)	3
2023	Pacific FC	1.CAN	4th CPL (23/1188/3g); 3rd Playoffs (3/129/1g); SF CanChamp (3/63/1g)	5

RICCI, AUSTIN — YORK UNITED FC
Forward. Born 1996, Richmond Hill, ON, CAN. Height 178 cm. Dominant right foot. Youth clubs: Richmond Hill SC, Ajax SC
School: Oakland University

SEASON	CLUB	NATION	HIGHLIGHTS (MP/MIN/G)	G
2014	Vaughan Azzurri	CAN	4th League1 Ontario	
2016	K-W United FC	CAN-4.US	USL PDL (7/439/3g)	3
2017	Michigan Bucks	4.USA	USL PDL; R3 US Cup	
2018	Vaughan Azzurri	CAN	5th League1 Ontario (8/616/5g); 1st Playoffs (4/360/1g)	6
2018	Michigan Bucks	4.USA	USL PDL	
2019	York9 FC	1.CAN	3rd CPL (9/200); CanChamp (2/36)	
2020	Valour FC	1.CAN	6th CPL (6/361)	
2021	Valour FC	1.CAN	5th CPL (16/1187/5g); QF CanChamp (2/154/3g)	8
2022	York United FC	1.CAN	6th CPL (3/63); SF CanChamp (1/24)	
2023	York United FC	1.CAN	5th CPL (26/1467/3g); QF CanChamp (2/51/1g)	4

RICCI, LUCA
Midfielder. Born 1998, LaSalle, QC, CAN. Grew up Dorval, QC, CAN. Height 166 cm. Dominant right foot. Youth clubs: NDG Concordia, Académie de l'Impact Montréal

SEASON	CLUB	NATION	HIGHLIGHTS (MP/MIN)
2012	Québec U-15	CAN	2nd Canada Soccer All Stars U-15
2013	Québec U-15	CAN	th Canada Soccer All Stars U-15
2018	Phoenix Rising FC	2.USA	W3rd USL (4/127); R2 US Cup (1/120)
2019	Impact de Montréal	1.CAN	18th MLS (0/0)
2019	Ottawa Fury FC	2.USA	E8th USL (0/0)
2021	FC Lanaudière	CAN	9th PLSQ (5/450)
2022	Pacific FC	1.CAN	4th CPL (6/230); QF CanChamp (1/67)

RICHARDSON, TOBY
Centre back. Born 2005, Ottawa, ON, CAN. Height 188 cm. Dominant Left foot. Youth clubs: West Ottawa SC

SEASON	CLUB	NATION	HIGHLIGHTS (MP/MIN)
2023	York United FC	1.CAN	5th CPL (0/0)
2023	Alliance United FC	CAN	8th League1 Ontario (3/220)

RIGGI, ALESSANDRO — CAM / ANGKOR TIGER FC
Winger. Born 1993, Montréal, QC, CAN. Height 162 cm. Dominant right foot. Youth clubs: CS Rivière-des-Prairies, CS Conquérants de Laval, Académie Impact Montréal, UC Sampdoria (Italy), Celta Vigo (Spain), CFR Cluj (Romania)

SEASON	CLUB	NATION	HIGHLIGHTS (MP/MIN/G)	G
2007	CS Conquérants de Laval	CAN	2nd Tide U-14 Cup	
	Québec U-14	CAN	1st Canada Soccer All Stars U-14	
2008	CS Conquérants de Laval	CAN	5th U-16 Cup	
	Québec U-16	CAN	1st Canada Soccer All Stars U-16	
2009	CS Conquérants de Laval	CAN	1st U-16 Cup	
	Québec U-16	CAN	2nd Canada Soccer All Stars U-16	
2009	Québec U-18	CAN	Gold at Canada Games (5/324)	
2015	FC Montréal	CAN-2.US	E10th USL (26/1660/9g)	9

2016	FC Montréal	CAN-2.US	E14th USL (22/1374/6g)	6
2017	Phoenix Rising FC	2.USA	W5th USL (20/1192/4g); Playoffs (1/23)	4
2018	Phoenix Rising FC	2.USA	W3rd USL (14/346/2g); R2 US Cup (1/65)	2
2020	HFX Wanderers FC	1.CAN	2nd CPL (7/395/1g)	1
2021	HFX Wanderers FC	1.CAN	4th CPL (16/621); QF CanChamp (1/60)	
2022	Valour FC	1.CAN	5th CPL (22/909/3g); CanChamp (1/45)	3
2023-24	Angkor Tiger FC	1.CAM	Cambodian Premier (current season)	

RIGOPOULOS, THEO — TORONTO FC II
Fullback. Born 2006, London, ON, CAN. Height 160 cm. Dominant right foot. Youth clubs: London Norwest, Red Star, North London SC, London Alliance SC, London Whitecaps, Toronto FC Academy

SEASON	CLUB	NATION	HIGHLIGHTS (MP/MIN)
2023	Toronto FC II	CAN-3.US	23rd MLS NEXT Pro (20/114)

ROBINSON, RYAN — VAUGHAN SC
Forward. Born 2001, Hamilton, ON, CAN. Height 173 cm. Dominant right foot. Youth clubs: Mount Hamilton YSC, Toronto FC Academy

SEASON	CLUB	NATION	HIGHLIGHTS (MP/MIN/G)	G
2018	TFC Academy	CAN	4th League1 Ontario (8/265)	
2021	Vaughan Azzurri	CAN	1st League1 Ontario (5/298/4g); SF Playoffs (1/90)	4
2022	HFX Wanderers FC	1.CAN	7th CPL (18/400); QF CanChamp (1/17)	
2023	Vaughan Azzurri	CAN	CanChamp (1/34)	

RODRIGUE, ADAM — CF MONTRÉAL U-23
Midfielder. Born 2005, Montréal, QC, CAN. Grew up in . Youth clubs: Académie CF Montréal

SEASON	CLUB	NATION	HIGHLIGHTS (MP/MIN/G)	G
2018	Impact de Montréal U-13	CAN	4th Concacaf Under-13 Champions League	
2022	CF Montréal U-23	CAN	6th PLSQ (5/250/1g)	1
2023	CF Montréal U-23	CAN	5th Ligue1 Québec	

ROGERS, SKYLER
Midfielder. Born 2004, Calgary, AB, CAN. Height 170 cm. Youth clubs: Calgary Foothills SC
School: Mount Royal University

SEASON	CLUB	NATION	HIGHLIGHTS (MP/MIN/G)	G
2019	Calgary Foothills FC U-15	CAN	2nd U-15 Cup	
2022	Cavalry FC	1.CAN	3rd CPL (3/25); QF CanChamp (0/0)	
	Alberta U-18	CAN	Bronze at Canada Games (3/240/2g)	2

ROLLOCKS, CYRUS — SCROSOPPI FC
Born 1998, Toronto, ON, CAN. Height 185 cm. Youth clubs: North Mississauga SC, Toronto FC Academy

SEASON	CLUB	NATION	HIGHLIGHTS (MP/MIN/G)	G
2012	North Mississauga U-14	CAN	1st U-14 Cup	
2015	TFC Academy	CAN	5th League1 Ontario (?/14g)	14
2016	TFC Academy	CAN	W3rd League1 Ontario (10/418/4g); USL PDL (13/778/4g)	8
2017	TFC Academy	CAN	W3rd League1 Ontario (17/1172/17g)	17
2018	Master's FA	CAN	10th League1 Ontario (6/423/3g)	3
2019	York9 FC	1.CAN	3rd CPL (9/292); CanChamp (2/24)	
2021	Oakville Blue Devils FC	CAN	3rd League1 Ontario (10/714; 2g); 2nd Playoffs (2/73)	2
2022	Scrosoppi FC	CAN	12th League1 Ontario (19/1613/6g)	6
	York United FC	1.CAN	6th CPL (2/32)	

ROMANO, ANDREW — TORONTO FC II
Goalkeeper. Born 2005, Vaughan, ON, CAN. Grew up in Vaughan, ON, CAN. Youth clubs: Vaughan SC, Toronto FC Academy

SEASON	CLUB	NATION	HIGHLIGHTS (MP/MIN)
2022	Toronto FC II	CAN-3.US	7th MLS NEXT Pro (0/0
	Ontario U-18	CAN	Silver at Canada Games (1/80)
2023	Toronto FC II	CAN-3.US	23rd MLS NEXT Pro (0/0)

ROMEO, ANTONIO ROCCO — VANCOUVER FC
Centre back. Born 2000, Toronto, ON, CAN. Grew up Richmond Hill, ON, CAN. Height 195 cm. Dominant right foot. Youth clubs: Bolton Wanderers SC, Woodbridge SC, Toronto FC Academy

FOOTBALLERS

SEASON	CLUB	NATION	HIGHLIGHTS (MP/MIN/G)	G
2016	Toronto FC II	CAN-2.US	E12th USL (1/29)	
2017	TFC Academy	CAN	W3rd League1 Ontario (15/1301/1g)	1
2018	TFC Academy	CAN	4th League1 Ontario (1/90)	
2018	Toronto FC II	CAN-2.US	E16th USL (12/1014)	
2018-19	HB Køge	2.DEN	7th 1. division (8/667)	
2019	Toronto FC II	CAN-3.US	7th USL League One (10/747/1g)	1
2020-21	HB Køge	2.DEN	6th 1. division (12/529); R3 DBU Pokalen (2/172/1g)	1
2021	Valour FC	1.CAN	5th CPL (16/1439/2g); QF CanChamp (2/180)	2
2022	Valour FC	1.CAN	5th CPL (23/1926/2g); CanChamp (1/90)	2
2023	Vancouver FC	1.CAN	7th CPL (25/2189); CanChamp (1/90)	

ROSE, FEDERICO — ARG / VÉLEZ SARSFIELD
Forward. Born 2004, Toronto, ON, CAN. Height 186. Youth clubs: North York Hearts SC, Toronto Boca Juniors, Woodbridge SC, CA Vélez Sarsfield (Argentina)

ROY, ZACHARY — ATLÉTICO OTTAWA
Right back. Born 2003, Saint-Bruno, QC, CAN. Height 183 cm. Dominant right foot. Youth clubs: CS St-Hubert
Honours: CPL Regular Season (2022)

SEASON	CLUB	NATION	HIGHLIGHTS (MP/MIN)
2021	CS Saint-Hubert	CAN	5th PLSQ (2/28)
2022	Atlético Ottawa	1.CAN	1st CPL (13/406); 2nd Playoffs (1/16)
2023	Atlético Ottawa	1.CAN	6th CPL (3/71)

RUBY, JAKE
Fullback. Born 2000, Vancouver, BC, CAN. Grew up North Vancouver, BC, CAN. Height 178 cm. Dominant right foot. Youth clubs: Lynn Valley SA, Mountain United FC, Vancouver Whitecaps FC Residency
School: Trinity Western University

SEASON	CLUB	NATION	HIGHLIGHTS (MP/MIN/G)	G
2019	Victoria Highlanders FC	CAN-4.US	USL League Two (9/798)	
2020	HFX Wanderers FC	1.CAN	2nd CPL (8/317)	
2021	HFX Wanderers FC	1.CAN	4th CPL (16/1246/1g); QF CanChamp (1/78)	
2022	HFX Wanderers FC	1.CAN	7th CPL (10/795)	
2023	HFX Wanderers FC	1.CAN	3rd CPL (8/557); 4th Playoffs (1/58)	

RUSHENAS, AIDEN
Goalkeeper. Born 2003, Toronto, ON, CAN. Height 188 cm. Youth clubs: North Toronto SC
School: Dalhousie University

SEASON	CLUB	NATION	HIGHLIGHTS (MP/MIN)
2022	Halifax Wanderers FC	1.CAN	7th CPL (0/0)
2023	Halifax Wanderers FC	1.CAN	3rd CPL (0/0); 4th Playoffs (0/0); CanChamp (0/0)

RUSSELL-ROWE, JACEN — USA / COLUMBUS CREW SC
Forward. Born 2002, Toronto, ON, CAN. Grew up Brampton, ON, CAN. Height 184 cm. Youth clubs: Brampton YSC, Toronto FC Academy
School: University of Maryland
Honours: MLS Cup (2023), MLS NEXT Pro Cup (2022)

SEASON	CLUB	NATION	HIGHLIGHTS (MP/MIN/G)	G
2018	TFC Academy	CAN	4th League1 Ontario (1/12)	
2019	Toronto FC II	CAN-3.US	7th USL League One (1/5)	
2022	Columbus Crew SC	1.USA	16th MLS (6/227)	
	Columbus Crew 2	3.USA	1st MLS NEXT Pro (19/1498/21g); 1st Playoffs (3/249/4g)	25
2023	Columbus Crew SC	1.USA	3rd MLS (21/527/4g); 1st MLS Cup (2/2); L32 Leagues (2/25)	4
	Columbus Crew 2	3.USA	5th MLS NEXT Pro (1/64)	

SABBATASSO, JERONIMO — ITA / EMPOLI FC
Midfielder. Born 2004, Buenos Aires, ARG. Grew up Buenos Aires, ARG & Toronto, ON, CAN. Height 180 cm. Youth clubs: Club Las Herras (Argentina), Richmond Hill SC, CA Independiente Inferiores (Argentina), FC Empoli (Italy)

SEASON	CLUB	NATION	HIGHLIGHTS (MP/MIN)
2022-23	ASD Termoli	4.ITA	F15th Serie D Girone F (0/0)

SADEK, AGHILAS — CS LONGUEUIL
Midfielder. Born 2008. Grew up in Longueuil, QC, CAN. Height 181 cm. Dominant right foot. Youth clubs: CS Longueuil

SALIBA, NATHAN-DYLAN — CF MONTRÉAL
Midfielder. Born 2004, Longueuil, QC, CAN. Height 171 cm. Youth clubs: CS Longueuil, Académie de l'Impact de Montréal

SEASON	CLUB	NATION	HIGHLIGHTS (MP/MIN/G)	G
2020	Impact de Montréal	Concacaf	QF Champions League (0/0)	
2022	CF Montréal	1.CAN	3rd MLS (0/0)	
	CF Montréal U-23	CAN	6th PLSQ (7/507/4g)	4
2023	CF Montréal	1.CAN	20th MLS (28/1768); 2nd CanChamp (3/65); Leagues (2/120)	

SALTER, SAMUEL — ATLÉTICO OTTAWA
Forward. Born 1999, Montréal, QC, CAN. Grew up Laval, QC, CAN. Height 186 cm. Dominant left foot. Youth clubs: Académie de l'Impact de Montréal, Étoiles de l'Est

SEASON	CLUB	NATION	HIGHLIGHTS (MP/MIN/G)	G
2017	Québec U-18	CAN	Bronze at Canada Games (4/266/4g)	4
2018	CS Saint-Hubert	CAN	6th PLSQ (12/919/4g)	4
2020	AS Blainville	CAN	1st PLSQ (8/694/8g)	8
2021	HFX Wanderers FC	1.CAN	4th CPL (21/811/3g); QF CanChamp (1/56)	3
2022	HFX Wanderers FC	1.CAN	7th CPL (27/1840/11g); QF CanChamp (2/180/1g)	12
2023	Atlético Ottawa	1.CAN	6th CPL (27/1475/7g); QF CanChamp (2/38)	7

SAMAKÉ, ABDOULAYE — VALOUR FC
Centre back. Born 1996, Bamako, MLI. Grew up Ottawa, ON, CAN. Height 186 cm. Dominant right foot. Youth clubs: Ottawa Gloucester Hornets SC, Ottawa South United SC, Académie de l'Impact de Montréal
School: University of Michigan
Honours: CPL Championship (2021)

SEASON	CLUB	NATION	HIGHLIGHTS (MP/MIN/G)	G
2015	FC Montréal	CAN-2.US	E10th USL (0/0)	
2016	Chicago Fire U-23	4.USA	USL PDL (6/?)	
2017	Chicago FC United	4.USA	USL PDL (10/?/1g); R3 US Cup	1
2018	Chicago FC United	4.USA	USL PDL (10/?/1g)	1
2019	AFC Ann Arbor	3.USA	NPSL (2/?)	
2020	Pacific FC	1.CAN	3rd CPL (3/88)	
2021	Pacific FC	1.CAN	1st CPL Championship &	
	Pacific FC	1.CAN	3rd CPL (24/2003); 1st Playoffs (1/76); SF CanChamp (3/241)	
2022	Pacific FC	Concacaf	L16 Concacaf League (2/17)	
	Pacific FC	1.CAN	4th CPL (19/1358); SF Playoffs (1/30); QF CanChamp (1/10)	
2023	Valour FC	1.CAN	8th CPL (17/1457/1g); CanChamp (1/90)	1

SAMUEL, DOMINIC — FORGE FC HAMILTON
Centre back. Born 1994, Toronto, ON, CAN. Height 178 cm. Dominant right foot. Youth clubs: East York SC, Sigma FC
School: Southern New Hampshire University
Honours: CPL Championship (2019, 2020, 2022, 2023)

SEASON	CLUB	NATION	HIGHLIGHTS (MP/MIN/G)	G
2015	Sigma FC	CAN	4th League1 Ontario	
2016	Rochester Rhinos	2.USA	E4th USL (26/1552); QF Playoffs (2/27); R4 US Cup	
2017	Sigma FC	CAN	W2nd League1 Ontario (17/1424/2g)	2
2018	Sigma FC	CAN	2nd League1 Ontario (16/1440/1g); 3rd Playoffs (1/90)	1
2019	Forge FC Hamilton	Concacaf	L16 Concacaf League (4/347)	
	Forge FC Hamilton	1.CAN	1st CPL (26/2134); CanChamp (2/180)	
2020	Forge FC Hamilton	Concacaf	QF Concacaf League (4/272)	
	Forge FC Hamilton	1.CAN	1st CPL (9/634)	
2021	Forge FC Hamilton	Concacaf	SF Concacaf League (7/621)	
	Forge FC Hamilton	1.CAN	1st CPL (26/1958); 2nd Playoffs (2/180); SF CanChamp (2/180)	
2022	Forge FC Hamilton	Concacaf	L16 Champions League (2/180)	
	Forge FC Hamilton	1.CAN	2nd CPL (18/978); 1st Playoffs (3/37); QF CanChamp (1/90)	
2023	Forge FC Hamilton	1.CAN	2nd CPL (19/1083); 1st Playoffs (2/111); SF CanChamp (3/180)	

FOOTBALLERS

SÁNCHEZ, JUAN PABLO — VALOUR FC
Midfielder. Born 2003, Hartford, CT, USA. Grew up Burlington, ON, CAN. Height 170 cm. Dominant right foot. Youth clubs: Toronto FC Academy, SC Salgueiros (Portugal)

SEASON	CLUB	NATION	HIGHLIGHTS (MP/MIN)
2021-22	SC Salgueiros	3.POR	C1st Campeonato Serie C; 4th Playoffs
2022-23	SC Salgueiros	3.POR	x- Campeonato Serie B
2023	Valour FC	1.CAN	8th CPL (21/1256); CanChamp (1/45)

SANGHA, GURMAN — USA / CROWN LEGACY FC
Forward. Born 2000, Vancouver, BC, CAN. Grew up in Burnaby, BC, CAN. Height 185. Youth clubs: Vancouver Wesburn, Vancouver Whitecaps FC Academy
School: University of Memphis, University of Portland

SEASON	CLUB	NATION	HIGHLIGHTS (MP/MIN)
2019	TSS Rovers FC	CAN-4.US	USL League Two (10/509)
2022	Vanc. Whitecaps FC Academy	3.CAN	3rd League1 BC

SANY-KANG, LOÏC — CF MONTRÉAL U-23
Midfielder. Born 2005, Yaoundé, CMR. Grew up in Montréal, QC, CAN.

SEASON	CLUB	NATION	HIGHLIGHTS (MP/MIN)
2022	CF Montréal U-23	CAN	6th PLSQ (0/0)
2023	CF Montréal U-23	CAN	5th Ligue1 Québec

SAPPLETON, SPENCER — TORONTO FC ACADEMY
Centre back. Born 2008, Toronto, ON, CAN. Height 187 cm. Dominant right foot. Youth clubs: East York SC, Toronto Dutch Connections FC, Toronto FC Academy

SAPUTO, JOEY — CF MONTRÉAL U-23
Forward. Born Montréal, QC, CAN. Height 175.
School: University of Connecticut

SEASON	CLUB	NATION	HIGHLIGHTS (MP/MIN/G)	G
2022	CF Montréal U-23	CAN	6th PLSQ (10/482/2g)	2
2023	CF Montréal U-23	CAN	5th Ligue1 Québec	

SARAKINIS, ALEXANDER — GRE / ILIAKOS VARTHOLOMIOU
Forward. Born 2003, Hamilton, ON, CAN. Grew up in Hamilton, ON, CAN. Youth clubs: FC Volos (Greece)

SARAKINIS, LUKAS — ENG / BOLTON WANDERRS
Forward. Born 2004, Hamilton, ON, CAN. Grew up in Hamilton, ON, CAN. Youth clubs: Bolton Wanderers (England)

SCHNEIDER, TREVOR — ALTITUDE FC
Midfielder. Born 2000, Langley, BC, CAN. Grew up in Coquitlam, BC, CAN. Height 178 cm. Youth clubs: Coquitlam SC, Vancouver Whitecaps FC Academy

SEASON	CLUB	NATION	HIGHLIGHTS (MP/MIN)
2019	Victoria Highlanders FC	CAN-4.US	USL League Two (5/270)
2023	Vancouver FC	1.CAN	7th CPL (0/0)
	North Vancouver Altitude FC	3.CAN	7th League1 BC (8/720)

SCHIAVONI, MATTEO — ACADÉMIE CF MONTRÉAL
Midfielder. Born 2005, Montréal, QC, CAN. Grew up in Montréal, QC, CAN. Dominant right foot. Youth clubs: CS Lachine, Académie de CF Montréal, Bologna FC (Italy)

SEASON	CLUB	NATION	HIGHLIGHTS (MP/MIN)
2022	CF Montréal U-23	CAN	6th PLSQ (6/348)

SCHILTE-BROWN, ETHAN
Centre back. Born 2005, Richmond, VA, USA. Grew up in Orlando, FL, USA. Height 190. Dominant right foot. Youth clubs: Lutz FC Tampa Rangers, Tampa Bay United, Orlando City SC Academy, Halifax Wanderers, Kilmarnock FC (SCO).

SEDIN, VALTER — VANCOUVER WHITECAPS FC ACADEMY
Midfielder. Born 2007, Vancouver, BC, CAN. Youth clubs: Vancouver Whitecaps FC Academy

SEASON	CLUB	NATION	HIGHLIGHTS (MP/MIN)
2023	Vanc. Whitecaps FC 2	CAN-3.US	21st MLS NEXT Pro (0/0)
	Vanc. Whitecaps FC Academy	3.CAN	3rd League1 BC (1/11)

SELEMANI, JOHNNY — VANCOUVER WHITECAPS FC ACADEMY
Forward. Born 2008, Edmonton, AB, CAN. Height 178 cm. Dominant left foot. Youth clubs: Edmonton Blue Quill Community, Edmonton KC Trojans SA

SHAFFELBURG, JACOB — USA / NASHVILLE SC
Winger. Born 1999, Kentville, NS, CAN. Grew up Port Williams, NS, CAN. Height 181 cm. Dominant left foot. Youth clubs: Valley United SC, FC Nashville Heroes (USA), Sporting Kansas City (USA for a month in 2014), Berkshire School (USA), Manhattan SC (USA), Toronto FC Academy
Honours: Concacaf champion (2021-22), Canadian Championship (2022/'20)
1st #CANMNT: 2020-01-10 at Irvine, CA, USA (v. BRB)

SEASON	CLUB	NATION	HIGHLIGHTS (MP/MIN/G)	G
2017	TFC Academy	CAN	W3rd League1 Ontario (1/44)	
	Nova Scotia U-18	CAN	7th Canada Games (3/171/1g)	1
2019	Toronto FC	Concacaf	L16 Champions League (1/33)	
	Toronto FC	1.CAN	9th MLS (10/672); 2nd CanChamp (2/119)	
	Toronto FC II	CAN-3.US	7th USL League One (15/1210/2g)	2
2020	Toronto FC	1.CAN	2nd MLS (4/125); L16 MLS is Back (1/15)	
2021	Toronto FC	Concacaf	QF Champions League (4/282)	
	Toronto FC	1.CAN	26th MLS (20/995/3g); 2nd CanChamp (3/257/1g)	4
	Toronto FC II	CAN-3.US	7th USL League One (1/85)	
2022('20)	Toronto FC	1.CAN	1st CanChamp (1/45)	
2022	Toronto FC	1.CAN	27th MLS (13/578); 2nd CanChamp (1/31)	
	Toronto FC II	CAN-3.US	7th MLS NEXT Pro (1/73)	
	Nashville SC	1.USA	9th MLS (8/510/2g); Playoffs (1/21)	2
2023	Nashville SC	1.USA	12th MLS (28/1318/3g); L16 MLS Playoffs (2/103); L16 (3/174); 2nd Leagues (6/199/1g)	4

SHOME, SHAMIT — CAVALRY FC
Midfielder. Born 1997, Edmonton, AB, CAN. Height 178 cm. Youth clubs: Edmonton Southwest United, FC Edmonton Academy
School: University of Alberta
Honours: Canadian Championship (2019), CPL North Star Shield (2023)
1st #CANMNT: 2020-01-7 at Irvine, CA, USA (v. BRB)

SEASON	CLUB	NATION	HIGHLIGHTS (MP/MIN/G)	G
2013	Alberta U-16	CAN	Canada Soccer All Stars U-16	
2016	FC Edmonton	2.USA	3rd NASL (26/1657); SF Playoffs (1/78); 5th CanChamp (1/59)	
2017	Impact de Montréal	1.CAN	17th MLS (1/8); 2nd CanChamp (0/0)	
2018	Impact de Montréal	1.CAN	15th MLS (5/249); SF CanChamp (1/84)	
2019	Impact de Montréal	1.CAN	18th MLS (27/1627/1g); 1st CanChamp (5/319)	1
2020	Impact de Montréal	Concacaf	QF Champions League (1/90)	
	Impact de Montréal	1.CAN	18th MLS (12/282); L16 MLS is Back (0/0)	
2021	FC Edmonton	1.CAN	7th CPL (27/2186); CanChamp (1/45)	
2022	FC Edmonton	1.CAN	8th CPL (24/1975)	
2023	Cavalry FC	1.CAN	1st CPL (17/1245); 2nd Playoffs (3/150); CanChamp (1/90)	

SILVA, MATTHEW
Goalkeeper. Born 1991, Mississauga, ON, CAN. Height 185 cm. Youth clubs: SC Toronto, Toronto Lynx
School: Le Moyne College
Honours: Gibraltar Rock Cup (2022-23)

SEASON	CLUB	NATION	HIGHLIGHTS (MP/MIN)
2010	Toronto Lynx	CAN-4.US	USL PDL
2011	Toronto Lynx	CAN-4.US	USL PDL
2012	Toronto Lynx	CAN-4.US	USL PDL
2013	Toronto Lynx	CAN-4.US	USL PDL
2014	Toronto Lynx	CAN-4.US	USL PDL
2015	Kaya FC	1.PHI	4th United Football League (1/90)
2016	Bodens BK	4.SWE	5th Division 2 Norrland
2017	Bodens BK	4.SWE	7th Division 2 Norrland
2018	Österlens FF	4.SWE	12th Division 2 Södra Götaland
2019	York9 FC	1.CAN	3rd CPL (1/90); CanChamp (0/0)

FOOTBALLERS

2020	Valour FC	1.CAN	6th CPL (0/0)
2021	Valour FC	1.CAN	5th CPL (4/360); QF CanChamp (2/180)
2022	United City FC	AFC	AFC Champions League (2/180)
	United City FC	1.PHI	1st Copa Paulino Alcantara
2022-23	Magpies FC Bruno's	UEFA	UEFA Qualifying Europa Conference League (2/180)
	Magpies FC Bruno's	1.GIB	3rd Gibraltar League (3/270); 1st Rock Cup (0/0)

SIMEON, NATHAN

Centre back. Born 2000, Montréal, QC, CAN. Grew up in Montréal, QC, CAN. Youth clubs: CS St-Laurent, Académie de CF Montréal, Montverde Academy (USA)
School: San Francisco University

SEASON	CLUB	NATION	HIGHLIGHTS (MP/MIN)
2016	St-Laurent U-16	CAN	4th U-16 Cup
2019	Orlando City B	3.USA	10th USL League One (15/1350)

SIMMONS, ELLIOT — VANCOUVER FC

Midfielder. Born 1998, Luton, ENG. Grew up Stittsville, ON, CAN. Height 185 cm. Dominant right foot. Youth clubs: Gouldbourn SC, Ottawa Fury FC Academy, Milton Keynes Dons Academy (England), Málaga CF (Spain)

SEASON	CLUB	NATION	HIGHLIGHTS (MP/MIN/G)	G
2018	Mikkelin Palloilijat	3.FIN	A7th Kakkonen Lohko A (20/1336)	
2019	HFX Wanderers FC	1.CAN	7th CPL (13/969); CanChamp (4/344)	
2020	Cavalry FC	1.CAN	4th CPL (10/630)	
2021	Cavalry FC	1.CAN	2nd CPL (25/1568/1g); QF CanChamp (2/180)	1
2022	Cavalry FC	1.CAN	3rd CPL (24/1682); SF Playoffs (2/177); QF CanChamp (2/180)	
2023	Vancouver FC	1.CAN	7th CPL (25/1832); CanChamp (1/90)	

SIMMONS, MALCOLM — VANCOUVER WHITECAPS FC 2

Forward. Born 2003.

SEASON	CLUB	NATION	HIGHLIGHTS (MP/MIN)
2023	Vanc. Whitecaps FC 2	CAN-3.US	21st MLS NEXT Pro (5/275)

SIROIS, JONATHAN — CF MONTRÉAL

Goalkeeper. Born 2001, LaSalle, QC, CAN. Grew up Saint-Hubert, QC, CAN. Height 180 cm. Youth clubs: CS St-Hubert, Académie de l'Impact de Montréal

SEASON	CLUB	NATION	HIGHLIGHTS (MP/MIN)
2020	Impact de Montréal	Concacaf	QF Champions League (0/0)
	Impact de Montréal	1.CAN	18th MLS (0/0); Playoffs (0/0)
	Vancouver Whitecaps FC	1.CAN	17th MLS (0/0)
2021	CF Montréal	1.CAN	18th MLS (0/0)
	Valour FC	1.CAN	5th CPL (24/2160); QF CanChamp (0/0)
2022	CF Montréal	1.CAN	3rd MLS (0/0)
	Valour FC	1.CAN	5th CPL (19/1710)
2023	CF Montréal	1.CAN	20th MLS (33/2887); 2nd CanChamp (3/270); Leagues (2/180)

SMITH, COURTNEY — SIMCOE COUNTY ROVERS FC

Forward. Born 1998, Brampton, ON, CAN. Height 180 cm. Dominant right foot. Youth clubs: Grand Valley MSA, Brampton East SC, ProStars FC, ETO FC Győr (Hungary)
School: Mississippi Gulf Coast Community College, University of South Carolina, Georgia Southern University, Houston Baptist University
Honours: League1 Ontario (2023)

SEASON	CLUB	NATION	HIGHLIGHTS (MP/MIN/G)	G
2016	ProStars FC	CAN	W8th League1 Ontario (11/917/2g)	2
2017	Master's FA	CAN	E5th League1 Ontario (2/56)	
2021	Port City FC	3.USA	NPSL	
2022	FC Edmonton	1.CAN	8th CPL (21/596/2g); CanChamp (1/28)	2
2023	Vaughan Azzurri	CAN	x- League1 Ontario (3/76)	
	Simcoe County Rovers FC	CAN	2nd League1 Ontario (5/196/1g); 1st Playoffs (2/46)	1

SMITH-DOYLE, GARETH

Forward. Born 2002, Calgary, AB, CAN. Height 188 cm. Youth clubs: Calgary Foothills SC. School: University of Calgary
Honours: CPL North Star Shield (2023)

SEASON	CLUB	NATION	HIGHLIGHTS (MP/MIN)
2017	Calgary Foothills SC U-15	CAN	2nd U-15 Cup
2022	Cavalry FC	1.CAN	3rd CPL (5/43)
2023	Cavalry FC	1.CAN	1st CPL (16/532/1g); 2nd Playoffs (0/0)

SMITH, JUSTIN — FRA / US AVRANCHES

Centre back. Born 2003, Paris, FRA. Grew up Voisins-le-Bretonneux, Yvelines, FRA. Height 190 cm. Youth clubs: OGC Nice (youth)

SEASON	CLUB	NATION	HIGHLIGHTS (MP/MIN)
2021-22	OGC Nice	1.FRA	5th Ligue 1 (0/0); Coupe (0/0)
	OGC Nice B	5.FRA	3rd National 3 Corse-Méditerranée
2022-23	US Quevilly-Rouen	2.FRA	11th Ligue 2 (6/94)
	US Quevilly-Rouen 2	5.FRA	7th National 3 Normandie
2023-24	US Avranches	3.FRA	Championnat National (current season)

SOLTANZADEH, SHAYAN — TORONTO FC II

Left winger. Born 2004. Grew up in Vaughan, ON, CAN. Height 183. Dominant right foot. Youth clubs: Vaughan SC, Toronto FC Academy

SEASON	CLUB	NATION	HIGHLIGHTS (MP/MIN)
2022	Toronto FC II	CAN-3.US	7th MLS NEXT Pro (0/0)
	Ontario U-18	CAN	Silver at Canada Games (4/122)
2023	Toronto FC II	CAN-3.US	23rd MLS NEXT Pro (0/0)

SON, JONGHYUN

Midfielder. Born 2003, Oakville, ON, CAN. Height 180 cm. Youth clubs: Sigma FC

SEASON	CLUB	NATION	HIGHLIGHTS (MP/MIN)
2019	Sigma FC	CAN	5th League1 Ontario (2/64); QF Playoffs (2/149)
2021	Forge FC Hamilton	CAN	SF Concacaf League (1/15)
	Forge FC Hamilton	1.CAN	1st CPL (6/61)m SF CanChamp (0/0)

SOW, KAREEM

Fullback & centre back. Born 2000, Ottawa, ON, CAN. Height 185 cm. Dominant left foot. Youth clubs: Ottawa Gloucester Hornets SC, Académie Impact de Montréal. School: Université de Montréal
Honours: U-Sports Championship (2018)

SEASON	CLUB	NATION	HIGHLIGHTS (MP/MIN)
2021	HFX Wanderers FC	1.CAN	4th CPL (11/900); QF CanChamp (0/0)
2022	HFX Wanderers FC	1.CAN	7th CPL (5/416); QF CanChamp (0/0)

ST. CLAIR, DAYNE — USA / MINNESOTA UNITED FC

Goalkeeper. Born 1997, Toronto, ON, CAN. Grew up Pickering, ON, CAN. Height 191 cm. Youth clubs: Ephinay Church SL, North Scarborough SC, Pickering FC, Vaughan SC. School: University of Maryland
Honours: Concacaf champion (2021-22)

CANADA INTERNATIONAL
1 FIFA World Cup: Group phase at Qatar 2022
1 Concacaf medal: Silver at CNL 2022-23
1st #CANMNT: 2021-06-5 at Bradenton, FL, USA (v. ARU)

SEASON	CLUB	NATION	HIGHLIGHTS (MP/MIN)
2012	Ontario U-15	CAN	1st Canada Soccer All Stars U-15
2013	Ontario U-18	CAN	Bronze at Canada Games (3/10)
	Ontario U-16	CAN	th Canada Soccer All Stars U-16
2014	Vaughan Azzurri	CAN	8th CS National Championships (4/264)
	Vaughan Azzurri	CAN	4th League1 Ontario
2015	Vaughan Azzurri	CAN	3rd League1 Ontario
2016	K-W United FC	CAN-4.US	USL PDL (6/540)
2017	K-W United FC	CAN-4.US	USL PDL (7/630)
2018	New York Red Bulls U-23	4.USA	USL PDL; QF Playoffs
2019	Minnesota United FC	1.USA	7th MLS (0/0); Playoffs (0/0); 2nd US Cup (0/0)
	Forward Madison FC	3.USA	4th USL League One (5/450)
2020	Minnesota United FC	1.USA	9th MLS (13/1170); SF Playoffs (3/270)
	San Antonio FC	2.USA	W3rd USL (5/450)

FOOTBALLERS

2021	Minnesota United FC	1.USA	11th MLS (4/360); Playoffs (1/90)
2022	Minnesota United FC	1.USA	11th MLS (32/2835); Playoffs (1/120)
	MLS All-Stars	1.USA	MLS All-Star Game (1/?)
2023	Minnesota United FC	1.USA	21st MLS (30/2700); L16 US Cup (0/0); QF Leagues (5/450)

ST-LOUIS, NATHANIEL

Winger & midfielder. Born 2000, Toronto, ON, CAN. Height 175 cm. Youth clubs: Mooredale SC, North Toronto SC, Markham SC, Vaughan SC.
School: Syracuse University, University of Alabama at Birmingham

SEASON	CLUB	NATION	HIGHLIGHTS (MP/MIN)
2023	Vancouver FC	1.CAN	7th CPL (4/71); CanChamp (1/9)

STAMATOPOULOS, KENNY   SWE / AIK FOTBOL

Goalkeeper. Born 1979, Kalamata, GRE. Grew up Markham, ON, CAN. Height 188 cm. Youth clubs: Markham SC, Scarborough Azzurri
Honours: Allsvenskan (2018)
1st #CANMNT: 2001-11-14 at Paola, MLT (v. MLT)

SEASON	CLUB	NATION	HIGHLIGHTS (MP/MIN)
1999-00	Kalamata FC	1.GRE	Kypello (1/90)
2000-01	Kalamata FC	1.GRE	15th Alpha Ethniki (1/90); Kypello (1/90)
2001-02	Kalamata FC	2.GRE	11th Beta Ethniki (7/551); Kypello (4/314)
2002-03	Kalamata FC	2.GRE	7th Beta Ethniki (2/158); R2 Kypello (2/180)
2003	Enköpings SK	1.SWE	14th Allsvenskan
2004	Enköpings SK	2.SWE	14th Superettan
2005	Bodens BK	2.SWE	14th Superettan
2006	Tromsø IL	1.NOR	10th Tippeligaen (10/892)
2007	Tromsø IL	1.NOR	x- Tippeligaen (4/307)
	Toronto FC	1.CAN	13th MLS (12/1080)
2008	Tromsø IL	1.NOR	3rd Tippeligaen (3/125)
2009	Lyn FK	1.NOR	16th Tippeligaen (6/540)
	Fredrikstad FK	1.NOR	14th Tippeligaen (11/990)
2010	AIK Fotboll	1.SWE	11th Allsvenskan (4/360); QF Cupen (1/120)
2011	AIK Fotboll	1.SWE	2nd Allsvenskan (6/540); R3 Cupen (1/90)
2012	AIK Fotboll	1.SWE	4th Allsvenskan (6/540); Cupen (0/0)
2013	AIK Fotboll	1.SWE	2nd Allsvenskan (26/2253); R2 Cupen (1/120)
2014	AIK Fotboll	1.SWE	3rd Allsvenskan (8/720); Cupen (2/180)
2015	AIK Fotboll	1.SWE	3rd Allsvenskan (3/270)
2016	AIK Fotboll	1.SWE	2nd Allsvenskan (0/0); QF Cupen (1/90)
2017	AIK Fotboll	1.SWE	2nd Allsvenskan (1/90); QF Cupen (0/0)
2018	AIK Fotboll	1.SWE	1st Allsvenskan (0/0); SF Cupen (1/90)
2019	AIK Fotboll	1.SWE	4th Allsvenskan (0/0)
2020	AIK Fotboll	1.SWE	9th Allsvenskan (0/0); QF Cupen (0/0)
2021	AIK Fotboll	1.SWE	2nd Allsvenskan (0/0); Cupen (0/0)
2022	AIK Fotboll	1.SWE	5th Allsvenskan (0/0)
2023	AIK Fotboll	1.SWE	11th Allsvenskan (0/0); QF Cupen (0/0)
2024	AIK Fotboll	1. SWE	Allsvenskan (current season)
CONTINENTAL FOOTBALL		UEFA	HIGHLIGHTS (MP/MIN)
2010-11	AIK Fotboll	UEFA	Qualifying Champions League (0/0); UEFA Europa League (0/0)
2012-13	AIK Fotboll	UEFA	UEFA Europa League (0/0)
2014-15	AIK Fotboll	UEFA	UEFA Europa League (0/0)
2015-16	AIK Fotboll	UEFA	UEFA Europa League (2/180)
2016-17	AIK Fotboll	UEFA	UEFA Europa League (0/0)
2017-18	AIK Fotboll	UEFA	UEFA Europa League (0/0)
2022-23	AIK Fotboll	UEFA	UEFA Qualifying Europa Conference League (0/0)

STAMPATORI, DANIEL

Fullback & midfielder. Born 2004, Mississauga, ON, CAN. Height 180 cm. Dominant right foot. Youth clubs: Sigma FC, Iona Catholic Secondary School. School: Lipscomb University

SEASON	CLUB	NATION	HIGHLIGHTS (MP/MIN)
2021	Sigma FC	CAN	9th League1 Ontario (8/534)

2022('20)	Forge FC Hamilton	1.CAN	2nd CanChamp (0/0)
2022	Forge FC Hamilton	1.CAN	2nd CPL (2/9)
2022	Sigma FC	CAN	9th League1 Ontario (10/478)
2023	Sigma FC	CAN	9th League1 Ontario (10/678)

STEFANOVIC, LAZAR — TORONTO FC II

Centre back. Born 2006, Clearwater, FL, USA. Grew up Oakville, ON, CAN. Height 184 cm. Dominant right foot. Youth clubs: Oakville SC, Toronto FC Academy

SEASON	CLUB	NATION	HIGHLIGHTS (MP/MIN)
2022	Toronto FC II	CAN-3.US	7th MLS NEXT Pro (1/45)
	Ontario U-18	CAN	Silver at Canada Games (4/320)
2023	Toronto FC	1.CAN	29th MLS (2/78); Leagues (1/90)
	Toronto FC II	CAN-3.US	23rd MLS NEXT Pro (25/2149)

STEVANOVIC, BRADEN — BELLE RIVER FC

Midfielder. Born 2006, Belle River, ON, CAN. Height 180 cm. Dominant left foot. Youth clubs: Belle River FC

STEWART-BAYNES, KIMANI — USA / COLORADO RAPIDS

Forward. Born 2005, Kingstown, VIN. Grew up in Toronto, ON, CAN. Height 175. Dominant right foot. Youth clubs: Unionville-Milliken SC, Thornhill Bolts SC, Vaughan SC. School: University of Maryland.

STOJADINOVIC, MARKO — TORONTO FC II

Centre back. Born 2004, Brampton, ON, CAN. Grew up Caledon, ON, CAN. Height 178 cm. Youth clubs: South Caledon SC, Toronto FC Academy

SEASON	CLUB	NATION	HIGHLIGHTS (MP/MIN)
2023	Toronto FC II	CAN-3.US	23rd MLS NEXT Pro (16/966)

STURING, FRANK — YORK UNITED FC

Centre back. Born 1997, Nijmegen, NED. Height 186 cm. Dominant right foot. Youth clubs: Oranje Blauw, NEC Nijmegen
1st #CANMNT: 2021-03-29 at Bradenton, FL, USA (v. CAY)

SEASON	CLUB	NATION	HIGHLIGHTS (MP/MIN/G)	G
2016-17	NEC Nijmegen	1.NED	16th Eredivisie (3/188)	
2017-18	NEC Nijmegen	2.NED	3rd Eerste Division (20/1755/1g); L16 Beker (2/180)	1
2018-19	NEC Nijmegen	2.NED	9th Eerste Division (7/369); R2 Beker (1/120)	
2019-20	NEC Nijmegen	2.NED	8th Eerste Division (14/676); R1 Beker (1/120)	
2020-21	FC Den Bosch	2.NED	19th Eerste Division (18/1465); R1 Beker (1/90)	
2021-22	SV Horn	2.AUT	12th 2.liga (21/1797/2g)	2
2022-23	SV Horn	2.AUT	4th 2.liga (23/1878); L16 OFB Pokalen (3/110)	2

SUKUNDA, ZACHARY — VALOUR FC

Fullback. Born 1995, Ottawa, ON, CAN. Height 174 cm. Youth clubs: AJ Auxerre (France), Académie de l'Impact de Montréal

SEASON	CLUB	NATION	HIGHLIGHTS (MP/MIN/G)	G
2015	FC Montréal	CAN-2.US	E10th USL (25/1960)	
2016	FC Montréal	CAN-2.US	E14th USL (21/1199/1g)	1
2017	Umeå FC	3.SWE	5th Ettan Norra (15/1114)	
2018	Hume City FC	2.AUS	x- Victoria Division	
	Northcote City FC	2.AUS	13th Victoria Division	
2019	HFX Wanderers FC	1.CAN	7th CPL (17/841); CanChamp (4/167)	
2020	Ekenäs IF	2.FIN	4th Ykkösen (19/1314/1g); Kuppi (5/439)	1
2021	PEPO Lappeenranta	3.FIN	2nd Kakkosen Lohko A (22/1941); L16 Kuppi (1/81)	1
2022	PEPO Lappeenranta	2.FIN	11th Ykkösen (24/2027/1g); Kuppi (2/116/2g)	3
2023	IF Gnistan	2.FIN	2nd Ykkösen (25/1490/1g); R5 Kuppi (3/128)	1

ŚWIDERSKI, GRÉGOIRE

Forward. Born 2005, Bordeaux, FRA. Height 190. Dominant right foot. Youth clubs: FC Saint-Médard en Jalles (FRA), FC Girondins de Bordeaux (FRA).

SYLVESTER, MALIK

Centre back. Born 2004, . Grew up Sherwood Park, AB, CAN. Height 188 cm. Youth clubs: St. Albert Impact, Edmonton BtB Academy
School: Oakland University

SEASON	CLUB	NATION	HIGHLIGHTS (MP/MIN)
2019	St. Albert Impact U-15	CAN	1st U-15 Cup
2022	FC Edmonton	1.CAN	8th CPL (1/2)

TABI, OBENG — CS ST-LAURENT

Fullback. Born 2000, Montréal, QC, CAN. Height 180 cm. Dominant left foot. Youth clubs: FS Salaberry, CS St-Laurent, CS Étoiles de l'Est. School: Louisiana State University Eunice

SEASON	CLUB	NATION	HIGHLIGHTS (MP/MIN)
2022	HFX Wanderers FC	1.CAN	7th CPL (19/1011); QF CanChamp (0/0)

TABLA, BALLOU — ATLÉTICO OTTAWA

Attacking midfielder. Born 1999, Abidjan, CIV. Grew up Montréal, QC, CAN. Height 175 cm. Youth clubs: Pte-aux-Trembles, CS Panellinios Montréal, Académie de l'Impact de Montréal, FC Barcelona (Spain)
Honours: Canadian Championship (2019, 2021), CPL Regular Season (2022)
1st #CANMNT: 2018-10-16 at Toronto, ON, CAN (v. DMA)

SEASON	CLUB	NATION	HIGHLIGHTS (MP/MIN/G)	G
2013	Panellinios Montréal FC U-14	CAN	1st U-14 Cup	
2016	FC Montréal	CAN-2.US	E14th USL (21/1707/5g)	5
2017	Impact de Montréal	1.CAN	17th MLS (21/1146/2g); 2nd CanChamp (3/205/1g)	3
2017-18	FC Barcelona B	2.ESP	20th Segunda División (12/322/1g)	1
2018-19	FC Barcelona B	3.ESP	x- Segunda División B Group 3 (18/957/2g)	2
	Albacete Balompié	2.ESP	4th Segunda División (2/37)	1
2019	Impact de Montréal	1.CAN	18th MLS (4/127); 1st CanChamp (0/0)	
2020	Impact de Montréal	Concacaf	QF Champions League (2/37)	
	Impact de Montréal	1.CAN	18th MLS (5/100/1g)	1
2021	CF Montréal	1.CAN	18th MLS (2/19); 1st CanChamp (2/76/2g)	2
2022	Atlético Ottawa	1.CAN	1st CPL (27/2031/6g); 2nd Playoffs (3/265/1g); CanChamp (1/83)	7
2022-23	Manisa FK	2.TUR	8th 1. Lig (14/759/3g)	3
2023-24	Manisa FK	2.TUR	x- 1. Lig (7/138/1g)	1
2024	Atlético Ottawa	1.CAN	CPL (current season)	

TAHID, TARYCK — VANCOUVER FC

Midfielder. Born 2007, Maple Ridge, BC, CAN. Grew up in Maple Ridge, BC, CAN. Height 178. Youth clubs: Abion FC, VanCity Pro FA

SEASON	CLUB	NATION	HIGHLIGHTS (MP/MIN)
2023	Vancouver FC	1.CAN	7th CPL (20/554/3g)

TAVARES, HUGO

Midfielder. Born 2003, Lac Mégantic, QC, CAN. Grew up Santarém & Porto, POR. Height 178 cm. Dominant right foot. Youth clubs: Associação Académica de Santarém, FC Paços de Ferreira
School: New Jersey Institute of Technology

TAVERNIER, KEVAUGHN — FORGE FC HAMILTON

Winger. Born 2006, Brampton, ON, CAN. Height 175. Dominant right foot. Youth clubs: Brampton YSC, Juventus Academy Toronto, Sigma FC

SEASON	CLUB	NATION	HIGHLIGHTS (MP/MIN/G)	G
2023	Forge FC Hamilton	1.CAN	2th CPL (2/72)	
	Sigma FC	CAN	9th League1 Ontario (10/499/2g)	2

TCHEMMOUN, RAYANE — CF MONTRÉAL U-23

Midfielder. Born 2004, Oran, ALG. Grew up in Montréal, QC, CAN. Height 188. Youth clubs: FC Laval

SEASON	CLUB	NATION	HIGHLIGHTS (MP/MIN)
2022	FC Laval	CAN	1st PLSQ (1/11)
	Québec U-18	CAN	Gold at Canada Games (4/300)
2023	CF Montréal U-23	CAN	5th Ligue1 Québec

TEIBERT, RUSSELL

Retired after the 2023 season
Midfielder. Born 1992, Niagara Falls, ON, CAN. Height 173 cm. Dominant left foot. Youth clubs: Niagara Falls SC, Oakville SC, Saltfleet SC, Clarkson SC, Toronto FC Academy, Vancouver Whitecaps FC Residency
Honours: Canadian Championship (2015, 2022, 2023)
1st #CANMNT: 2012-08-15 at Lauderhill, FL, USA (v. TRI)

SEASON	CLUB	NATION	HIGHLIGHTS (MP/MIN/G)	G
2006	Ontario U-14	CAN	1st Canada Soccer All Stars U-14	
2008	Ontario U-16	CAN	2nd Canada Soccer All Stars U-16	
2010	Vancouver Whitecaps	CAN	5th USSF2 (1/45)	
2011	Vancouver Whitecaps FC	1.CAN	18th MLS (11/503); 2nd CanChamp (4/232)	
2012	Vancouver Whitecaps FC	CAN-2.US	Playoffs (0/0); 2nd CanChamp (0/0)	
	Vancouver Whitecaps FC	1.CAN	11th MLS (4/117); 2nd CanChamp (4/360)	
2013	Vancouver Whitecaps FC	1.CAN	13th MLS (24/1777/2g); 3rd CanChamp (2/210)	2
2014	Vancouver Whitecaps FC	1.CAN	Playoffs (0/0); 9th MLS (29/1971)	
2015	Vancouver Whitecaps FC	1.CAN	3rd MLS (23/1346); QF Playoffs (1/90); 1st CanChamp (3/270)	
2015-16	Vancouver Whitecaps FC	Concacaf	16th Champions League (3/206)	
2016	Vancouver Whitecaps FC	1.CAN	16th MLS (11/696); 2nd CanChamp (4/235)	
2016-17	Vancouver Whitecaps FC	Concacaf	SF Champions League (4/360)	
2017	Vancouver Whitecaps FC	1.CAN	8th MLS (12/731); SF CanChamp (2/180)	
2018	Vancouver Whitecaps FC	1.CAN	14th MLS (23/1604/1g); 2nd CanChamp (4/360)	1
2019	Vancouver Whitecaps FC	1.CAN	23rd MLS (27/2202); CanChamp (1/64)	
2020	Vancouver Whitecaps FC	1.CAN	17th MLS (20/1585); L16 MLS is Back (1/90)	
2021	Vancouver Whitecaps FC	1.CAN	12th MLS (33/2421/1g); Playoffs (1/90); CanChamp (1/1)	1
2022	Vancouver Whitecaps FC	1.CAN	17th MLS (29/2043); 1st CanChamp (4/304/1)	1
2023	Vancouver Whitecaps FC	Concacaf	QF Champions League (3/171); L32 Leagues Cup (2/30)	
	Vancouver Whitecaps FC	1.CAN	13th MLS (7/147); L16 MLS Playoffs (0/0); 1st CanChamp (3/217)	

TEMGUIA, MÉLÉ
Centre back. Born 1995, Dramstadt, GER. Grew up Montréal, QC, CAN. Height 188 cm. Youth clubs: Verts de Sherbrooke, Académie de l'Impact de Montréal

SEASON	CLUB	NATION	HIGHLIGHTS (MP/MIN/G)	G
2015	FC Montréal	CAN-2.US	E10th USL (19/1494)	
2016	FC Montréal	CAN-2.US	E14th USL (4/129)	
2017	FC Cincinnati	2.USA	E6th USL (1/62); SF US Cup (0/0)	
2018	Hume City FC	2.AUS	x- Victoria Division	
	Valentine Phoenix	2.AUS	11th Northern NSW Division	
2019	FC Edmonton	1.CAN	4th CPL (27/2430/2g); CanChamp (2/180/1g)	3
2020	FC Edmonton	1.CAN	8th CPL (5/450)	
2021	FC Edmonton	1.CAN	7th CPL (21/1409); CanChamp (1/61)	
2022	Forward Madison FC	3.USA	9th USL League One (16/417/1g)	1
2023	PEPO Lappeenranta	3.FIN	Kakkosen Lohko A (current season); 5R Kuppi (1/68)	

THERRIEN, JORDAN   CF MONTRÉAL U-23
Midfielder. Born 2004, Montréal, QC, CAN. Grew up Rosemère, QC, CAN. Height 165 cm. Youth clubs: CS Lorraine-Rosemère, Académie Impact de Montréal

SEASON	CLUB	NATION	HIGHLIGHTS (MP/MIN)
2022	CF Montréal U-23	CAN	6th PLSQ (10/463)

THOMAS, AMONI
Right back. Born 2006. Grew up in Edmonton, AB, CAN. Youth clubs: Edmonton Warriors SC, Vancouver Whitecaps FC Academy

SEASON	CLUB	NATION	HIGHLIGHTS (MP/MIN)
2023	Vanc. Whitecaps FC 2	CAN-3.US	21st MLS NEXT Pro (3/81)
	Vanc. Whitecaps FC Academy	3.CAN	3rd League1 BC (1/5)

THOMAS, SIMON
Goalkeeper. Born 1990, Victoria, BC, CAN. Height 190 cm. Dominant right foot. Youth clubs: Bays United SC, Victoria Metro United, Vancouver Whitecaps FC Residency
Honours: USL First Division (2008), OBOS-ligaen (2017)
1st #CANMNT: 2013-01-26 at Tucson, AZ, USA (v. DEN)

SEASON	CLUB	NATION	HIGHLIGHTS (MP/MIN)
2004	Lower Island U-14	CAN	4th Tide U-14 Cup
2006	British Columbia U-16	CAN	3rd Canada Soccer All Stars U-16
2008	Vancouver Whitecaps FC	CAN-2.US	2nd USL First Division (0/0); 1st Playoffs (0/0)
	Vanc. Whitecaps Residency	CAN-4.US	USL PDL
2009	Vancouver Whitecaps FC	CAN-2.US	7th USL First Division (0/0)

2010	Vancouver Whitecaps FC	CAN-2.US	5th USSF2 (1/9); SF Playoffs (0/0); 2nd CanChamp (0/0)
2013	Vancouver Whitecaps FC	1.CAN	2nd CanChamp (0/0)
2014-15	Newport County FC	4.ENG	x- EFL League Two (0/0); R1 Lg.Cup (0/0)
2015	Strømmen IF	2.NOR	8th OBOS-ligaen (28/2445); L16 Cup (4/420)
2016	FK Bodø/Glimt	1.NOR	15th Tippeligaen; SF Cup (4/360)
2017	FK Bodø/Glimt	2.NOR	1st OBOS-ligaen (8/720); R3 Cup (3/300)
2018	Kongsvinger IL	2.NOR	x- OBOS-ligaen (5/450); R3 Cup (1/90)
2019	KFUM-Kameratene Oslo	2.NOR	4th OBOS-ligaen (4/527); QF Cup (4/360)
2020	KFUM-Kameratene Oslo	2.NOR	x- OBOS-ligaen (7/571)
	Sarpsborg	1.NOR	12th Eliteserien (1/90)
2021	Tromsø IL	1.NOR	11th Eliteserien (0/0); R2 Cup (1/90)
2022	Tromsø IL	1.NOR	7th Eliteserien (1/90); QF Cup (3/300)
2023	Tromsø IL	1.NOR	Elitserien (3/262); L16 Cup (4/390)

THOMPSON, KOSI   TORONTO FC

Midfielder. Born 2003, North York, ON, CAN. Height 180 cm. Dominant right foot. Youth clubs: Vaughan SC, Toronto FC Academy

Honours: Canadian Championship (2022/'20)

SEASON	CLUB	NATION	HIGHLIGHTS (MP/MIN/G)	G
2021	Toronto FC II	CAN-3.US	7th USL League One (27/1532/1g)	1
2022('20)	Toronto FC	1.CAN	1st CanChamp (1/90)	
2022	Toronto FC	1.CAN	27th MLS (24/1625/1g); 2nd CanChamp (3/248)	1
2023	Toronto FC	1.CAN	x- MLS (14/580/1g); QF CanChamp (1/10); Leagues (1/32)	1
	Toronto FC II	CAN-3.US	23rd MLS NEXT Pro (1/90)	
	Lillestrøm SK	1.NOR	6th Elitserien (4/109)	

THOMPSON, LENNON

Midfielder. Born 2005. Grew up in Surrey, BC, CAN. Youth clubs: Unity FC

SEASON	CLUB	NATION	HIGHLIGHTS (MP/MIN)
2023	Vancouver FC	1.CAN	7th CPL (3/48)
	Langley Unity FC	1.CAN	4th League1 BC (2/75)

THOMPSON, ROGER

Centre back & right back. Born 1991, Clarendon, JAM. Grew up Brampton, ON, CAN. Height 191 cm. Dominant Bight foot. Youth clubs: Brampton East SC, Vaughan SC

School: University of Cincinnati

SEASON	CLUB	NATION	HIGHLIGHTS (MP/MIN/G)	G
2005	Ontario U-14	CAN	1st Canada Soccer All Stars U-14	
2007	Ontario U-16	CAN	2nd Canada Soccer All Stars U-16	
2013	IFK Mariehamn	1.FIN	4th Veikkausliiga (30/2700); SF Kuppi (3/300); Liigacup (6/549/1g)	1
2013-14	IFK Mariehamn	UEFA	UEFA Qualifying Europa League (2/180)	
2014	IFK Mariehamn	1.FIN	5th Veikkausliiga (20/1181); SF Kuppi (2/180); SF Liigacup (4/360)	
2014-15	KSV Baunatal	4.GER	Regionalliga	
2015	Trelleborgs FF	3.SWE	7th Ettan Södra (9/738)	
2016	Trelleborgs FF	2.SWE	7th Superettan (17/859)	
2017	Ljungskile SK	3.SWE	7th Ettan Södra (25/2250); QF Cupen (1/90)	
2018	Ljungskile SK	3.SWE	6th Ettan Södra (13/903)	
2019	York9 FC	1.CAN	3rd CPL (10/802); CanChamp (2/180)	
2020	York9 FC	1.CAN	5th CPL (7/630)	
2021	York United FC	1.CAN	4th CPL (9/546); QF CanChamp (1/90)	
2022	York United FC	1.CAN	6th CPL (14/1023); SF CanChamp (1/43/1g)	1
2023	York United FC	1.CAN	5th CPL (15/1166/1g); QF CanChamp (1/25)	1

TIMÓTEO, WESLEY   HALIFAX WANDERERS FC

Midfielder. Born 2000, Montréal, QC, CAN. Height 175 cm. Dominant left foot. Youth clubs: CS Panellinios Montréal, Académie de l'Impact de Montréal, Esperança de Lagos (Portugal), CF Belenenses (Portugal), GD Estoril Praia (Portugal)

SEASON	CLUB	NATION	HIGHLIGHTS (MP/MIN/G)	G
2013	Panellinios Montréal FC U-14	CAN	1st U-14 Cup	
2020-21	PO Xylotymbou	2.CYP	12th B Division (26/1506); R1 Cup (1/8)	1

| | 2022 | FC Edmonton | | 1.CAN | 8th CPL (27/1925); CanChamp (1/90) | |
| | 2023 | Halifax Wanderers FC | | 1.CAN | 3rd CPL (24/1584); 4th Playoffs (1/32); CanChamp (1/75) | |

TINIAKOS, VASILIOS — CF MONTRÉAL U-23
Midfielder. Born 2003, Montréal, QC, CAN.

SEASON	CLUB	NATION	HIGHLIGHTS (MP/MIN/G)	G
2022	CF Montréal U-23	CAN	6th PLSQ (15/761/2g)	2
2023	CF Montréal U-23	CAN	5th Ligue1 Québec	

TISSEUR, JORDAN
Goalkeeper. Born 2000, Montréal, QC, CAN. Grew up Candiac, QC, CAN. Height 186 cm. Dominant right foot. Youth clubs: Cosmos de Candiac, Académie de l'Impact de Montréal
School: Université de Montréal

SEASON	CLUB	NATION	HIGHLIGHTS (MP/MIN)
2019	Ottawa Fury FC	CAN-2.US	E8th USL (0/0)
2022	FC Laval	CAN	1st PLSQ (21/1886)
2023	Valour FC	1.CAN	8th CPL (0/0); CanChamp (0/0)

TISSOT, MAXIM — ATLÉTICO OTTAWA
Midfielder & fullback. Born 1992, Aylmer, QC, CAN. Grew up Gatineau, QC, CAN. Height 180 cm. Dominant left foot.
Youth clubs: CS Aylmer, FC Outaouais, Académie de l'Impact de Montréal
Honours: Canadian Championship (2013, 2014), CPL Championship (2020), CPL Regular Season (2022), NASL Championship (2017)
1st #CANMNT: 2015-01-16 at Orlando, FL, USA (v. ISL)

SEASON	CLUB	NATION	HIGHLIGHTS (MP/MIN/G)	G
2006	Québec U-14	CAN	5th Canada Soccer All Stars U-14	
2008	Québec U-16	CAN	1st Canada Soccer All Stars U-16	
2009	Québec U-18	CAN	Gold at Canada Games (4/119)	
2013	Impact de Montréal	1.CAN	11th MLS (6/303/1g); 1st CanChamp (2/180)	1
2013-14	Impact de Montréal	Concacaf	Champions League (2/180)	
2014	Impact de Montréal	1.CAN	19th MLS (20/762/2g); 1st CanChamp (3/93)	2
2014-15	Impact de Montréal	Concacaf	2nd Champions League (7/154)	
2015	Impact de Montréal	1.CAN	7th MLS (11/581/1g); 2nd CanChamp (3/213)	1
2016	Impact de Montréal	1.CAN	x- MLS (7/517/1g); SF CanChamp (0/0)	1
	FC Montréal	CAN-2.US	x- USL (1/90)	
	Ottawa Fury FC	2.USA	10th NASL (19/1664/2g)	2
2017	Richmond Kickers	2.USA	x- USL (4/339)	
	D.C. United	1.USA	x- MLS (1/90)	
	San Francisco Deltas	2.USA	2nd NASL (26/2171); 1st Playoffs (2/180); R4 US Cup (1/60)	
2018	Ottawa Fury FC	2.USA	E10th USL (2/48); SF CanChamp (2/44)	
2019	Ottawa Fury FC	2.USA	E8th USL (15/830); SF CanChamp (3/147/1g)	1
2020	Forge FC Hamilton	CAN	QF Concacaf League (2/95)	
	Forge FC Hamilton	1.CAN	1st CPL (10/386/1g)	1
2021	Forge FC Hamilton	CAN	SF Concacaf League (5/227)	
	Forge FC Hamilton	1.CAN	1st CPL (12/533); 2nd Playoffs (1/14)	
2022	Atlético Ottawa	1.CAN	1st CPL (27/2180/3g); 2nd Playoffs (3/269); CanChamp (1/56)	3
2023	Atlético Ottawa	1.CAN	6th CPL (15/1066/2g); QF CanChamp (1/90/1g)	3

TOMY, CADEN
Midfielder. Born 2001, Winnipeg, MB, CAN. Height cm. Youth clubs: Winnipeg South End United, WSA Winnipeg

SEASON	CLUB	NATION	HIGHLIGHTS (MP/MIN)
2021	Valour FC	1.CAN	5th CPL (4/33); QF CanChamp (1/1)

TOUSSAINT, CÉDRIC — PACIFIC FC
Midfielder. Born 2001, Drummondville, QC, CAN. Grew up Montréal, QC, CAN. Height 173 cm. Dominant right foot.
Youth clubs: AS Pointe-aux-Trembles, CS Rivière-des-Prairies, CS Panellinios, CS Mercier-Hochelaga-Maisonneuve, Académie Impact Montréal

SEASON	CLUB	NATION	HIGHLIGHTS (MP/MIN)
2021	York United FC	1.CAN	4th CPL (24/1470); QF CanChamp (1/42)
2022	York United FC	1.CAN	CPL (14/776); SF CanChamp (3/227)
	Pacific FC	Concacaf	L16 Concacaf League (2/81)

FOOTBALLERS

SEASON	CLUB	NATION	HIGHLIGHTS (MP/MIN/G)	G
	Pacific FC	1.CAN	4th CPL (9/554); SF Playoffs (2/135)	
2023	Pacific FC	1.CAN	4th CPL (23/1672); 3rd Playoffs (3/72); SF CanChamp (2/145)	

TRAFFORD, CHARLIE — CAVALRY FC

Midfielder. Born 1992, Calgary, AB, CAN. Height 193 cm. Dominant right foot. Youth clubs: Calgary Foothills SC, Vancouver Whitecaps FC Residency, De Graafschap (Netherlands)
School: York University
Honours: CPL North Star Shield (2023), I liga polska (2016-17)
1st #CANMNT: 2015-10-13 at Washington, DC, USA (v. GHA)

SEASON	CLUB	NATION	HIGHLIGHTS (MP/MIN/G)	G
2006	Calgary Foothills U-14	CAN	5th Tide U-14 Cup	
2008	Alberta U-16	CAN	3rd Canada Soccer All Stars U-16	
2009	Calgary Foothills U-18	CAN	1st Sony U-18 Cup	
2010	Calgary Foothills U-18	CAN	2nd Sony U-18 Cup (5/?)	
2013	IFK Mariehamn	1.FIN	4th Veikkausliiga (8/333/2g)	2
2014	Turun Palloseura	1.FIN	x- Veikkausliiga (5/282); L16 Kuppi (2/180); Liigacup (3/234)	
	Kuopion Palloseura	1.FIN	7th Veikkausliiga (21/1816/3g)	3
2015	Kuopion Palloseura	1.FIN	7th Veikkausliiga (28/2141/5g); SF Kuppi (3/156); Liigacup (4/315/1g)	6
2015-16	Korona Kielce	1.POL	12th Ekstraklasa (3/150)	
2016-17	Korona Kielce	1.POL	x- Ekstraklasa (0/0); R2 Puchar (1/120)	
	Sandecja Nowy Sącz	2.POL	1st 1.liga (8/170)	
2017	Rovaniemen Palloseura	1.FIN	x- Veikkausliiga (6/451)	
2017-18	Inverness Caledonian Thistle	2.SCO	5th Championship (26/1829); 4R SFA Cup (1/58)	
2018-19	Inverness Caledonian Thistle	2.SCO	3rd Championship (24/1382/1g); SF Playoffs (4/360/1g); SF Cup (6/283); Lg.Cup (3/172)	2
2019-20	Inverness Caledonian Thistle	2.SCO	2nd Championship (20/1527); QF Cup (3/269/1g); Lg.Cup (3/266)	1
2020-21	Hamilton Academical FC	1.SCO	12th Premiership (16/806); R3 SFA Cup (0/0); Lg.Cup (1/90)	
2021-22	Wrexham FC	WAL (5.ENG)	x- National League (0/0)	
2022	Cavalry FC	1.CAN	3rd CPL (23/1535); SF Playoffs (1/13); QF CanChamp (2/73)	
2023	Cavalry FC	1.CAN	1st CPL (25/1731); 2nd Playoffs (3/300); CanChamp (1/68)	

TRAFFORD, MASON

Centre back. Born 1986, Boynton Beach, FL, USA. Grew up North Vancouver, BC, CAN. Height 193 cm. Dominant left foot. Youth clubs: North Shore Selects, Vancouver Whitecaps FC Residency
School: University of Nevada, Las Vegas
Honours: NPSL Championship (2018)
1st #CANMNT: 2013-01-26 at Tucson, AZ, USA (v. DEN)

SEASON	CLUB	NATION	HIGHLIGHTS (MP/MIN/G)	G
2008	Vancouver Whitecaps FC	CAN-2.US	2nd USL First Division (14/514); 1st Playoffs (3/243)	
2009	Vancouver Whitecaps FC	CAN-2.US	7th USL First Division (23/1240); 2nd CanChamp (3/122)	
2010	Real Maryland FC	2.USA	6th USL 2nd Division; R2 US Cup (1/90)	
	IFK Mariehamn	1.FIN	12th Veikkausliiga (6/540/1g)	1
2011	IFK Mariehamn	1.FIN	7th Veikkausliiga (28/2317/1g); SF Kuppi (2/180); Liigacup (2/180)	1
2012	IFK Mariehamn	1.FIN	4th Veikkausliiga (30/2693); QF Kuppi (4/280); Liigacup (1/90)	
2013	Guizhou Zhicheng	1.CHN	16th China League One (29/?)	
2014	Ottawa Fury FC	2.USA	8th NASL (27/2349); 5th CanChamp (2/180)	
2015	Ottawa Fury FC	2.USA	2nd NASL (25/2250/1g); 2nd Playoffs (2/188); 5th CanChamp (1/82)	1
2016	Miami FC	2.USA	7th NASL (31/2766); R3 US Cup (1/90)	
2017	Miami FC	2.USA	1st NASL (26/2171); SF Playoffs (1/120); QF US Cup (5/450)	
2018	Miami FC 2	3.USA	NPSL; 1st NPSL Playoffs; R2 US Cup	
2019	Cavalry FC	1.CAN	2nd CPL (22/1891); SF CanChamp (6/540)	
2020	Cavalry FC	1.CAN	4th CPL (8/520)	
2021	Cavalry FC	1.CAN	2nd CPL (13/1062); SF Playoffs (1/120); QF CanChamp (2/162)	
2022	Cavalry FC	1.CAN	3rd CPL (21/1747/1g); SF Playoffs (2/180); QF CanChamp (2/180)	1

TRIANTAFILLOU, SIMON — BURLINGTON SC

Midfielder. Born 1999, Burlington, ON, CAN. Height 183 cm. Dominant right foot. Youth clubs: Sigma FC
School: Syracuse University, Providence College

SEASON	CLUB	NATION	HIGHLIGHTS (MP/MIN/G)	G
2016	Sigma FC	CAN	W2nd League1 Ontario (10/577)	

SEASON	CLUB	NATION	HIGHLIGHTS (MP/MIN)	
2017	Sigma FC	CAN	W2nd League1 Ontario (8/156)	
2018	Sigma FC	CAN	2nd League1 Ontario (6/258)	
2019	Sigma FC	CAN	5th League1 Ontario (14/1218/3g)	3
2022	Forge FC Hamilton	Concacaf	L16 Champions League (0/0)	
	FC Edmonton	1.CAN	8th CPL (26/1866); CanChamp (1/90)	
2023	Burlington SC	CAN	5th League1 Ontario (8/584)	

TSAI, JACOB

Goalkeeper. Born 2004, . Grew up Winnipeg, MB, CAN. Height cm. Youth clubs: Winnipeg Bonivital SC

SEASON	CLUB	NATION	HIGHLIGHTS (MP/MIN)
2018	Winnipeg Bonivital SC U-15	CAN	4th U-15 Cup
2019	Winnipeg Bonivital SC U-15	CAN	4th U-15 Cup
2021	Valour FC	1.CAN	QF CanChamp (0/0)
2022	Manitoba U-18	CAN	8th Canada Games (2/160)

TWARDEK, KRIS — ATLÉTICO OTTAWA

Forward. Born 1997, Toronto, ON, CAN. Grew up Ottawa, ON, CAN. Height 185 cm. Youth clubs: West Carleton SC, Ottawa South United, Everton FC (England), Millwall FC (England)
1st #CANMNT: 2017-10-8 at Houston, TX, USA (v. SLV)

SEASON	CLUB	NATION	HIGHLIGHTS (MP/MIN/G)	G
2015-16	Milwall FC	3.ENG	4th League One (0/0)	
2016-17	Milwall FC	3.ENG	x- League One (0/0); R2 Lg.Cup (0/0); R2 EFL Trophy (3/158)	
	Braintree Town FC	5.ENG	22nd National League (12/747)	
2017-18	Milwall FC	2.ENG	x- EFL Championship (2/12); R3 FA Cup (1/15)	
	Carlisle United FC	4.ENG	10th League Two (12/541)	
2018	Sligo Rovers FC	1.IRL	7th Premier (11/642); R1 FAI Cup (1/90); SF Lg.Cup (1/90)	
2019	Sligo Rovers FC	1.IRL	7th Premier (36/2526/2g); SF Cup (4/360/4g); R2 Lg.Cup (1/73)	6
2020	Bohemian FC Dublin	1.IRL	2nd Premier (13/1149/1g); R2 FAI Cup (1/62)	1
2020-21	Bohemian FC Dublin	UEFA	UEFA Europa League Qualifying (1/120)	
	Jagiellonia Białystok	1.POL	9th Ekstraklasa (15/668)	
2021-22	FK Senica	1.SVK	x- Slovenská liga (18/1422); R4 Cup (3/138)	
2022	Bohemian FC Dublin	1.IRL	6th Premier (29/1951/1g); QF FAI Cup (3/157)	1
2023	Bohemian FC Dublin	1.IRL	6th Premier (19/879); 2nd FAI Cup (2/46/1g)	1

UGBO, IKÉ — ENG / SHEFFIELD WEDNESDAY FC

Forward. Born 1998, London, ENG. Grew up Brampton, ON, CAN & London, ENG. Height 185 cm. Dominant right foot. Youth clubs: Brampton East SC, Woodbridge SC, Chelsea FC (England)
Honours: Concacaf champion (2021-22)

CANADA INTERNATIONAL

1 FIFA World Cup: Group phase at Qatar 2022
1st #CANMNT: 2021-11-12 at Edmonton, AB, CAN (v. CRC)

SEASON	CLUB	NATION	HIGHLIGHTS (MP/MIN/G)	G
2017-18	Barnsley FC	2.ENG	x- Championship (16/741/1g); R3 Lg.Cup (2/167/1g)	2
	Milton Keynes Dons FC	3.ENG	23rd League One (15/981/2g); R4 FA Cup (2/180)	2
2018-19	Scunthorpe United FC	3.ENG	23rd League One (15/837/1g); R2 FA Cup (1/90)	1
2019-20	Roda JC	2.NED	17th Eerste Division (28/2338/13g); R2 Beker (1/78)	13
2020-21	Club Brugge KS	2.BEL	16th Championnat (32/2725/16g); QF Beker (2/15)	16
2021-22	KRC Genk	UEFA	UEFA Europa League (5/169/1g)	1
	KRC Genk	2.BEL	Championnat (18/608/3g); L16 Beker (2/133/2g)	5
	ES Troyes AC	1.FRA	16th Ligue 1 (14/821/5g)	5
2022-23	ES Troyes AC	1.FRA	19th Ligue 1 (25/885/2g); R3 Coupe (1/90)	2
2023-24	Cardiff City FC	WAL-2.ENG	x- Championship (20/937/4g); EFL Cup (2/18)	4
	Sheffield Wednesday FC	2.ENG	Championship (current season)	

UMAR, MUSLIM — THUNDER BAY CHILL

Forward. Born 2003, . Grew up Edmonton, AB, CAN. Height cm. Youth clubs: Edmonton Internazionale SC, Edmonton BTB Academy, FC Edmonton Academy, Vancouver Whitecaps FC Academy. School: University of Portland

SEASON	CLUB	NATION	HIGHLIGHTS (MP/MIN)
2021	York United FC	1.CAN	4th CPL (1/45)

FOOTBALLERS

VASCONCELOS, CAMILO
Midfielder. Born 2005, Cambridge, ON, CAN. Height 170 cm. Dominant right foot. Youth clubs: Cambridge SC, Guelph United FC

SEASON	CLUB	NATION	HIGHLIGHTS (MP/MIN/G)	G
2022	Guelph United FC	CAN	7th League1 Ontario (10/656/2g)	2
2023	Halifax Wanderers FC	1.CAN	3rd CPL (1/45); 4th Playoffs (0/0)	
	Guelph United FC	CAN	6th League1 Ontario (11/769/4g)	4

VELLIOS, DEYLEN — VANCOUVER WHITECAPS FC ACADEMY
Right back. Born 2002, Burnaby, BC, CAN. Height 176 cm. Youth clubs: South Burnaby Metro SC, Vancouver Whitecaps FC Academy

SEASON	CLUB	NATION	HIGHLIGHTS (MP/MIN)
2022	Whitecaps FC	3.CAN	3rd League1 BC
	Vanc. Whitecaps FC Academy	3.CAN	3rd League1 BC
2023	Vanc. Whitecaps FC Academy	3.CAN	3rd League1 BC (11/990)

VERHOEVEN, NOAH — ATLÉTICO OTTAWA
Midfielder. Born 1999, New Westminster, BC, CAN. Grew up Surrey, BC, CAN. Height 173 cm. Dominant left foot. Youth clubs: Surrey United SC, Guru Nanak SC, Vancouver Whitecaps FC Residency

SEASON	CLUB	NATION	HIGHLIGHTS (MP/MIN/G)	G
2017	Vanc. Whitecaps FC 2	CAN-2.US	W14th USL (1/16)	
2018	Fresno FC	2.USA	W12th USL (23/1085); R4 US Cup (1/120)	
2019	Pacific FC	1.CAN	5th CPL (24/1850); CanChamp (1/32)	
2020	Pacific FC	1.CAN	3rd CPL (3/170)	
2021	York United FC	1.CAN	4th CPL (26/2009); SF Playoffs (1/90); QF CanChamp (2/152)	
2022	York United FC	1.CAN	6th CPL (24/1838); SF CanChamp (3/194)	
2023	Atlético Ottawa	1.CAN	6th CPL (25/1323/1g); QF CanChamp (2/105)	1

VERHOVEN, ZACHARY — ATLÉTICO OTTAWA
Midfielder. Born 1998, Surrey, BC, CAN. Height 175 cm. Dominant right foot. Youth clubs: Surrey United SC, Surrey Guildford United SC, Vancouver Whitecaps FC Residency
School: University of British Columbia
Honours: CPL Regular Season (2022)

SEASON	CLUB	NATION	HIGHLIGHTS (MP/MIN/G)	G
2013	British Columbia U-15	CAN	Canada Soccer All Stars U-15	
2015	Surrey United SC U-18	CAN	3rd U-18 Cup	
2017	TSS Rovers FC	CAN-4.US	USL PDL (11/767/2g)	2
2018	TSS Rovers FC	CAN-4.US	USL PDL (10/616/3g)	3
2019	Pacific FC	1.CAN	5th CPL (22/1285/2g); CanChamp (2/148)	2
2020	Pacific FC	1.CAN	3rd CPL (9/316/1g)	1
2021	Atlético Ottawa	1.CAN	8th CPL (25/1540/1g); CanChamp (1/10)	1
2022	Atlético Ottawa	1.CAN	1st CPL (12/384/2g); 2nd Playoffs (3/39/1g); CanChamp (1/56)	3
2023	Atlético Ottawa	1.CAN	6th CPL (22/768/3g); QF CanChamp (1/8)	3

VILSAINT, JULES-ANTHONY — CF MONTRÉAL
Forward. Born 2003, Montréal, QC, CAN. Grew up Laval, QC, CAN. Height 190 cm. Youth clubs: Delta Dragon Laval, CS St-Laurent, CS Panellinios Montréal, Lille OSC (France), Royal Antwerp FC (Belgium)

SEASON	CLUB	NATION	HIGHLIGHTS (MP/MIN)	
2018	Panellinios Montréal FC U-15	CAN	2nd U-15 Cup	
2023	CF Montréal	1.CAN	20th MLS (11/408/1g); 2nd CanChamp (1/6); Leagues (1/31)	1
	CF Montréal U-23	CAN	5th Ligue1 Québec	

VISCOSI, JONATHAN
Goalkeeper. Born 1991, Ottawa, ON, CAN. Height 188 cm. Dominant right foot. Youth clubs: Ottawa South United SC
School: Rio Grande Community College, University Buffalo
Honours: Ykkösen (2017)

SEASON	CLUB	NATION	HIGHLIGHTS (MP/MIN)
2010	Albany BWP Highlanders	4.USA	USL PDL
2011	Ottawa Fury SC	CAN-4.US	USL PDL
2012	Des Moines Menace	4.USA	USL PDL

2013-14	Tiverton Town FC	ENG	x- Southern League (13/?)	
	Carlton Town FC	ENG	10th Northern Premier; Division One South	
2014-15	Brackley Town FC	ENG	x- Conference League North	
	Chester FC	4.ENG	12th Conference League Premier (1/4)	
2015-16	Southport FC	5.ENG	16th National League (6/?)	
2016	Oskarshamns AIK	3.SWE	10th Ettan Södra (8/720); R2 Cupen (0/0)	
2017	Turun Palloseura	2.FIN	1st Ykkösen (27/2430); Kuppi (5/450)	
2018	Turun Palloseura	1.FIN	11th Veikkausliiga (32/2850); Cupen (4/360)	
2019	San Antonio FC	2.USA	W11th USL (2/138); R3 US Cup (2/180)	
2020	IK Sirius	1.SWE	10th Allsvenskan (3/270); Cupen (1/79)	
2021	Dalkurd FF	3.SWE	2nd Ettan Norra (28/2520); Cupen (3/270)	
2022	Dalkurd FF	2.SWE	16th Superettan (17/1530); R2 Cupen (1/90)	
2023	Vaasan Palloseura	1.FIN	Veikkausliiga (2/106); L16 Kuppi (4/360); Liigacup (2/180)	

VITÓRIA, STEVEN   POR / GD CHAVES

Centre back. Born 1987, Toronto, ON, CAN. Grew up Sudbury & Mississauga, ON, CAN. Height 195 cm. Youth clubs: Sudbury Lions, Toronto CS Azzurri, Mississauga SC Falcons, Dixie SC, Kleinburg Nobleton SC, Glen Shields SC, Woodbridge SC, FC Porto (Portugal)

Honours: Concacaf champion (2021-22), Primeira (2013-14), Taça de Portugal (2014), Taça da Liga Portuguesa (2014), Primeira (2008-09, 2011-12), Puchar Polski (2019)

CANADA INTERNATIONAL
1 FIFA World Cup: Group phase at Qatar 2022
1 Concacaf medal: Silver at CNL 2022-23
1st #CANMNT: 2016-02-5 at Carson, CA, USA (v. USA)

SEASON	CLUB	NATION	HIGHLIGHTS (MP/MIN/G)	G
2007-08	SC Olhanense	2.POR	5th Primeira (17/1150); R1 Taça da Liga (1/18)	
2008-09	SC Olhanense	2.POR	1st Primeira (19/1324/1g); Taça da Liga (6/530)	1
2009-10	SC Covilhã	2.POR	14th Primeira (24/1901/2g); R3 Taça (2/180); Taça da Liga (4/360)	2
2010-11	GD Estoril Praia	2.POR	10th Primeira (25/1730/1g); R3 Taça (1/90); Taça da Liga (5/480)	1
2011-12	GD Estoril Praia	2.POR	1st Primeira (27/2416/7g); L16 Taça (2/240/1g); Taça da Liga (7/630/2g)	10
2012-13	GD Estoril Praia	1.POR	5th Primeira (27/2418/11g); Taça da Liga (3/270/2g)	13
2013-14	SL Benfica	UEFA	2nd UEFA Europa League (0/0)	
	SL Benfica	1.POR	1st Primeira (1/90); 1st Taça (1/90); 1st Taça da Liga (3/212)	
	Benfica B	2.POR	5th Primeira (7/616/3g)	3
2015	Philadelphia Union	1.USA	18th MLS (18/1575/1g); 2nd US Cup (0/0)	1
2016-17	Lechia Gdańsk	1.POL	4th Ekstraklasa (8/516); L16 Puchar (1/120)	
2017-18	Lechia Gdańsk	1.POL	13th Ekstraklasa (14/1183/1g); R2 Puchar (1/90)	1
2018-19	Lechia Gdańsk	1.POL	3rd Ekstraklasa (15/742/1g); 1st Puchar (5/308/1g)	2
2019-20	Moreirense FC	1.POR	8th Primeira (19/1538/5g); R4 Taça (1/90); R2 Taça da Liga (1/90)	5
2020-21	Moreirense FC	1.POR	8th Primeira (19/1388/3g); L16 Taça (3/300/1g)	4
2021-22	Moreirense FC	1.POR	16th Primeira (18/1425/2g); 2nd Playoff (1/90); L16 Taça (1/90/1g)	3
2022-23	GD Chaves	1.POR	7th Primeira (31/2646/7g); R3 Taça (1/120); Taça da Liga (1/90)	7
2023-24	GD Chaves	1.POR	Primeira (current season); R3 Taça (1/120)	

VOJVODIC, KYLER   VANCOUVER WHITECAPS FC ACADEMY

Forward. Born 2006, New Westminster, BC, CAN. Grew up Port Coquitlam, BC, CAN. Height 170 cm. Dominant right foot. Youth clubs: Port Coquitlam Eurorite SA, Vancouver Whitecaps FC Academy
Honours: League1 BC (2023)

SEASON	CLUB	NATION	HIGHLIGHTS (MP/MIN)
2019	Vancouver Whitecaps U-13	Concacaf	Concacaf Under-13 Champions League
2023	Vanc. Whitecaps FC 2	CAN-3.US	21st MLS NEXT Pro (1/33)
	Vanc. Whitecaps FC Academy	3.CAN	3rd League1 BC (1/90); 1st Playoffs (2/40)

VOLCY, CHARLES-ÉTIENNE   CF MONTRÉAL U-23

Winger. Born 2004, Montréal, QC, CAN. Grew up Blainville, QC, CAN. Height 180 cm. Youth clubs: AS Blainville, Académie de l'Impact de Montréal

SEASON	CLUB	NATION	HIGHLIGHTS (MP/MIN)
2022	CF Montréal U-23	CAN	6th PLSQ (5/128)
2023	CF Montréal U-23	CAN	5th Ligue1 Québec

FOOTBALLERS

VOYTSEKHOVSKYY, MARKI — YORK UNITED FC
Midfielder. Born 2003, Lviv, UKR. Grew up Mississauga, ON, CAN. Height 183 cm. Youth clubs: FC Shakhtar Donetsk (Ukraine), Rush Academy, Guelph United FC

SEASON	CLUB	NATION	HIGHLIGHTS (MP/MIN/G)	G
2022	ProStars FC	CAN	6th League1 Ontario (21/1520/10g); QF Playoffs (1/90)	10
2023	York United FC	1.CAN	5th CPL (7/167/1g); QF CanChamp (1/13)	1

WALKER, KEEGAN — TORONTO FC II
Winger. Born 2004, Oakville, ON, CAN. Grew up in Oakville, ON, CAN. Height 175. Youth clubs: Toronto FC Academy. School: University of Wisconsin-Green Bay

SEASON	CLUB	NATION	HIGHLIGHTS (MP/MIN)
2022	Toronto FC II	CAN-3.US	7th MLS NEXT Pro (1/29)
2023	Toronto FC II	CAN-3.US	23rd MLS NEXT Pro (0/0)

WALKES, RESHAUN — TORONTO FC II
Forward. Born 1999, Brampton, ON, CAN. Grew up in Brampton, ON, CAN. Height 183. Youth clubs: Ajax SC, Toronto Eagles SC, Dixie SC, Richmond Hill SC, Erin Mills SC
School: Sheridan College, Lewis and Clarke Community College, University of Texas Rio Grande Valley

SEASON	CLUB	NATION	HIGHLIGHTS (MP/MIN/G)	G
2018	Master's FA	CAN	10th League1 Ontario (9/480/3g)	3
2019	Master's FA	CAN	4th League1 Ontario (8/687/3g)	3
2021	Des Moines Menace	4.USA	USL League Two (11/107/1g); 1st Playoffs (2/108)	1
2022	Toronto FC II	CAN-3.US	7th MLS NEXT Pro (17/394/6g); SF Playoffs (2/75)	6
2023	Toronto FC II	CAN-3.US	23rd MLS NEXT Pro (23/1033/6g)	6

WATERMAN, JOEL — CF MONTRÉAL
Centre back. Born 1996, Surrey, BC, CAN. Grew up Aldergrove, BC, CAN. Height 185 cm. Dominant right foot. Youth clubs: Aldergrove YSA, Langley United SA, Surrey United SC, Kitsap Pumas, TSS Rovers
School: Trinity Western University
Honours: Canadian Championship (2021), USL PDL Championship (2018)

CANADA INTERNATIONAL
1 FIFA World Cup: Group phase at Qatar 2022
1st #CANMNT: 2022-11-11 at Isa Town, BHR (v. BHR)

SEASON	CLUB	NATION	HIGHLIGHTS (MP/MIN/G)	G
2012	Surrey United U-16	CAN	1st U-16 Cup	
2013	British Columbia U-18	CAN	Silver at Canada Games (5/110)	
2014	Surrey United SC U-18	CAN	1st U-18 Cup	
2016	Kitsap Pumas	4.USA	USL PDL (11/?); R4 US Cup (2/156)	
2017	TSS Rovers FC	CAN-4.US	USL PDL (11/938)	
2018	Calgary Foothills SC	CAN-4.US	USL PDL (14/1109); 1st Playoffs (3/42)	
2019	Cavalry FC	1.CAN	2nd CPL (22/1720/1g); SF CanChamp (3/181)	1
2020	Impact de Montréal	Concacaf	QF Champions League (3/208)	
	Impact de Montréal	1.CAN	18th MLS (7/549); L16 MLS is Back (0/0)	
2021	CF Montréal	1.CAN	18th MLS (22/1854); 1st CanChamp (3/270)	
2022	CF Montréal	1.CAN	3rd MLS (30/2673/3g); QF Playoffs (2/161); SF CanChamp (1/90)	3
	CF Montréal	Concacaf	QF Champions League (3/244)	
2023	CF Montréal	1.CAN	20th MLS (28/2375/1g); 2nd CanChamp (3/270); Leagues (2/180)	1

WATHUTA, SYDNEY
Forward. Born 2004, Vancouver, BC, CAN. Height 190. Dominant right foot. Youth clubs: Vancouver Whitecaps FC Academy
Honours: League1 BC (2023)

SEASON	CLUB	NATION	HIGHLIGHTS (MP/MIN)	
2022	Vanc. Whitecaps FC Academy	3.CAN	3rd League1 BC	
2023	Vanc. Whitecaps FC 2	CAN-3.US	21st MLS NEXT Pro (2/66)	
	Vanc. Whitecaps FC Academy	3.CAN	3rd League1 BC (10/652/2g); 1st Playoffs (2/180/2g)	4

WATSON, JALEN — TORONTO FC II
Fullback. Born 2000, Mississauga, ON, CAN. Grew up in Mississauga, ON, CAN. Height 183. Youth clubs: Brampton East SC, Erin Mills SC, Vancouver Whitecaps FC Academy. School: Penn State University

SEASON	CLUB	NATION	HIGHLIGHTS (MP/MIN)
2023	Pacific FC	1.CAN	4th CPL (0/0)
	Toronto FC II	CAN-3.US	23rd MLS NEXT Pro (2/64)

WHITE, ANTHONY — VANCOUVER FC
Centre back. Born 2003, Port Moody, BC, CAN. Height 188 cm. Dominant left foot. Youth clubs: Port Moody SC, Coquitlam Metro-Ford SC
School: University of Toronto

SEASON	CLUB	NATION	HIGHLIGHTS (MP/MIN)
2022	TSS Rovers FC	3.CAN	2nd League1 BC; 1st Playoffs
2023	Vancouver FC	1.CAN	7th CPL (20/1500); CanChamp (0/0)

WHITE, ERIC
Right back. Born 2003, New Westminster, BC, CAN. Grew up Coquitlam, BC, CAN. Height 186 cm. Dominant right foot. Youth clubs: Coquitlam Metro-Ford SC, Vancouver Whitecaps FC Academy

SEASON	CLUB	NATION	HIGHLIGHTS (MP/MIN)
2022	Vanc. Whitecaps FC 2	CAN-3.US	14th MLS NEXT Pro (10/546)
2023	Vanc. Whitecaps FC Academy	3.CAN	5th League1 BC (12/701)

WILLIAMS, MICHAEL
Goalkeeper. Born 2006.

SEASON	CLUB	NATION	HIGHLIGHTS (MP/MIN)
2023	York United FC	1.CAN	5th CPL (0/0)

WILSON, ARMAAN — HFX WANDERERS FC
Midfielder. Born 2002, Kleinburg, ON, CAN. Grew up in Toronto, ON, CAN. Height 191. Youth clubs: Vaughan SC, Woodbridge SC
School: Providence College

SEASON	CLUB	NATION	HIGHLIGHTS (MP/MIN)
2015	Epic FC Toronto U-14	CAN	1st U-14 Cup
2019	Woodbridge SC U-17	CAN	2nd U-17 Cup
2022	Woodbridge Strikers SC	CAN	11th League1 Ontario (7/567)
2023	Halifax Wanderers FC	1.CAN	3rd CPL (11/336/1g); 4th Playoffs (0/0)

WOTHERSPOON, DAVID — SCO / DUNDEE UNITED FC
Midfielder. Born 1990, Perth, SCO. Grew up Bridge of Earn, SCO. Height 172 cm. Dominant right foot. Youth clubs: Abernethy Cubs, Bridge of Earn Boys, St. Johnstone Academy, Glasgow Celtic, Hibernian FC
Honours: Concacaf champion (2021-22), Scottish Cup (2014, 2021), Scottish Lg.Cup (2021)

CANADA INTERNATIONAL
1 FIFA World Cup: Group phase at Qatar 2022
1 Concacaf medal: Silver at CNL 2022-23
1st #CANMNT: 2018-03-24 at San Pedro del Pinatar, ESP (v. NZL)

SEASON	CLUB	NATION	HIGHLIGHTS (MP/MIN/G)	G
2009-10	Hibernian FC	1.SCO	4th Premier (33/2725/1g); QF Cup (4/354); L16 Lg.Cup (2/180)	1
2010-11	Hibernian FC	1.SCO	10th Premier (26/2219/2g); R4 Cup (2/38); L16 Lg.Cup (1/10)	2
2011-12	Hibernian FC	1.SCO	11th Premier (30/1858); 2nd Cup (4/218/1g); QF Lg.Cup (3/300)	1
2012-13	Hibernian FC	1.SCO	7th Premier (34/2293/4g); 2nd Cup (3/251); R2 Lg.Cup (1/45)	4
2013-14	St. Johnstone FC	1.SCO	6th Premiership (38/2875/1g); 1st Cup (5/348); SF Lg.Cup (3/180)	1
2014-15	St. Johnstone FC	1.SCO	4th Premiership (35/2730); L16 Cup (2/109); QF Lg.Cup (1/14)	
2015-16	St. Johnstone FC	1.SCO	4th Premiership (35/2830/9g); R4 Cup (1/90); SF Lg.Cup (3/171)	9
2016-17	St. Johnstone FC	1.SCO	4th Premiership (32/1893/1g); L16 Cup (2/135); QF Lg.Cup (3/210/1g)	2
2017-18	St. Johnstone FC	1.SCO	8th Premiership (35/2364/3g); L16 Cup (2/97); L16 Lg.Cup (1/90)	3
2018-19	St. Johnstone FC	1.SCO	7th Premiership (29/1841/2g); L16 Cup (2/180); QF Lg.Cup (4/352)	2
2019-20	St. Johnstone FC	1.SCO	6th Premiership (21/1290/3g); QF Cup (3/255); Lg.Cup (1/45)	3
2020-21	St. Johnstone FC	1.SCO	5th Premiership (37/2499/3g); 1st Cup (5/408); 1st Lg.Cup (7/602/3g)	6
2021-22	St. Johnstone FC	1.SCO	11th Premiership (10/779); R4 SFA Cup (0/0); SF Lg.Cup (2/142)	
2022-23	St. Johnstone FC	1.SCO	9th Premiership (22/720); R4 SFA Cup (1/6); Lg.Cup (0/0)	
2023-24	Inverness Caledonian Thistle	2.SCO	x- Championship (10/795/4g); R3 SFA Cup (1/19/1g)	5
	Dundee United FC	2.SCO	Championship (current season)	

CONTINENTAL FOOTBALL		COMPETITION	HIGHLIGHTS (MP/MIN)
2010-11	Hibernian FC	UEFA	UEFA Europa League (2/97)

FOOTBALLERS

SEASON	CLUB	NATION	HIGHLIGHTS (MP/MIN/G)	G
2013-14	St. Johnstone FC	UEFA	UEFA Europa League (4/361)	
2014-15	St. Johnstone FC	UEFA	UEFA Europa League (4/371)	
2015-16	St. Johnstone FC	UEFA	UEFA Europa League (1/90)	
2017-18	St. Johnstone FC	UEFA	UEFA Europa League (2/78)	
2021-22	St. Johnstone FC	UEFA	UEFA Qualifying Europa Conference League (1/1)	
	St. Johnstone FC	UEFA	UEFA Qualifying Europa League (1/90)	

WRIGHT, BRIAN — YORK UNITED FC
Forward. Born 1995, Ajax, ON, CAN. Height 183 cm. Dominant right foot. Youth clubs: Ajax SC
School: University of Vermont
Honours: CPL Regular Season (2022)

SEASON	CLUB	NATION	HIGHLIGHTS (MP/MIN/G)	G
2016	Burlingame Dragons	4.USA	USL PDL (7/317/2g)	2
2017	New England Revolution	1.USA	15th MLS (2/45); QF US Cup (3/186)	
	Tulsa Roughnecks	2.USA	W7th USL (3/186)	
2018	New England Revolution	1.USA	16th MLS (10/258/1g); R4 US Cup (1/90)	1
2019	New England Revolution	1.USA	14th MLS (2/10)	
	Birmingham Legion FC	2.USA	E10th USL (26/2055/6g); Playoffs (2/180)	6
2020	Birmingham Legion FC	2.USA	E7th USL (16/744/3g); Playoffs (0/0)	3
2021	Atlético Ottawa	1.CAN	8th CPL (23/1164/6g); CanChamp (1/72/1g)	7
2022	Atlético Ottawa	1.CAN	1st CPL (25/1313/7g); 2nd Playoffs (3/120); CanChamp (1/17)	7
2023	York United FC	1.CAN	5th CPL (26/1370/2g); 5th Playoffs (1/1); QF CanChamp (2/55)	2

WRIGHT, LOWELL — VANCOUVER WHITECAPS FC 2
Forward. Born 2003, Brampton, ON, CAN. Height 180 cm. Dominant right foot. Youth clubs: Brampton YSC, Woodbridge SC, Slgma FC, Toronto FC Academy

SEASON	CLUB	NATION	HIGHLIGHTS (MP/MIN/G)	G
2019	Woodbridge Strikers SC	CAN	8th League1 Ontario (3/76/1g); QF Playoffs (1/11)	1
2020	York9 FC	1.CAN	5th CPL (4/131/1g)	1
2021	York United FC	1.CAN	4th CPL (26/1309/6g); SF Playoffs (1/26); QF CanChamp (2/115)	6
2022	York United FC	1.CAN	6th CPL (9/580); SF CanChamp (2/127)	
	Vanc. Whitecaps FC 2	CAN-3.US	14th MLS NEXT Pro (1/22)	
2023	Vanc. Whitecaps FC 2	CAN-3.US	21st MLS NEXT Pro (14/879/4g)	4

YAO, KARIFA
Centre back. Born 2000, Montréal, QC, CAN. Height 193 cm. Dominant right foot. Youth clubs: CS Fabrose Laval, CS Chomedey, CS Étoiles de l'Est, Académie Impact de Montréal
Honours: Canadian Championship (2019, 2023)

SEASON	CLUB	NATION	HIGHLIGHTS (MP/MIN/G)	G
2019	Impact de Montréal	1.CAN	18th MLS (0/0)	
2020	Impact de Montréal	Concacaf	QF Champions League (/0)	
	Impact de Montréal	1.CAN	18th MLS (2/127); L16 MLS is Back (0/0); Playoffs (0/0)	
2021	Cavalry FC	1.CAN	2nd CPL (25/2035); SF Playoffs (1/120/1g); QF CanChamp (2/92)	1
2022	CF Montréal	1.CAN	3rd MLS (0/0)	
	Cavalry FC	1.CAN	3rd CPL (24/2108/1g); SF Playoffs (2/167); QF CanChamp (2/180)	1
2023	Vancouver Whitecaps FC	Concacaf	QF Champions League (2/101); L32 Leagues Cup (1/55)	1
	Vancouver Whitecaps FC	1.CAN	13th MLS (1/1); 1st CanChamp (1/8)	
	Vanc. Whitecaps FC 2	CAN-3.US	21st MLS NEXT Pro (7/630)	

YEATES, STEFFEN — PACIFIC FC
Midfielder. Born 2000, Toronto, ON, CAN. Grew up Vaughan, ON, CAN. Height cm. Youth clubs: Vaughan SC, Toronto FC Academy
School: University of Connecticut, Oregon State University

SEASON	CLUB	NATION	HIGHLIGHTS (MP/MIN/G)	G
2017	TFC Academy	CAN	W3rd League1 Ontario (8/343)	
2018	Toronto FC II	CAN-2.US	E16th USL (4/196)	
	TFC Academy	CAN	4th League1 Ontario (6/343/1g)	1
2022	Toronto FC	1.CAN	27th MLS (2/31)	
	Toronto FC II	CAN-3.US	7th MLS NEXT Pro (22/1599/3g)	3
2023	Pacific FC	1.CAN	4th CPL (28/1625/1g); 3rd Playoffs (1/68); SF CanChamp (3/184)	1

YEO, TENENA ISMAËL CF MONTRÉAL U-23
Born 2005, Abidjan, CIV. Grew up in .., QC, CAN. Youth clubs: FS Salaberry, CS St-Laurent

SEASON	CLUB	NATION	HIGHLIGHTS (MP/MIN)
2022	CS Saint-Laurent U-17	CAN	1st U-17 Cup
	CS St-Laurent	CAN	2nd PLSQ (0/0
2023	CF Montréal U-23	CAN	5th Ligue1 Québec

YESLI, RAYANE VALOUR FC
Goalkeeper. Born 1999, Tizi-Ouzou, ALG. Grew up Montréal, QC, CAN. Height 200 cm. Dominant right foot. Youth clubs: CS Dollard, CS Notre-Dame-de-Grâce, CS Pannelinios Montréal, Académie de l'Impact de Montréal, US Vibonese (Italy). School: Université de Montréal

SEASON	CLUB	NATION	HIGHLIGHTS (MP/MIN)
2019	CS Fabrose	CAN	4th PLSQ (8/720)
2020	CS Fabrose	CAN	6th PLSQ (6/540)
2021	AS Blainville	CAN	CanChamp (1/90)
	AS Blainville	CAN	2nd PLSQ (4/360)
2022	Valour FC	1.CAN	5th CPL (9/810); CanChamp (1/90)
2023	Valour FC	1.CAN	8th CPL (26/2340); CanChamp (1/90)

YOUNG, SEAN PACIFIC FC
Midfielder. Born 2001, Victoria, BC, CAN. Height 186 cm. Youth clubs: Bays United SC, Vancouver Island Wave
Honours: CPL Championship (2021)

SEASON	CLUB	NATION	HIGHLIGHTS (MP/MIN/G)	G
2019	Victoria Highlanders FC	CAN-4.US	USL League Two (12/1029/1g)	1
2020	Pacific FC	1.CAN	3rd CPL (9/460)	
2021	Pacific FC	1.CAN	3rd CPL (24/1053/1g); 1st Playoffs (2/51); SF CanChamp (2/12)	1
2022	Pacific FC	Concacaf	L16 Concacaf League (4/168)	
	Pacific FC	1.CAN	4th CPL (23/1459/1g); SF Playoffs (2/89)	1
2023	Pacific FC	1.CAN	4th CPL (26/1905/4g); 3rd Playoffs (3/270); SF CanChamp (3/257)	4

ZAJAC, MARCEL VAUGHAN SC
Midfielder. Born 1998, Toronto, ON, CAN. Grew up Mississauga, ON, CAN. Height 182 cm. Dominant right foot. Youth clubs: Erin Mills SC, Sigma FC
School: University of Akron
Honours: CPL Championship (2019, 2020)

SEASON	CLUB	NATION	HIGHLIGHTS (MP/MIN/G)	G
2015	Sigma FC	CAN	4th League1 Ontario (?/12g)	12
2016	Sigma FC	CAN	W2nd League1 Ontario (13/956/5g)	5
2017	Sigma FC	CAN	W2nd League1 Ontario (6/425/3g)	3
2018	Sigma FC	CAN	2nd League1 Ontario (8/498/7g)	7
2019	Forge FC Hamilton	Concacaf	L16 Concacaf League (3/74)	
	Forge FC Hamilton	1.CAN	1st CPL (22/1074/1g); CanChamp (1/28)	1
2020	Forge FC Hamilton	Concacaf	QF Concacaf League (0/0)	
	Forge FC Hamilton	1.CAN	1st CPL (4/232)	
2021-22	Olimpia Elbląg	3.POL	9th 2.liga (2/22)	
2022	Guelph United FC	CAN	7th League1 Ontario (15/1120/6g); CanChamp (1/90)	6
2023	Vaughan Azzurri	CAN	3rd League1 Ontario (6/284/3g)	

ZANATTA, DARIO
Forward. Born 1997, Victoria, BC, CAN. Height 175 cm. Youth clubs: Victoria Gorge SA, Victoria Capitals, Vancouver Whitecaps FC Residency, Heart of Midlothian FC (Scotland)

SEASON	CLUB	NATION	HIGHLIGHTS (MP/MIN/G)	G
2011	Victoria Capitals U-14	CAN	5th U-14 Cup	
2015-16	Heart of Midlothian FC	1.SCO	3rd Premiership (13/341); L16 SFA Cup (1/6); QF Lg.Cup (0/0)	
2016-17	Heart of Midlothian FC	UEFA	UEFA Qualifying Europa League (0/0)	
	Heart of Midlothian FC	1.SCO	5th Premiership (1/13); R4 SFA Cup (2/25); L16 Lg.Cup (0/0)	
	Queen's Park FC	3.SCO	6th League One (9/770/4g)	4
2017-18	Heart of Midlothian FC	1.SCO	6th Premiership (1/6/1g); Lg.Cup (0/0)	1
	Raith Rovers FC	3.SCO	2nd League One (25/1571/7g); SF Playoffs (1/30)	7
2018-19	Alloa Athletic	2.SCO	8th Championship (34/2863/6g); 4R SFA Cup (2/158/1g)	7

2019-20	Heart of Midlothian FC	1.SCO	x- Lg.Cup (3/193)	
	Partick Thistle FC	2.SCO	10th Championship (23/1302/3g); R4 SFA Cup (2/105)	3
2020-21	Ayr United FC	2.SCO	8th Championship (13/391); R3 SFA Cup (0/0); L16 Lg.Cup (5/271/1g)	1
2021-22	Raith Rovers FC	2.SCO	5th Championship (31/2058/8g); L16 SFA Cup (3/180); QF Lg.Cup (6/465/2g)	10
2022-23	Raith Rovers FC	2.SCO	x- Championship (2/36); Lg.Cup (3/219)	
	Hamilton Academical FC	2.SCO	9th Championship (27/1205/1g); 2nd Playoffs (4/214/2g); L16 SFA Cup (3/119)	3
2023-24	Hamilton Academical FC	3.SCO	x- League One (9/327/1g)	1

ZATOR, DOMINICK — POL / KORONA KIELCE

Right back and centre back. Born 1994, Calgary, AB, CAN. Height 189 cm. Dominant right foot. Youth clubs: Calgary Cal-Glen SC, Calgary Foothills SC. School: University of Calgary

Honours: USL PDL Championship (2018)

1 Concacaf medal: Silver at CNL 2022-23

SEASON	CLUB	NATION	HIGHLIGHTS (MP/MIN/G)	G
2015	Calgary Foothills SC	CAN-4.US	USL PDL	
2016	Calgary Foothills SC	CAN-4.US	USL PDL (12/993/1g); 2nd PDL Playoffs (5/480/1g)	2
2017	Vanc. Whitecaps FC 2	CAN-2.US	W14th USL (8/685)	
2018	Calgary Foothills SC	CAN-4.US	USL PDL (11/912); 1st PDL Playoffs (4/390/1g)	1
2019	Cavalry FC	1.CAN	2nd CPL (29/2425/1g); SF CanChamp (8/720/2g)	1
2020	Cavalry FC	1.CAN	4th CPL (10/900/1g)	1
2021	Vasalunds IF	2.SWE	15th Superettan (5/242)	
	York United FC	1.CAN	4th CPL (24/2046/1g); SF Playoffs (1/90); QF CanChamp (2/180)	1
2022	York United FC	1.CAN	6th CPL (28/2506/1g); SF CanChamp (3/270)	1
2022-23	Korona Kielce	1.POL	13th Ekstraklasa (17/1510/1g)	1
2023-24	Korona Kielce	1.POL	Ekstraklasa (current season); Puchar (current)	

ZEBIE, BRUNO

Midfielder. Born 1995, Paris, FRA. Grew up Edmonton, AB, CAN. Height 165 cm. Youth clubs: CS St-Hubert, Edmonton Juventus, FC Edmonton Academy

School: University of AlbertaŽ

Honours: USL PDL Championship (2018), U-Sports Championship (2016)

SEASON	CLUB	NATION	HIGHLIGHTS (MP/MIN/G)	G
2009	Edmonton Juventus	CAN	1st U-14 Cup	
	Alberta U-14	CAN	4th Canada Soccer All Stars U-14	
2010	Edmonton Juventus U-16	CAN	4th U-16 Cup	
2011	Edmonton Juventus U-16	CAN	7th U-16 Cup	
	Alberta U-16	CAN	4th Canada Soccer All Stars U-16	
2015	FC Edmonton	2.USA	7th NASL (1/14)	
	Edmonton Green & Gold	CAN	4th CS National Championships (5/404)	
2016	FC Edmonton	2.USA	3rd NASL (1/90)	
2017	Calgary Foothills SC	CAN-4.US	USL PDL (14/1237/1g)	1
2018	Calgary Foothills SC	CAN-4.US	USL PDL (12/897/1g); 1st PDL Playoffs (4/376)	1
2019	FC Edmonton	1.CAN	4th CPL (23/1767/1g); CanChamp (2/180)	1
2020	Cavalry FC	1.CAN	4th CPL (10/477)	
2022	Edmonton Green & Gold	CAN	2nd CS National Championships	

ZOUHIR, RIDA — CF MONTRÉAL

Midfielder. Born 2003, Montréal, QC, CAN. Height 180 cm. Dominant right foot. Youth clubs: CS Braves d'Ahuntsic, Académie Impact de Montréal

Honours: Canadian Championship (2021)

SEASON	CLUB	NATION	HIGHLIGHTS (MP/MIN/G)	G
2020	Impact de Montréal	Concacaf	QF Champions League (0/0)	
2021	CF Montréal	1.CAN	18th MLS (2/16); 1st CanChamp (2/91)	
2022	CF Montréal	Concacaf	QF Champions League (2/84)	
	CF Montréal	1.CAN	3rd MLS (5/117); SF CanChamp (1/28)	
	CF Montréal U-23	CAN	6th PLSQ (2/135/2g)	2
2023	CF Montréal	1.CAN	x- MLS (5/218); 2nd CanChamp (1/90)	
	San Antonio FC	2.USA	W4th USL (25/1755/8g)	8

2024 CANADIAN SOCCER MATCH CALENDAR

FEBRUARY 2024

SEASON	DATE	LOCAL KO	CITY	HOME TEAM		AWAY TEAM	VENUE
CCC	2024-02-07	20.00	Hamilton, ON	Forge FC Hamilton	1-3	CD Guadalajara	Tim Hortons (11,513)
CCC	2024-02-07	19.00	Langford, BC	Vancouver Whitecaps FC	1-1	Tigres UANL	Starlight (5,763)
CCC	2024-02-13	21.00	Guadalajara, JA	CD Guadalajara	2-1	Forge FC Hamilton	Akron (25,059)
CCC	2024-02-14	20.00	Monterrey, NL	Tigres UANL	3-0	Vanc. Whitecaps FC	Universitario (24,988)
CCC	2024-02-21	19.00	Langford, BC	Cavalry FC	0-3	Orlando City SC	Starlight (2,484)
MLS	2024-02-24	19.30	Orlando, FL	Orlando City SC	0-0	CF Montréal	Exploria (24,249)
MLS	2024-02-25	14.30	Cincinnati, OH	FC Cincinnati	0-0	Toronto FC	TQL (25,513)
CCC	2024-02-27	18.00	Orlando, FL	Orlando City SC	3-1	Cavalry FC	Exploria (5,141)

MARCH 2024

SEASON	DATE	LOCAL KO	CITY	HOME TEAM		AWAY TEAM	VENUE
MLS	2024-03-02	16.30	Vancouver, BC	Vancouver Whitecaps FC	1-1	Charlotte FC	BC Place (29,624)
MLS	2024-03-02	19.30	Frisco, TX	FC Dallas	1-2	CF Montréal	Toyota (19,096)
MLS	2024-03-03	14.00	Foxborough, MA	New England Revolution	0-1	Toronto FC	Gillette (29,293)

Concacaf Champions Cup Round of 16 (1st Leg) from 5 to 7 March 2024

MLS	2024-03-09	14.00	Toronto, ON	Toronto FC	1-0	Charlotte FC	BMO Field (26,345)
MLS	2024-03-09	19.30	San Jose, CA	San Jose Earthquakes	0-2	Vancouver Whitecaps FC	PayPal (16,045)
MLS	2024-03-10	17.00	Fort Lauderdale, FL	Inter Miami CF	2-3	CF Montréal	DRV PNK (21,212)

Concacaf Champions Cup Round of 16 (2nd Leg) from 12 to 14 March 2024

MLS	2024-03-16	14.00	Chicago, IL	Chicago Fire FC	4-3	CF Montréal	Soldier (14,874)
MLS	2024-03-16	19.30	Frisco, TX	FC Dallas	1-3	Vancouver Whitecaps FC	Toyota (19,096)
MLS	2024-03-16	19.30	New York, NY	New York City FC	2-1	Toronto FC	Yankee (18,623)

MEN'S INTERNATIONAL MATCH CALENDAR from 18 to 26 March 2024 (inc. Copa América Play-In Series)

MLS	2024-03-23	16.30	Vancouver, BC	Vancouver Whitecaps FC	1-2	Real Salt Lake	BC Place (22,178)
MLS	2024-03-23	19.30	Toronto, ON	Toronto FC	2-0	Atlanta United FC	BMO Field (25,768)
MLS	2024-03-30	19.30	Washington, DC	D.C. United	1-0	CF Montréal	Audi (18,402)
MLS	2024-03-30	19.30	Toronto, ON	Toronto FC	1-3	Kansas City	BMO Field (24,382)
MLS	2024-03-30	19.30	Vancouver, BC	Vancouver Whitecaps FC	3-2	Portland Timbers FC	BC Place (24,693)

APRIL 2024

SEASON	DATE	LOCAL KO	CITY	HOME TEAM	AWAY TEAM	VENUE
Concacaf Champions Cup Quarterfinals (1st Leg) from 2 to 4 April 2024						
MLS	2024-04-06	16.30	Vancouver, BC	Vancouver Whitecaps FC	Toronto FC	BC Place
MLS	2024-04-06	19.30	Seattle, WA	Seattle Sounders FC	CF Montréal	Lumen

Concacaf Champions Cup Quarterfinals (2nd Leg) from 9 to 11 April 2024

CPL	2024-04-13	13.00	Ottawa, ON	Atlético Ottawa	York United FC	TD Place
CPL	2024-04-13	16.00	Hamilton, ON	Forge FC Hamilton	Cavalry FC	Tim Hortons
CPL	2024-04-13	16.00	Langford, BC	Pacific FC	Halifax Wanderers FC	Starlight
MLS	2024-04-13	19.30	Montréal, QC	CF Montréal	FC Cincinnati	Saputo

2024 CANADA

Season	Date	Local KO	City	Home Team	Away Team	Venue
MLS	2024-04-13	19.30	Charlotte, NC	Charlotte FC	Toronto FC	Bank of America
MLS	2024-04-13	19.30	Vancouver, BC	Vancouver Whitecaps FC	Los Angeles Galaxy	BC Place
CPL	2024-04-14	14.00	Langley, BC	Vancouver FC	Winnipeg Valour FC	Willoughby
CPL	2024-04-18	19.00	Langley, BC	Vancouver FC	Halifax Wanderers FC	Willoughby
CPL	2024-04-19	19.00	Langford, BC	Pacific FC	Winnipeg Valour FC	Starlight
CPL	2024-04-20	14.00	Ottawa, ON	Atlético Ottawa	Cavalry FC	TD Place
MLS	2024-04-20	19.30	Montréal, QC	CF Montréal	Orlando City SC	Saputo
MLS	2024-04-20	19.30	Seattle, WA	Seattle Sounders FC	Vancouver Whitecaps FC	Lumen
MLS	2024-04-20	19.30	Toronto, ON	Toronto FC	New England Revolution	BMO Field
CPL	2024-04-21	16.00	Toronto, ON	York United FC	Forge FC Hamilton	York Lions

Concacaf Champions Cup Semifinals (1st Leg) from 23 to 25 April 2024
Canadian Championship Preliminary Round from 23 April to 2 May 2024

Season	Date	Local KO	City	Home Team	Away Team	Venue
CanChamp	04-23	19.00	Calgary, AB	Cavalry FC	Vancouver FC	ATCO
CanChamp	04-24	19.30	Toronto, ON	Toronto FC	Simcoe County Rovers FC	BMO Field
CPL	2024-04-26	19.00	Toronto, ON	York United FC	Vancouver FC	York Lions
CPL	2024-04-27	14.00	Halifax, NS	Halifax Wanderers FC	Atlético Ottawa	Wanderers
CPL	2024-04-27	16.00	Hamilton, ON	Forge FC Hamilton	Winnipeg Valour FC	Tim Hortons
MLS	2024-04-27	19.30	Columbus, OH	Columbus Crew SC	CF Montréal	Lower.com
MLS	2024-04-27	19.30	Harrison, NJ	New York Red Bulls	Vancouver Whitecaps FC	Red Bull Arena
MLS	2024-04-27	19.30	Orlando, FL	Orlando City SC	Toronto FC	Exploria
CPL	2024-04-28	15.00	Calgary, AB	Cavalry FC	Pacific FC	ATCO

MAY 2024

SEASON	DATE	LOCAL KO	CITY	HOME TEAM	AWAY TEAM	VENUE

Concacaf Champions Cup Semifinals (2nd Leg) from 30 April to 2 May 2024
Canadian Championship Preliminary Round from 23 April to 2 May 2024

Season	Date	Local KO	City	Home Team	Away Team	Venue
CanChamp	05-01	19.00	Ottawa, ON	Atlético Ottawa	Winnipeg Valour FC	TD Place
CanChamp	05-01	19.00	Langford, BC	Pacific FC	Victoria Highlanders FC	Starlight
CanChamp	05-01	19.00	Hamilton, ON	Forge FC Hamilton	York United FC	Tim Hortons
CanChamp	05-02	19.00	Halifax, NS	Halifax Wanderers FC	CS St-Laurent	Wanderers
CPL	2024-05-03	19.00	Calgary, AB	Cavalry FC	Vancouver FC	ATCO
CPL	2024-05-04	16.00	Langford, BC	Pacific FC	York United FC	Starlight
MLS	2024-05-04	19.30	Nashville, TN	Nashville SC	CF Montréal	GEODIS
MLS	2024-05-04	19.30	Toronto, ON	Toronto FC	FC Dallas	BMO Field
MLS	2024-05-04	19.30	Vancouver, BC	Vancouver Whitecaps FC	Austin FC	BC Place
CPL	2024-05-05	14.00	Ottawa, ON	Atlético Ottawa	Winnipeg Valour FC	TD Place
CPL	2024-05-07	11.00	Hamilton, ON	Forge FC Hamilton	Halifax Wanderers FC	Tim Hortons
CPL	2024-05-10	19.00	Toronto, ON	York United FC	Winnipeg Valour FC	York Lions
CPL	2024-05-11	15.00	Halifax, NS	Halifax Wanderers FC	Cavalry FC	Wanderers
CPL	2024-05-11	14.00	Langford, BC	Pacific FC	Forge FC Hamilton	Starlight
MLS	2024-05-11	19.30	Montréal, QC	CF Montréal	Inter Miami CF	Saputo
MLS	2024-05-11	19.30	Los Angeles, CA	Los Angeles FC	Vancouver Whitecaps FC	BMO Field
MLS	2024-05-11	19.30	Toronto, ON	Toronto FC	New York City FC	BMO Field
CPL	2024-05-12	14.00	Langley, BC	Vancouver FC	Atlético Ottawa	Willoughby
MLS	2024-05-15	19.30	Montréal, QC	CF Montréal	Columbus Crew SC	Saputo
MLS	2024-05-15	19.30	Commerce City, CO	Colorado Rapids	Vancouver Whitecaps FC	Dick's
MLS	2024-05-15	19.30	Nashville, TN	Nashville SC	Toronto FC	GEODIS
CPL	2024-05-17	19.00	Langford, BC	Pacific FC	Atlético Ottawa	Starlight
CPL	2024-05-18	16.00	Hamilton, ON	Forge FC Hamilton	Vancouver FC	Tim Hortons
CPL	2024-05-18	17.00	Calgary, AB	Cavalry FC	York United FC	ATCO
MLS	2024-05-18	19.30	Seattle, WA	Seattle Sounders FC	Vancouver Whitecaps FC	Lumen
MLS	2024-05-18	19.30	Toronto, ON	Toronto FC	CF Montréal	BMO Field

Season	Date	Local KO	City	Home Team	Away Team	Venue
CPL	2024-05-20	16.00	Halifax, NS	Halifax Wanderers FC	Winnipeg Valour FC	Wanderers
CPL	2024-05-24	19.00	Toronto, ON	York United FC	Halifax Wanderers FC	York Lions
CPL	2024-05-25	15.00	Ottawa, ON	Atlético Ottawa	Forge FC Hamilton	TD Place
CPL	2024-05-25	13.00	Langley, BC	Vancouver FC	Pacific FC	Willoughby
MLS	2024-05-25	19.30	Montréal, QC	CF Montréal	Nashville SC	Saputo
MLS	2024-05-25	19.30	Toronto, ON	Toronto FC	FC Cincinnati	BMO Field
MLS	2024-05-25	19.30	Vancouver, BC	Vancouver Whitecaps FC	Inter Miami CF	BC Place
CPL	2024-05-26	15.00	Calgary, AB	Cavalry FC	Winnipeg Valour FC	ATCO
MLS	2024-05-29	19.30	Montréal, QC	CF Montréal	D.C. United	Saputo
MLS	2024-05-29	19.30	Kansas City, KS	Kansas City	Vancouver Whitecaps FC	Children's Mercy
MLS	2024-05-29	19.30	Chester, PA	Philadelphia Union	Toronto FC	Subaru

JUNE 2024

SEASON	DATE	LOCAL KO	CITY	HOME TEAM	AWAY TEAM	VENUE
CPL	2024-06-01	16.00	Hamilton, ON	Forge FC Hamilton	York United FC	Tim Hortons
CPL	2024-06-01	16.00	Langford, BC	Pacific FC	Cavalry FC	Starlight
MLS	2024-06-01	19.30	Washington, DC	D.C. United	Toronto FC	Audi
MLS	2024-06-01	19.30	Chester, PA	Philadelphia Union	CF Montréal	Subaru
MLS	2024-06-01	19.30	Vancouver, BC	Vancouver Whitecaps FC	Colorado Rapids	BC Place
CPL	2024-06-02	14.00	Ottawa, ON	Atlético Ottawa	Halifax Wanderers FC	TD Place
CPL	2024-06-02	16.00	Winnipeg, MB	Winnipeg Valour FC	Vancouver FC	IG Field

Concacaf Champions Cup Final on Sunday 2 June 2024

MEN'S INTERNATIONAL MATCH CALENDAR 2024 from 3 to 11 JUNE

CPL	2024-06-08	15.00	Halifax, NS	Halifax Wanderers FC	Pacific FC	Wanderers
CPL	2024-06-08	15.00	Calgary, AB	Cavalry FC	Forge FC Hamilton	ATCO
CPL	2024-06-09	14.00	Winnipeg, MB	Winnipeg Valour FC	Atlético Ottawa	IG Field
CPL	2024-06-09	18.00	Toronto, ON	York United FC	Vancouver FC	York Lions
CPL	2024-06-14	19.00	Winnipeg, MB	Winnipeg Valour FC	Pacific FC	IG Field
CPL	2024-06-15	13.00	Ottawa, ON	Atlético Ottawa	York United FC	TD Place
CPL	2024-06-15	17.00	Halifax, NS	Halifax Wanderers FC	Forge FC Hamilton	Wanderers
MLS	2024-06-15	19.30	Montréal, QC	CF Montréal	Real Salt Lake	Saputo
MLS	2024-06-15	19.30	Foxborough, MA	New England Revolution	Vancouver Whitecaps FC	Gillette
MLS	2024-06-15	19.30	Toronto, ON	Toronto FC	Chicago Fire FC	BMO Field
CPL	2024-06-16	14.00	Langley, BC	Vancouver FC	Cavalry FC	Willoughby

MEN'S INTERNATIONAL MATCH CALENDAR : 2024 CONMEBOL COPA AMÉRICA from 20 JUNE to 14 JULY

CPL	2024-06-19	19.00	Toronto, ON	York United FC	Pacific FC	York Lions
MLS	2024-06-19	19.30	Montréal, QC	CF Montréal	New York Red Bulls	Saputo
MLS	2024-06-19	19.30	Toronto, ON	Toronto FC	Nashville SC	BMO Field
CPL	2024-06-21	19.00	Calgary, AB	Cavalry FC	Atlético Ottawa	ATCO
MLS	2024-06-22	19.30	Commerce City, CO	Colorado Rapids	CF Montréal	Dick's
MLS	2024-06-22	19.30	Harrison, NJ	New York Red Bulls	Toronto FC	Red Bull
MLS	2024-06-22	19.30	Portland, OR	Portland Timbers FC	Vancouver Whitecaps FC	Providence
CPL	2024-06-23	16.00	Hamilton, ON	Forge FC Hamilton	Winnipeg Valour FC	Tim Hortons
CPL	2024-06-23	14.00	Langley, BC	Vancouver FC	Halifax Wanderers FC	Willoughby
CPL	2024-06-27	18.30	Winnipeg, MB	Winnipeg Valour FC	York United FC	IG Field
CPL	2024-06-27	19.30	Langford, BC	Pacific FC	Vancouver FC	Starlight
CPL	2024-06-28	19.00	Ottawa, ON	Atlético Ottawa	Forge FC Hamilton	TD Place
MLS	2024-06-29	19.30	Atlanta, GA	Atlanta United FC	Toronto FC	Mercedes-Benz
MLS	2024-06-29	19.30	Montréal, QC	CF Montréal	Philadelphia Union	Saputo
MLS	2024-06-29	19.30	Vancouver, BC	Vancouver Whitecaps FC	St. Louis CITY FC	BC Place

2024 CANADA

JULY 2024

SEASON	DATE	LOCAL KO	CITY	HOME TEAM	AWAY TEAM	VENUE
CPL	2024-07-01	16.00	Halifax, NS	Halifax Wanderers FC	Cavalry FC	Wanderers
MLS	2024-07-03	19.30	St. Paul, MN	Minnesota United FC	Vancouver Whitecaps FC	Allianz
MLS	2024-07-03	19.30	New York, NY	New York City FC	CF Montréal	Citi
MLS	2024-07-03	19.30	Toronto, ON	Toronto FC	Orlando City SC	BMO Field
CPL	2024-07-05	19.00	Hamilton, ON	Forge FC Hamilton	Vancouver FC	Tim Hortons
CPL	2024-07-06	16.00	Toronto, ON	York United FC	Halifax Wanderers FC	York Lions
MLS	2024-07-06	19.30	Montréal, QC	CF Montréal	Vancouver Whitecaps FC	Saputo
MLS	2024-07-06	19.30	Columbus, OH	Columbus Crew SC	Toronto FC	Lower.com
CPL	2024-07-07	14.00	Ottawa, ON	Atlético Ottawa	Pacific FC	TD Place
CPL	2024-07-07	16.00	Winnipeg, MB	Winnipeg Valour FC	Cavalry FC	IG Field
CPL	2024-07-11	19.00	Halifax, NS	Halifax Wanderers FC	Pacific FC	Wanderers
CPL	2024-07-12	19.00	Langley, BC	Vancouver FC	Atlético Ottawa	Willoughby
CPL	2024-07-13	14.00	Calgary, AB	Cavalry FC	York United FC	ATCO
MLS	2024-07-13	19.30	Montréal, QC	CF Montréal	Atlanta United FC	Saputo
MLS	2024-07-13	19.30	St. Louis, MO	St. Louis CITY FC	Vancouver Whitecaps FC	CITYPARK
MLS	2024-07-13	19.30	Toronto, ON	Toronto FC	Philadelphia Union	BMO Field
CPL	2024-07-14	19.00	Hamilton, ON	Forge FC Hamilton	Pacific FC	Tim Hortons

CONMEBOL Copa América Final on Sunday 14 July 2024

MLS	2024-07-17	19.30	Fort Lauderdale, FL	Inter Miami CF	Toronto FC	DRV PNK
MLS	2024-07-17	19.30	Harrison, NJ	New York Red Bulls	CF Montréal	Red Bull
MLS	2024-07-17	19.30	Vancouver, BC	Vancouver Whitecaps FC	Kansas City	BC Place
CPL	2024-07-18	19.00	Halifax, NS	Halifax Wanderers FC	Winnipeg Valour FC	Wanderers
CPL	2024-07-20	13.00	Langley, BC	Vancouver FC	York United FC	Willoughby
MLS	2024-07-20	19.30	Montréal, QC	CF Montréal	Toronto FC	Saputo
MLS	2024-07-20	19.30	Vancouver, BC	Vancouver Whitecaps FC	Houston Dynamo FC	BC Place
CPL	2024-07-21	14.00	Ottawa, ON	Atlético Ottawa	Winnipeg Valour FC	TD Place
CPL	2024-07-21	15.00	Calgary, AB	Cavalry FC	Forge FC Hamilton	ATCO

MLS All-Star Game on Wednesday 24 July 2024 in Columbus, Ohio

CPL	2024-07-26	19.00	Toronto, ON	York United FC	Atlético Ottawa	York Lions
CPL	2024-07-26	19.00	Langley, BC	Vancouver FC	Cavalry FC	Willoughby
CPL	2024-07-27	19.00	Hamilton, ON	Forge FC Hamilton	Halifax Wanderers FC	Tim Hortons
CPL	2024-07-28	14.00	Langford, BC	Pacific FC	Winnipeg Valour FC	Starlight

Leagues Cup (Group Phase) kicks off on Friday 26 July 2024 (MLS clubs Vancouver, Toronto and Montréal).

LC	2024-07-26	20.00	Orlando, FL	Orlando City SC	CF Montréal	Inter&Co
LC	2024-07-27	20.00	East Rutherford, NJ	New York Red Bulls	Toronto FC	Red Bull Arena
LC	2024-07-30	19.00	Montréal, QC	Atlético de San Luis	CF Montréal	Stade Saputo
LC	2024-07-30	19.30	Los Angeles, CA	Los Angeles FC	Vancouver Whitecaps FC	BMO Stadium

OLYMPIC FOOTBALL TOURNAMENT from 24 JULY to 10 AUGUST 2024

AUGUST 2024

SEASON	DATE	LOCAL KO	CITY	HOME TEAM	AWAY TEAM	VENUE
CPL	2024-08-02	19.00	Langford, BC	Pacific FC	York United FC	Starlight
CPL	2024-08-03	19.00	Ottawa, ON	Atlético Ottawa	Cavalry FC	TD Place
LC	2024-08-03	19.00	Vancouver, BC	Vancouver Whitecaps FC	Club Tijuana Xolos	BC Place
LC	2024-08-04	20.00	Toronto, ON	CF Pachuca	Toronto FC	BMO
CPL	2024-08-04	14.00	Winnipeg, MB	Winnipeg Valour FC	Forge FC Hamilton	IG Field
CPL	2024-08-05	16.00	Halifax, NS	Halifax Wanderers FC	Vancouver FC	Wanderers

Leagues Cup Round of 32 from 7 to 9 August 2024

CPL	2024-08-10	14.00	Calgary, AB	Cavalry FC	Halifax Wanderers FC	ATCO
CPL	2024-08-10	19.00	Hamilton, ON	Forge FC Hamilton	Atlético Ottawa	Tim Hortons

CPL	2024-08-11	14.00	Langley, BC	Vancouver FC	Pacific FC	Willoughby
CPL	2024-08-11	19.00	Winnipeg, MB	Winnipeg Valour FC	York United FC	IG Field

Leagues Cup Round of 16 from 12 to 13 August 2024

Leagues Cup Quarterfinals from 16 to 17 August 2024

CPL	2024-08-16	19.00	Toronto, ON	York United FC	Cavalry FC	York Lions
CPL	2024-08-17	14.00	Winnipeg, MB	Winnipeg Valour FC	Halifax Wanderers FC	IG Field
CPL	2024-08-17	13.00	Langford, BC	Pacific FC	Atlético Ottawa	Starlight
CPL	2024-08-18	14.00	Langley, BC	Vancouver FC	Forge FC Hamilton	Willoughby

Leagues Cup Semifinals from 20 to 21 August 2024

CPL	2024-08-23	19.00	Toronto, ON	York United FC	Forge FC Hamilton	York Lions
CPL	2024-08-24	15.00	Halifax, NS	Halifax Wanderers FC	Atlético Ottawa	Wanderers
CPL	2024-08-24	15.00	Calgary, AB	Cavalry FC	Pacific FC	ATCO
MLS	2024-08-24	16.30	Vancouver, BC	Vancouver Whitecaps FC	Los Angeles FC	BC Place
MLS	2024-08-24	19.30	Montréal, QC	CF Montréal	New England Revolution	Saputo
MLS	2024-08-24	19.30	Houston, TX	Houston Dynamo FC	Toronto FC	Shell Energy
CPL	2024-08-25	14.00	Winnipeg, MB	Winnipeg Valour FC	Vancouver FC	IG Field

Leagues Cup Final on Saturday 25 August 2024

CPL	2024-08-30	19.00	Hamilton, ON	Forge FC Hamilton	Pacific FC	Tim Hortons
CPL	2024-08-30	19.00	Calgary, AB	Cavalry FC	Winnipeg Valour FC	ATCO
CPL	2024-08-31	19.00	Ottawa, ON	Atlético Ottawa	Vancouver FC	TD Place
MLS	2024-08-31	19.30	Austin, TX	Austin FC	Vancouver Whitecaps FC	Q2
MLS	2024-08-31	19.30	Cincinnati, OH	FC Cincinnati	CF Montréal	TQL
MLS	2024-08-31	19.30	Toronto, ON	Toronto FC	D.C. United	BMO Field

SEPTEMBER 2024

MEN'S INTERNATIONAL MATCH CALENDAR 2024 from 2 to 10 SEPTEMBER

SEASON - DATE - LOCAL KO - CITY				HOME TEAM	AWAY TEAM	VENUE
CPL	2024-09-02	16.00	Halifax, NS	Halifax Wanderers FC	York United FC	Wanderers
CPL	2024-09-06	19.00	Langley, BC	Vancouver FC	York United FC	Willoughby
CPL	2024-09-07	19.00	Hamilton, ON	Forge FC Hamilton	Cavalry FC	Tim Hortons
CPL	2024-09-07	19.00	Langford, BC	Pacific FC	Halifax Wanderers FC	Starlight
MLS	2024-09-07	19.30	Vancouver, BC	Vancouver Whitecaps FC	FC Dallas	BC Place
CPL	2024-09-09	19.00	Winnipeg, MB	Winnipeg Valour FC	Atlético Ottawa	IG Field
CPL	2024-09-13	19.00	Toronto, ON	York United FC	Winnipeg Valour FC	York Lions
CPL	2024-09-14	15.00	Halifax, NS	Halifax Wanderers FC	Forge FC Hamilton	Wanderers
CPL	2024-09-14	14.00	Langford, BC	Pacific FC	Vancouver FC	Starlight
MLS	2024-09-14	19.30	Montréal, QC	CF Montréal	Charlotte FC	Saputo
MLS	2024-09-14	19.30	Toronto, ON	Toronto FC	Austin FC	BMO Field
MLS	2024-09-14	19.30	Vancouver, BC	Vancouver Whitecaps FC	San Jose Earthquakes	BC Place
CPL	2024-09-15	15.00	Calgary, AB	Cavalry FC	Atlético Ottawa	ATCO
MLS	2024-09-18	19.30	Houston, TX	Houston Dynamo FC	Vancouver Whitecaps FC	Shell Energy
MLS	2024-09-18	19.30	Foxborough, MA	New England Revolution	CF Montréal	Gillette
MLS	2024-09-18	19.30	Toronto, ON	Toronto FC	Columbus Crew SC	BMO Field
CPL	2024-09-20	19.00	Toronto, ON	York United FC	Cavalry FC	York Lions
CPL	2024-09-21	14.00	Winnipeg, MB	Winnipeg Valour FC	Halifax Wanderers FC	IG Field
CPL	2024-09-21	13.00	Langley, BC	Vancouver FC	Forge FC Hamilton	Willoughby
MLS	2024-09-21	19.30	Montréal, QC	CF Montréal	Chicago Fire FC	Saputo
MLS	2024-09-21	19.30	Commerce City, CO	Colorado Rapids	Toronto FC	Dick's
MLS	2024-09-21	19.30	Carson, CA	Los Angeles Galaxy	Vancouver Whitecaps FC	Dignity Health
CPL	2024-09-22	14.00	Ottawa, ON	Atlético Ottawa	Pacific FC	TD Place

2024 CANADA

CPL	2024-09-28	16.00	Hamilton, ON	Forge FC Hamilton	York United FC	Tim Hortons
CPL	2024-09-28	17.00	Calgary, AB	Cavalry FC	Vancouver FC	ATCO
MLS	2024-09-28	19.30	Montréal, QC	CF Montréal	San Jose Earthquakes	Saputo
MLS	2024-09-28	19.30	Chicago, IL	Chicago Fire FC	Toronto FC	Soldier
MLS	2024-09-28	19.30	Vancouver, BC	Vancouver Whitecaps FC	Portland Timbers FC	BC Place
CPL	2024-09-29	14.00	Ottawa, ON	Atlético Ottawa	Halifax Wanderers FC	TD Place
CPL	2024-09-30	19.00	Winnipeg, MB	Winnipeg Valour FC	Pacific FC	IG Field

OCTOBER 2024

SEASON	DATE	LOCAL KO	CITY	HOME TEAM	AWAY TEAM	VENUE
MLS	2024-10-02	19.30	Atlanta, GA	Atlanta United FC	CF Montréal	Mercedes-Benz
MLS	2024-10-02	19.30	Toronto, ON	Toronto FC	New York Red Bulls	BMO Field
MLS	2024-10-02	19.30	Vancouver, BC	Vancouver Whitecaps FC	Seattle Sounders FC	BC Place
CPL	2024-10-05	15.00	Halifax, NS	Halifax Wanderers FC	Vancouver FC	Wanderers
CPL	2024-10-05	14.00	Langford, BC	Pacific FC	Cavalry FC	Starlight
MLS	2024-10-05	16.30	Vancouver, BC	Vancouver Whitecaps FC	Minnesota United FC	BC Place
MLS	2024-10-05	19.30	Charlotte, NC	Charlotte FC	CF Montréal	Bank of America
MLS	2024-10-05	19.30	Toronto, ON	Toronto FC	Inter Miami CF	BMO Field
CPL	2024-10-06	13.00	Winnipeg, MB	Winnipeg Valour FC	Forge FC Hamilton	IG Field
CPL	2024-10-06	17.00	Toronto, ON	York United FC	Atlético Ottawa	York Lions

MEN'S INTERNATIONAL MATCH CALENDAR 2024 from 7 to 15 OCTOBER

Toyota National Championships from 9 to 14 October

CPL	2024-10-10	19.00	Toronto, ON	York United FC	Pacific FC	York Lions
CPL	2024-10-12	16.00	Hamilton, ON	Forge FC Hamilton	Atlético Ottawa	Tim Hortons
CPL	2024-10-12	17.00	Calgary, AB	Cavalry FC	Halifax Wanderers FC	ATCO
CPL	2024-10-13	14.00	Langley, BC	Vancouver FC	Winnipeg Valour FC	Willoughby
CPL	2024-10-19	TBD	Halifax, NS	Halifax Wanderers FC	York United FC	Wanderers
CPL	2024-10-19	TBD	Ottawa, ON	Atlético Ottawa	Vancouver FC	TD Place
CPL	2024-10-19	TBD	Winnipeg, MB	Winnipeg Valour FC	Cavalry FC	IG Field
CPL	2024-10-19	TBD	Langford, BC	Pacific FC	Forge FC Hamilton	Starlight
MLS	2024-10-19	18.00	Montréal, QC	CF Montréal	New York City FC	Saputo
MLS	2024-10-19	19.00	Sandy, UT	Real Salt Lake	Vancouver Whitecaps FC	America First

CPL Playoffs (dates to be announced)
MLS Playoffs (dates to be announced)

NOVEMBER 2024

MEN'S INTERNATIONAL MATCH CALENDAR 2024 from 11 to 19 NOVEMBER

DECEMBER 2024

MLS Cup Final on Saturday 7 December 2024

PUBLICATIONS BY UP NORTH PRODUCTIONS

Canada from Bronze to Gold

A Canadian soccer guide to the Women's National Team and their story to the top of women's football, from Olympic Bronze at London 2012 and Rio 2016 to Olympic Gold at Tokyo 2020 (2021). Includes year-by-year stories, stats and results from 2010 to 2021, plus player vignettes for all 40 medal winners including Sophie Schmidt, Desiree Scott and Christine Sinclair.

Canadian Soccer's All-Time Top 100 Women's Footballers

The top 100 women's footballers from more than 40 years of Canadian soccer. Profiles and statistics from their international careers including FIFA World Cups and the Olympic Games. Also features Canada's ultimate FIFA World Cup squad and 28 future FIFA World Cup hopefuls. The world's all-time international goalscoring record holder Christine Sinclair is featured on the cover.

This Day In Canadian Soccer History

A day-by-day history to Canadian Soccer in club football. "On This Day" vignettes featuring Canadian clubs, Canadian heroes like Christine Sinclair and Alphonso Davies, and greats of the game who played in Canada like Pelé, Maradona, Eusébio, Ferenc Puskás and Sir Stanley Matthews. Features champions, records and achievements in Canadian soccer from both at home and around the world.

www.ingramcontent.com/pod-product-compliance
Lightning Source LLC
Chambersburg PA
CBHW072200070526
44585CB00015B/1231